THE CHINESE IN PHILIPPINE LIFE

1850–1898

YALE SOUTHEAST ASIA STUDIES, 1

Tan Quien-sien, also known as Don Carlos Palanca Tan Chuey-liong. From *Fei-lü-p'in Min-li-la Chung-hua Shang-hui san-shih chou-nien chi-nien k'an,* ed. Huang Hsiao-ts'ang (Manila, 1936).

The Chinese in Philippine Life

1850-1898

by EDGAR WICKBERG

New Haven and London, Yale University Press, 1965

For Ellen Goldstein Wickberg

Preface

One of the most fascinating and significant phenomena in the modern history of Asia has been the development of overseas Chinese communities, economically powerful, socially and culturally resistant to assimilation by their host countries, and tied in many ways to China. The existence of these communities presents the historian with the important task of identifying periods of significant change in their institutional lives and in their relations with both their host societies and their "mother country," China.

In the case of one group of overseas Chinese, those in the Philippines, the latter half of the nineteenth century was just such a transition period. For the Philippines as a whole it was a time of considerable economic and social change. Many of the most important features of Philippine economy and society in the middle of the twentieth century may be traced back to developments in that period. Indeed, it may be no exaggeration to say that the formative years of modern Philippine economy and society were those of the half century from 1850 to 1898.

The economic and social changes of those years could not but have affected the resident Chinese. Changes in China affected them too. At the end of the nineteenth century the status of the Philippine Chinese—both with respect to their host society and with respect to China—had been redefined in terms that were to remain substantially the same down to the present day. Thus, if we can speak of the late nineteenth century as a formative period in the development of contemporary Philippine economy and society, it is no less possible to find in the same period the origins of the present status of the Philippine Chinese community. The purpose of this study is to describe the economic and social position of the Chinese in the Philippines as of 1850 and to determine how it was affected by the ensuing changes of 1850–98.

The choice of 1850 and 1898 as terminal dates is mostly a matter of convenience. There are no dates that can be called "turning points" for every aspect of the subject at hand. At mid-century the tempo of Chinese immigration to the Philippines began to accelerate, and, for the first time in their long history of residence in the Philippines, the Chinese began to spread out into every corner of the archipelago, thus posing the problems to be discussed here. The year 1898 marks the end of Spanish rule in the Philippines. The transition in colonial policy from Spanish to American makes this a logical dividing point, although not the only possible one.

Despite the significance of the subject and the period, a study of the nineteenth-century Philippine Chinese community has never been attempted in any systematic or detailed fashion. The few intensive studies that have been made of the Philippine Chinese have concentrated on the problems of the twentieth-century community.[1] Historians, who might be expected to correct this condition, have not been attracted to the subject.

The same is true of broader changes in the economy and society of the Philippines in the late nineteenth century—changes which provide the background and framework for the study of the Philippine Chinese community. Historians and others have barely begun to give systematic treatment to these phenomena. Illustrative of this point is the fact that for the present study I have had to base my discussion of the Philippine economy primarily upon an unpublished Ph.D. dissertation. While scholars in the Philippines continue to focus their attention on the politics and personalities of the rising nationalist movement in the late nineteenth century, many other important features of the time remain unstudied. The present study is, therefore, an attempt to begin the exploration of a hitherto neglected phase in the development of the Philippine Chinese community,

---

1. Notable examples are: Jacques Amyot, S.J., "The Chinese of Manila: A Study of Adaptation of Chinese Familism to the Philippine Environment" (Ph.D. dissertation, Dept. of Anthropology, University of Chicago, mimeo., 1960); George Weightman, "The Philippine Chinese: A Cultural History of a Marginal Trading Community" (Ph.D. dissertation, Cornell, 1960); Huang Yen-hsing, *Hirippin kakyō* (The Philippine Chinese) (2 vols. Tokyo, 1943–44); Mantetsu Tōā Keizai Chōsa Kyoku, *Hirippin ni okeru kakyō* (The Overseas Chinese in the Philippines) (Dairen, 1939); Japan, Koain, Seimubu, "Firippin ni okeru kakyō chōsa" (A Survey of the Overseas Chinese in the Philippines), *Jōhō*, 11 (Feb. 1940), 31–123; Huang Ming-te, *Fei-lü-p'in hua-ch'iao ching-chi* (The Economy of the Overseas Chinese in the Philippines) (Taipei, 1957); Chang Ch'i-yun, et al., *Chung-Fei wen-hua lun-chi* ("Symposium of the Sino-Philippine Culture") (2 vols. Taipei, 1960); Eufronio Alip, *Ten Centuries of Philippine–Chinese Relations: Historical, Political, Social, Economic* (Manila, 1959), Ch'en Lieh-fu, *Fei-lü-p'in hua-ch'iao chiao-yu* (Overseas Chinese Education in the Philippines) (Taipei, 1958).

within the context of the almost neglected history of nineteenth-century Philippine economy and society. If it raises questions and suggests themes for further study it will have served its purpose.

There is another justification for this study: the introduction of unpublished materials from the Philippine National Archives, acquired on microfilm during 1952 and 1953, when the writer was a Fulbright scholar in the Philippines. Material from these archives has never been systematically used, whether for a study of the Philippine Chinese or for any other topic. Perhaps this volume will, in a small way, suggest the possibilities of this hitherto untapped source of information, both for studies of the Philippine Chinese under Spain's administration, and for other problems in the study of the Philippines.

The use of this Philippine archival material as a major source, while expanding the possibilities of treatment of the subject, also imposed certain limitations upon the study. Given the disorganization of the Philippine National Archives, it was not possible to be as systematic in collecting research material for this topic as one ought to be. Many questions of importance had to be left unanswered simply because of inability to locate material about them. It is to be hoped that further archival work, by the writer or others, may clear up many of the points left at issue.

A number of obligations have been incurred in preparing this book —too many to give all of them the acknowledgment they deserve. I hope those not mentioned will understand that I list here only major contributors. Former Director of Public Libraries Luis Montilla and the staff of the Philippine National Archives facilitated my use of their collection with the utmost freedom. Srta. Consuelo del Castillo of the Archivo del Ministerio de Asuntos Exteriores, Madrid, lent understanding and efficient assistance. For providing primary material from sources other than these two archives I am indebted to Dr. Pao Shih Tien, Principal of Chiang Kai Shek High School, Manila, to Rev. Juan Velasco, O.P., National Director of Chinese Missionaries in the Philippines, to Robert Irick, to Rev. Pablo Fernández O.P., Rev. Jean Desautels, S.J., and Rev. Jacques Amyot, S.J. For assistance in miscellaneous ways I am happy to thank Thomas R. McHale, Benito Legarda, Jr., Fernando Zóbel de Ayala, John S. Carroll, P. Y. Wu and Peter Schran. The editors of the *Journal of Southeast Asian History* and *Pacific Affairs* have kindly granted permission to use material originally published in those journals.

Joseph Levenson did more than direct the study in its original dissertation form; he played a major part in shaping my thinking about historical problems. I am especially grateful to him for that. G. William Skinner and Donn V. Hart gave generously of their time and knowledge in reading the manuscript. Because of them there are fewer embarrassing moments here than there would otherwise have been. I wish also to thank my colleague, Karl Lo, for writing the characters in the Glossary and Bibliography. Finally, a special acknowledgment is due Harry Benda for his efforts toward the publication of this volume.

Parts of this study were completed with the assistance of the Ford Foundation, the Center for Chinese Studies of the University of California, and the Social Science Research Council. I am happy to express my thanks for their support and to absolve them and the previously named individuals of responsibility for errors and shortcomings. I alone assume that.

Contents

Abbreviations used in the notes

AMAE: Archivo del Ministerio de Asuntos Exteriores, Madrid

BR: Blair and Robertson, *The Philippine Islands, 1493–1898*

CWHKCC: *Chang Wen-hsiang-kung ch'üan-chi* (Collected Works of Chang Chih-tung)

CSMJPKJC: *Ch'u-shih Mei-Jih-P'i-kuo jih-chi* (Diary of an Embassy to the United States, Spain, and Peru) by Tsui Kuo-yin, in *Hsiao-fang-hu-chai yü-ti ts'ung-ch'ao*

IMH-AS: Chinese government archives deposited at the Institute of Modern History, Academia Sinica, Taiwan

LWCKCC: *Li Wen-cheng-kung ch'üan-chi* (Collected Works of Li Hung-chang)

PNA: Philippine National Archives

SCJC: *San-chou jih-chi* (Diary of Three Continents) by Chang Yin-huan

WCSL: *Ch'ing-chi wai-chiao shih-liao* (Historical Materials on Foreign Relations in the Late Ch'ing Period, 1875–1911)

PART ONE

Historical Patterns

1

The Philippine Chinese before 1850

Before 1750

Long before 1850 the Chinese had been significantly involved in the economic and social affairs of the Philippines. Direct contact between China and the Philippines existed from at least the Sung period (960–1279). By Ming times (1368–1644) the *tung-yang chen-lu,* or eastern route of the Chinese junk trading system, had been established, passing through the western side of the Philippine Archipelago enroute from South China to Sulu, Borneo, and the Moluccas. Through the junk trade several points in the Philippines enjoyed regular commercial and cultural contacts with the Chinese.[1] Passengers on the junks, whether

1. The most comprehensive examination of sources relating to early Sino–Philippine contacts is found in Wu Ching-hong, "A Study of References to the Philippines in Chinese Sources from Earliest Times to the Ming Dynasty," *Philippine Social Sciences and Humanities Review,* 24 (1959), 1–181, continued in the same author's "Supplements to a Study of References to the Philippines in Chinese Sources from Earliest Times to the Ming Dynasty (?–1644)," *University of Manila Journal of East Asiatic Studies,* 7 (1958), 307–93. Some other important works on Sino–Philippine relations in the pre-Spanish period and the cultural consequences thereof are Wada Sei, "The Philippine Islands as Known to the Chinese Before the Ming Dynasty," *Memoirs of the Research Department, Tōyō Bunkō,* Series B, No. 4 (1929); H. O. Beyer, "Early History of Philippine Relations with Foreign Countries, Especially China," in E. A. Manuel, *Chinese Elements in the Tagalog Language* (Manila, 1948); Narita Setsuo, *Zōho kakyō shi* (Revised History of the Overseas Chinese) (Tokyo, 1942); Olov R. T. Janse, "Notes on Chinese Influence in the Pre-Spanish Philippines," *Harvard Journal of Asiatic Studies,* 7 (1944); Fay-Cooper Cole and Berthold Laufer, *Chinese Pottery in the Philippines* (Chicago, 1912); Berthold Laufer, "Relations of the Chinese to the Philippine Islands," *Smithsonian Miscellaneous Collection,* 50 (1908); Wu Ching-hong, "Hua-ch'iao tui-yü Fei-lü-p'in wen-hua ti kung-hsien," (Contributions of the Overseas Chinese to Philippine Culture), *Ta-lu tsa-chih,* 9, 11 (December 1954), 18–21; Liu Chi Tien, *Chung-Fei kuan-hsi shih* (History of Sino–Philippine Relations) (Taipei, 1964); Robert B. Fox, "The Calatagan Excavations," *Philippine Studies,* 7 (1959), 325–90; and Kamer Aga-Oglu, "Ming Porcelain from Sites in the Philippines," *Asian Perspectives,* 5 (1961), 243–52.

merchants or otherwise, occasionally settled in various parts of the
Philippines, at least on a temporary basis. But nothing is known about
how such settlers may have fitted into the economic and social life of
their host societies. At Jolo, in the Archipelago of Sulu, an important
trading center for the raw products of neighboring regions, there were
a Chinese wharf and lodging quarter.[2] In the Manila area, the Spanish
conquerors of 1570 found a small settlement of about 150 Chinese.[3]
But no other information is available about these settlements or the
existence of other Chinese colonies.

The arrival of the Spanish conquerors in the Philippines in the 1560s
meant new opportunities for the Chinese. In Fukien province, on
China's southeastern coast, shipowning merchants immediately realized
the potential economic significance of the newly-developing Manila
Galleon trade between the Philippines and Mexico. The way was open
for Chinese vessels to carry goods from China to Manila, there to be
loaded for markets in Mexico. The Spaniards, unlike the Portuguese,
possessed no trading station on the China coast. Nor did they handle
the China–Manila carrying trade in their own vessels. Instead, they
developed a pattern of waiting for the yearly monsoon winds to bring
the Chinese junks to Manila, bearing silks and other luxury goods from
China to be transshipped to Mexico on the Manila galleon. On the
galleon's return voyage Mexican silver was brought to Manila, from
whence it was taken to China by the Chinese junk traders in repayment
for the luxury goods they had brought. Both the Chinese and the
Manila Spaniards, who acted as middlemen, profited enormously from
this arrangement.[4]

Shipowning merchants were not the only Chinese who came to the
Philippines. Soon other Chinese—merchants and artisans—were migrating to the archipelago, attracted by the sophisticated economy newly
established at Manila and other centers of Spanish residence. The
provisioning of the Spanish settlements with needed goods and services
was an open field for Chinese enterprise. Not only merchants and
artisans but fishermen and market gardeners settled in the Manila area
and supplied the needs of the Spaniards. By 1603, barely thirty-two
years after the founding of Manila as a Spanish settlement, the Chinese

2. Najeeb Saleeby, *History of Sulu* (Manila, 1908), pp. 137–38. On page 138 is
a nineteenth century map showing the Chinese pier. See also *Fei-lü-p'in Min-li-la
Chung-hua shang-hui san-shih chou-nien chi-nien k'an* ("Thirtieth Anniversary Publication, Manila Chinese Chamber of Commerce"), ed. Huang Hsiao-ts'ang (Manila,
1936) (hereafter: Huang Hsiao-ts'ang), p. *chia* 2.

3. Anon., "Relation of the Conquest of Luzon," BR, 3, 168.

4. The Galleon trade and its ramification are discussed in detail in W. L. Schurz,
The Manila Galleon (New York, 1939).

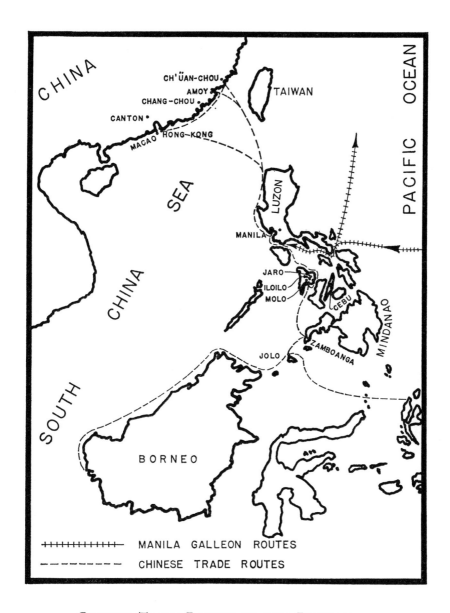

CHINESE TRADE ROUTES TO THE PHILIPPINES

population there was estimated at 20,000—in contrast to perhaps 1,000 Spaniards. Even before that, the Chinese had achieved a virtual monopoly in the retail commercial and industrial life of this settlement and were moving in the same direction in the other parts of the archipelago where Spaniards had established themselves.[5]

The establishment of Spanish rule over parts of the archipelago, and the immigration of Chinese to areas where Spaniards were settled[6] resulted in the development, broadly speaking, of not one but three economic systems in the Philippines: a "Western economy," a "native economy," and a "Chinese economy." The major interest of the Western economy was speculation in the Manila Galleon trade. Neither the Galleon trade with Mexico nor the Manila trade with China involved Philippine products in any large quantity. The Spaniards of the pre-1750 period were, therefore, uninterested in the development of cash crops grown on Philippine soil, devoting themselves to trade in foreign commodities. Their exports were Chinese luxury goods to Mexico and Mexican silver to China; their imports, silver from Mexico and staple and luxury goods from China to meet the demands of Philippine Spaniards.

The native economy was a subsistence one, of mostly local orientation and concern. But it was affected by the Western economy in areas near Spanish settlements, especially in the Manila area where the overwhelming majority of Spaniards took up residence. The Spaniards of Manila drew upon the area surrounding Manila Bay for provisions. The native economy in this area was also affected by the imports of Chinese cloths and Mexican silver reaching the area in exchange for the provisions sent to the Spaniards.

As for the Chinese economy, besides maritime trading between China and the Philippines, it included artisanry, both in Spanish settlements and in the nearby native villages, and the important function of provisioning the Spaniards. In this function, the Chinese acted as a link between the Western economy and the native economy, taking Chinese imports to the villages in exchange for local products for the Spanish community.[7]

5. Archbishop Benavides to Philip III, Dec. 16, 1603, BR, *12*, 150; Bishop Salazar, "The Chinese and the Parian in Manila," BR, *7*, 227; Antonio de Morga, *Sucesos de las Islas Filipinas*, ed. W. E. Retana (Madrid, 1910), p. 224; Yanai Kenji, "Hi-tō shinajin no chihō hatten ni tsuite," (On the Geographical Expansion of the Philippine Chinese), *Nampō Minzoku*, 7 (1942), 6–7.

6. Yanai, "Hi-tō shinajin," pp. 7–8, 20; Antonio de Morga, "Report of Conditions in the Philippines," June 8, 1598, BR, *10*, 81–82; Morga, *Sucesos*, p. 224.

7. Schurz, pp. 48–49, 56; Morga, "Report," pp. 81, 85–86; "Wearing of Chinese Stuffs," BR, *8*, 79–94; Real Decreto, June 16, 1679, Miguel Rodríguez Berriz, *Dic-*

This plurality in economic life was paralleled by cultural pluralism. In areas penetrated by the Spaniards there quickly came to be cultural communities of Spaniards, *indios*,[8] and Chinese. Formal social distinctions between and among these cultural groups were built into the administrative structure by the Spaniards. "Spaniard," "*indio*," and "Chinese," became terms of legal status. And when in the eighteenth century a sizable number of Chinese–indio half-castes, or *mestizos*[9] appeared, a legal classification was created for them too.

This policy of formalized social classification ought not to be labeled simply "divide-and-rule." It was, rather, a Spanish application of the Roman traditional concept of recognition of cultural differences within the empire. To the Spaniards, at least in the pre-nineteenth-century period, it was important to classify individuals according to assumed cultural differences. Thus, in Latin America, offspring of mixed marriages were carefully classified as *zambos, pardos,* and so forth. To do otherwise was not so much to sow the seeds of revolution as it was to allow social malfunctioning, helter-skelter living, and "perversion of customs."[10]

This formalization and legalization of cultural differences as social differences did not result in a strictly fragmented society. Individuals

---

cionario de la administración de Filipinas, anuario 1888 (2 vols. Manila, 1888), 1, 560; Ch'en Ching-ho, *Shih-liu shih-chi chih Fei-lü-p'in hua-ch'iao* (The Philippine Chinese in the Sixteenth Century) (Hong Kong, 1963), pp. 96–100. Although the native weaving industry of Central Luzon was damaged by imports of Chinese cloth, native textile manufacturing outside this area seems to have survived without much damage. Since water transport was so easy, the provinces around Manila Bay quickly became involved in provisioning the city and were therefore affected by its Western economy. As far away as Pampanga natives were influenced, leaving their lands to work for silver in Manila. Benito Legarda, Jr., "Foreign Trade, Economic Change, and Entrepreneurship in the Nineteenth Century Philippines" (Unpub. Ph.D. dissertation, Harvard, 1955), p. 99.

8. Use of the term indio to refer to Malayan natives of the Philippines is made here for purposes of clarity and is intended to reflect no discredit upon the Filipinos of today. "Filipino," as a term of national identification, is a post-1898 usage. In the Spanish period the term "Filipino" was ordinarily applied to Spaniards born in the Philippines. The ethnic classification term for Malayan natives of the archipelago was indio.

9. In the Philippines there were both Chinese mestizos and Spanish mestizos. But since the number of Spaniards in the islands was not large, Spanish mestizos were never as numerous as Chinese mestizos. Nor were they as important. The unmodified term mestizo, as used herein, refers to the Chinese mestizo. For a brief comparison between the Chinese mestizo and the Spanish mestizo, see my article "The Chinese Mestizo in Philippine History," *Journal of Southeast Asian History,* 5, 1 (March 1964), 62–100.

10. An anti-gambling proclamation of 1800, for instance, uses this as a major argument. Berriz, *Anuario 1888,* 2, 346.

within each group readily interacted with those of other groups and, the Spanish group excepted, individuals could change status and move from group to group. Moreover, a culturally and socially unifying factor was present: Spanish Catholicism. The Spanish colony in the Philippines was, from the very beginning, as much a religious mission as it was a commercial venture. The sense of a religious–cultural mission to Catholicize and hispanize the Philippines and all its inhabitants was a very real part of Spain's imperial philosophy. Spanish policy thus combined the recognition of present cultural pluralism with the universal propagation of a culturally unifying religious doctrine.

It must be emphasized that this cultural pluralism and social classification existed only in those areas where Spaniards and Chinese settled. For the rest of the archipelago, indigenous society, although not unaffected by the Spanish conquest and Spanish cultural influence,[11] underwent no change of the kind described.

In dealing with the Chinese, Spain's policies revealed the basic compromise between religious–cultural ideals and economic interest characteristic of her action in the Philippines. Economic interest decreed the presence of Chinese merchants and artisans, who filled occupations which the Spaniards scorned and for which the indios were believed unsuited. No less necessary was the China–Manila trade carried on by the Chinese, as part of the Manila Galleon trading system, in which many powerful Spanish residents had sizable investments. There were also the taxes and miscellaneous contributions of the Chinese, of interest both to government and to private individuals and institutions.[12]

Balanced against economic interest was the mandate to Catholicize and hispanize the Philippines and all its inhabitants. It appeared to the Spaniards that the Chinese could not easily be converted or hispanized. Moreover, intimate contact between unconverted Chinese and barely-converted indios stood as a possible threat to the lasting conversion of the latter, which was, after all, the major Spanish concern.[13]

Another factor conditioning Spanish attitudes and policy toward the Chinese was the Iberian experience with the Moors and Jews, groups

---

11. See J. L. Phelan, *The Hispanization of the Philippines* (Madison, 1959), passim.

12. For quantitative information on the economic importance of the Chinese, see Pierre Chaunu, *Les Philippines et le Pacifique des Iberiques (xvie, xviie, xviiie siècles)* (Paris, 1960), pp. 77–83, 92–93, 147–220, 267; Horacio de la Costa, S. J., *The Jesuits in the Philippines* (Cambridge, 1961), pp. 206, 216, 272–73, 400; PNA, Gremios de naturales, mestizos, y chinos, 16-5-5; Gov.-gen. Tello to Philip III, July 12, 1599, BR, *10*, 251; Manuel Azcárraga y Palmero, *La libertad de comercio en las Islas Filipinas* (Madrid, 1871), pp. 100, 102; Giovanni Gemelli Careri, *A Voyage to the Philippines* (Manila, 1963), pp. 10, 24.

13. De la Costa, p. 207.

that were both economically necessary and culturally difficult to assimilate. There the Spanish had tried segregation, hispanization, and expulsion. Bringing this experience with them to the Philippines, the Spanish used some of the same methods in dealing with the Chinese. Not surprisingly, within a few years after the Spanish conquest, the relations between the Chinese and the Spaniards fell into a pattern of distrust and latent hostility. Basic to this pattern was a prevailing condition of economic interdependence coupled with seemingly irreconcilable cultural differences. Within this context, the term *sangley,*[14] the Spanish name for the Chinese immigrants, quickly came to apply to an invidious cultural stereotype, and the Chinese became not simply one of two ethnic groups of equal status under the Spanish, but a despised cultural minority.[15]

While considered a cultural minority in the Spanish plan, the Chinese were still, compared with the Spaniards, a numerical majority and hence potentially dangerous. Thus, if the indios seemed to need protection from the Chinese for religious–cultural reasons, no less did the Manila Spaniards need it for security reasons. Here was another argument in favor of establishing controls over the Chinese. Therefore, as Spain's Chinese policy took form there were three major elements: taxation, control, and conversion.

Prior to the nineteenth century, Spanish taxation policy in the Philippines was based on the philosophy of taxing heaviest those groups best able to pay (Spaniards always excepted). The Chinese were assumed to have greater earning potential than the indios and so were taxed more heavily. Spanish policy also recognized occupational differences. Indios, who were primarily engaged in agriculture, might fulfill their tax obligations with tribute grain and obligatory labor service. Chinese, whose occupational specialties usually involved the use of money, paid in cash. The annual tax of 81 *reales,* or slightly more than 10 *pesos,* which the Chinese paid, was made up of 8 pesos for a residence permit, 5 reales for head tax, and a "community chest" contribution of 12 reales.[16] The basic tax on the indios was the 10 real tribute. Added to

14. Probably derived from *shang-lü*: "merchant *traveler.*" Y. Z. Chang, "Sangley, the Merchant Traveller," *Modern Language Notes,* 52 (1937), 189. See also Victor Purcell, *The Chinese in Southeast Asia* (London and New York, 1951), p. 585, and Fuchiwaki Hideo, "Shina Hirippin tsūshō-jō no 'sangley' ni tsuite" (On 'Sangley' in China–Philippine Commerce), *Rekishi to chiri, 33* (1934).

15. The development of Spanish attitudes toward the Chinese during the first three or four decades after the conquest is traced in Margaret Wyant Horsley, "Sangley: The Formation of Anti-Chinese Feeling in the Philippines" (Ph.D. dissertation, Columbia University, 1950). A broader discussion of problems of the same period with the addition of Chinese source material is found in Ch'en Ching-ho, passim.

16. Purcell, pp. 598–99. Eight reales were equal to one peso.

this were miscellaneous levies for religious instruction and the "community chests," the total being about 14 reales, or less than 2 pesos, payable in goods or in cash.[17]

Although the Chinese paid higher taxes than the indios, heavy taxation was less a point of Sino–Spanish friction than was arbitrary taxation. Special levies were frequent; so were forced labor drafts of Chinese for rowers of galleys. The Spanish crown issued a series of laws from 1594 to 1627 with the objective of protecting the Chinese from undue exactions.[18] But Spain was a long way from Manila, and these regulations were difficult to enforce. The practice of extralegal taxation imposed without notice was one cause of the occasional Chinese uprisings in the early Spanish period.

More basic to the occurrence of uprisings and Spanish reprisals against the Chinese was the prevailing pattern of economic interdependence combined with cultural animosity mentioned above. Attitudes of distrust periodically found violent expression in Chinese uprisings and Spanish massacres [19] or expulsion laws. In 1603 the entire Manila Chinese colony of 20,000 was wiped out in a massacre following a Chinese revolt. The incident resulted from the visit of three officials from China, who claimed they had come seeking a mountain of gold. This curious explanation aroused Spanish fears of an invasion from China, which would be aided by the local Chinese. Outnumbered twenty to one by the local Chinese alone, the Spaniards prepared for the worst. A rumor spread that a preventive massacre of the Manila Chinese was being planned. A Chinese uprising followed, and the Spaniards put it down, proceeding then to massacre almost all of the immigrant population.[20] But before long, though royal orders from Spain tried to limit it to 6,000, the Chinese population, drawn by the economic opportunities at Manila, was as large as ever.

In 1639 a group of Chinese who were being forced to work crown lands in Laguna province rose up and moved on Manila. They were joined by the Manila Chinese, who were provoked to rebellion by arbitrary tax demands and by the economic hardships accompanying a bad year in the Galleon trade. The rebellion was put down harshly.

17. Phelan, pp. 95, 97; Tomás de Comyn, "Estado de las Islas Filipinas en 1810," in *Las Islas Filipinas. Progresos en 70 años,* ed. J. F. del Pan (Manila, 1878), p. 114.

18. Purcell, pp. 586–88; *Recopilación de leyes de los reynos de las Indias* (2d ed. 4 vols. Madrid, 1756), *libro* 6, *título* 18, *leyes* 1–13.

19. The word "massacre" is used with due caution. It is Spanish sources, not Chinese, that record the systematic killing of thousands of Chinese in these incidents.

20. Liu Chi Tien, *Hua-ch'iao yü Fei-lü-p'in* (The Overseas Chinese and the Philippines) (Manila, 1955), pp. 37–41; Schurz, pp. 86–87; Laufer, pp. 267–72; de la Costa, pp. 207–16.

It was estimated that of perhaps 30,000 Chinese residents, 20,000 or more were killed.[21]

In 1662, the anti-Manchu adventurer, Cheng Ch'eng-kung, or Koxinga, sent an envoy from his stronghold in Formosa to Manila, demanding tribute from the Spaniards. The Spaniards responded by hastily calling in all troops from outlying islands and preparing for an invasion. Once again, rumor had it that a massacre of local Chinese was planned. This time the Manila Chinese began to flee into adjacent provinces. The prudent action of Governor Manrique de Lara prevented wholesale slaughter, but many Chinese who remained in hiding were killed. Governor-general and council now agreed that in accordance with royal orders of 1606 and 1622, which had never been observed, the number of Chinese was to be limited to 6,000.[22]

In 1686 a small group of restless, newly-arrived immigrants attempted to revolt, partly as a protest against restrictive Spanish laws, partly for plunder. Most of the Manila Chinese did not join them, and the rebellion prove abortive. Nevertheless, the expulsion of all but 6,000 Chinese was once again ordered.[23] But it is doubtful that the order was carried out.

From 1594 to 1766 expulsions were frequently ordered from Spain and somewhat less frequently carried out in the Philippines.[24] The Chinese, however undesirable culturally, continued to be considered essential economically. Expulsions did not reduce the Chinese population to the legally permitted 6,000. But these expulsion orders probably helped to hold down the number of Chinese to about 20,000, of which some 50 per cent were in the Manila area.[25]

For those Chinese who stayed in the Philippines the Spanish control system took the form of attempts at segregation. At Manila, the Parián, a kind of Chinese ghetto, was built outside the city walls—distant enough for military security, but near enough for economic convenience. At first, all Chinese were supposed to stay close to this Manila "China-

21. Anon., *Relación verdadera del levantamiento que los sangleyes o chinos hizieron en las Filipinas, y de las vitorias que tuvo cõtra ellos . . . 1640 y 1641* (Sevilla, 1642), pp. 1–4; Juan de la Concepción, R.A., *Historia general de Filipinas* (14 vols. Manila, 1788–92), 5, 429; Liu Chi Tien, *Hua-ch'iao*, pp. 41–45; de la Costa, pp. 389–92.

22. Liu Chi Tien, *Hua-ch'iao*, pp. 45–47; "Anonymous Relation of Events in Manila, 1662–63," BR, 36, 218–60; de la Costa, p. 484.

23. Casimiro Díaz, O.S.A., "The Augustinians in the Philippines, 1670–1694," BR, 42, 248–50.

24. "Anonymous Relation of Events in Manila, 1662–3," BR, 36, 259; José Ma. Zamora y Coronado, *Biblioteca de legislación ultramarina en forma alfabética* (7 vols. Madrid, 1844–49), 6, 101.

25. Population estimates for various periods are given in Purcell, pp. 576–79 and BR, 29, 209 n., 257.

town." But it soon became possible for Catholic Chinese to receive permission to reside away from the Spanish capital, and, except for an abortive attempt to recall them to Manila in the 1680s, they were allowed to wander about the Islands almost as they wished. Non-Catholics, too, were occasionally allowed in areas adjacent to Manila, but more often restricted to the Parián.[26]

Even if a policy of rigid segregation had been attempted it would probably have failed to keep the unconverted Chinese and the converted indio away from each other. Like the Spanish, the indios in Spanish areas of settlement had come to be economically dependent upon the Chinese. Economic relations between the two groups, and between individuals in the two groups, were constant. Social interaction was inevitable in the course of economic relations. There was no way to keep indio and Chinese completely apart.

Given the physical mobility allowed the Catholic Chinese, Chinese expansion into the provinces proceeded steadily, and by the mid-eighteenth century small numbers of Chinese could be found scattered about in several areas of the Philippines: in Central Luzon, particularly the provinces of Cavite, Laguna, Bulacan, Pampanga, Bataan, and Pangasinan; in the Ilocos region, centering around Vigan; on the island of Panay; and at the Spanish settlements of Cebu, Naga, and Zamboanga. In these areas of Spanish settlement other Pariáns, or Pariancillos, sprang up: notably, the Parián at Cebu, and Pariancillos at Arevalo and Capiz on Panay, at Naga in Camarines Sur, and at Vigan, Ilocos Sur.[27]

26. *Recopilación, lib.* 6, *tít.* 18, *ley* 3. A royal decree of 1628 allowed Chinese to travel in the islands, but the Ordinances of Good Government of Governors Corcuera (1642) and Cruzat (1696) ordered their restriction to the Manila Parián. Purcell, p. 598; "Ordinances of Good Government," BR, 50, 200. The Chinese term for the Parián is discussed in Liu Chi Tien, *Fei-lü-p'in Hua-ch'iao shih-hua* (Historical Stories of the Chinese in the Philippines) (Taipei, 1958), pp. 12–13.

27. This information is derived from Berriz, *Anuario 1888, 1,* 566; Joaquín Rodríguez San Pedro, *Legislación ultramarina* (16 vols. *Madrid,* 1865–69), 2, 470; Ferdinand Blumentritt, *Die Chinesen auf den Philippinen* (Leitmeritz, 1879), p. 32; Bartolomé de Letona, O.S.F., "Description of the Filipinas Islands," 1662, BR, *36,* 214; Yanai Kenji, "Ma-ni-ra no iwayuru 'Parian' ni tsuite," (On the So-called 'Parian' of Manila), Taihoku Teikoku Daigaku Bunsei Gakubu, *Shigakka kenkyū nempō,* 5 (1938), esp. p. 201; Yanai Kenji, "Ma-ni-ra Tondo-ku no shinajin no hatten," (The Growth of the Chinese in Tondo ward of Manila), *Minami Ajiya gakuhō,* 2 (1943), passim; Yanai Kenji, "Hi-tō shinajin," pp. 6–24; PNA, Ilocos; Real Haber, 1762; also location of concentrations of Chinese mestizos given in Joaquín Martínez de Zúñiga, O.S.A., *Estadismo de las Islas Filipinas,* ed. W. E. Retana (2 vols. Madrid, 1893), *1,* 44 ff., 306, 334–35, 460, 539; *2,* 20–203; Juan Delgado S.J., *Historia sacro-profana, política y natural de las Islas del poniente llamadas Filipinas* (Manila, 1892), pp. 27–46; Comyn, p. 186.

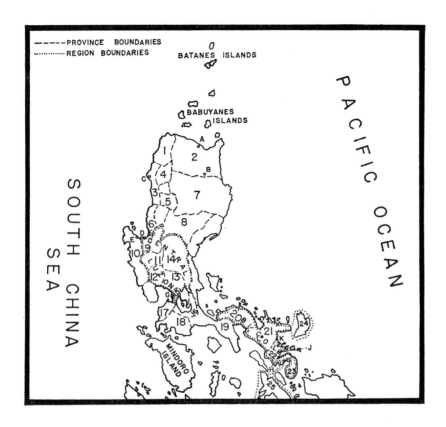

THE ISLAND OF LUZON IN THE SPANISH PERIOD

PROVINCES

1	Ilocos Norte
2	Cagayan
3	Ilocos Sur
4	Abra
5	Lepanto
6	Union
7	Isabela
8	Nueva Vizcaya
9	Pangasinan
10	Zambales
11	Tarlac
12	Pampanga
13	Bulacan
14	Nueva Ecija
15	Tondo
16	Laguna
17	Cavite
18	Batangas
19	Tayabas
20	Camarines Norte
21	Camarines Sur
22	Albay
23	Sorsogon
24	Catanduanes
25	Masbate

TOWNS

A	Aparri
B	Tuguegarao
C	Vigan
D	Lingayen
E	Sual
F	Dagupan
G	Manila
H	Albay
J	Legaspi
K	Tabaco
L	Naga

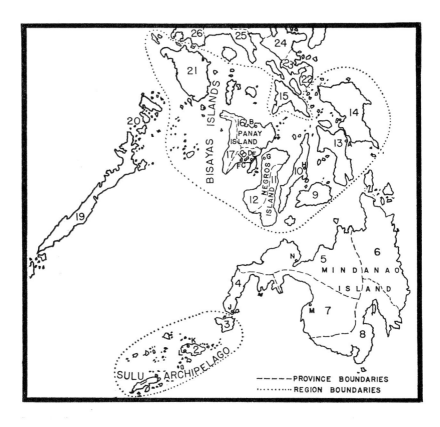

THE BISAYAS, MINDANAO, AND SULU IN THE SPANISH PERIOD

ISLANDS AND PROVINCES

1	Tawi Tawi Island	14	Samar Island
2	Jolo Island	15	Masbate Island
3	Basilan Island	16	Capiz
4	Zamboanga	17	Antique
5	Misamis	18	Iloilo
6	Surigao	19	Paragua (Palawan) Island
7	Cotabato	20	Calamianes Island
8	Davao	21	Mindoro Island
9	Bohol Island	22	Sorsogon
10	Cebu Island	23	Albay
11	Negros Oriental	24	Camarines Sur
12	Negros Occidental	25	Tayabas
13	Leyte Island	26	Batangas

TOWNS

A	Tacloban
B	Capiz
C	Molo
D	Jaro
E	Iloilo
F	Arevalo
G	Bacolod
H	Cebu
J	Zamboanga
K	Jolo
L	Maymbung
M	Cotabato
N	Misamis

One source of Chinese geographical expansion was a Spanish attempt to settle Chinese in rural areas adjacent to Manila in order to assist in the agricultural development of Central Luzon, especially during the second, third, and fourth decades of the seventeenth century. The general freedom conceded to the Catholic Chinese was a more important explanation. What to do with Catholic Chinese was always something of a dilemma for the Spaniards. Despite repeated demonstrations to the contrary, the Spaniards persisted in the hope that the act of baptism would somehow make those who accepted it easier to control.

Spanish religious policy with respect to the Chinese had three objectives: extension of the Faith, inculcation of loyalty, and encouragement of eventual assimilation. To the Spaniards it was clear that their mandate to Catholicize and hispanize the peoples of the Philippines included the Chinese people. In this context, the objectives of the Spanish religious orders, particularly the Dominicans, were of importance. Their aims included both effective conversion of the Philippine Chinese and, of greater concern to them, access to China as a mission field.[28] It appears that for the sake of the latter objective, the religious consistently protected and favored the Chinese in the Philippines, both Catholic and non-Catholic, in the hope that word of this might reach officials in China who would then be disposed to admit them as missionaries.[29] Even after the Spanish religious had broken into the China field in the 1630s this policy was followed lest the opportunity, once gained, be lost. When, in 1686, it was decreed that all Chinese were to be expelled from the Philippines within six months, a suspension of the order was necessary, prompted by fear that the K'ang Hsi emperor would revoke permission to proselytize in South China.[30] The protection of non-Catholics as well as Catholic Chinese in the Philippines suggests a subordination of the local effort to the larger mission.

Besides the general mandate to proselytize, there was the loyalty theme. Catholicism was a central value in Spanish culture, and the close association of Church and State made acceptance of the Faith in a Spanish country a kind of swearing of allegiance to the monarch. If by this means a hard core of loyal Catholic Chinese merchants and artisans could be created in the Philippines, it would solve all problems:

28. Purcell, p. 593.

29. Governor Tello to Philip III, July 12, 1599, BR, 10, 251; Bishop Salazar, "Carta-Relación . . . ," June 24, 1590, Archivo del bibliófilo filipino, ed. W. E. Retana (5 vols. Madrid, 1895–1905), 3, 55; T. H. Pardo de Tavera, Una memoria de Anda y Salazar (Manila, 1899), p. 23.

30. Proclamation of the audiencia, 1686, quoted in Real Cédula, July 23, 1744, Berriz, Anuario 1888, 1, 567. See also Real Decreto, Dec. 30, 1696, quoted in same cédula.

religious–cultural ideals and economic interest could be harmonized and security achieved.

But Spanish attempts to achieve their objectives by converting the Chinese met with only moderate success. There were never more than three to four thousand Catholic Chinese at any one time, while the Chinese population as a whole was often as large as 20 to 30 thousand.[31] Even in this rather small quantity, the quality of the conversions was questionable. No doubt there were sincere converts. But acceptance of baptism was a shrewd business move for a Chinese. Besides reduced taxes, land grants, and freedom to reside almost anywhere, one acquired a Spanish godparent, who could be counted upon as a bondsman, creditor, patron, and protector in legal matters.

By 1759 a royal official was suggesting that Catholic Chinese should be restricted to the Manila area, since so many Chinese were asking for baptism merely as a means of moving to the provinces, away from the close surveillance of Manila officials.[32] Casimiro Díaz, an Augustinian, writing in the 1690s, declared that visiting Catholic Chinese from Fukien would lose their faith if not kept away from local Chinese converts.[33] And the no doubt biased opinion of the English visitor, Captain Alexander Hamilton, is still worthy of quotation:

> All Chinese who go there for commerce get a little brass image hung about their neck, with a string of beads in their hands, and learning to cross themselves, cry *Jesu Sancta Malia* (for they cannot pronounce Maria, because the letter R is excluded the Chinese alphabet); I say, when they have got all those forenamed qualifications, they are good Spanish Christians. And when they have feathered their nest by cheating the Spaniards, and taken their leave of Manila . . . at their passing by a mountain dedicated to the Virgin Mary, they throw their beads overboard, and thank the Virgin for her kindness to them.[34]

During the "crisis years" of Sino–Spanish relations in the Philippines, the reactions of the Catholic Chinese were mixed. The leader of the 1603 Chinese rebellion was Juan Suntay (Ontal), a wealthy Catholic. But another Catholic, Juan Bautista de Vera Eng Kang, headman of the

31. Diego de Aduarte, O.P., "History of the Dominican Province of the Holy Rosary," 1640, BR, 32, 85; Concepción, 13, 356–57; Gregorio López et al., "Status of Missions," BR, 17, 216; Purcell, pp. 576–80; de la Costa, p. 483.

32. Francisco Viana to governor-general, Nov. 9, 1759, PNA, Reales Órdenes, caja 24, número 107.

33. "The Augustinians in the Philippines, 1670–1694," BR, 42, 253.

34. "A New Account of the East Indies," in A General Collection of the Best and Most Interesting Voyages and Travels in All Parts of the World, ed. John Pinkerton (17 vols. London, 1808–14), 8, 512.

Chinese community, sought to mediate between the two sides. And when the rebels moved on Binondo the Spanish defenders were assisted by recruits from among the Catholic Chinese there. In the 1639 Chinese uprising, churches were looted and images overturned. A few of the participants were Catholics. But the Chinese of Binondo were herded into their church by the Dominicans and remained at peace.[35] Neither the 1662 nor the 1686 crises seems to have involved the Catholics.

But Catholic Chinese were very much involved in Chinese support of the English invaders of the Philippines in 1762–64. In 1762, as part of the Seven Years' War, in which England and Spain were on opposite sides, the English East India Company dispatched a squadron from Madras to the Philippines. Manila was occupied for the remainder of the war, and the Spanish government forced into exile in Pampanga province. The English attempted, with considerable success, to woo the Chinese to their side. Because an expulsion of 1755 had removed most non-Catholics, the majority of the Chinese who remained were avowedly of that faith, and might have been expected to show some sympathy toward Spain. Nevertheless, they served with the English forces as fighters and laborers, and an armed body of 5,000 Chinese made an unsuccessful assault on the Spanish government-in-exile.[36] After the English left the Philippines and the Spaniards returned to Manila, the Spanish government issued the last of many Chinese expulsion orders in 1766. All Chinese who had sided with the English were expelled; but Catholic Chinese who had done so were particularly censured because "they apostasized, abandoning the Catholic Religion . . . proclaiming and applauding the aforesaid British nation as being better than the Spaniards, having neither priests, Mass, sermons, Confession, nor prayer. They threw off from their necks the Rosary and rid themselves of all the signs of Catholics." [37]

But although a nominal acceptance of Catholicism did not cause a Chinese to identify himself with Spain, this is not to say that the Chinese were the unassimilable cultural minority the Spaniards popularly believed them to be. Assimilation was a constant process throughout the period of Spanish rule. It was facilitated by the almost complete

35. See notes 20 and 21; also Pablo Pastells, S.J., "Historia general de Filipinas," in Pedro Torres Lanzas and Francisco Navas del Valle, eds., *Catálogo de los documentos relativos á las Islas Filipinas existentes en el Archivo de Indias de Sevilla* (9 vols. Barcelona, 1925–36), 5, lxxxi; Aduarte, in BR, *31*, 186; Díaz, in BR, *42*, 219 n., 228 n.; de la Costa, pp. 208–09.

36. Marqúes de Ayerbe, "Sitio y conquista de Manila por los ingleses en 1762," *Tres hechos memorables de la marina española en el siglo xviii* (Madrid, 1907), p. 112; José Montero y Vidal, *Historia general de Filipinas* (3 vols. Madrid, 1887–95), *2*, 54, 83; Liu Chi Tien, *Hua-ch'iao*, pp. 47–51.

37. Real Cédula, April 17, 1766, PNA, Reales Órdenes, caja 29, núm. 9.

absence of Chinese women, which led to a high rate of Chinese–indio intermarriage, both legally recognized and otherwise. Given this pattern of intermarriage, the direction of social assimilation was toward the native element, not the European. But cultural assimilation was a more complex matter. To a Chinese, who considered himself a representative of a superior culture, there was little attractiveness about indio culture. But Spanish religious–cultural policies mitigated the existing cultural pluralism by making Spanish culture, in however diluted a form, available to non-Spanish groups and individuals. Thus, for a Philippine Chinese, the direction of cultural assimilation could be and was toward a hispanized Philippine culture, not a pure indio culture.

In the early years of Spanish rule the government, while trying to keep apart unconverted Chinese and indias, attempted to encourage intermarriage when both partners were Catholics. As an inducement to marriage with benefit of clergy, uncultivated tracts of land in Manila's suburbs were offered to Catholic Chinese who married indias.[38] But farming was of limited interest to the Chinese. It is probable that this inducement to baptism and marriage was not particularly attractive and that consensual unions of Chinese and indias were a common practice, as indeed they were later.

In the Spanish attempt to assimilate the Chinese by marrying Catholic Chinese to indias, special notice should be taken of the mission parish activities of the Dominicans and Jesuits in Binondo and Santa Cruz, across the river from both the Spanish city of Manila and the Parián. Binondo was founded as a Chinese town in 1594. A royal order for the expulsion of all Chinese had been received, but Governor Dasmariñas, realizing the city's need for at least a small group of Chinese, purchased a tract of land across the river from the city and gave it to a group of prominent Chinese merchants and artisans as the basis for a new settlement, once the Parián was deserted. The land was given in perpetuity, to be tax free and inalienable, with limited self-governing privileges attached.[39]

Although the original purpose of the grant was simply to insure the availability of goods and services for Manila, without reference to religious or cultural questions,[40] the enterprise of the Dominicans, who took Binondo as their parish, soon made of it a community of married Catholic Chinese. Non-Catholic Chinese in the Binondo area were missionized, baptized, married, and added to the community of married

38. This offer was made in 1620. *Recopilación*, lib. 6, tít. 18, ley 8.

39. L. P. Dasmariñas, "Donazión," March 29, 1594, PNA, Gremios, 16-5-5.

40. On this point, Dasmariñas' "Donazión" is in conflict with Jesús Gayo, O.P., "Ensayo histórico-bibliográfico," in *Doctrina christiana; Primer libro impreso en Filipinas* (Manila, 1951), p. 70.

Catholics. By 1600 this group had reached a size of perhaps five or six hundred.[41] There were high hopes that the mestizo progeny of these Chinese would excel in higher education and help the Dominicans in the spiritual conquest of China.[42]

This Catholic Chinese community was confirmed in its privileges repeatedly during the seventeenth century. As early as 1602 a claim to the area occupied by the community was filed by a group of indios, but the issue was decided in favor of the Chinese. When the Parián was destroyed during the Chinese uprising of 1639, Governor Fajardo rebuilt it in Binondo. But the Catholic Chinese, with the aid of their mestizo offspring, protested vigorously and the Parián was removed to its old location. In 1686 a long-standing dispute involving land claims in Binondo by the Jesuits and the Hospital of San Juan de Dios was decided in favor of the Catholic Chinese and mestizos, and non-Chinese settlers in Binondo were directed to pay rent to them.[43]

Clearly, Binondo, by the seventeenth century, was intended to be a settlement for Catholic Chinese and their mestizo descendants, and ultimately, in the continued absence of Chinese women, an all-mestizo community. But such a community, once developed beyond a certain point, could not be dissolved with ease and its members assimilated into indio society. This was true even after indios began to settle in Binondo. The result was what might be expected: acculturation without complete assimilation and the formation of separate communities of Chinese, mestizos, and indios within Binondo.

At first, when their numbers were small, the mestizos sided with the Chinese against the indios, and in 1687 the two formed the Gremio de Chinos de Binondo, a kind of combined municipal governing corporation and religious sodality, headed by ten Chinese "captains" and five mestizo "captains." [44] Later, as the mestizos became the leading element in Binondo, they broke away from the Chinese, forming their own Gremio de Mestizos de Binondo in 1741.[45] There were now three *gremios* in Binondo, each claiming superiority in civil and ceremonial affairs within the town. The mestizos made good their claim.

While this was going on in Binondo, the Jesuits had established a similar "reduction," or mission settlement, primarily for Catholic Chinese, in Santa Cruz between 1619 and 1634. Little is known about the

41. Morga, *Sucesos*, p. 225; Gregorio López, et al., "Status of Missions in the Philippines," BR, 17, 216; Gayo (p. 73) gives 800.

42. Francisco de Montilla, O.F.M. (c.1600), quoted in Gayo, pp. 72–73.

43. "Auto de audiencia," March 13, 1686, and "Petición al gobernador," March 22, 1657, in "Testimonio de varios documentos," PNA, Gremios, 16-5-5. See also Gayo, pp. 27, 90.

44. "Ordenanza de 10 julio 1687 para Binondo," PNA, Gremios, 16-5-5.

45. "Petición de naturales," Nov. 19, 1888, PNA, Gremios, 16-5-5.

history of this community, except that the three-gremio arrangement that developed in Binondo occurred there as well.[46]

Both the Binondo and Santa Cruz communities of married Chinese Catholics were segregated from the non-Catholics of the Parián. Marriage was considered to be of such importance as a means of assimilation that whenever Catholic Chinese residing in the provinces were ordered to return to Manila, unmarried Catholics were sent to the Parián, but married Catholics to Binondo or Santa Cruz. And although some effort was made to keep unmarried Catholic Chinese who lived in the Parián separated somehow from the non-Catholics there (an impossible feat), it was considered more important to segregate those who were both baptized and married.[47]

Questions of policy and legality aside, intermarriage was a first step toward assimilation. The mestizo offspring of the Chinese, reared by their Catholic mothers, were almost all Catholics. They identified themselves with the Philippines and with Spain, not with China. The mestizos of Binondo, in particular, actively assisted in suppressing the Chinese rebellion of 1639, and repeatedly thereafter made proud claims that they always supported Spain against the Chinese. But all mestizos, not just those in Binondo, seem to have been consistent in their support of the Spaniards, against the Chinese, the English, or anyone else. As late as the early 1800s there was a mestizo military unit in Manila, the Regimiento del Real Príncipe, jointly financed by the Spanish government and a rich mestizo.[48]

Thus, while Spain's policy was to keep apart non-Catholic Chinese and Catholic indios, and to bring together Catholic Chinese and Catholic indios, the policy was irrelevant in terms of the outcome; the growth of a hispanized, Catholic, pro-Spanish group of Chinese mestizos.

1750–1850

In modern Philippine history a kind of watershed occurs around the middle of the eighteenth century. The determinants of this demarcation are economic change and social change.

46. de la Costa, pp. 373–74, 513–14. There were said to be 800 to 1,000 Catholic Chinese in Santa Cruz in 1638. Royal Order, March 15, 1638, BR, *29*, 102–03.

47. Real Decreto, June 17, 1679, San Pedro, *2*, 466; "Ordinances of Good Government," BR, *50*, 200; Real Cédula, March 26, 1697, and Real Cédula, Feb. 8, 1702 in Berriz, *Anuario 1888, 1*, 562–63.

48. *Relación verdadera . . . 1640 y 1641*, p. 2; BR, *29*, 258; Community of mestizos to governor-general, March 31, 1884, PNA, Gremios, 16-5-5; Jean François de Galaup de la Perouse, *A Voyage Around the World in the Years 1785, 1786, 1787, and 1788* (3d ed. 3 vols. London, 1807), *1*, 521; Rafael Comenge, *Cuestiones filipinas. 1.ª parte. Los chinos* (Manila, 1894), p. 224; *Catálogo de la exposición cartográfica y documental de Filipinas* (Madrid, 1946), p. 58; Comyn, p. 203.

In the late eighteenth century the two systems of "native economy" and "Western economy" began to move closer together. This was the period of the earliest Spanish attempts to encourage cash crops for export: sugar, indigo, and tobacco in particular. Neither of the first two products proved very important during the eighteenth century. But tobacco as a government monopoly was, along with customs receipts and indio tributes, a major source of revenue for the Spanish government. The Western economy was changing in other ways. Although some of the old dependence on the Manila Galleon system remained, even this system was being modified, losing its entrepot character. More and more Philippine products were being loaded for Mexico, cutting into the silks-for-silver exchange. Of more importance, Spain was beginning to take the initiative in its economic relations with the Chinese.

The foundation of the Royal Philippine Company in 1785 began the era of sending Spanish ships to China for cargoes rather than awaiting the arrival of the junk fleet. Another change was the opening of Manila in 1789 to non-Spanish European vessels carrying Asian trade goods.[49] Prior to this time, Spanish colonial policy had prohibited the entry of non-Spanish European vessels into the Philippines. This prohibition, and the Spanish reluctance to send ships of their own to China, had meant that China–Philippines trade had been almost entirely dependent upon the junk fleet from Amoy and Ch'üan-chou in Fukien.[50] During the eighteenth century the junk trade to Manila had declined, as other parts of Southeast Asia (notably Netherlands India) became more attractive to the Chinese. Now the competition of Spanish and other European vessels (especially English), plying between Manila and China, reduced the junk trade still further. During the period 1797–1812 the average number of junks arriving annually at Manila was eight, as contrasted with average annual arrivals of nineteen European vessels. This figure of eight stands in dramatic contrast to the annual fleets of twenty or thirty junks in the early seventeenth century.[51]

49. Schurz, pp. 58, 412–13.

50. There were some native craft that went to China, but infrequently. For an example, see Chao Ch'üan-ch'eng, "A Ship's Voyage from Luzon to China in the Eighteenth Century," in *Chinese Social History*, ed. E-tu Zen Sun and John DeFrancis (Washington, 1956).

51. Chaunu (pp. 147–98) traces the rise and decline of the junk trade from 1577 to 1787. See also M. A. P. Meilink-Roelofsz, *Asian Trade and European Influence in the Indonesian Archipelago between 1500 and about 1630* ('S-Gravenhage, 1962), p. 264; Blumentritt, *Die Chinesen*, pp. 31–33; Zúñiga, *1*, 260; Herónimo de Salazar y Salcedo to Philip III, July 5, 1603, BR, *12*, 83; Schurz, p. 71; J. C. van Leur, "On Early Asian Trade," in *Indonesian Trade and Society. Essays in Asian Social and Economic History* (The Hague, 1955), p. 129; "Informe de la junta de comercio," Nov. 7, 1843, PNA, Reales Órdenes, caja 99, núm. 37. In terms of value of cargo,

Spanish initiative in the carrying trade brought Spain into the Canton trading system, somewhat belatedly, alongside the other Europeans. Thus, while the junks continued to come from Amoy, Spanish vessels could trade only at Canton. The total effect of this arrangement on the nature of Chinese immigration to the Philippines cannot as yet be determined. But one new feature was the presence of a small body of Cantonese from Macao, called in Manila *macanistas* ("macaos"), who were brought there by European vessels.[52] To this extent, at least, immigration was becoming more diversified geographically and less dependent upon the junk trade.

Within the Philippines, Spanish initiative took the form of attempts to replace the Chinese in retail trade. The social background to these efforts was as follows. By the eghteenth century the Manila Galleon trade, which had previously been open to most of the Spanish citizens of the city, had become the monopoly of a small wholesale commercial guild. Those not included looked about for other economic opportunities; so did the rising group of urbanized mestizos and indios. It was in the interest of these groups that in 1755 the expulsion of most of the Chinese in the Philippines was ordered and carried out. Most non-Catholic Chinese were expelled, both from the provincial areas and from Manila, leaving perhaps 5,000 to 10,000 Chinese in the Philippines, almost all of them in Manila.

The Spanish governor-general now attempted to organize a commercial company to handle retail trading. The Spaniards and mestizos who participated raised 76,500 pesos. But the commercial company, a victim of financial troubles, was a failure after only one year. Still, the Spaniards tried to keep the Chinese out of retail trade for some years thereafter.[53]

Meanwhile, Chinese refugees from the 1755 expulsion settled in the Sulu Archipelago or around the mouth of the Cotabato River in Mindanao, areas as yet unconquered by the Spanish. In Mindanao they became rice millers, carpenters, and palm wine distillers. They also exchanged Chinese goods, imported through Sulu, for rice and other Mindanao products to be shipped to the Sulu and China markets. In all these activities, the Chinese were assisted by high-interest loans made

---

Chinese vessels were doing about 13 per cent of the total import business at Manila in the first decade of the nineteenth century. PNA, Cuenta del peso marcante, 14-50-1 and 47-22-7.

52. Bando, July 24, 1822, Berriz, *Anuario 1888, 1,* 778–79.

53. Schurz, pp. 43, 96; Concepción, *14,* 163–65; Feodor Jagor, *Travels in the Philippines* (London, 1875), p. 347; Bando, Dec. 6, 1786, PNA, Bandos, 41–14–3.

them by local Moro *datus*. In the Sulu area, Moro sea-trading was in decline as the result of Spanish attacks on Moro vessels. The Chinese took over this trade.[54]

During the century from 1750 to 1850 Spanish methods of controlling the Chinese underwent basic changes. The segregation of non-Catholic Chinese from Catholic Chinese, indios, and Spaniards was abandoned. When the Manila Parián was torn down in 1790 to make room for new fortifications for the walled city of Manila, its inhabitants were permitted to scatter over most of the province of Tondo (which included, roughly, parts of the present city of Manila, and the present Rizal province) and into Cavite. The result was that most of them moved to Binondo and Santa Cruz, thus breaking down the old system of separating Catholic and non-Catholic Chinese.[55] The principle of separation on the basis of religion was already largely discredited in Spanish thinking, a victim of the Spanish disillusionment of 1762–64. Separation now was by "transient" or "resident." Transient traders were housed in the Alcaicería de San Fernando, a combined customs house, wholesale mart, and living compound, erected in Binondo in the late 1750s. Strict legislation attempted to keep them separated from the resident Chinese. But in fact, from the 1790s onward Binondo became a great Chinese and mestizo town in which permanently residing Chinese, mestizos, and indios rubbed shoulders with newcomers from China.[56]

Outside the Manila area there were fewer Chinese than ever. The expulsion of 1755 had left only a very few Catholic Chinese in some

54. Purcell, pp. 610–12; Saleeby, pp. 137–38. There was also direct migration from southern Fukien to Sulu beginning at this time. Chuang Wei-chi, et al., "Fuchien Chin-chiang chuan-ch'ü Hua-ch'iao shih tiao-ch'a pao-kao" (Report of an Investigation into the History of the Overseas Chinese of the Special District of Chinchiang in Fukien), *Hsia-men ta-hsüeh hsüeh-pao, she-hui k'o-hsüeh pan*, 1 (June 1958), 109–11.

55. Real Decreto, May 14, 1790, PNA, Reales Órdenes, caja 49, núm. 96; PNA, Reales Órdenes, caja, 74, núm. 23; Zúñiga, 1, 214. By the 1828 census, 90 per cent of all Chinese in the Philippines were in Tondo province, of which Binondo was the main urban center. Purcell, p. 614; Manuel Buzeta, O.S.A. and Felipe Bravo, O.S.A., *Diccionario geográfico, estadístico, histórico de las Islas Filipinas* (2 vols. Manila, 1850–51), 1, 136.

56. Real Órden, July 31, 1758, PNA, Reales Órdenes, caja 24, núm. 120; Charles III to gov.-gen., Aug. 4, 1759, PNA, Reales Órdenes, caja 25, núm. 55; Real Decreto, Aug. 19, 1776, PNA, Reales Órdenes, caja 35, núm. 69; Buzeta, 1, 138; 2, 258–59; Rafael Díaz Arenas, *Memorias históricas y estadísticas de Filipinas* (Manila, 1850), cuaderno 10: "edificios públicos." A floor plan of the Alcaicería de San Fernando is given in Pedro Ortiz Armengol, *Intramuros de Manila* (Madrid, 1958), p. 133. For a time there was also an Alcaicería de San José within the walled city of Manila to provide necessary craftsmen's services. Real Decreto, May 14, 1790, PNA, caja 49, núm. 96.

of the more important provincial towns.[57] And although, after 1790, it was again possible for non-Catholics as well as Catholics to settle in the provinces—provided, in this case, that they adhered strictly to agriculture—few Chinese took advantage of this opportunity.[58] There were, here and there, colonies of Chinese farmers or miners founded by enterprising Spaniards. But they were almost all short-lived.[59] Few Chinese on their own initiative availed themselves of the opportunity to reside in the provinces, and even those few were closely watched by local authorities.

Nor were there any independent farming and mining *kongsi* associations of Chinese, such as those used by the Chinese at this time in the development of rural Malaya, South Siam, and West Borneo. Two reasons for their absence might be (1) the continuity of mostly Hokkien (Fukienese) immigration, which had established certain occupations as "Chinese," and made gravitation to them the line of least resistance; and (2) the Spanish unwillingness to allow the establishment of such autonomous "states within the state."

In the century from 1750 to 1850 Spanish immigration policy moved from limitation to encouragement. After 1766 there were no more expulsions. A cautious figure of 4,000 "necessary" Chinese was set in 1790.[60] The actual Chinese population exceeded this, and possibly also the figure of 5,000 which appears in official statistics of the period.[61] But the size of the population seems to have been stable and was probably much less than the normal Chinese population during the preceding two centuries.

By the 1830s a Spanish desire to make more from the Philippine colony by developing it economically—in agriculture, commerce, and industry—led to a gradual trend toward encouragement of Chinese immigration.[62] A much larger Spanish population, stronger military forces, and the absence of any Chinese revolt since 1762 lent confidence to the Spaniards and overcame their former insecurity.

57. Circular, April 26, 1758, Berriz, *Anuario 1888*, 1, 576. In 1787 it was believed that there were 427 Chinese in the provinces. Real Cédula, March 16, 1816, Berriz, *Anuario 1888*, 1, 594.

58. Superior Decreto, Jan. 24, 1804, San Pedro, 2, 467–70; Real Decreto, May 14, 1790, PNA, caja 49, núm. 96.

59. Real Órden, April 1, 1785, PNA, Reales Órdenes, caja 44, núm. 14; Díaz Arenas, *Memorias históricas*, cuad. 9: "minas."

60. Real Decreto, May 14, 1790, PNA, caja 49, núm. 96.

61. Liu Chi Tien, *Hua-ch'iao*, p. 56. Zúñiga (1, 263) argues that there were 20,000 Chinese in the Philippines.

62. Superior Decreto, Aug. 31, 1839, San Pedro, 2, 474–75; Real Audiencia Chancillería de las Islas Filipinas, *Colección de autos acordados de la Real Audiencia Chancillería de Filipinas* (5 vols. in 2, Manila, 1861–66), 1, 389; 2, 139; San Pedro, 2, 479; Real Órden, Feb. 16, 1851, PNA, Reales Órdenes, caja 109, núm. 93.

Unquestionably the most important social phenomenon of the century 1750–1850 was the rise of the Chinese mestizo to a position of economic and social prominence.[63] The development of the two communities of Catholic Chinese at Binondo and Santa Cruz, and the pre-1750 scattering of Chinese in Luzon and parts of the Bisayas had left a mestizo residue. By 1810 there were perhaps 120,000 mestizos in a total Philippine population of about 2,500,000.[64] Of more significance than their numerical strength (they formed, after all, only 5 per cent of the total population) was the fact that the mestizos were concentrated in the most westernized, most economically advanced parts of the Philippines. Over 60 per cent of the mestizos in the Philippines resided in the three Central Luzon provinces of Tondo, Bulacan, and Pampanga. The province of Tondo alone accounted for almost 30 per cent of the mestizo population in the Philippines. And although these were heavily populated provinces, the number of mestizos relative to the total population was not insignificant. In Tondo, mestizos made up about 15 per cent of the population; in Bulacan and Pampanga they accounted for about 11 per cent each. In other, less populated provinces within the same general region of Central Luzon, the mestizos, although not numerous in absolute terms, were an important percentage of the provincial population. In Bataan 15 per cent of the population was mestizo. Twelve per cent of Cavite's population was mestizo.

But away from Central Luzon there were no large concentrations of mestizos. In other parts of Luzon there were mestizos—some in almost every province; but in the Bisayas and Mindanao mestizos were few, both in absolute terms and relative to the local population. Indeed, something like 90 per cent of the mestizos in the Philippines lived in Luzon, and in only a few spots in the other islands—notably the provinces of Cebu, Iloilo, Samar, and Capiz—were mestizos of any significance.

This pattern of mestizo geographical distribution may be partly explained by reference to the pattern of Chinese settlement. The province of Tondo in the early nineteenth century included the towns of Binondo and Santa Cruz as well as the present province of Rizal. We have already noted the importance of Binondo and Santa Cruz in Chinese and mestizo affairs. Beyond them stretched the suburban towns to which Chinese could usually migrate, however strict the government's policies. When residence restrictions were eased, the natural avenues of expansion were those of the trade routes that linked Manila and the Manila Bay perimeter with the Central Luzon plains. The pattern

63. For detailed discusion of this development, see Wickberg, "The Chinese Mestizo," passim.
64. Comyn, p. 186.

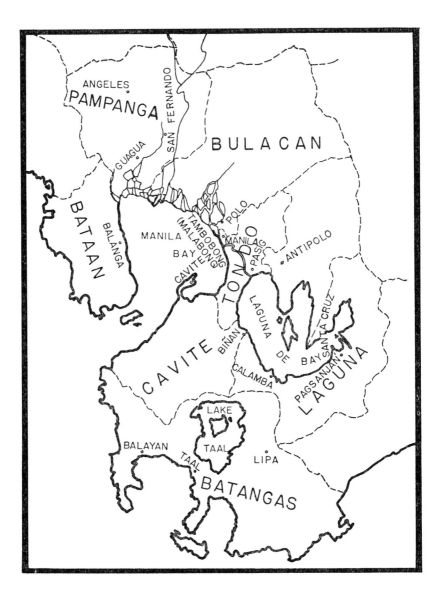

MANILA AND ADJACENT PROVINCES IN THE MIDDLE
NINETEENTH CENTURY

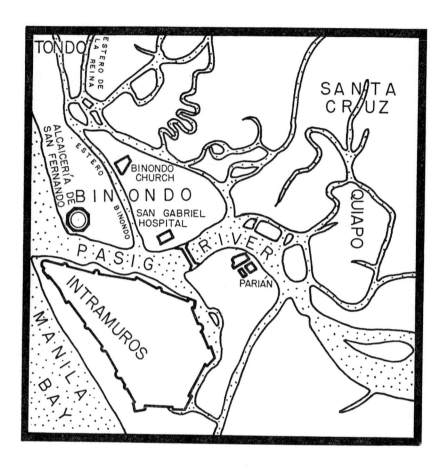

MANILA IN THE LATE EIGHTEENTH CENTURY

of Central Luzon settlement by the Chinese is therefore not surprising and the pattern of mestizo distribution in this area may largely be
explained as a consequence of Chinese settlement patterns. However,
one should note that since the mestizos were relatively free to move
about, their areas of residence were not entirely predetermined by where
their paternal ancestors had lived. Nevertheless, mestizos were found
usually in those areas where Spanish settlement had created economic
opportunities, and in this they were like their Chinese ancestors. Thus,
the largest bodies of mestizos in the Bisayas were those around Cebu
City and in two settlements in Iloilo province: Molo and Jaro. All of
these settlements were in areas of early Spanish colonization.[65]

Turning from the size and distribution of the mestizo population
about 1800 to its occupational characteristics, we find that most of the
mestizos of the Manila area were retail merchants or artisans. Away
from Manila, the characteristic mestizo occupations were wholesaling,
retailing, and landholding.[66]

The reduction of the Manila Chinese population by the expulsions of
1755 and 1766 meant less economic competition for the mestizos who
lived there. Although the Spaniards were never able to drive a sizable
wedge into the Chinese dominance of Manila's retail trade, the mestizos
were. By 1800, mestizos and Chinese shared the function of retailing
imported goods and local products. In Manila mestizos were also found
in many trades hitherto exclusively Chinese: carriage-makers, carpenters,
stone masons, printers, shoemakers, and tailors.[67] Presumably, some of
their businesses were inherited from their Chinese fathers. But apparently few if any mestizos inherited a position in the business of
wholesaling the imports and exports of the Chinese junk fleet. That
was done through the Alcaicería de San Fernando, exclusively by the
Chinese. Imports and exports in European vessels, whether from China
or elsewhere, were handled by the Spanish.[68]

Outside Manila, the 1755 and 1766 expulsions had drained the
provinces of most of the Chinese that had resided there. Accordingly,
there were even fewer Chinese than in Manila to provide economic
competition for other social groups. Taking advantage of the situation,
some mestizos and indios now took over from the Chinese the job

65. Wickberg, "The Chinese Mestizo," pp. 73–74.

66. Ibid., pp. 74–79.

67. Zúñiga, *1*, 266, 272, 294.

68. Ibid., *1*, 271–72; Schurz, Appendix 1; Jean Mallat de Bassilan, *Les Philippines. . . .* (2 vols. Paris, 1846), *2*, 321; Díaz Arenas, *Memorias históricas*, cuad. 10:
"edificios públicos."

of provisioning Manila by collecting the produce of nearby provinces and shipping it to the city.[69]

The mestizos and rich indios were also involved in the local or native economy away from Manila in a way the Chinese probably had never been. Partly this was due to the development of certain cash crops, which had to be collected and shipped to Manila for export. These the mestizos and rich indios purchased wholesale and held for speculation on the Manila market. Their major competitors in this trade were the Spanish governors of provinces, who acquired crops for speculation by insisting that the indios of their provinces pay their tribute in kind rather than cash.[70] Another reason for mestizo involvement in the native economy was the increasing complexity of the local trade itself. This was especially true in the Bisayas. There the towns of Molo, Jaro, and Cebu became not only the headquarters for the purchase of Bisayan export crops and local products going to Manila, but the main distribution centers for intra-Bisayan trade as well. The manipulators of this Bisayan trade were the mestizos of those towns.[71]

Another important area of mestizo interest, especially in Central Luzon, was landholding. Spanish writers during the early decades of the nineteenth century especially noted the landholding and land-use activities—and the wealth—of the mestizos of Central Luzon. Zúñiga, in particular, repeatedly points out the role of the Central Luzon mestizos as lessees (*inquilinos*) of rice-producing lands—lands that were often part of estates belonging to religious orders. Some of the lands in question were sublet by the inquilinos for amounts in excess of the rent owed by the inquilino to the landowner. Others were worked according to the *kasamahan* system, by which the actual tiller received a percentage of the crop, the inquilino taking the rest, from which he paid his rent.[72]

Mestizos were also acquiring outright ownership of indio lands in Central Luzon. By providing loans for the expenses of fiestas, baptisms, and litigation, with rice lands as security, the mestizos were in a position to obtain the lands by foreclosure when the indio borrower de-

69. Buzeta, 1, 251.

70. Comyn, pp. 50, 113–14; Zúñiga, 1, 296, 340, 349, 404; Buzeta, 1, 251. Both indios and mestizos were involved in transporting the government's tobacco to Manila. Jagor, p. 122.

71. Zúñiga, 2, 57, 88, 49; Buzeta, 2, 393. Agents of the mestizos of Cebu were sent east to Leyte and Samar, south to Surigao and Misamis, and west to Negros and Panay. Mallat, 1, 311–20. See also PNA, Provincial Documents, leg. 117, núm. 4; Sir John Bowring, A Visit to the Philippine Islands (London, 1859), pp. 114, 359–403.

72. Zúñiga, 1, 45–48, 334–35, 398.

faulted, as was often the case. As early as 1768 there were laws against such practices.[73] But it was not easy to break the power of the mestizo moneylender, who lived close to the indio and knew his needs.

Thus, mestizos in Central Luzon were much involved in questions of land tenure and usage. This is not the place for a detailed discussion of the mestizo and land use.[74] But it is worth pointing out in passing that students of the modern Philippine land problem and the economic background to the Philippine Revolution would do well to explore the activities of the Chinese mestizo.

Besides the occupations mentioned, there were a few mestizos, both in Manila and in the provinces, who were members of the professions, notably lawyers and secular clergy. This is not to say that all members of these small professional classes were mestizos; indios were also prominent. But for our purposes it is important to note that there was in process of development in this period a mestizo intellectual elite, hand in hand with an indio intelligentsia, though both were still very small in size.[75]

In any locality where mestizos were sufficiently numerous, separate mestizo gremios, or municipal corporations, were established alongside those of the indios, each endowed with limited self-governing powers.[76] There appear to have been only two places, Binondo and Santa Cruz, where the presence of a large number of Chinese resulted in the existence of three gremios. But there were many towns where a previous wave of Chinese immigration, now receded, had left enough mestizos to set up a two-gremio (mestizo and indio) situation.[77]

The political distinctions made by establishing separate gremios were paralleled by legal distinctions. A mestizo was defined as a person whose

73. "Ordinances of Good Government," BR, 50, 241; Real Decreto, May 14, 1790, Berriz, *Anuario 1888, 1,* 591; "Contratos usurarios," *Revista general de legislación y jurisprudencia, 25* (Madrid, 1864), 176.

74. References for such a discussion are found in Wickberg, "The Chinese Mestizo," pp. 74–79, 81–82, 91–93.

75. On educational opportunities for mestizos and indios, see BR, *45,* 121–230; de la Costa, pp. 577, 579. On the mestizo response to those opportunities see San Pedro, *2,* 523; Valentín González Serrano, *España en Filipinas* (Madrid, 1896), p. 18. The size of the secular clergy is given in Comyn, p. 159. See also BR, 50, 59.

76. Manuel Azcárraga y Palmero, *La reforma del municipio indígena en Filipinas* (Madrid, 1871), p. 7. For Binondo and Santa Cruz the date was 1741. "Petición de naturales," Nov. 19, 1888, PNA, Gremios, 16-5-5; "List of Gobernadorcillos of Mestizos of Santa Cruz, 1741–1889," *Philippine Historical Review, 1,* No. 4 (Aug. 1905), No. 5 (Sept. 1905).

77. Robert MacMicking, *Recollections of Manilla and the Philippines During 1848, 1849, and 1850* (London, 1852), p. 38; PNA, Provincial Documents, leg. 117, núm. 70; leg. 56, núm. 11; Gregorio Sancianco y Goson, *El progreso de Filipinas. Parte económica* (Madrid, 1881), pp. 180–81.

father was Chinese or mestizo. Thus, the children of a Chinese parent immediately moved into the mestizo classification. And since mestizos were regarded as indigenous subjects of Spain rather than as Chinese,[78] they, along with the indios, were regarded as tribute-paying *indigenes*. They had the same legal rights as the indios to participate in local government. When there were not enough mestizos in a given town to justify a separate mestizo gremio, mestizos of that locality could participate individually in local government as freely as the indios. They were also free, as were the indios, to change their place of residence. By contrast, the Chinese, where sufficiently numerous, could govern themselves; but they could never participate in a mostly indio town government. Nor did they possess the right to change residence.[79]

The mestizos, clearly, did not share the legal liabilities of the Chinese. In fact, the only liability attached to being a mestizo seems to have been in the realm of taxation. By the eighteenth century, when mestizos were numerous enough to be recognized and classified, their head tax or tribute was set at 20 reales, or twice that of the indios. The addition of miscellaneous taxes like those paid by the indios brought the total mestizo contribution to 24 reales, or 3 pesos.[80] There was some ambiguity about mestizo labor obligations. In some parts of the Philippines mestizos owed labor services; elsewhere they did not.[81]

It is evident that the mestizo tax schedule recognized both the relative earning capacity and the occupational specialties of the mestizo, as compared with the indio and the Chinese. The mestizo might be engaged in agriculture or commerce, or perhaps both. Either way, he would probably earn more than the indio and less than the Chinese.

Culturally, the mestizo was unique. Unlike the *baba* of Malaya or the *peranakan* of Java, the Chinese mestizo in the Philippines was not a special kind of local Chinese. He was a special kind of Filipino. The law identified him as such and so did he. The legal identification with the Philippines was automatic upon birth; he was not required to dissociate himself from identification with China upon reaching majority; indeed, the reverse was the case. It took a special effort for a mestizo to identify himself with China, an effort the majority did not wish to make, given the mestizo cultural outlook.[82]

Mestizo culture was a blend of Chinese, Spanish, and indio culture. One of the most interesting ways to observe mestizo usages is to look

78. Azcárraga, *Reforma*, p. 92.
79. *Recopilación*, lib. 6, tít. 18, ley 3; Purcell, p. 598; BR, 50, 200.
80. Comyn, p. 114.
81. *Informe secreto de Sinibaldo de Mas* (Manila, 1963), p. 103.
82. Wickberg, "The Chinese Mestizo," p. 89.

at the way surnames were formed. Sometimes mestizos retained the surname of the Chinese father, making such Chinese surnames as Tan and Lim Filipino surnames by their association with persons who identified themselves as Filipinos and were accepted as such. Another common practice was to create a new Filipino surname by combining parts of the full name of the Chinese parent. Thus, where the name of the Chinese was Yap Tin-chay, the mestizo descendants might choose to create a new surname, Yaptinchay, for themselves. Or, if Yap Tin-chay had been popularly known as Yap Tinco, using the Hokkien polite suffix *k'o* with his personal name, the new surname might be Yaptinco. There are today a great many Filipino surnames that end in "co." Almost all of them have this derivation. Finally, since Catholic Chinese also acquired a Spanish name upon baptism, the mestizo descendants might simply drop the Chinese part of the name and use only the Spanish part. Thus, the descendants of José Castro Ongchengco might simply be known by the name Castro. There is no evidence that those who adopted the Spanish name were accepted any more readily into Philippine society than those who retained a version of the Chinese name. All surnames and their bearers seem to have been accorded equal welcome.

Most mestizos spoke the Philippine dialect of the region where they lived. Most did not speak Chinese.[83] Those who had business relations with their Chinese relatives undoubtedly spoke some Chinese. In Manila, a local patois in which Hokkien, Cantonese, and Tagalog were mixed was spoken by many Chinese and also mestizos. It was a kind of lingua franca of the Chinese, not a specifically mestizo patois.[84] Rich mestizos who ostentatiously rejected Chinese culture spoke a Philippine dialect and Spanish.

The dress worn by the mestizos was a unique blend of Spanish, indio, and Chinese, a style also affected by the Spanish mestizos in the Philippines. The men wore a knee-length *camisa de chino* shirt, which was allowed to hang outside the trousers. By the middle of the nineteenth century it was common for mestizo males to wear top hats, supposedly the exclusive status mark of a *gobernadorcillo*. The characteristic dress of the women, which was called the "mestiza dress," was a combination of Spanish and indio, with little if any discernible Chinese influence.

Almost no information is available about kinship patterns and terminology among the mestizos. Apparently, the household formed when a

83. Azcárraga, *Reforma,* p. 91; Sancianco, p. 173.

84. Jacques Amyot, S.J., "The Chinese of Manila: A Study of Adaptation of Chinese Familism to the Philippine Environment," (Ph.D. dissertation, Dept. of Anthropology, University of Chicago, mimeo., 1960), p. 71.

Chinese married an india or mestiza was, as is the case in Manila today, closer to the Philippine pattern than the Chinese, in that many of the wife's kin were likely to be included. Characteristically, the Chinese husband was used and perhaps abused by his indio or mestizo in-laws, who found it financially advantageous to have such a moneymaker as a relative.[85] In child-rearing, the mother's influence was decisive. The father often returned to China, leaving mother and children with an economic stake but without his presence. Observers of the mestizos universally noted their combination of cultural attributes: a love of ostentation and a devotion to Catholicism (they were almost all Catholics) and to Spanish culture (the last characteristic being much more noticeable among the richest mestizos), combined with a financial acumen that they were said to have "inherited" from their Chinese fathers.[86] Undoubtedly, there were instances of Chinese fathers instructing mestizo sons in business methods.[87] But the Chinese immigrant was most likely to marry or live with an india or mestiza who happened to have some business sense herself and could help him run his business. It is not an unlikely supposition that the business training of mestizo offspring frequently came from the mother.

In social terms, those whose behavior and attitudes corresponded to what has just been described, who defined themselves as mestizos, and whose social relations were primarily with others who so defined themselves, were mestizos, whatever the law might say. According to the law, male descendants of Chinese paternal ancestors were classified as mestizos, generation after generation. Female descendants might change status according to their marriages. A mestiza marrying a mestizo or a Chinese remained in the mestizo classification, as did her children. But if she married an indio or Spaniard she and her children assumed her husband's classification.[88]

For male descendants intermarriage was not a way to change one's classification. But there was a procedure by which one could do so. The lineage history of the Filipino national hero, José Rizal, is relevant here. By lineage, Rizal might be considered a fifth-generation Chinese mestizo. His paternal ancestor, a Catholic Chinese named Domingo Lamco, married a Chinese mestiza. Their son and grandson both married Chinese mestizas. This grandson, having achieved wealth and status in

85. Ibid., p. 155.

86. Del Pan, *Las Islas Filipinas,* pp. 399–400; Mallat, 2, 134–35; Buzeta, 2, 244; Commenge, pp. 214–15.

87. Liu Chi Tien, *Fei-lü-p'in Hua-ch'iao,* p. 44.

88. *Chinos. Sus reglamentos y sus contribuciones,* comp. *El Faro Administrativo* (Manila, 1893), pp. 13–14; PNA, Provincial Documents, leg. 56, núm. 11.

his locality, was able to have his family transferred from the mestizo *padron,* or tax-census register, to that of the indios. Thus, Rizal's father, and Rizal himself, were considered indio.[89]

The legal procedure followed seems to have been that commonly used in the Spanish American empire in the late eighteenth century and known there as *dispensa de ley,* or *gracias al sacar.*[90] Whatever the formalities, it is important to know that such a mechanism existed. More information must become available before we can generalize about the frequency of this practice. We know that it existed and could also be used by indios to achieve legal recognition as mestizos down to about 1840.[91] It seems logical to infer that in areas where mestizos were not numerous enough to form gremios, changes of status from mestizo to indio were frequent and occurred within a very few generations (in the Rizal case, the third generation). In such places, the prestige that was attached to being a mestizo in Manila or in most parts of Central Luzon scarcely existed. Mestizo status meant only the liability of an extra tax burden for those who lived with indios and considered themselves part of the indio community.

It was another story in Manila and in most of Central Luzon. Here, the richer mestizos carefully maintained their distinctiveness, which they partly accomplished by seeming to be more hispanized and pro-Spanish than the indios. In the so-called "mestizo towns," like Tambobong (Malabong) and Pasig in Tondo province, Binan, Santa Cruz, and Pagsanjan in Laguna province, and Molo and Jaro in Iloilo province, mestizos were the richest element and politically dominant. There were good reasons for maintaining their separate identity. Individually and corporately they ostentatiously endowed the local church, the center of Spanish culture, while scorning association with the indios.[92] It was in these parts of the Philippines that mestizos had prestige, and it was here that one hears of many indios wishing to change status to mestizo, despite the extra tax burden.

But there is no reason to assume that the less successful descendants of Chinese in Manila and Central Luzon, although automatically possessed of the legal status of mestizo and membership in the mestizo gremios, necessarily had any important stake in identifying themselves with either the mestizo community or its political–cultural organization.

89. Austin Craig, *Rizal's Life and Minor Writings* (Manila, 1927), pp. 7–23.

90. A brief outline of the *gracias al sacar* procedure, with references, is found in J. F. King, "The Case of José Ponciano de Ayarza: A Document on *Gracias al Sacar,*" *Hispanic American Historical Review,* 31 (1951), 640–47.

91. *Informe Secreto de Sinibaldo de Mas,* p. 110.

92. Zúñiga, *1,* 44, 204, 334–35; Mallat, *1,* 245; *2,* 135; MacMicking, p. 61; "Remarks on the Philippine Islands, 1819–1822," BR, *51,* 102–06; PNA, Provincial Documents, leg. 117, núm. 70; leg. 56, núm. 11; Bowring, pp. 114–15.

For them, too, despite their geographic location, assimilation might occur rapidly.

Manila offers a special case. Chinese coming to the Philippines almost always arrived at Manila. Wherever else they might not be permitted to go, they were always allowed to stay at Manila unless there was a general expulsion. Thus, unlike other parts of the archipelago, Manila had a Chinese population that was constantly being replenished. Moreover, the mestizos of Binondo lived next to the Chinese and could hardly avoid contact with them. The gremio hall of the mestizos was but a few blocks down Calle San Fernando from the Tribunal de Sangleyes. And the Catholic Chinese and mestizos were co-parishioners and sat together opposite the indios in Binondo Church.[93] These facts must have had some bearing upon the orientation of the mestizos who lived in Binondo. The law said the child of a Chinese was automatically classed as a mestizo and a member of the mestizo gremio. But if he was of a Manila family of low socioeconomic status (and it may be assumed that the lower the socioeconomic status the lower the level of hispanization was likely to be), and if he grew up in Manila where there were always many Chinese with their claims of cultural superiority as compared with the indios, it was then possible for the Chinese community to reclaim him. We have no quantitative information about movement from mestizo to Chinese. But it is noteworthy that the "one known case" of a mestizo's seeking Chinese status was that of a rich and well-known member of the Gremio de Mestizos de Binondo.[94] For someone of that socioeconomic status, such a movement must indeed have been rare. But it is likely to have been much less rare at lower levels. In the end, the deciding factors in assimilation may well have been the relative level of hispanization and the relative availability of direct contact with Chinese culture as an alternative. Those who were heavily hispanized stopped in the mestizo gremios and stayed there. Those who were moderately hispanized might pause in the mestizo community and classification and then move on to total assimilation as indios. Those in Manila who were lightly hispanized and in contact with the Chinese cultural alternative might pause for a generation and then move into the Chinese community.

A lengthy speculative discussion has been presented here despite the lack of source material to support a definitive factual presentation. I have done this because the subject of mestizo social mobility is vital to our understanding of the social history of the Philippines and therefore must be dealt with as part of a volume that purports to discuss social

93. PNA, Gremios, 16-5-5.
94. Comenge, p. 229; Huang Hsiao-ts'ang, p. *chia* 198.

change in the Spanish period. I offer the foregoing as a tentative model of social change, based on what we know of similar problems in the contemporary Chinese community of the Philippines and in historical and contemporary Chinese communities elsewhere.

Some of the relations of the mestizos with the indios and Chinese have been touched upon above. Mestizo–indio relations were prejudiced by the frequent position of the mestizo as inquilino, moneylender, and sharp wholesaler in his dealings with the indio. There were, too, the competitive jousts of a local prestige nature between the mestizo and indio gremios, especially in Binondo.[95]

Mestizo–Chinese relations are less easy to pinpoint. The majority of the mestizos, identifying themselves with the Spanish Philippines, adopted Spanish prejudices along with Spanish culture. Their attitudes toward the Chinese depended upon their degree of hispanization. The greater the hispanization the more willing they were to side with the Spaniards—and perhaps with the indios too—against the Chinese.

Spanish records, which are our major source of information about this period, say little of Chinese–indio relations. Undoubtedly, the Chinese regarded the indios as culturally inferior barbarians. For their part, the indios quickly developed an antipathy toward the Chinese, based upon cultural norms acquired from the Spanish—notably, Catholicism. The troops that suppressed the Chinese uprisings and massacred the sangleyes for the Spaniards were indio. In return, the Chinese of Cebu helped finance the suppression of the indio rebellion of Dagohoy in the eighteenth century. But there is evidence of Chinese aid to an indio revolt in Pangasinan in the 1660s, and after the 1755 expulsion of Chinese many of the sangleyes retired to Mindanao, where they aided the Moros—indios who had not been influenced by the cultural biases introduced by the Spaniards—against the Spanish forces.[96]

But despite culturally-based antipathies, intermarriage was a continuous process. The Catholic indio and the non-Catholic or nominally Catholic Chinese must have had mixed feelings about intermarriage, as they do today. For each partner, his cultural ideals denied the possibility, but his economic interest affirmed the desirability.[97]

Information about the internal structure of the Philippine Chinese community prior to 1850 is difficult to obtain. We do know something

95. Sinibaldo de Mas, "Internal Political Condition of the Philippines, 1842," BR, 52, 64; PNA, Gremios, 16-5-5; Th. Aube, "Manille et les Philippines," *Revue des deux mondes*, 22 (1848), 345, speaks of the "profound aversion" of indios to mestizos—even greater than indio dislike of the Spanish.

96. Díaz, in BR, 42, 255; Real Decreto, Dec. 29, 1772, PNA, Reales Órdenes, caja 33, núm. 95; Liu Chi Tien, *Hua-ch'iao*, pp. 55-56; Purcell, p. 600.

97. George Weightman, "The Philippine Chinese: A Cultural History of a Marginal Trading Community" (Ph.D. dissertation, Cornell, 1960), p. 247.

about the formal organization of the Chinese community at Manila, especially in its dealings with the Spanish government. Almost from the beginning, the Spaniards adopted the familiar Asian practice [98] of appointing a headman, called in the Philippines gobernadorcillo, or *capitán*. The duties of this official were to act as judge in petty civil actions where both parties were Chinese, collect taxes for the Spaniards, keep order, and act as intermediary between the Chinese community and the Spanish government. His jurisdiction included all Chinese in the Manila area, whether inmates of the Parián or residents of Binondo and Santa Cruz. To assist him, two or three subalterns were chosen.[99] The *gobernadorcillo de chinos* was immediately responsible to two Spanish officials. One was a special justice who handled Chinese criminal cases and civil suits involving large sums. The other was the *fiscal*, or crown attorney, who was concurrently Protector of the Chinese and Protector of the Indians.[100]

The formal organization of the Chinese community itself was according to occupational gremios. At various times there were anywhere from twenty to forty of these.[101] Each was represented by a *cabeza* or *cabecilla*,[102] these headmen being collectively known as the *cabecillas de oficios*, or (roughly) "occupational foremen." As a group, the cabecillas de oficios, together with a *cabecilla principal*, who stood over them, made up a *principalia*, or board of notables, which was responsible for making nominations for the office of gobernadorcillo. They also signed petitions presented by the gobernadorcillo to the Spanish government.[103]

It is impossible to determine whether these occupational gremios were actually trade and craft guilds with social and economic functions. They may have been merely artificial organizations established for purposes of tax collecting and representation in dealing with the Spaniards. The titles of the cabecillas are of no help, being usually

98. See Seiichi Iwao, "Li Tan, Chief of the Chinese Residents at Hirado, Japan in the Last Days of the Ming Dynasty," *Memoirs of the Research Dept., Tōyō Bunkō*, Ser. B, *17* (1958), 27 ff.; also J. K. Fairbank, *Trade and Diplomacy on the China Coast* (2 vols. Cambridge, 1953), *1*, 36.

99. Mallat, *1*, 354; MacMicking, pp. 40–41; Liu Chi Tien, *Hua-ch'iao*, p. 51.

100. *Recopilación*, lib. 5, tít. 3, ley 24; lib. 6, tít. 18, ley 6. One reason for the high community chest tax on the Chinese, as contrasted with that of the indios and mestizos was that the salaries of these officials were supplied from that source. *Recopilación*, lib. 6, tít. 18, ley 12; Purcell, p. 598.

101. PNA, Reales Órdenes, 37-1-3; Bando, June 6, 1807, Berriz, *Anuario 1888, 1*, 777–78; Bando, July 24, 1822, in ibid., 778–79; Real Cédula, Sept. 24, 1747, ibid., p. 572; Bando, Sept. 25, 1812, ibid., p. 594.

102. The term *cabecilla* had a variety of uses in the Philippines. A rough translation would be "boss," "foreman," or "ringleader." Besides the usage mentioned in the text there were other applications, which will be discussed below.

103. PNA, Reales Órdenes, 37-1-3; PNA, Capellanías, 34-1-19.

phonetic representations of the Spanish titles. Thus (in Amoy Hokkien pronunciation): *bí-tiàm kah-li-si* (rice dealers' cabeza), *gîn-tiàm kah-li-si-iâ* (silversmiths' cabecilla), and so on.[104] Of cultural interest is a note of similarity between these headmen and the *hong* merchants of Canton. Like the hong merchants, the cabecillas considered themselves agents of the government and so entitled to the style of *kuan* ("official"), in its South Chinese form appearing as the suffix *qua*. Hence, in the Philippines were found names like Benito Tengqua and Sebastián de Niqua.[105]

At some time during the eighteenth century the office of gobernadorcillo became purely honorary, and real power was assumed by the cabecilla principal. Spanish dealings with the Chinese community now passed through his hands, as did Chinese taxes going to the Spaniards. The profits from tax collection were sufficient to cause a scramble for the office of cabecilla principal.[106] But the tax was not collected to the satisfaction of the Spaniards, and in 1809 this function was thrown open to quinquennial contract bidding by all Chinese. This served to reduce the power of the cabecilla principal, as well as the attraction of the office. By the 1830s the cabecilla principal was a defunct institution and the office of gobernadorcillo was beginning to reassert itself.[107]

In the pre-1850 period there may have been organizations based on kinship or common place of origin in China; but nothing is known about this. Up to 1800, the Manila community—and, for that matter, the Philippine Chinese community as a whole—seems to have possessed a considerable homogeneity. Immigration was dependent upon the junk trade, and the junk trade route was a direct line from Ch'üan-chou or Amoy to the Philippines. It is likely that almost all the immigrants were Hokkiens from the Amoy-Ch'üan-chou area. The Cantonese, or macanistas, introduced after 1800, probably did not disturb the stability of the Manila community. Their numbers were few, and they maintained a certain aloofness from the rest of the Chinese.[108]

104. PNA, Reales Órdenes, 37-1-3.

105. Ibid.; PNA, "Legajo 15"; cf. Fairbank, *1*, 50.

106. In 1790 it was ruled that the cabecilla could collect the tribute in the form of products of the respective industries of the Chinese rather than in cash. Berriz, *Anuario 1888, 1*, 574, 584, 590–91, 597; Zúñiga, *1*, 262–63.

107. Comyn, pp. 115-16; Liu Chi Tien, *Fei-lü-p'in Hua-ch'iao,* p. 32. The 1828 tax law put an end to tax collection by contract and returned this function to the gobernadorcillo de chinos. Berriz, *Anuario 1888, 1*, 597. The legislation of the 1830s and 1840s referring to the control of Chinese immigration places responsibility in the hands of the gobernadorcillo and the Warden of the Alcaicería de San Fernando. The cabecilla principal is not mentioned.

108. *Los chinos en Filipinas*, ed. *La Oceanía Española* (Manila, 1886), p. 18; Gabriel García Ageo, "Memorandum on the Chinese in the Philippines," in *Report*

The loci of community leadership and power are difficult to determine. There is no information available at present on how the cabecillas de oficios and the cabecilla principal were chosen. We do have some fragmentary information about one of the ways in which power was exercised. By the nineteenth century there were two rival secret societies in Manila, whose membership and control were vested in the wealthy elements in Chinese society. Each of the societies had its military auxiliary, the "sam-sings." These "sam-sings" spent part of their time fighting each other, and the rest in violence against individual Chinese or in plunder. Penniless newcomers were particularly subject to the demands the secret societies made—and the benefits they conferred.[109] The origins of the two secret societies are unknown. There may be a connection between them and two "musical associations," the Lang Chun Hui and the Chang Ho Hui, which were formed in 1824. Whatever the case, one may infer on the basis of the known role of secret societies in other Chinese communities that the secret societies were at once both the major agencies of political control and the most important instruments of social aid to the newcomer.[110]

As mentioned above, the relations between the Philippine Chinese and the Spaniards were occasionally marked by rebellions and massacres during the seventeenth and eighteenth centuries. In some of these events, relations with China were involved. The anti-Manchu adventurer, Cheng Chih-lung, and his son, Cheng Ch'eng-kung, or Koxinga, maintained relations with the Chinese in the Philippines, and relied upon Sino–Philippine trade for economic support. Cheng Chih-lung is believed to have been involved in the 1639 Philippine Chinese uprising. His son demanded tribute of the Philippines in 1662, with consequences already discussed above.[111]

We may assume that just as Cheng Chih-lung found it worth his

of the Philippine Commission to the President (4 vols. Washington, 1900–01), 2, 434; PNA, Capitación de chinos, 1830, sect. 3. A separate tax register was kept for the macanistas.

109. Comenge, pp. 136–40. It is not known whether any connection existed between these secret societies and the famous Hung Men secret society, which is known to have been established in Manila after 1850.

110. Liu Chi Tien, Hua-ch'iao, p. 62; Huang Hsiao-ts'ang, pp. chia 2, chia 197; "Fei-lü-p'in Hua-ch'iao shih-lüeh" (Short History of the Philippine Chinese), in Fei-lü-p'in Hua-ch'iao shang-yeh ming-lu ("Philippine–Chinese Business Guide and Pictorial Directory") (Manila–Cebu, 1953), p. 3. Cf. Maurice Freedman, "Immigrants and Associations: Chinese in Nineteenth century Singapore," Comparative Studies in Society and History, 3 (1960), esp. pp. 37–38.

111. Relación verdadera . . . 1640 y 1641, p. 1. Cheng Chih-lung is referred to as "Iquan." Liu Chi Tien, Hua-ch'iao, pp. 41–47. Wang Gungwu, A Short History of the Nanyang Chinese (Singapore, 1959), p. 14.

trouble to divert part of the China–Philippines junk trade in his direction, Chinese officials in Fukien and Kwangtung were no less aware
than he of the importance of the junk trade in the economies of their
provinces. Such an awareness might help explain the curious visit of
the three mandarins from Fukien who came to Manila in 1603 looking
for a mountain of gold, an event that touched off the uprising and
massacre of that year. It is also noteworthy that an envoy of the
governor-general in Kwangtung came to Manila in 1658 to discuss
commercial relations, and that a Spanish commercial envoy was sent to
Kwangtung eleven years after that.[112]

Assuming that local governments in Southeastern China were somewhat concerned about the trade, did the imperial government of China
show any interest in either the trade or the Chinese settlers? It is well
known that at various times in Chinese history overseas trade and
migration were prohibited by the Chinese government. Trade led to
emigration, and emigration tended to weaken the Chinese system of
social control. Those who migrated left not only their families and
ancestral tombs, they avoided taxes and labor obligations due the
government.[113] Nevertheless, prohibitions on emigration were relaxed
from time to time; but there is little evidence of a sustained Chinese
interest in the welfare of subjects who had gone overseas. This apparent
lack of interest in the overseas Chinese prior to the late nineteenth
century has been explained as Confucian scorn for those who would
desert the tombs of their ancestors. Such people were not considered
worthy of China's protection. This is the explanation given in a letter
from a Fukien official to the Spanish governor-general after the 1603
massacre.[114]

But another argument has it that China was really interested during
the seventeenth century, both because of the Ming-Manchu struggle
and the emigration of Ming loyalists to Southeast Asia, and because of
the importance of the junk trade to the economy of Southeastern China.
By this analysis, explanations of disinterest are not to be taken literally;
they are mere rationalizations for China's weakness and inability to
protect the overseas Chinese.[115]

There is something to be said for this argument. But it fails to explain
why the Ch'ing dynasty, during its period of greatest strength, the

112. Chaunu, p. 166, n. 8; de la Costa, p. 488. See also Meilink-Roelofsz, p. 265.
113. Jung-pang Lo, "China as a Seapower, 1127–1368," (Ph.D. dissertation, University of California, 1957), pp. 432–33; Wolfram Eberhard, *Social Mobility in
Traditional China* (Leiden, 1962), p. 19.
114. Morga, *Sucesos,* p. 157.
115. Wang Gungwu, pp. 11–16; Lo, p. 433.

eighteenth century, neglected the overseas Chinese and reinstituted the prohibition on emigration.

On the eve of 1850, Chinese economic penetration in the Philippines, once promising, had been inhibited by Spanish restrictions and the Chinese adherence to the English in 1762. In the mid-eighteenth century, at the very time when the Philippine economy was beginning to offer new opportunities for any group able to seize them, Chinese merchants had been excluded from the provinces and limited to the Manila area. The mestizos had reaped the benefits instead, and were now expanding their interests, apparently on the way to economic dominance.[116] In the process of this development, the mestizos (and some indios) had muddled the neat picture of an economic pluralism congruent with a cultural pluralism. The "Chinese economy" was no longer completely Chinese.

In Manila, the social position of the Chinese was slightly improved. The walls of the Parián ghetto had come down and the threat of massacre was now remote. The greater freedom of movement and association within the Manila area and the small size of the Chinese population may have brought about an increase in the rate of assimilation. Of this we cannot be sure. It is certain that the rate of intermarriage did not decline. The growth rate of the mestizo population kept pace with that of the Philippine population as a whole.

Given the removal of pressures from the outside during the early nineteenth century, the Chinese community was during this period less a community than a group, many of whose individuals had social ties with non-Chinese that were as strong as those with other Chinese. Without outside pressures or outside opportunities defined in community terms, there was little need for community-wide mobilizing organizations and community-wide institutions for dealing with the government or with other sources of pressure. There was little need—and few if any such institutions existed.

But changes were already underway. The trend of Spanish policy was toward encouragement of Chinese immigration. This trend would have far-reaching effects.

116. Mallat, 2, 135. "Almost all the retail commerce is in their hands and they may be counted the middle class of the Philippines." Sinibaldo de Mas, *Informe sobre el estado de las Islas Filipinas* (2 vols. Madrid, 1843), 1, 138. Zamora, writing in the 1840s, said: "Those who seem called to occupy the place of the Chinese are their mestizos." Zamora, 6, 103. Mas, at the same time, said: "The Chinese mestizos will, within a century, have grown to at least one million by natural increase and immigration from China, and will possess the greater part of the wealth of the islands." "Internal Political Condition," BR, 52, 64.

PART TWO

Economic Expansion

2

Growth of the Chinese Economy

Background

During the fifty-year period from 1820 to 1870 Philippine economic life underwent a fundamental transformation. The essence of this change was the development of an export crop economy, in which the three economies described in Part One—the Western, native, and Chinese—were linked in a system covering the entire archipelago. To put it another way, in 1820 there were three economies in the Philippines, in mutual association only in a few geographical regions; in 1870 there were still three economies—Western, native, and Chinese—but one could speak of a larger Philippine economy, a system prevailing over most of the archipelago, of which these three were parts.

The developments of this half century accelerated a process set in motion much earlier. Ever since the latter half of the eighteenth century Spanish policy had favored development of cash crops for export. But in the pre-1820 period there had been no real urgency about it. The Philippine government had derived its revenue mostly from customs duties on the China–Manila trade and the Manila Galleon trade with Mexico. When revenue did not meet expenses, which was often the case, Mexico, also a part of the Spanish Empire, supplied a subsidy. The encouragement of export crop production in the eighteenth century was primarily an attempt to provide some source in the Philippines for making up the deficits without resorting to Mexico. The government's tobacco monopoly, established in 1782, had managed to accomplish this.[1]

1. Schurz, *Manila Galleon*, pp. 43, 53–60, 181–82; Gregorio Zaide, *Philippine Political and Cultural History* (2 vols. Manila, 1949), 2, 28–29; Legarda, "Foreign Trade," p. 168.

Nevertheless, the demise of the Manila Galleon trade in 1815 and the end of the private entrepôt trade between Manila and Mexico in 1820 removed an important source of Philippine customs revenue. Of more importance, the independence of Mexico from Spain in 1821 cut off the Philippines from its source of subsidies should tobacco fail. Therefore, when, in the 1820s, the Spanish government reexamined Philippine economic policy after the loss of Spain's American empire, the pressure toward exploitation of Philippine resources was somewhat greater than before.

Moreover, the independence of the American colonies and the difficult conditions attending the Carlist Civil War in Spain produced a sizable body of unemployed Spaniards who sought new opportunities and were ready to migrate to the remaining colonies of Cuba, Puerto Rico, and the Philippines. If the Philippine economy could be stimulated in some way it might provide opportunities for these emigrés. This kind of thinking underlay an 1844 measure which did away with the trade privileges of Philippine provincial governors. It was hoped that this policy change would stimulate the internal trade of the Islands, and that any Spaniards who wished to participate in this trade would have as competitors only the mestizos and a few rich indios.[2] If the Chinese had not flooded into the provincial areas in the post-1850 period, this might have been the case.

If these imperial considerations made Philippine economic development seem important in the 1820s, other conditions had changed in a way that made such a development possible. Eighteenth-century Spanish efforts to promote cash crops had been inhibited by the existence of monopoly trading systems and restrictive commercial laws, and the absence of any entrepreneurial element with the necessary facilities of organization and access to capital and markets. By the 1830s both these problems were on their way to solution.

In the eighteenth-century Philippines, trade had been limited by law to exchanges with other Asian countries, Spanish America, and Spain, none of which were logical markets for Philippine cash crops.

2. *Los chinos en Filipinas*, pp. 110, 112. Manuel Bernaldez Pizarro suggested Spanish factories be established in the provinces for purchasing agricultural produce, so as to break the power of the mestizo trader in internal commerce. "Reforms Needed in Filipinas," 1827, BR, 51, 246. Díaz Arenas noted that as of 1850 the Spaniards had shown little inclination to seize upon the new opportunities. *Memorias históricas*, cuad. 5: "población." Later in the century, as more Spaniards went abroad to non-Spanish places like Algeria and South America, there were protests that they should be coming to the Philippines. See, for example, Carlos Recur, *Filipinas: Estudios administrativos y comerciales* (Madrid, 1879), p. 65; *Los chinos en Filipinas*, p. 33; and *China en Filipinas. Colección de artículos publicados en el Diario de Manila. . . .* (Manila, 1889), p. 94.

Termination of the Manila Galleon trading system removed one impediment to more liberalized commerce. Another impediment was the monopolistic Royal Philippine Company, chartered in 1785, with the promotion of Philippine export crops as one of its functions. The decree that dissolved this company in 1834 also included a provision formally opening Manila to the trade of the world.[3]

While Spanish encouragement of economic development took the almost passive form of relaxation of trade regulations, the more positive function of entrepreneurship was provided by the entry at Manila of North American and non-Spanish European merchant firms, particularly after 1820. Their arrival came about as the culmination of a long process of liberalization in trade and residence laws beginning in the late eighteenth century. Spain's traditional colonial policy prohibited both the trade and residence of non-Spanish Europeans in Spanish colonies. But in 1789 Manila had been opened to the trade of European ships carrying goods to and from Asian countries only. In 1809 a British business firm was allowed to establish itself in Manila, and five years later trade and residence rights at Manila were granted to firms of some other countries. Finally, in 1834, it was decreed that persons of any nationality, trading with any foreign port, might trade and reside at Manila. Application had to be made individually, and trade and residence were restricted to Manila. But a beginning had been made.[4]

Foreign enterprise, particularly North American and British, played a key role in the transformation of the Philippine economy. Besides acting as exporters of raw materials and importers of manufactures, foreign firms provided machinery, made advances on crops, insured ships' cargoes, and received funds for investment from other merchant houses. Their efforts were largely responsible for the development of certain crops to export status—in particular, sugar, *abaca* (Manila hemp), and coffee. Through them, too, the products of European factory industry —especially Manchester and Glasgow textiles—penetrated to every corner of the Philippines.

In the early 1820s, local produce first assumed the leading place in Philippine exports, and European factory goods appeared among Philippine imports for the first time. Fifty years later, sugar and abaca were overwhelmingly the major exports, British textiles were the leading item on the import list, the domestic textile industry was in decline, and the Philippines, which had been a rice exporter, had become an importer

3. Benito Legarda, Jr., "American Entrepreneurs in the 19th Century Philippines," *Explorations in Entrepreneurial History*, 9 (1957), 142; Zaide, *1*, 325–38; *2*, 31–34; Schurz, pp. 412–16.

4. Mas, *Informe*, 2: "comercio exterior," 2; Schurz, pp. 57–58; Zaide, 2, 64–65; Montero, *Historia*, 2, 394; J. Lannoy, *Iles Philippines* (Bruxelles, 1849), p. 165.

of its basic foodstuff. The transition to an export crop economy had been completed.[5]

The Expansion of Chinese Immigration and Residence

Although European and American entrepreneurs were already initiating the process of broad economic change in the Philippines as early as the 1820s, the Chinese did not assume a role in the new economic activities until about midcentury. For them to do so required some changes in the conditions of the 1820s. In large part, this was a matter of liberalizing Spanish policy in Chinese affairs.

During a period of roughly thirty years, beginning in the early 1830s, Spain's policy toward Chinese immigration and settlement underwent a fundamental revision. Basically, the change was from a policy of limiting new immigration and restricting the activities of Chinese already in the country to one of openly encouraging immigration, easing restrictions, and providing attractive opportunities for profit. The fundamental motivation for this policy change was the same as that underlying the general liberalization of trade and residence regulations: the desire to develop the Philippines economically. All segments of Spanish opinion seemed ready to concede that the Chinese would be useful in realizing this goal. There was less agreement on how they were to be used, and whether the danger to Philippine society implied in letting down barriers to Chinese immigration was greater than the benefits. How many Chinese should be let in? Should they be restricted as to occupation and residence? Or should the bars simply be lowered and events allowed to take their course? These questions were debated throughout the rest of the Spanish period.

The first movement in the direction of liberalization was in the realm not of immigration but of trade. A decree of 1832 attempted to relieve Chinese junk merchants arriving at Manila of some of the annoying procedures and petty taxes to which they exclusively had been subjected. It was ruled that Chinese ships thereafter should pay only those taxes other countries' vessels paid. Subsequent decrees of 1837 and 1843 confirmed this.[6]

Legislation of this kind was intended in part to encourage further

---

5. Legarda, "American Entrepreneurs," pp. 142, 149-51. A more detailed discussion of the role of foreign enterprise in the transformation of the Philippine economy is found in Legarda's "Foreign Trade," esp. Chaps. 4-6.

6. Real Órden, April 11, 1832, quoted in Real Cédula, April 20, 1837, PNA, Reales Órdenes, caja 93, núm. 30; Bando, Dec. 13, 1843, quoted in Real Órden, Jan. 28, 1844, caja 100, núm. 75; Superior Decreto, Dec. 13, 1843, San Pedro, *Legislación ultramarina*, 2, 477-78.

development of the China–Manila junk trade, for what it could contribute to the economic development of the Philippines. However, it is likely that an indirect and more important benefit hoped for was reciprocally favorable treatment of Spanish traders in China. Ever since the early 1820s the Philippine government had sought to obtain a trade treaty between Spain and China which might allow greater privileges to Spanish vessels at Chinese ports. In the wake of the Opium War treaty settlement, Spain struggled to acquire for herself the benefits China had given other countries. Not until 1864 did China deign to grant a treaty to Spain. During the long struggle that preceded this pact, Spain may well have sought favor with China by granting better treatment to both Chinese junk merchants and Chinese residents in the Philippines.

We know, for instance, that in the late 1840s those who favored allowing the Philippine Chinese to use opium argued that to deny this convenience to China's subjects might jeopardize Spanish chances for a trade treaty with China. And by the 1850s, at least, Spanish discussions on how to treat the Philippine Chinese were made explicitly within the context of reciprocity. Thus, one could say that Spanish policy toward the Philippine Chinese was liberalized not only to encourage Chinese assistance in Philippine economic development, but to aid that development indirectly by promoting Spanish trade with China.[7]

Ever since the mid-eighteenth century, Chinese migrating to the Philippines had found their economic activities hampered by restrictions on occupational pursuits and limitations on geographical mobility. While Chinese within the Manila area had free choice of occupation, only those dedicated to agricultural pursuits could reside in the provinces. The policy in force was essentially a negative one—punishing with residence restrictions those who did not enter the occupations favored by the government. Such a policy did not really encourage Chinese activity in agriculture, as it was intended to do. It offered no positive inducements. Access to residence in the provinces was not a bonus of any kind; it was a necessary precondition to agricultural activity. Beginning with the tax law of 1828, Spanish policy moved away gradually from this negative course toward one of positive encouragement. As mentioned in Part I, the 1828 tax law was a kind of tacit recognition that, Spanish

7. See Real Órden, July 4, 1846, San Pedro, 2, 478; Comenge, *Cuestiones filipinas*, p. 162; "Voto consultivo de la audiencia," 1859, PNA, Acuerdos de audiencia, 17-16-20; Real Cédula, April 20, 1837, caja 93, núm. 30; Reales Órdenes in caja 97, núm. 2, 3, 100, and caja 99, núm. 37; Sinibaldo de Mas, *La Chine et les puissances Chretiennes* (2 vols. Paris, 1861), 2, 114–20; Jerónimo Bécker, *Historia de las relaciones exteriores de España durante el siglo XIX* (3 vols. Madrid, 1924–26), 2, 668; Ramón Jordana y Morera, *La inmigración china en Filipinas* (Madrid, 1888), p. 23.

efforts notwithstanding, the Chinese were continuing to gravitate toward mercantile occupations. The Spanish acceptance of the idea that the Chinese could not be forced into agriculture led eventually to a more positive policy of tax preference for those who did go into farming. Those who did not were penalized, not by residence restriction but by higher taxes. In this fashion, the Spanish hoped to accomplish two things at once: subsidization of agricultural development and an increase in tax revenue.

The process of change in the occupational and residence laws was a gradual one. The tax law of 1828 established the principle of taxation according to occupational classification, and applied high rates to those in commerce, but it did not specifically mention agricultural occupations. Residence laws were also unaffected. But by 1830 royal treasury officials in Manila were urging relaxation of residence and occupational restrictions, and in 1834 the crown ordered that means be devised to do this.[8]

This royal directive immediately provoked debate, in which, speaking broadly, two points of view became clear. Those holding liberal views believed that the encouragement of Chinese immigration and the dispersion of Chinese throughout the Philippine provinces could not but benefit economic life. They differed among themselves as to what, if any, restrictions to put on the Chinese in the provincial areas. Some believed that restrictions of some kind ought to be established to keep Chinese in the provinces from forming large communities beyond the reach of Spanish military power. Others recommended an unqualified open door policy. Liberals also seem to have become aware quite early that the presence of more Chinese offered possibilities not only for economic development but also for revenue increase. This kind of thinking resulted in the establishment of a government opium monopoly in 1843. Some years later, Rafael Comenge, an ardent conservative, decried what he considered an obsession with the Chinese as an object of revenue, and Gabriel García Ageo sarcastically remarked that the "most advanced classes" favored using Chinese immigration to fill the government treasury "even at the cost of converting the archipelago into a Chinese colony with a Spanish flag." [9]

8. Comenge, p. 256; Montero, *Historia*, 3, 27; Zamora, *Biblioteca legis. ultra.*, 6, 102.

9. Opinion of *fiscal* [crown attorney], cited in Acuerdo de audiencia, Feb. 23, 1850, PNA, Reales Órdenes, caja 100, núm. 75; Opinion of fiscales, cited in "Voto consultivo de la audiencia," PNA, Acuerdos de audiencia, 17-16-20. Queen Isabel II, usually on the side of the Spanish liberals, ordered in 1851 that the Philippine governor-general encourage Chinese immigration by every possible means, "regardless of professions." Real Órden, Feb. 16, 1851, PNA, Reales Órdenes, caja 109, núm. 98; Comenge, pp. 151, 365, 416; García Ageo, "Memo. on Chin. in Phil.," p. 437. See also Jordana, pp. 35, 45.

Conservatives were quick to point out that this emphasis on economic development and revenue was apt to be in fundamental contradiction to Spanish policies of protecting the indio from the Chinese. As mentioned in Part I, Spain's policy traditionally had been a kind of compromise between economic interest and her mission to Catholicize and hispanize the indio. So long as the Chinese were restricted to those areas where Spaniards were concentrated, particularly Manila, they could be segregated, watched, and their relations with the indios controlled. Thus, economic interest and religious–cultural mission could be harmonized and kept in balance. Now, conservatives were prepared to concede the desirability of Chinese settlement in the provinces—but only as agricultural laborers, and only then if there were sufficient provisions for controlling their activities. If given free residence and occupational choice in the provinces, they argued, the Chinese would contaminate the indios with their religion and take over all internal trade and small industry. The Spanish would thus be unfaithful not only to their religious–cultural obligation to the indios, but to an economic obligation toward them as well. Better, they said, to have an economically backward country than a Chinese colony flying the Spanish flag.[10]

Some liberals attempted to answer this argument with the claim that, far from damaging the indio, the presence of Chinese in every town would serve as a stimulus and an education to him. In other words, they argued that exposure to Chinese competition would teach the indio the value of hard work. The Chinese was needed as agricultural labor precisely because the indio did not work hard enough. Surely he would respond to the competitive stimulus.

In this sense, the Chinese were to be used as teachers of the indio—agents of cultural change, as it were. And if the Philippines was to be developed economically, the indios should not be protected from closely associating with the Chinese, but encouraged to do so. This line of argument appears repeatedly as late as the 1890s, when it was already apparent that the indios had not responded in the fashion predicted and

10. Opinion of Governor-general Norzagaray, c. 1859, in "The Chinese in the Philippines," *Report of the Philippine Commission to the President* (4 vols. Washington, 1900–01), *1*, 152. Bernaldez Pizarro contrasted the asceticism and benign influence of the Spanish friar with the "greed and ambition of the European trader, the mestizo, and the Chinese." Economic development, he said, should be in the hands of Spaniards or indios. Bernaldez Pizarro, pp. 203–06, 250–51. See also "Voto consultivo de la audiencia," 1859, PNA, Acuerdos de audiencia, 17-16-20. The opposition of the religious orders to the presence of Chinese in the provinces is also indicated in this document. Rafael Comenge, an arch-conservative of the 1890s, bemoaned the abandonment of the wise paternalism of the Laws of the Indies, urged in the 1830s by newcomers from Spain who did not understand the Philippine situation. Comenge, pp. 407-10.

conservative predictions about trade and industry had been in large part realized.[11]

The liberal–conservative controversy went in favor of the liberals with the Philippine governor-general's decree of 1839, which gave the Chinese "complete liberty to choose the occupation that best suits them," whatever their place of residence. The doors to the provinces were now opened wide. Licenses to reside in the provinces, or to change residence from one province to another, could now be obtained by application either to the governor-general at Manila or to provincial governors. But trips between Manila and the provinces for collection of produce continued to be subject to restrictions. Travel permits of three months' duration could be obtained, and in special cases might even be extended a short time. But while three months was surely enough time for anyone traveling to and from provinces adjacent to Manila, it was insufficient for those whose business took them to the Bisayas. The transmittal of goods from all parts of the archipelago to Manila for export was becoming an ever larger business, and these travel restrictions were hampering Chinese participation in it. Moreover, any Chinese wishing a travel permit had to pay the equivalent of first-class tax, according to the 1828 scale, for each month the permit was in force.[12] If a Chinese had an "overhead" of 30 pesos for a three-month permit, his enterprise would require substantial financing to be attempted and a high rate of return to be successful.

The 1839 law also suggested the desirability of using the Chinese as settlers in such uncolonized areas as the Calamianes island group, the provinces of Caraga (present Davao) and Misamis in Mindanao, and around the Spanish *presidio* at Zamboanga. The proposed settlements were to be essentially penal colonies composed of Chinese who had not paid their taxes.[13]

11. Opinion of fiscales, cited in "Voto consultivo de la audiencia," 1859; Buzeta, *Diccionario de las Islas Fil.*, 1, 184; Opinion of "Ministros de los cajas," in Zamora, 6, 102–03. Foreign merchants and their representatives, interested in the development of the export crop economy in the Philippines, sometimes parroted these arguments. See Lannoy, p. 109, and John Foreman, *The Philippine Islands* (2nd ed. New York, 1899), p. 119. See also the argument that the Chinese were needed to teach industries to the indios. José Jimeno Agius, *Población y comercio de las Islas Filipinas* (Madrid, 1884), p. 19 n. The most extreme liberal suggestion was that intermarriage between the Chinese and other elements in Philippine society ought to be encouraged, on the assumption this would help produce a "superior" mestizo society. Mas, "Internal Political Condition," BR, 52, 86–87, and Raimundo Geler, *Islas Filipinas* (Madrid, 1869), summarized in W. E. Retana, *Aparato bibliográfico de la historia general de Filipinas* (3 vols. Madrid, 1906), 2, 752. See also Lannoy, p. 168.

12. San Pedro, 2, 474.

13. Ibid., pp. 474–75.

Contrary to what one might expect, the legislation of 1839 did not result in an immediate influx of Chinese into every part of the Philippines. Instead, the overall Chinese population, which had been gaining at the rate of something over 500 persons per year since 1828, suddenly dropped off by half, from an 1839 figure of 11,575, to an 1840 mark of 5,729. The reasons for this are not clear, but it is likely that the Opium War was, in some fashion, a factor. From 1840 through 1847 there were fluctuations but no solid gain, and the 1847 Chinese population of 5,736 was at almost the same level as that of 1828. Only in 1848 did a steady rise begin. Nor was there an immediate change in the geographical distribution of the Chinese population. In 1828, of the 5,708 Chinese in the Philippines, 5,279, or approximately 93 per cent, were in the Manila area. In 1849, when the Chinese population had increased to 8,757, about 92 per cent of these (8,064) were in the Manila area.[14] Thus, both large-scale increase in the overall Chinese population and the greater distribution of Chinese in the provinces were phenomena of the post-1850 period. This fact indicates that a simple liberalization of the occupational and residence law was not, by itself, enough to encourage large-scale Chinese immigration and settlement in the provinces. Other conditions were necessary.

A possible influence on Chinese immigration and penetration into the interior of the Philippines was the 1844 law that prohibited provincial governors from participating in trade. In some provinces governors had had almost monopolistic control of internal commerce, and this law, when strictly enforced, permitted new opportunities for any group able to seize them.[15]

There was still the problem of restrictions on trips between Manila and the provinces. Although the Chinese were never allowed complete freedom of movement without paying high prices for it, decrees of the governor-general in 1847–48 provided some loosening of restrictions, extending the period of transit to some provinces from three months to twelve. The specific reason for this change was the predicament of Chinese from Manila who went to trade at Samar. If granted only three months' license, they had to go and return at the time when monsoon winds made sea travel from Samar to Manila easiest and hence the

14. Díaz Arenas, *Memorias históricas,* cuad. 5: "población." Díaz seems to have obtained most of his figures from the official guides (*Guías oficiales*). Official figures are probably more accurate during the 1830s and 1840s than later, when large-scale immigration and illegal entries were common. See also Mas, *Informe, 1,* 138.

15. *Los chinos en Filipinas,* pp. 110, 112; O. D. Corpuz, *The Bureaucracy in the Philippines* (Quezon City, 1957), pp. 101–03. On the practices of the governors before 1844 see Legarda, "Foreign Trade," pp. 319–21.

greatest number of ships were available for cargo at Samar. But precisely because of the monsoon this was the time when prices were highest at Samar. In the season of the favorable monsoon, the mestizos of Cebu sent their agents to buy produce at Samar. Backed by "colossal" capital, they could afford to pay almost any price. A Manila Chinese merchant, on the other hand, could pay only a small price. He was indebted to a lender in Manila, he had to pay the freight to Manila of whatever he bought, and still make a profit. Therefore, royal officials in Manila suggested that Chinese travel permits for anywhere in the Bisayas be extended to as long as twelve months. In this way a Chinese could go from Manila during the counter-monsoon when the prices were low, buy his goods, and wait until the monsoon, when cargo ships were available, to send them on to Manila.[16]

The motives for the royal officials' recommendation and Governor Clavería's favorable action are nowhere made explicit. But it is likely that prices, rather than equitable treatment, were the determining factor. It is reasonable to assume that the high prices paid by the Cebu mestizos would be passed on by them to merchants at Manila, which would not only be contrary to the interests of the latter but would result in higher prices for Philippine goods in world markets. It would therefore be in the interest of lower prices that the mestizo brokerage monopoly be challenged.[17]

But the mestizos of Cebu had an advantage besides large capital; they also were shipowners, and hence could forward goods to Manila cheaper than a Chinese who had to pay freight on someone else's vessel. This advantage could be overcome by either selling or consigning vessels to Chinese for ventures from Manila to the Bisayas. Apparently such a practice was a threat to the Cebu mestizos' brokerage business, since we find them in 1859 protesting that the Spanish law which prohibited "foreign" ownership of vessels in Manila's maritime fleet should be applied to the Chinese.

In another protest of the same year, the mestizos of Cebu urged that the Chinese be forbidden to be consignees of Spanish boats and that no captain of an interisland trading vessel be allowed to carry cargoes con-

16. PNA, Provincial Documents, ley 117, núm. 4.

17. Jagor (*Travels in the Philippines,* p. 303) mentions the existence of a high brokerage fee charged by the Cebu mestizos. MacMicking notes (*Recollections of Manilla,* p. 258) that government taxes on provincial goods coming to Manila, when added to export duties, helped make Philippine produce too expensive in competition with the same products grown elsewhere. Writing in the late 1870s Jimeno Agius argued in favor of having Chinese merchants in the interior on the grounds that their competition with other traders kept prices down. Jimeno Agius, p. 19 n.

signed to Chinese. They further recommended that Chinese commerce in the provinces be restricted to retail shopkeeping, and that the Chinese be denied trading in abaca, sugar, *almáciga* (mastic), sapanwood, sea cucumbers, wax, tortoise shell and other articles sent from the provinces to Manila. The royal officials at Manila answered the first of these protests with a simple affirmation that laws excluding foreigners from owning vessels engaged in coastwise trade did include the Chinese. The second protest was referred to the governor-general and maritime agencies for study. It is not known whether there was ever a reply.[18]

Whatever the Manila authorities might dispose, in the long run the trend of Spanish policy (up to the middle 1870s, at least) was away from protecting the rights of domestic trading firms and in the direction of establishing the same rights and obligations for foreigners. In 1859 all foreigners doing business in the Philippines were declared to be subject to Spanish commercial law and commercial courts. Chinese coastal traders were to be included in the *matricula de comercio* (register of merchants) of Manila, along with Spaniards, Americans, and non-Spanish Europeans. A regulation of 1865 on the subject of Chinese wholesalers tacitly recognized Chinese boat ownership by requiring that Chinese shipowners keep their records in Spanish. Finally, a law of 1870, allowing foreigners to own all classes of movable property, did not except boat ownership.[19]

Thus, the Chinese were useful to those who wished to challenge a mestizo commercial monopoly. But the most widely advertised claims of their usefulness were in the realms of plantation labor and frontier colonization. The idea of using Chinese as agricultural labor was, of course, nothing new. Agricultural colonies of Chinese had been tried in Laguna in the seventeenth century and in Pampanga late in the eighteenth century. Neither of these ventures had succeeded.[20] The

18. "Circular del gobierno superior," May 21, 1859, Berriz, *Anuario 1888, 1,* 604–05; Petition of Cebu merchants and ship-owners, 1859, PNA, Acuerdos de audiencia, 17-16-20. The ownership of boats by Chinese using assumed names dates from at least the 1820s. Bernaldez Pizarro, p. 232.

19. Real Cédula, July 26, 1863, Berriz, *Anuario 1888, 1,* 607–08; Montero, *Historia, 3,* 470. The law of 1870 is cited in Opinion of the Consejo de Ultramar, May 11, 1887, PNA, Reales Órdenes, caja 155, núm. 354. Legarda notes that the 1870 law was promulgated "during the high-water mark of nineteenth century Spanish liberalism." "Foreign Trade," p. 344. See also Jagor, p. 347. A publication of 1875 lists six Chinese as consignees of sailing vessels for coastwise shipping. Ramón González Fernández and Federico Moreno Jérez, *Manual del viajero en Filipinas* (Manila, 1875), p. 276.

20. *Relación verdadera . . . 1640 y 1641,* p. 1; Craig, *Rizal's Life,* pp. 67–68; Real Órden, April 1, 1785, PNA, Reales Órdenes, caja 44, núm. 14; Díaz Arenas, *Memorias históricas,* cuad. 5: "población."

general effort, after 1790, to push Chinese into agricultural activity had also failed, mostly because sufficient inducements were not offered. From the 1820s on, the question of using the Chinese in agriculture was again discussed, but this time within the framework of two specific possibilities: plantation labor and frontier colonization.[21]

It was with these two objectives in mind that the Philippine government finally decreed in 1850 preferred tax status for Chinese agricultural laborers. Instead of paying 6 pesos' tribute (or headtax), plus 6 reales' "community chest" tax, plus one or another of the rates established in the 1828 industrial tax, a Chinese agricultural laborer in Luzon was to be exempt from the industrial tax and pay only a reduced headtax and "community chest" fee totaling 13 reales, or about $1\frac{1}{2}$ pesos. Plantation laborers in the Bisayas were to pay only 6 reales, or less than 1 peso. Chinese who settled as agricultural colonists on the frontier, whether in Luzon, the Bisayas, or Mindanao, were to be charged only the standard 12 real tax paid by the indios.[22]

These tax inducements were established to do two things: to foster development of plantations growing export crops—particularly sugar, indigo, and abacá—and to populate hitherto uncolonized regions. In the case of the first objective, subsequent legislation widened the scope of this law to include Chinese miners, woodcutters, fishermen, and boat builders. Furthermore, these tax privileges were extended to Chinese mestizos who planted export crops, provided they worked their own lands; mestizo landlords who used to kasamahan system were not included.[23]

The idea seems to have been that owners of large haciendas would import laborers from China. Apparently, this rarely happened. In the first place, there were few large haciendas in the Philippines in the 1850s. Those that existed were generally owned by the religious orders,[24] which were opposed to the spread of the Chinese into the countryside, fearing it would adversely affect the indios. It is true that a few landowners, like the energetic Domingo Roxas, imported some Chinese laborers to work their estates. But in the main, those who owned or leased land seemingly lacked the means to import coolies, or else preferred traditional methods of exploiting their holdings. MacMicking,

21. See Mas, "Internal Political Condition," pp. 67–68; Real Órden, Jan. 28, 1844, PNA, Reales Órdenes, caja 100, núm. 75 (which discusses encouraging the immigration of Chinese in family groups); Bernaldez Pizarro, p. 251; Bando, Aug. 31, 1839, Berriz, Anuario 1888, 1, 603.

22. Superior Decreto, Dec. 5, 1850, San Pedro, 2, 485.

23. Ibid.

24. Mallat, Les Philippines, 2, 365.

writing shortly after the 1850 decree, accurately predicted the failure of this Spanish attempt to encourage plantation agriculture, pointing out that there were few people in the Philippine colony with sufficient capital to start a large-scale plantation. As he predicted, Philippine agriculture remained mostly on a small-unit basis.[25]

When few landowners showed interest, some persons who did not own land came forward with speculative brokerage enterprises to import and settle Chinese coolies as agricultural colonists. Examples of such enterprises may be seen in the activities of Juan Bautista Marcaida, a Manila Spanish merchant. In 1849 Marcaida and his two Spanish associates were given special permission to import, tribute-free for fifteen years, 176 Chinese men and six Chinese women to act as agricultural colonists of the Batanes and Babuyanes Islands north of Luzon. Encouraged by the apparent success of his project, Marcaida was back the following year with a sweeping scheme to open new lands for Spain and new vistas of profit for himself. His plan was to pay all expenses for the importation of 1,000 Chinese. These were to be furnished with whatever animals and machinery were appropriate to the industry they would undertake. Public lands could be leased to them. Profits would be split 50-50 between the Chinese and Marcaida's "enterprise."

Since they were neither *hacenderos* nor produce wholesalers, Marcaida and his friends were not so much interested in the development of agricultural products in the Philippines; their point of view was simply that Chinese labor was now considered a valuable commodity in the Philippines, and hence offered possibilities for speculation and fortune. Sinibaldo de Mas, Spain's number one "China Hand," wrote Marcaida from Macao, encouraging these enterprises. With 200 to 300 Chinese to work for him, Mas believed, a man would soon have a fortune. It is doubtful that it worked out that way for Marcaida. The Batanes-Babuyanes experiment was gone without a trace twenty years later, and one hears nothing more of his proposal of 1850.[26]

From the standpoint of establishing the Chinese in agriculture, the

25. MacMicking, pp. 151–55. On Domingo Roxas, see PNA, Libro de informes, 1833, 48a-3-9, pp. 76v–77. See also a request from Mariano Rojas, cited in Real Órden, June 14, 1848, in Berriz, *Anuario 1888, 1,* 604. In both these cases, requests for permission to bring in Chinese plantation laborers were made before the 1850 law. On the attitude of the religious orders, see "Voto consultivo," 1859. On the essentially small-scale nature of Philippine agriculture during this period, see Legarda, "Foreign Trade," pp. 307, 311–12.

26. Juan Bautista Marcaida, *Empresas agrícolas, con chinos, en Filipinas* (Manila, 1850), esp. preface and pp. 3–21. A statistical publication of 1875 lists no Chinese for Batanes and Babuyanes. Agustín de la Cavada y Méndez de Vigo, *Historia geográfica, geológica y estadística de Filipinas* (2 vols. Manila, 1876), *2,* 10.

1850 legislation had a large loophole—perhaps an intentional one. Chinese entering the Philippines under this new plan had to show on arrival where and for whom they were going to work. But once they had arrived at the work site they were not obliged to work for the person in whose name they had been imported, unless he had previously bound them to a contract. Instead they were free to do whatever they wished, having only to pay the higher tax rate associated with non-agrarian occupations if they should go into commerce.[27] Thus, whoever wished to bring into a province—for whatever purpose—a larger number of Chinese than would otherwise have been allowed, could use "plantation labor" as the means.

The frontier colonization idea was hardly more successful than "plantation labor." A Chinese agricultural settlement was established and maintained for a time in the Calamianes Islands; a trading colony was settled in Zamboanga.[28] But the idea of using Chinese as frontier colonists conflicted with other Spanish objectives. Contact between natives and Chinese in frontier zones was believed to jeopardize subsequent Spanish efforts to conquer and Christianize those areas.[29] Thus, the frontier colonization projects proposed for Mindanao and Palawan in the last years of the Spanish period involved either agricultural colonists from Spain or a combination of these and Chinese laborers to work for them. It is doubtful that many of these projects were carried to fruition.[30]

On the whole, Spanish attempts to induce the Chinese into agricultural activities ended, as before, in failure. Some Chinese did become vegetable gardeners near towns. But otherwise, Chinese continued to go into commerce and industries because of personal connections and the known opportunities for profit. In 1870, at perhaps the high point of Chinese activity in agriculture, there were slightly less than 500 Chinese employed in agricultural occupations, out of a Chinese population of over 40,000.[31]

27. Superior Decreto, Dec. 5, 1850, San Pedro, 2, 485–86. See also Comenge, p. 261, where it is asserted that Chinese on completion of contracts could settle on public lands and farm for themselves, continuing to pay the same low rate as contract laborers.

28. Comenge, p. 410.

29. AMAE, China, 1889. Reclamación del gobierno chino, Ultramar to Estado, June 27, 1891.

30. Real Órden, May 13, 1884, Berriz, Anuario 1888, 1, 773; "Sesión de 9 mayo 1888 de la Sociedad Geográfica de Madrid," Boletín de la Sociedad Geográfica de Madrid, 24 (1888), 394.

31. China en Filipinas, p. 231; Comenge, p. 263; González and Moreno, p. 51; Census of the Philippine Islands Taken Under the Direction of the Philippine Commission in the Year 1903 (4 vols. Washington, 1905) (hereafter: Census of 1903), 2, 985.

A more significant attraction to Chinese immigration and enterprise was the opening of new ports to world trade between 1855 and 1860. Manila, as the single port of foreign commerce, had drawn on all the provinces for export goods and had, in turn, acted as the distributor of imports. The opening of Sual in Pangasinan and Zamboanga in western Mindanao did little to change this. But when Cebu and Iloilo were opened, trade patterns were altered. Now there were three major foreign trade ports, rather than one. Moreover, agriculture and industry in the areas around Cebu and Iloilo were stimulated by access to direct exporting and importing, and there were new economic opportunities of many kinds.[32]

One of the most attractive opportunities presented the Chinese during the post-1850 period was access to the government's tax-collecting monopoly contracts. A measure of 1857 allowed foreigners to bid on government contracts. Before long, most monopoly contractors on both the municipal and provincial levels were Chinese, and their profits were considerable.[33] It might be added that a monopoly contractor, as a government agent, was entitled to whatever troops were necessary to protect his monopoly and presumably his person as well. A Chinese going into a province as a monopoly contractor thus had some protection for his other interests.

The Chinese also benefited from a general law of 1863 which allowed all foreigners to practice whatever occupations they wished, and gave them rights of land ownership and inheritance in the Philippines. A subsequent law, in 1870, extended these rights to movable property as well.[34]

One deterrent to Chinese settlement in the provinces had always been the insecurity of property. The danger might take the form of robbery by professionals or casual village vandalism. Without a consulate to support him, a Chinese could only bribe the locally powerful and hope for the best. The creation of the Guardia Civil in 1868 improved the situation. In subsequent years, as additional units of this security police force were created, more and more provinces were kept in some kind of order, which benefited commerce. Sea trade was expedited by the post-1850 activities of steam warships, which put an end to large-scale Moro piracy in most parts of the archipelago.[35] Finally, the opening of the Suez Canal in 1869 and the promulgation the same year of a liberal

32. Conrado Benitez, *History of the Philippines* (rev. ed. Boston and New York, 1954), pp. 234–38; Legarda, "Foreign Trade," pp. 203–04.

33. Montero, *Historia, 3,* 265, n. 2; *Los chinos en Filipinas,* pp. 20–21.

34. Montero, *Historia, 3,* 389; Legarda, "Foreign Trade," p. 344; Opinion of Consejo de Ultramar, PNA, caja 155, núm. 354.

35. Montero, *Historia, 3,* 560, n. 1.

tariff—one that did away with some of the preferences hitherto given
to Spanish shipping—did much to stimulate Philippine trade and provide economic opportunities.[36]

But if all the changes just described served to provide an attractive
atmosphere for Chinese enterprise, Chinese immigration required other
stimuli in China to put it into motion. The founding of Hong Kong in
1842 was probably of importance in this respect. Wang Gungwu has
called attention to Hong Kong's position as a kind of "base" for the
enterprises of the overseas Chinese, especially in Southeast Asia. So long
as Chinese law made emigration illegal, Hong Kong was a convenient
point of exit and reentry for emigrants.[37] But in the absence of any
dependable information we cannot say how early or in just what fashion
it assumed this function, especially with respect to the Philippines.

One factor in the Chinese situation that stimulated emigration to the
Philippines after 1850 was the unsettled condition attendant upon the
T'ai-p'ing Rebellion of 1850–64. Although Fukien was not directly
involved in this revolt, parts of the province were affected, especially
Changchou, which the retreating rebels sacked in 1864–65.[38] The economic and social conditions prevailing during the T'ai-p'ing Rebellion
were undoubtedly responsible for increased emigration to the Philippines
and, for that matter, to other parts of the world.[39]

Some authors have claimed that the expansion of Chinese emigration
to the Philippines resulted from a clause in the Sino–Spanish treaty of
1864 which gave most-favored-nation rights to Chinese merchants going
to the Philippines.[40] I find this argument unconvincing. It is doubtful
that agreements at the treaty level meant much to coolie or merchant
emigrants. To them it was apparent that without a consulate or any
other visible sign of China's interest, only their own resources and
those of the other Chinese in the Philippines could aid them. China's
interest in the overseas Chinese was just beginning in the 1860s. Moreover, although the Ch'ing government had defeated the T'ai-p'ing Rebellion it had required Western aid to do so, and in the Second Anglo-
Chinese War China's weakness again had been demonstrated. Under
these circumstances one would hardly expect that in the 1860s overseas

36. Legarda, "Foreign Trade," pp. 304–05, 337.

37. Wang Gungwu, Short History of Nanyang Chinese, pp. 22–24.

38. Pablo Fernández, O.P., Dominicos donde nace el sol (Barcelona, 1958), p. 422.

39. Wang Gungwu, p. 25; SCJC, ch. 4, pp. 47a–47b; Chuang Wei-chi, "Fu-chien
Chin-chiang chuan-ch'ü hua-ch'iao shih tiao-ch'a pao-kao," 113–14.

40. Lü Shih-p'eng, "Hsi-ling shih-ch'i Fei-lü-p'in hua-ch'iao chih shang-yeh huo-
tung" (Commercial Activities of the Philippine Chinese in the Spanish Period) Ta-lu
tsa-chih, 13 (1956), 399; Khin Khin Myint Jensen, "The Chinese in the Philippines
During the American Regime, 1898–1946" (Ph.D. dissertation, University of Wisconsin, 1956), p. 41.

Chinese would place great reliance upon China's interest in them or her ability to provide aid.

Perhaps the decisive factor in the expansion of Chinese emigration to the Philippines was neither improved opportunities in the archipelago nor the urgency of the situation in China, but simply the improvement of transportation. By the 1870s Manila was linked to Hong Kong by regular, direct steamship service. The steerage class fares established were low enough and the service frequent and rapid enough to allow a great deal of travel back and forth. Steamship service also made possible a sizable volume of coolie broker emigration. And once in Manila, transportation to the provinces was facilitated by the interisland steamer system inaugurated in the early 1870s.[41]

Whatever the reasons, Chinese immigration figures soared after 1850 and the immigrants scattered into almost every province. In 1847 there had been a Chinese population of about 5,700. By 1864 it had increased to better than 18,000. The census of 1876 showed over 30,000. But the apogee of nineteenth-century immigration was reached in the decade 1876–86, during which the Chinese population increased to an official figure of about 66,000, and an unofficial calculation of over 90,000. There seems to have been some tapering off thereafter. Official figures of the nineteenth century usually undervalue the size of the Chinese population, but the figures of about 59,000 in 1891 and roughly 50,000 in 1894 suggest some decline. As for geographical distribution, in 1849 92 percent of the Chinese were in the Manila area. By 1873 this figure was reduced to about 50 per cent; in 1886 it stood at 77 per cent. The official tax records of 1891 not only show some Chinese in every province, but indicate that only 61 per cent of the Chinese population resided in the Manila area. The 1894 census data shows only 48 per cent in Manila. Of course it must be remembered that Manila was the center for arrivals and departures, and contained a large floating population. The number of Chinese in Manila was apt to fluctuate wildly from year to year, or even within a given year. Nevertheless, these figures serve as indicators of a tendency toward settlement in the provinces.[42]

41. Jagor, p. 4; *The Chronicle and Directory for China, Japan, and the Philippines, 1873* (Hong Kong, 1873), pp. 249, 404. See González and Moreno, pp. 139–40, 274–76, 474; and Montero, *Historia, 3,* 619.

42. Díaz Arenas, *Memorias históricas,* cuad. 5: "población"; González and Moreno, pp. 51, 93; Juan Mencarini, "The Philippine Chinese Labor Question," *Journal of the China Branch of the Royal Asiatic Society, 33* (1899–1900), 181; Jimeno Agius, p. 19; *Los chinos en Filipinas,* pp. 95–96, 102; PNA, Presupuestos de ingresos y pagos de varios conceptos (1891), 4-14-1; *Guía oficial de Filipinas, 1896* (Manila, 1896), p. 213; PNA, Padrones de chinos, 1892–97.

Nature of the New Chinese Economy

The two most salient features of the new Chinese economy were its geographical extent and the new forms it assumed. The old Chinese economy, in the pre-1750 period, had been in operation in those parts of the Philippines where Spaniards were settled, specifically, on Luzon: the Central Plains region, and the areas around the towns of Vigan (in Ilocos) and Naga (in the Bicol region); in the Bisayas and Mindanao: on the island of Panay, and around the Spanish settlements at Cebu and Zamboanga. In the century from 1750 to 1850 the Chinese had been forced to withdraw from those areas, and the scope of the Chinese enonomy had been narrowed to include only the Manila area and nearby Cavite province.

After 1850 the new Chinese economy extended its reach over all the archipelago, beyond the limits of Spanish settlement. In so doing, it brought into the general system of Philippine trade areas where the native economy had been hitherto unaffected by outside influences. In this way, it could be said that Chinese economic penetration helped to unify the Philippines by linking native economy and Western economy throughout the Islands. But at the same time it served to extend the problems of economic and cultural pluralism to all parts of the archipelago.

When the bars were lowered and the Chinese pushed into the provinces again, many of them went to areas where Chinese had penetrated earlier. But the attractions of the export crop business drew many Chinese into provinces where there had probably never been Chinese settlements. The official tax record of 1891 shows that over 10 per cent of the Chinese in the Philippines were located in the abaca-producing provinces of Albay, Leyte, and Samar, where previously there had not been any significant number of Chinese. Two other hemp provinces, Cebu and Camarines Sur, where some Chinese had lived before 1750, also attracted new immigrants. If one adds them to the three provinces just mentioned, the proportion of Chinese in the abaca region reaches between 12 per cent and 15 per cent. Somewhat less spectacular than abacá's attraction was that of the sugar industry. Negros Occidental had had no Chinese residents in pre-1750 times; Iloilo had. By 1881, these two provinces—one a major producer, the other an exporter of sugar—had perhaps 4 per cent of the total Chinese population, according to the official figures. The tobacco provinces of Cagayan and Isabela had had almost no Chinese population before 1850 and very little prior to the disestablishment of the government tobacco monopoly in 1880.

By 1891 the official figures showed almost 1,000 Chinese in Cagayan and nearly 600 in Isabela.[43]

Even in those provinces that were not large producers or export centers of cash crops, there were opportunities for small Chinese shops or itinerant peddlers, selling imported cloths and collecting such raw produce as they could market. The Spaniards assisted the expansion of the Chinese economic frontier by expanding their own political frontier. In the late nineteenth century the Spanish government made a fairly sustained military effort against the unconquered native peoples of Mindanao. Chinese trade followed the Spanish flag. Spanish garrisons in Cotabato and Misamis had to be provisioned, a job for the Chinese. And once an area was conquered by Spanish forces, there was security for traders to move in. Thus, the official figures for 1891 list 476 Chinese in Misamis, 155 in Cotabato, and 254 in Surigao.[44]

This geographical expansion was accompanied by changes in the nature of Chinese economic activities. As described in Part I, the old Chinese economy included the functions of maritime traders, provisioners and retail dealers in urban settlements, distributors of Chinese imports in the areas adjacent to Spanish settlements, and artisans in both Spanish settlements and native communities. In the new Chinese economy, the most important new activity was that of commercial agent, or middleman. In this role Chinese collected produce for export, selling it, usually to Europeans, for shipment to world markets on European ships. They also acted as wholesalers of imported goods, distributing them in the provinces. In addition, the Chinese partly reclaimed their position as provisioners of urban areas from the mestizos and indios, who had usurped it from 1750 to 1850. Chinese artisans began to enter a few new trades. Some Chinese became processors of Philippine produce. Others took away from the mestizos the latter's position in coastwise trade. Chinese became monopoly contractors and coolie labor brokers. Finally, at the end of the Spanish period, Chinese became, on their own account, importers of European goods and exporters of cash crops to world markets.

Alongside this new Chinese economy, parts of the old persisted. The traditional imports from China were continued, both for the use of the Chinese communities in the Philippines and for the wider Philippine market, and an old export trade of minor importance in such exotica as

---

43. PNA, Presupuestos . . . 1891, 4-14-1.

44. Ibid. Del Pan, *Las Islas Filipinas*, p. 384. Del Pan wrote: "From the commercial point of view, Mindanao, excepting the two districts of Surigao and Misamis, seems to be a territory garrisoned by Spaniards so some Chinese can make their fortunes with greater security." Ibid. See also *China en Filipinas*, p. 195.

birds' nests and sea cucumbers for the China market was carried on, although on European ships now instead of Chinese junks. With this general survey as background, let us separately examine each kind of Chinese activity.

3

Foreign Trade

The Character of Philippine Foreign Trade

Nineteenth-century Philippine foreign trade, according to Spanish trade balance sheets, was chiefly with five areas: Spain, China, Great Britain, the United States, and something called "British East Indies." Import figures for 1846 show that in terms of value China was first in Philippine import trade, followed by Singapore, Spain, the United States, and Britain. But the following year Britain leaped to third place, and by midcentury was in first place, a spot which it occupied for most of the rest of the century. China appears to have been in second place for most years between 1850 and 1898, and Spain maintained third place in imports down to the 1890s. The United States remained far down the list of importers, averaging about 1.5 to 2.5 per cent of Philippine imports.

As for exports, in 1846 Great Britain was first, with China a close second, and the United States third. Shortly after, the United States took the lead and retained it during most of the half century that followed, with Britain second. China competed with "British East Indies" for third place.[1]

1. The 1846 figures are found in Lannoy, Annex 3. A table of percentage distribution of Philippine trade by countries for 1846–94 is found in Legarda, "Foreign Trade," pp. 235–38. See also Legarda's general discussion, pp. 240–48. A table of absolute values by country in Philippine trade, 1854–95, expressed in US dollars, is found in *Census of 1903, 4,* 568–69, 572–73. Statistics for 1874–99, apparently taken from Spanish customs records and expressed in Mexican pesos, are given in *Fei-lü-p'in Min-li-la Chung-hua Shang-hui wu-shih chou-nien chi-nien k'an* ("Golden Book, 1955. A Fiftieth Anniversary Publication of the Philippine Chinese General Chamber of Commerce") (Manila, 1955), p. *keng* 168.

From the 1840s on, the patterns of Philippine trade were much influenced by the existence of Singapore and Hong Kong. Since these were both free ports, and strategically located with respect to Philippine commerce, it is not surprising that this happened. But there was also some positive encouragement provided by Spanish policy, which gave tariff preference to imports in Spanish vessels. The result of this policy was that foreign merchants made use of Singapore and Hong Kong as transshipment points where their merchandise from Europe could be loaded onto Spanish ships for the rest of the journey to Manila. This practice, of course, also encouraged the growth of the Spanish merchant marine. But even after 1870, when the tariff differential was reduced and more foreign vessels participated in the carrying trade to Manila, Hong Kong and Singapore continued to be transshipment points both for European goods going to the Philippines and Philippine produce enroute either to China or to markets in Europe or the United States.[2]

The existence of Hong Kong and Singapore is responsible for some confusion in Philippine trade statistics. Singapore was first entered as a separate item. Between 1873 and 1887 it appeared as part of "British East Indies." Thereafter, it was restored to independent listing. Hong Kong appeared first as part of "China," later (1873–87) as part of "British East Indies," and still later (1888–98) under "China" again.

Given the entrepôt nature of Singapore and Hong Kong trade, it is difficult to unravel the actual origin or destination of much of Philippine trade during the late nineteenth century. Singapore, for instance, overstates its volume and undervalues the trade of Britain, continental Europe, and India, which was transshipped through it. Hong Kong is even more confusing.

Hong Kong was a transshipment point for trade with Europe, North America, and China. Therefore, when included under "China," it causes an understatement of North American and European trade and an overstatement of China's trade. It is the inclusion of Hong Kong that boosts "China" to second place in imports and third place in exports. But it is impossible to determine the magnitude of this overstatement. The years 1873–87, when Hong Kong was included in "British East Indies," are of no help, because this arrangement cuts out not only Hong Kong's entrepôt trade to the West but also its transshipments to China. China is therefore undervalued for those years. China Maritime Customs statistics for 1873–87 list only direct trade, hence also excluding trade via Hong Kong. In the absence of Hong Kong statistics on trade with the

2. Legarda, "Foreign Trade," pp. 226–28.

Philippines there is no way Philippine–China commerce can be accurately measured.[3]

Nevertheless, we can make some observations. Legarda's table of percentage shares in Philippine trade shows that China's trade with the Philippines declined relative to that of other countries. If we check this with the Maritime Customs figures we find that Philippine imports from China remained at an almost constant level. But after 1872, and especially after 1880, there was a decline in Philippine exports to China. In other words, it appears that after 1850 Philippine imports from China suffered a relative decline, and in the same period—especially after 1880—exports to China suffered both a relative and an absolute decline.

Reasons for these trends are not difficult to find. The expansion of imports in the Philippines took place especially in cotton textiles, which were first on the import list from 1870 to the end of the century.[4] Chinese handicraft industry was simply unable to compete with European factory industry for a place in this newly opened import market.[5] China's diminished status as an export market for Philippine goods probably was due primarily to the termination of rice exports from the Philippines to China after 1870, when the archipelago ceased to have a rice surplus. Another factor was the absence of a large market in China for most of the export crops now being produced in the Philippines.[6]

Chinese Organizations and Philippine Foreign Trade

While China's position in Philippine trade underwent a relative decline, Chinese traders in the Philippines were able to expand their activities. The success of North European and American entrepreneurs in introducing manufactured goods to the Philippine market and extracting export crops was dependent not only on their organization and access to capital and markets. Efficient distribution of imports and purchasing of export crops were equally essential. Since the personnel of the foreign

3. China Maritime Customs statistics are found in *Liu-shih-wu nien lai Chung-kuo kuo-chi mao-i t'ung-chi* ("Statistics of China's Foreign Trade During the Last Sixty-Five Years") (in Chinese and English), ed. by Yang Shui-liu (C. Yang), Hou Hou-p'ei (H. B. Hau), and others. National Research Institute of Social Sciences, Academia Sinica, Monograph No. 4 (1931), Table XV, p. 102.

4. Legarda, "Foreign Trade," pp. 267–70.

5. Huang Hsiao-ts'ang, p. *i* 71. Another author says that the decline in China's share of Philippine trade was due to the lack of support of overseas Chinese enterprise by the Ch'ing government. Lü Shih-p'eng, p. 396.

6. Legarda, "Foreign Trade," p. 249.

firms wished to reside in Manila, it was necessary to have wholesaling agents in the provinces. But in the 1840s the largest share of wholesaling was done not by merchants based at Manila, but by those based elsewhere on Luzon or in the Bisayas, such as the mestizos of Cebu and Molo. In other words, most of the wholesaling was done by provincial shipowners who made trips to Manila, rather than by Manila shipowners who made trips to the provinces.[7] The new export crop economy demanded a wholesaling system based at Manila (so long as it was the only port open to foreign trade) and able to reach all parts of the archipelago. For this purpose, the Chinese proved well suited. Years later, the head of a European importing firm in Manila said of the Chinese distributors and purchasing agents:

> The firms here, with very few exceptions, only sell in Manila and to the Chinese, who are the intermediaries for the provinces. . . . For importers and exporters it would not have been possible to do any work at all; in fact, the trade of the islands, small as it is compared to what it might be, has depended entirely upon the Chinese, because on one side they sell to the men in the interior, and barter with the natives for produce in exchange for imports— they go into the interior; they have opened up communications; you will see the Chinese hawker everywhere; he will go to the last nook and corner, and he will offer his goods. . . . A European can not work outside here for any length of time.[8]

The Chinese had the right combination of patience, adaptability, pioneering spirit, economic sophistication, and organization to be

7. "Nearly the whole of the coasting trade is in the hands of the Indians, or Mestizos of Chinese descent, called Sangleys, although several Spaniards and European Mestizos at Manilla also own a better class of ships than those described. . . . Still, from some cause or other, they do not appear to carry on the trade so successfully as the provincial ship-owners, most of whom have only one or two small vessels, which they keep constantly running between their native place and Manilla." MacMicking, p. 256. See also Rafael Díaz Arenas, *Memoria sobre el comercio y la navegación de las Islas Filipinas* (Cádiz, 1838) (hereafter: Díaz Arenas, *Memoria*), p. 24. I am aware that two other sources (Mallat, *1*, 321–22, and Buzeta, *1*, 251) say most of the coastwise trade was in the hands of mestizos and indios from Manila. But I think the two sources cited above are more reliable on this point. It is well known that Buzeta used information gathered from the works of Mallat and Sinibaldo de Mas, adding almost nothing of his own. Apparently he relied here upon Mallat. Mallat, although a good observer, was a visitor to the Philippines. His contemporary, Díaz Arenas, was a Spanish official particularly concerned with economic matters. Mallat may have been thinking either of the transportation of the government's tobacco to Manila, contracted for by the mestizos and indios of Manila, or of the provisioning trade of Manila, which was in the hands of the mestizos and indios of that area, especially the mestizos of Tambobong. MacMicking's independent observation lends weight to Díaz Arenas' interpretation.

8. Testimony of A. Kuensle, *Report of the Philippine Commission, 2,* 227–29.

markedly successful distributors and purchasing agents. In fact, they were so well suited to this role that one is led to wonder whether their position in it was arrived at accidentally or by design of those who favored an export crop economy. There is no direct evidence of the latter possibility. But the law of 1839, permitting residence anywhere in the Philippines regardless of occupation, and the extension of travel permits for trade in the Bisayas are two phenomena which suggest that interest in the Chinese was commercial as well as agrarian and fiscal.

Liberalized travel and residence laws provided the Chinese commercial agents with needed access to the provinces. But to make this kind of Chinese activity successful there were other preconditions; specifically, dependable, long-term financing and effective economic organization.

In the pre-1850 period it is doubtful that there was much capital available within the Chinese community. Few enterprises were sufficiently lucrative. One could borrow at 6 per cent from the Chinese "community chests," [9] but after 1755 these funds were not large. Outside the community, individual Spaniards provided venture capital to individual Chinese in the middle and late eighteenth century.[10] But there appears to have been nothing systematic or organized about this practice. In the pre-nineteenth-century Philippines there were no banks, and the principal sources of loan capital for sizable ventures were the *obras pías,* or pious foundations. But these were absolutely forbidden to the Chinese. During the second quarter of the nineteenth century a few private banking businesses were initiated in Manila; it is not known whether they lent to Chinese.[11]

Benito Legarda has pointed out that the key function of the North European and North American entrepreneurs in Manila was banking. Funds were deposited with them by rich families, the Church, Manila businessmen, and even by the native banks just mentioned. Such funds were loaned out, mostly in the form of crop advances.[12] But advances were also made to Chinese wholesalers to help them dispose of European imports and to buy up produce for export. Soon, another source of funds became available to the Chinese. In 1851 the Banco Español–Filipino de Isabel II was founded for the purpose of encouraging the use of savings for commercial investment. Most of the funds from the

9. Witness the case of Nicolás Lim Simco, who borrowed 2,000 pesos from the Chinese *caja* in 1835 at 6 per cent, the principal to be repaid within two years. PNA, Chinos, Cajas de comunidad, 4-17-5.

10. Real Cédula, July 23, 1744, Berriz, *Anuario 1888, 1,* 570; Zúñiga, *Estadismo, 1,* 263–64.

11. On the *obras pías,* see Schurz, pp. 167–72. The "banks" of Gorricho, Rodríguez, and Tuason are briefly discussed in Legarda, "Foreign Trade," pp. 359–60. See also Zaide, 2, 69–70.

12. Legarda, "Foreign Trade," pp. 359–442.

obras pías were transferred to it and the government added other funds of its own, making it a government-regulated, quasi-official institution. Although the bank's first transaction was the discounting of a promissory note for a Chinese, it is doubtful that there were many dealings with Chinese until non-Chinese persons of known responsibility began to act as their cosigners. When European merchant firms were asked by the bank to name Chinese businessmen who were good risks, they not surprisingly proposed those Chinese who did business with them as jobbers and purchasing agents, the English merchants being especially alert to this opportunity. The European firms now became guarantors for Chinese borrowers from the bank, forwarding their payments to the bank, and assuming responsibility for settlement with the bank in case the Chinese defaulted.[13]

For Chinese dealers who concentrated entirely on distributing or re-tailing imports, obtaining goods on credit was more important than access to cash loans. Hence, a European or American firm usually ad-vanced imported goods to Chinese dealers in an interesting credit sys-tem which worked as follows. A Chinese would ask one of the merchant firms for a rather modest amount of goods on credit of perhaps three to six months' term. As soon thereafter as possible, he made a token repayment of a portion of the debt, asking then for a larger advance. Again, only part of this was repaid, and additional credit secured. The process continued in this fashion, so that some Chinese dealers were constantly in debt to foreign firms. It was estimated in one year that the total Chinese debt of this kind amounted to 10,000,000 *francs* (about 2,140,000 pesos).[14] This procedure is perhaps similar to that T'ien Ju-k'ang found among the Chinese in Sarawak:

> One of the Chinese Towkays expressed his view, gained after many years experience, that the secret of doing good business was not to make a high profit out of one's customers, but to get other

13. Petition of the gobernadorcillo and principales of the Gremio de Chinos de Manila, May 15, 1877, PNA, Cabezas de barangay, chinos, 49-1-10; *Los chinos en Filipinas*, pp. 22–25, 88; Montero, *Historia, 3,* 171; *Bank of the Philippine Islands. 75th Anniversary. Souvenir of the First Bank Established in the Far East* (Manila, 1928), p. 11. Branches of two English banks, the Chartered Bank of India, Australia, and China, and the Hongkong and Shanghai Bank, were established in Manila in 1872 and 1875, respectively. It is not known whether Chinese could borrow from them.

14. Some Chinese made "monthly purchases to the extent of ten or fifteen thousand dollars from one person, nearly all the goods being sold to them on credits of three, four, or six months after the date of purchase and delivery of the merchandise." MacMicking, p. 25. See also, Foreman, p. 126. The debt estimate is that given in Edmond Plauchut, "L'Archipel des Philippines," *Revue des deux mondes, 21* (1877), 893–94.

people's money as capital, since only in this way was it possible to build up a large scale business. There is also a saying which may be translated: "Buy for ten, sell for seven, give back three, keep four." This refers, with some exaggeration, to a custom which at first sight appears singularly uneconomical. Having bought an article on credit for $10 a man may sell it to his customer for $7 and then pay $3 of this back to his creditor. He then has $4 in his pocket—an effective way of doing business without money, and a vivid illustration of the importance of actual cash in a system where so much of the finance structure consists of debts.[15]

From the point of view of a Chinese, a system of constant indebtedness bound the creditor to him and insured the future availability of credit on the assumption that only in this way could the total investment be regained. Thus, what had been intended as short-term credit became long-term credit. From the European merchant's point of view, this system was usable only so long as it was the only way to deal with Chinese middlemen, and only so long as Chinese business defaults were kept to a reasonable minimum. During the first few decades after 1850 the system seems to have worked fairly well. But before long all too many Chinese dealers overextended their operations and ended in bankruptcy. The foreign business houses, when they were lucky, could settle for between 10 per cent and 30 per cent of the debt; otherwise, they got nothing. The wave of bankruptcies of Chinese traders resulted in establishment in the 1880s of a "get tough" policy of strictly cash dealings, which continued to the end of the Spanish period.[16] How rigidly this policy was adhered to is not known.

The credit system just described was an important factor in the British preeminence in Philippine trade, as it was also in the Chinese penetration. British merchants were particularly active in advancement of credit (as well as loans) to the Chinese. The investment paid off in what was almost an informal Anglo–Chinese economic partnership. There was much truth in the complaint of J. F. Del Pan that the commerce of Manila had acquired a "special Anglo–Chinese seal that dis-

15. Ju-k'ang T'ien, *The Chinese of Sarawak: A Study of Social Structure.* London School of Economics Monographs on Social Anthropology, *12* (London, 1953), 65 n.

16. Foreman, p. 126; Testimonies of Charles Ilderton Barnes, R. W. Brown, and A. Kuensle, *Report of the Philippine Commission, 2,* 187, 205, 227–29; Frederic H. Sawyer, *The Inhabitants of the Philippines* (London, 1900), p. 290. Once before something similar had happened. Prior to the mid-1840s the Chinese settled accounts on a weekly basis. But Chinese had sent so much in remittances to China that they failed to keep up with payments, and a system was adopted by which credit was given only after signature of a term-note endorsed by three bondsmen. Lannoy, p. 112.

tinguishes it," and in the sweeping remark of Carlos Recur: "From the commercial point of view, the Philippines is an Anglo–Chinese colony with a Spanish flag."[17]

No less important than financing was economic organization. The most characteristic element of this was what might be called the cabecilla system. We have encountered the term cabecilla in Part I, meaning "head of an occupational gremio." After 1850 the word acquired new meanings, one of which was "head of a firm," or "employer." In this usage it is a rough equivalent to the term *towkay* (owner of a business), generally used among the Chinese of Southeast Asia. In the Philippines after 1850, a cabecilla was usually a large wholesaler of imported goods and export produce. Ordinarily, he was established in Manila, where he dealt with the foreign business houses. He was apt to have several agents located in the provinces, who ran stores as retail outlets for the imported goods he had acquired, at the same time buying up crops for the cabecilla to wholesale to the foreign business houses.[18]

The cabecilla assisted his agents by extending them a line of credit. But in the cabecilla–agent relationship, credit was not likely to be the long-term arrangement described above. The tightest rein was kept upon the cabecilla's retail outlets in the Manila area, which had to settle accounts with him once a week. Because of this arrangement, it was said that Sunday was the best day for shopping in Manila, since cabecilla accounts were settled on that day or the next, and the agent would cut prices to clear his stock that day if possible.[19] But although the credit relationship appears to have been close, in another way agents maintained a fairly independent existence. The cabecilla–agent connection was usually kept secret. Agents whose businesses failed were considered independent, and ultimate responsibility to creditors was concealed as much as possible.[20]

The cabecilla–agent system offered a number of advantages to all parties concerned. The foreign merchant could be assured that by dealing with a cabecilla who had numerous agents his imported goods would receive the broadest possible distribution, and a wide network of pur-

17. *Los chinos en Filipinas*, p. 25; Recur, p. 110.

18. MacMicking, p. 23; *Los chinos en Filipinas*, pp. 23, 87. The same system is reported for the 1930s. Albert Kolb, *Die Philippinen* (Leipzig, 1942), p. 410.

19. Francisco de Moya y Jiménez, "Las Islas Filipinas en 1882," *Revista de España*, 93 (1883), 189; Ferdinand Blumentritt, "Die Chinesen Manilas," *Globus*, 62 (1890), 100.

20. Comenge (p. 179) notes that for doing business within the Chinese community the firm would be in the name of the cabecilla; in its relations with Spanish officials the business was registered in the agent's name. See also *Los chinos en Filipinas*, p. 88.

chasing agents would funnel Philippine produce to him in return. To the cabecilla, this system provided, besides a broad scale for his operations, certain tax and emergency advantages. The 1852 "shop" tax, which replaced the 1828 "industrial" tax, was essentially a levy on places of business—whether wholesale trade, retail trade, or artisanry. But it specifically excluded wholesalers who had no shop for selling their goods.[21] Since a cabecilla did not sell to independent retailers, but simply supplied goods to his agents, and since he had no store for selling to the foreign business houses, the shop tax did not apply to him. He might be taxable for some of his other operations, but as a middleman commission merchant, he was exempt.

The emergency advantages connected with business failure have been adverted to above. If the agent overextended his operations he was on his own. The cabecilla was still responsible to the foreign business house, of course. But creditors in the region where the agent had operated did not know the identity of the cabecilla in Manila, and were left to collect from the agent if they could. The best way to protect both cabecilla and agent was to use boys under 18 as agents. Spanish Philippine law provided that no one under 18 (the age of majority for males) was legally liable for debts. Since it was the practice for Chinese to bring over younger relatives in their teens, this legal provision fitted in perfectly with Chinese custom. The Spanish response was to forbid business activities by minors. When this failed to be effective, the Spaniards resigned themselves to the inevitable, and in 1889 lowered the age of majority for Chinese to 14. Those of this age and over paid full taxes and assumed full legal responsibility.[22]

The agent, too, found this system advantageous. Usually he had neither the capital nor the access to credit to start his own business. These he could get from the cabecilla, who started him in business, kept him supplied with whatever he needed, and provided a sure outlet for the produce the agent bought.

Finally, the system was advantageous to consumers and producers, who bought from the agent and sold him produce. The agent's store, most often a general merchandise store called *tienda de sari-sari,* was established in market towns. But, unlike the periodic markets held in these towns once or twice per week, the Chinese sari-sari store was open all the time. Another consumer advantage was the readiness of the Chinese to offer credit to his customers. From a producer's point

21. Decreto, Nov. 6, 1852, Montero, *Historia, 3,* 162.
22. *Chinos. Sus reglamentos* . . . , pp. 20, 51; AMAE, China, 1889. Reclamación del gobierno chino, Ultramar to Estado, June 27, 1891.

of view, the Chinese store was also an improvement over previous marketing systems. As early as the 1780s producers of export crops had been receiving cash advances from agents of the Royal Philippine Company and mestizo wholesalers.[23] The Chinese storekeeper continued this practice. But because he also had something to sell, a producer who needed supplies rather than cash could barter with him, which would take the form of credit at the Chinese store instead of cash advances against crops.[24] Moreover, negotiations were facilitated by the fact that the Chinese storekeeper, unlike the agents of previous wholesalers, was usually present in the nearest market town.

In handling imported textiles, the cabecilla system assumed a peculiar form at the top which is worthy of comment, especially since textiles were the major Philippine import. Whenever a cargo of textiles arrived the leading textile cabecillas associated themselves for the purpose of acquiring and distributing the imported goods. Once the textiles had been purchased, the associated cabecillas divided them among themselves, setting aside some to be given to Manila textile wholesalers who were of less importance than they, and others to be sent to cabecillas whose operations were centered in such provincial capitals as Cebu and Iloilo, rather than Manila. One hears of this textile cabecilla association as early as the 1840s, and it was still in operation as late as the mid-1880s. Its purpose appears to have been twofold: first, to present a united front in bargaining with the European importers, and thus control prices; second, to assure the distribution of textiles to all Chinese textile wholesalers. Thus, Chinese who were not known to the foreign merchants, and so could not join the association, would still be assured of a supply.[25]

23. Legarda, "Foreign Trade," p. 170.

24. Letters to Central Revenue Administration by merchants of Tacloban (Leyte), 1883, and Jaro, Iloilo, and other towns in Iloilo province, 1887, PNA, Chinos, 22-22-12. Any kind of regular crop purchasing would have been an improvement over the previous practice. Bernaldez Pizarro wrote in 1827: "the agriculture of Filipinas at this time depends on the irregular and transient stimulus which is furnished to it by the peripatetic capital of the mestizo, who buys only in the years when he calculates that he must, in view of the condition of the crops and the market, make a profit" (p. 245).

25. "There prevails a broad unity of purpose among the Chinese merchants, who act in concert so as not to compete with each other in the purchase of merchandise from Europe, which they divide among themselves, and give to those of them who, being less known, or having a more restricted scope of business, do not enjoy the same trust in the foreign business houses." Lannoy, p. 112. See also Mallat, 2, 161, and Jordana, p. 37. Non-Chinese observers of this practice believed that along with equitable distribution in Manila went equitable distribution in the provinces, through key men in each province. By this means, all Chinese textile shops throughout the

This method of association for purchase and distribution of an incoming cargo is curiously reminiscent of the system used by the Manila Spaniards for purchasing Chinese junk cargoes during the sixteenth and seventeenth centuries. Under this system, called *pancada,* representatives of the city of Manila purchased and allocated Chinese silks arriving on the junks. Again, the purpose seems to have been to control prices and insure equitable distribution. It is possible that both the pancada and the cabecilla association of the nineteenth century were manifestations of some general practice in Asian trade.[26] More work is needed on this point.

This textile cabecilla association seems to have been a temporary organization, convoked specifically for purchasing and distributing imported cloths. It may have been a temporary kongsi, like those organized in Indonesia for single transactions (e.g. fishermen's kongsi, organized for marketing their catch).[27] It is true that textile "guilds" existed. But none of these predates the middle 1880s, and it is doubtful that this temporary association could be identified with any of these guilds.

Although the guilds, or commercial associations, probably were not directly related to the temporary cabecilla association, they are of interest in themselves, because they indicate how textile distributors and retailers in Manila organized for mutual business protection. By the mid-1870s, three areas of textile retailing had developed in Manila: (1) the Escolta–San Vicente–Nueva area, which specialized in quality imported goods in large stores; (2) the Calle Rosario area, where imported textiles of somewhat cheaper quality were usually sold from tables or racks in the doorways of larger shops; (3) the Calle Tabora–Divisoria area, mostly consisting of stalls in the Divisoria Market, where the cheapest imported cloths were sold. The Rosario textile merchants organized the Fu Lien I Pu Shang Hui about 1885. At about the same time, over a three-year period, (1885–88), the Tabora–Divisoria merchants organized the Kuan Ti Yeh Hui, or Kuan Fu Tzu Hui, with Kuan Ti, the God of War and Commerce, as patron. The Escolta–San Vicente–Nueva merchants founded the I Ho Chü Pu Shang Hui in

Philippines sold exactly the same merchandise at the same prices. Moya, pp. 186–87; "The Chinese in the Philippines," p. 158. It is doubtful that the system of buying and distribution was ever this airtight.

26. Schurz, pp. 74–78, 115, 133. For the *"pancado"* in seventeenth century Japan, see J. C. van Leur, "The World of Southeast Asia: 1500–1650," in *Indonesian Trade and Society,* pp. 208, 214–15.

27. Lea Williams, "Chinese Entrepeneurs in Indonesia," *Explorations in Entrepreneurial History,* 5 (1952), 52–53.

1894–95.[28] The specific reason for organizing this last association was protection in dealings with non-Chinese businessmen. A certain Chinese cloth merchant had returned to China, leaving his business in charge of his son. A German merchant, believing the business had failed, attempted to put a lien upon it, and tried by diplomatic means to confiscate some real estate in China partly owned by the Chinese merchant. The Escolta–San Vicente–Nueva textile merchants, led by Tan Samto, organized the I Ho Chü association, boycotted the German merchant, and thus put him out of business.[29] Besides boycotts, the I Ho Chü, and the other two textile associations, were organized for mutual aid and benefit. Money was collected from members and an emergency fund developed. But membership was small, and until after 1900 the three textile associations remained separate from one another.[30]

Returning to the cabecilla system, it appears that this institution penetrated most parts of the archipelago. In 1877, when the Spanish government was attempting to revise the system of Chinese officers, inventories were made of the properties of Chinese reputed to be wealthy. The proposed new system provided for officers wealthy enough to guarantee from their own pockets quotas of taxes to be collected from the Chinese in their areas. In seven provinces—Camarines Sur, Leyte, Pangasinan, Iloilo, Bulacan, Batangas, and Zambales—it was discovered that all of the supposedly wealthiest Chinese shopowners were, or claimed to be, not owners of valuable merchandise, but agents of cabecillas in Manila. Since these Chinese were not eager to hold office, one might be skeptical of their claims that the properties inventoried did not really belong to them, but they were able to produce documentary evidence, including the names of the Manila cabecillas.[31]

The opening of ports other than Manila to world trade during the late 1850s caused some modifications in the cabecilla network; cabecillas established themselves at Cebu and Iloilo, as well as Manila. In Cebu, one important Chinese exporter, Lucio Herrera Uy Mayan, had as many as 45 employees—some at work in Cebu City, others in smaller com-

28. Huang Hsiao-ts'ang, pp. chia 74, chia 99, chia 160; Liu Chi Tien, *Hua-ch'iao*, p. 62. The kinds of shops, by location in Manila, are described in Blumentritt, "Die Chinesen Manilas," 97–100, which follows Isabelo de los Reyes' *Tipos de Manila*.

29. Huang Hsiao-ts'ang, p. chia 160.

30. Comenge, p. 136; Huang Hsiao-ts'ang, pp. chia 74, chia 99.

31. PNA, Cabezas de barangay, chinos, 49-1-10. See also PNA, Chinos, elecciones, 37-2-2. A writer of the 1880s estimated that in one province there were 300 Chinese who were agents of cabecillas. *China en Filipinas*, pp. 15–16. Nicholas Loney, British vice-consul at Iloilo, found some 30 Chinese established at Molo in 1859, who were "mostly connected with others at Manila, either as partners or agents." Bowring, *Visit to the Philippine Islands*, pp. 400-03.

munities in that province.[32] But Cebu and Iloilo were important mostly for export trade—Cebu for abaca and sugar, Iloilo for sugar, native textiles, and sapanwood. The import trade, particularly the textile imports, apparently continued to be funneled through the Manila cabecillas.[33]

The cabecilla–agent system dealt a blow to the wholesaling trade of the mestizos of Cebu and Molo–Jaro—in the latter case, a fatal blow. In pre-1850 days, the produce of the Bisayas was carried by mestizo shipowners of Cebu and Molo–Jaro to Manila. The first Chinese ventures, as pointed out above, were in the form of voyages from Manila to the Bisayas. But the cabecilla–agent system made it unnecessary for the Chinese trader in Manila to voyage to the Bisayas and try to compete with people who knew the local conditions better than he.[34] Now he had his agents in position to be in constant touch with local conditions. Moreover, the opening of Iloilo and Cebu made unnecessary the shipping of many products to Manila for export. The mestizo shipowners of Molo–Jaro found that Chinese cabecillas and agents could buy up and handle raw products for export through Iloilo or through Manila more cheaply than they could. The mestizos also found it was easier to let the Chinese market their textile manufactures than to do it themselves. The result was that many mestizos shifted their interests from commerce to agriculture.[35]

At this point a word of caution is in order. Chinese economic organization in the Philippines did not take the form of a single, well-planned, all-inclusive network, the controlling threads of which were

32. PNA, Padron de chinos: Cebú, 1894. Uy Mayan appears in the *Guía oficial* for 1891 under "Importers and Exporters" as "Lucio Herrera Uy-Singchiong" (Part 3, p. 140). Biographical information on Uy Mayan is found in "Fei-lü-p'in hua-ch'iao shih-lüeh," pp. 30–31. On Iloilo cabecillas, see Case of Quieng Deco, Bacolod, 1877, PNA, Cabezas de barangay, chinos, 49-1-10.

33. Jagor, pp. 301–02; Jimeno Agius, p. 87.

34. MacMicking notes that provincial shipowning traders could buy produce "at greatly lower terms, when buying them by little at a time, than it would be possible for the agent of a merchant in Manilla to do, whose operations it would probably be necessary should be conducted upon a more extensive and quicker scale, and whose knowledge of the district and of the vendors could seldom be equal to that of a native Sangley, or Indian born among them." MacMicking, pp. 256–57.

35. Benitez, pp. 238–39; Robustiano Echaúz, *Apuntes de las isla de Negros* (Manila, 1894), p. 24. Jagor estimated that by the 1860s the Chinese had taken over half of the wholesaling of products for export. Jagor, p. 347. In Cebu it was not merely Chinese competition that damaged the mestizo wholesale trade. By Jagor's time, foreign merchants were buying export produce direct from the producers, thus cutting out the high brokerage fee of the mestizos. Jagor, pp. 303–05. See also Nicholas Loney's comments of 1859 on changing trade patterns, in Bowring, pp. 406–11.

held by a few hands in Manila, Iloilo, and Cebu. There was no single, airtight system, in which every Chinese wholesaler and retailer participated. The cabecilla–agent system was the characteristic, and in some ways the most efficient, method of handling imported goods and export produce. But if one tries to establish this as *the* distributing and collecting system of the Chinese in the Philippines, a great many exceptions will be found.

To begin with, not all the Chinese wholesalers were both distributors of imports and collectors of export produce. Many were engaged in one or the other function. Furthermore, agents were not all employees of wholesalers in Manila. Some agents were business partners; the Manila partner furnished the capital, the agent partner furnished the "legwork." Nor were all Chinese traders in the provinces agents of a cabecilla in Manila, Cebu, or Iloilo. Some operated tiendas that were branch stores not of a Manila store, but of one in another town in the same province. Finally, there were Chinese retailers in Manila and in the provinces who were supplied not by cabecillas or other middlemen, but directly by importing firms. In Manila, some retailers went directly to the foreign business houses and bought textiles on credit, rather than getting their goods from the cabecillas who had bought them as a group. In the provinces, some independent dealers could get direct delivery by Manila merchants. Thus, because Aldecoa y Compañía, a trading and shipowning firm in Manila, maintained a wharf at Surigao, Chinese there could stock their warehouses directly through Aldecoa.[36]

In surveying the reasons for Chinese success in wholesaling imports and exports, financial and organizational considerations seem preeminent. For that matter, when one attempts to explain Chinese success in any form of commercial effort, economic sophistication, the credit system, and the patronage organization are likely to be of as much or more significance than the usual catalog of virtues such as hard work and low overhead.[37]

Thus far we have been concerned with the role of the Chinese as wholesalers in Philippine foreign trading. At this point it is worth asking

36. Case of Santiago Galay Tan Chungco, Zambales, 1879, PNA, Defraudadores de la contribución industrial, 26-17-12; "Albay" in PNA, Cabezas de barangay, chinos, 49-1-10; Plauchut, p. 894; Case of Lo Sangco, Surigao, 1895, PNA, Contribución industrial, 5-8-3.

37. See Hugo L. Miller, *Economic Conditions in the Philippines* (2nd ed. Boston and New York, 1920), p. 421. Hardly any work has been done along these lines. A brief beginning is Maurice Freedman, "The Handling of Money: A Note on the Background to the Economic Sophistication of Overseas Chinese," *Man*, 59 (1959), 64–65.

whether these Chinese wholesalers could be considered *compradores*. The term compradores is often loosely used to indicate any Asian merchant or merchant firm that acts as middleman between Western trading firms and the internal commerce of the area in question. It is apparently in this sense that Legarda uses it in asserting that "Most of the local merchants acted as compradores for the foreign firms" in Manila.[38] Naosaku Uchida, in an attempt to designate periods of Chinese economic enterprise in Southeast Asia, has spoken of an era of "compradore capital," when Chinese capital was subordinated to Western capital, which was superior in volume, techniques (warehouses, marine insurance, etc.), and access to markets. The era of "compradore capital" is said to have arrived with the establishment of law and order in the interiors of Southeast Asian countries and the consequent penetration of "intensively organized Western capital." This period occurred toward the end of the nineteenth century.[39] Here, as with Legarda, if one uses a loose, "Asian middleman" definition, this generalization could apply to the Philippines during the late nineteenth century. But attempts to show a similarity between Chinese compradores in China and Chinese compradores in Southeast Asia raise difficulties.

The compradore in China possessed certain occupational attributes. (1) He had a knowledge of the language, internal markets, and centers of production of the country; (2) As Uchida puts it, "In dealing with Western capital, he established a material credit relationship by furnishing guarantees in money or properties; in dealing with Chinese capital he operated on the basis of personal credit, which was favored in the Chinese communities. Hence the system was in a sense a hybrid of Western and Chinese societies." [40] (3) The compradore was contractually and physically attached to a Western firm, which paid him a monthly salary and allowed him office space.[41]

When we apply these criteria to the Philippines, we find that the Chinese in general satisfied the first; normally, Chinese merchants learned enough words in Philippine dialects and in Spanish to do their business, and they quickly learned much more about internal markets and producers than a foreign businessman in Manila would know. But when we attempt to apply the second and third points, the parallel

38. Legarda, "Foreign Trade," p. 442.
39. Naosaku Uchida, *The Overseas Chinese. A Bibliographical Essay Based on the Resources of the Hoover Institution*. Hoover Institution Bibliographical Series, 7 (Stanford, 1959), 48. See also Naosaku Uchida, "Economic Activities of the Chinese in Southeast Asia," *Asian Affairs*, 1 (1956), 56–57.
40. Uchida, *Overseas Chinese*, p. 48.
41. Ibid.

breaks down. Western business firms advanced Philippine Chinese credit or cash without security, and sometimes without even promissory notes.[42] In the Philippines, it appears that Chinese wholesalers operated on personal—not material—credit in their dealings with everyone: foreign merchants, natives, Spaniards, and other Chinese. Finally, on the third point, it is not known that any Chinese commission firm ever attached itself contractually or physically to a Western firm. Therefore, it may be concluded that if compradore is loosely defined as "Asian middleman," the Chinese commission wholesalers in the Philippines were compradores. But an attempt to apply a strict definition based on the Chinese phenomenon cannot be sustained.[43]

The China–Philippines Trade in Transition

If the characteristic role of the Philippine Chinese in foreign trade after 1850 was that of middleman, this fact does not deny the existence of a foreign trade carried on by the Chinese themselves, incorporating both a persistence of certain old trade patterns and the development of some new trade practices. One of the most important features was the continuance of the traditional trade with China.

The venerable Chinese junk trade with the Philippines had been, in pre-Spanish times, a matter of bartering Chinese porcelain, silks, iron and tin ware, and beads for Philippine pearls, carabao horns, hempen cloth, tortoise shell, yellow wax, dyewoods, and cotton.[44] After the arrival of the Spaniards at Manila, this trade had expanded considerably, becoming one end of Manila's entrepôt trade, in which Chinese silks were traded for Mexican silver. But the China–Manila junk trade always included a direct trade in imports of Chinese goods for Philippine consumption and exports of Philippine raw products to markets in China. In the greatest days of the China–Manila junk trade, imports included such items as linens, cotton cloth, jewelry, hardware, furniture, wheat flour, salt meat, fresh fruit, live fowl, and an almost infinite variety of knickknacks.[45] Philippine exports to China are not well documented.

42. Plauchut, pp. 893–94.

43. For further discussion on the overseas Chinese as compradores, see Suzuki Sōichirō, "Kakyō to baiben" (Overseas Chinese and Compradores), *Tō-A keizai ronsō,* I (1942), 162–81. Suzuki admits that Southeast Asian Chinese middleman firms were not attached to or salaried by individual Western firms. Ibid., p. 166.

44. Schurz, p. 69; Declaration of Juan de Alcega, 1591, BR, 8, 82; Friedrich Hirth and W. W. Rockhill, *Chau Ju-Kua: His Work on the Chinese and Arab Trade in the Twelfth and Thirteenth Centuries, entitled Chu-fan-chï* (St. Petersburg, 1912), pp. 161–62.

45. Schurz, pp. 73–74.

We do know that by 1810 they included swallows' nests and sea cucumbers (holothuria), which were considered delicacies in China, carabao horns, salt fish, sugar, *sibucao* (or sapanwood, used for dyeing textiles), and cotton.[46] Cotton was taken to China, woven, and returned to compete with native Philippine textiles. For a time in the late sixteenth century these Chinese cotton textile imports had caused considerable damage to the native textile industry in some regions, but native textile producers had managed to survive.[47]

Up to the 1750s, the China–Philippines trade was carried almost exclusively in Chinese junks, and buying and selling of cargoes was usually done by Chinese merchants aboard the junks. It was possible for cargoes from China to come consigned to individual Spaniards and Chinese importers residing in Manila. However, cargoes usually were not consigned to anyone in Manila but were brought aboard the junks by merchants, who disposed of them for whatever they might bring and then purchased goods to be taken back to China. Sometimes there were as many as 40 or 50 merchants of this kind aboard a single junk, each in charge of a cargo which might be his own or that of a backer in China.[48] It was particularly for the purpose of handling this kind of trading that the Alcaicería de San Fernando was established in the late 1750s and early 1760s. Here the incoming merchants could reside as long as needed to dispose of their goods and acquire return cargoes.[49]

When Spanish and other European vessels began to run between China and Manila in the 1790s, they immediately cut into the entrepôt part of the junk trade—that is, the importing of silks, bound eventually for Mexico, and the exporting of Mexican silver to China. But it is not clear when these vessels began to carry goods belonging to the direct trade. Since the junk trade was well into its decline by 1800 it is likely that European ships were already carrying goods in the direct trade by that time. The exact effect of this upon the methods of importing and exporting used by the Philippine Chinese cannot at present be determined. We do know that goods imported on European vessels were not brought by merchants who came to do their own trading, as on the junks. They were consigned to Chinese importers residing in Manila.

46. Comyn, "Estado de las Islas Fil. en 1810," p. 194.

47. Schurz, pp. 48–49; Legarda, "Foreign Trade," pp. 261–78, esp. pp. 262–66 and 272.

48. Schurz, pp. 76–78; Lannoy, p. 106. See also Friedrich Ratzel, *Die Chinesische auswanderung* (Breslau, 1876), pp. 254–55.

49. Real Cédula, July 23, 1744, Berriz, *Anuario 1888, 1,* 570. See also, Bando, May 2, 1777, ibid., p. 585, and Buzeta, *1,* 138; *2,* 258–59; Díaz Arenas, *Memorias históricas,* cuad. 10: "edificios públicos."

Thus, as the junk trade waned, the Chinese were losing the carrying part of the China–Philippines trade. But the Philippine Chinese and the Chinese of Amoy and Macao remained the exporters and importers of almost all this trade, handling it now increasingly by consignment and less by personal venture on junks.[50]

Our first clear picture of the China–Philippines trade in transition— part junk trade, part Western carrying trade—is obtained in the 1840s. Since the trade statistics for 1846 include Hong Kong, "cotton goods," which account for 25 per cent of the imports from "China," must be regarded as partly European cottons via Hong Kong and partly cottons from China. Likewise, "woolens" and "hardware," items of moderate importance, were probably partly from Europe, partly from China. But we can be fairly certain that the other imports listed did in fact come from China. These included, in order of value: silks and raw silk, specie, linen, paper, paper umbrellas, porcelain, edible goods, furniture, iron, and a number of smaller items, such as glassware, jewelry, and tea.[51] These goods were imported for the use of the Philippine Chinese communities as well as the broader Philippine market, and we have no way of determining what percentage of imports went to which market. Undoubtedly, some of the edible goods, furniture, hardware, porcelain, paper goods, and cotton textiles were consumed by the resident Chinese. Opponents of the Chinese always insisted that the local Chinese communities were completely supplied from China, that they used nothing produced in the Philippines.[52] It is probable that a large share of their supplies did come from China. Yet there is no reason to believe the estimate that in the 1890s one third of all Philippine customs revenue was paid by imports brought in by the Chinese for their own use.[53]

Many other items—silk, umbrellas, glassware, and jewelry—were probably aimed at the larger market. Raw silk was used by the native textile industry; Bowring found in 1859 that the textile industry of Iloilo province imported 400,000 pesos' worth of raw silk per year.[54] Parenthetically, this fact indicates an interesting reversal of the previous export of Philippine raw cotton to be woven by Chinese textile manu-facturers for the Philippine market. The Philippine textile craftsmen had survived to a day when they imported from China (although Philip-

50. Díaz Arenas, *Memoria*, p. 20; *Los chinos en Filipinas*, pp. 72–73.

51. Lannoy, p. 106 and Annex 3. See also, Mallat, 2, 344.

52. Mallat, 2, 144; Blumentritt, "Die Chinesen Manilas," p. 98; *Los chinos en Filipinas*, pp. 11, 30; *China en Filipinas*, p. 89. Buzeta (2, 247) attempts to refute this argument.

53. Mencarini, p. 167.

54. Bowring, p. 394.

pine cloths never became a serious competitor in the China market).
Paper umbrellas were widely used in the Philippines. Glassware and
jewelry, like linens, hardware, porcelain, and furniture, had been imported since the sixteenth century. Since that time, too, a substantial part
of Manila's edible goods had come from China. A large proportion of
the paper goods imported was used by the government's cigarette factory
in Manila.[55]

In 1846 exports to China, in order of value, included: rice, gold dust,
specie, sea cucumbers, tobacco, sapanwood, cotton, cabinet woods,
abaca, *piña* cloth (native textile made of pineapple fibers), swallows'
nests, carabao horn, salt fish, and small quantities of liquid indigo and
tortoise shell.[56] With the probable exception of abaca and gold dust,
these were goods intended for the China market, not transshipment
elsewhere. Abaca was probably transshiped through Hong Kong to
North America or Europe; the gold dust was for the trading operations
of the Chinese of Macao.[57]

Western shipping continued to reduce the junk trade. Fewer junks
shuttled between Amoy and Manila; more Western vessels carried the
cargoes of the China–Philippines trade between Macao and Manila and,
in later years, between Hong Kong and Manila.[58] But on whatever kind
of vessels or over whatever routes, this trade continued to be controlled
at either end by Chinese: the Chinese of Amoy, Macao and Hong Kong,
at one end, and those of Manila at the other.[59] Only one product among
direct exports to China, rice, was handled by Westerners.[60]

Rice became an export item in the early 1830s. As a result of rice
shortages in China, the Ch'ing government waived duties at Whampoa
on ships carrying rice cargoes of 3,000 *piculs* or more. The Philippines,
having a rice surplus, was in a position to take advantage of this opportunity. Between 1830 and 1850 the Philippine rice trade to China
boomed; so did the Spanish merchant fleet trading to China. From three
or four ships in 1830, the Spanish merchant marine at Manila expanded

55. Díaz Arenas, *Memoria*, p. 75; MacMicking, pp. 219, 227.
56. Lannoy, p. 106 and Annex 3; Mallat, 2, 330–33, 345.
57. Díaz Arenas, *Memoria*, p. 23.
58. The Amoy junk trade, with Siam and the Straits as well as with the Philippines, decreased as the trade through Hong Kong increased. Karl von Scherzer,
*Fachmännische berichte über die österreichisch-ungarische expedition nach Siam, China
und Japan (1868–1871)* (Stuttgart, 1872), p. 270. See also, Díaz Arenas, *Memorias
históricas*, cuad. 8: "minas." Mas (*Informe, 2*, "comercio exterior," 5) notes that of
154 vessels coming to the Philippines in 1839 only 4 were Chinese. Of 187 arrivals
the following year only 4 were Chinese. Buzeta (*2*, Appendix: "cuadro sinóptico")
shows 4 Chinese junk arrivals and departures for what is probably 1849 or 1850.
59. Mallat, 2, 335; Díaz Arenas, *Memoria*, p. 21; MacMicking, pp. 227, 268.
60. MacMicking, pp. 227, 268.

to over thirty within less than ten years. Rice became the major Philippine export to China, and for the first time in its history China–Philippines trade began to show balances favorable to the Philippines. In the past, specie had always gone to China to redress the normally unfavorable balance. Now, in years of rice surplus, specie went from China to Manila to redress China's unfavorable balance.[61]

Rice exporting was the one aspect of the China trade handled by Westerners, in Western vessels. But once the Western merchant had disposed of his cargo at Macao, he did not use his profits to make up a return cargo on his own account. Instead he gave funds to Chinese in Macao, who made up a cargo for his ship, consigning it to some Chinese importer in Manila. The Western merchant collected his share of the profits after thirty days.[62]

In the later days of the China–Philippines trade, after 1850, there were a number of changes in trade goods and in methods. By 1870 the junks stopped coming to Manila.[63] The end of this trade had been foreshadowed by the law of 1843 that put the handling of junk cargoes on the same basis as those of other vessels, sending the junks to the regular customs house instead of the Alcaicería de San Fernando.[64] The Alcaicería, having outlived its usefulness, was torn down some years later. From 1850 to 1880, Spanish sailing vessels carried a large share of the Philippine trade to Hong Kong and Amoy, but after 1880 they were displaced by British-owned steamships.[65]

The small trade in birds' nests and sea cucumbers increased slightly, and by the 1880s Philippine abaca, coffee, sugar, tobacco, and particularly cigars were beginning to find a market at Shanghai.[66] These increases did not keep pace with those in other branches of Philippine trade, however, and as a result the China–Philippines trade declined relative to Philippine trade with other areas. But the important thing to remember is that whatever the value of trade, the products carried, or the means of transport in the China–Philippines trade, the Chinese continued to maintain control.[67]

61. Ibid., pp. 268, 271; PNA, Reales Órdenes, caja 111, núm. 90; Mallat, 2, 330; Mas, La Chine, 2, 431; Díaz Arenas, Memoria, pp. 16–18.

62. Díaz Arenas, Memoria, p. 21.

63. Los chinos en Filipinas, p. 126.

64. Montero, Historia, 3, 62–63.

65. Los chinos en Filipinas, pp. 71–72.

66. Legarda, "Foreign Trade," p. 249; "Xangae" [extract from report of Spanish consul in Shanghai, Fernando Lames de Bonilla], Boletín de la Sociedad Geográfica de Madrid, 24 (1888), 354–55. See also Louis-M. Rabaud, "Rapport sur Hong-Kong," La mission lyonnaise d'exploration commerciale en Chine, 1895–97 (Lyons, 1898), p. 180.

67. Los chinos en Filipinas, pp. 72–73; PNA, Reales Órdenes, caja 128, núm. 137.

If the Philippine end of the China–Philippines trade was monopolized by Philippine Chinese importers and exporters, it was no less true that these Chinese had concentrated their efforts on trade with China, to the near exclusion of any importing or exporting relations with other countries. The Philippine Chinese had been content to act as middlemen between the European exporter–importer and Philippine internal markets. But by the 1880s and 1890s Chinese importers and exporters at Manila, Iloilo, and Cebú were beginning to expand their operations to include dealings with Japan and with Western countries.

If one compares customs records of the 1850s and the 1890s, some striking differences appear. Chinese who were large importers and exporters in the 1850s, like José Castro Ongchengco, Tan-nu, and Antonio Tong, imported tea, porcelain, baskets, and paper from China. They exported to China birds' nests, sea cucumbers, tortoise shell, sulphur, ebony, and carabao horns.[68] A different picture appears in the 1890s. Lorenzo Uy-Duco imported cottons from Hong Kong in 1892, and Tan Quien-sien imported lamps, paper lanterns, fancy woods, and dried vegetables from Japan in 1893. Tan Quien-sien, Ong Jun Goo, Francisco Ong Posuy, and Po Gui-yao exported sugar to Hong Kong. Francisco Manzano Yap-Tico sent sugar cargoes to Japan. Tan Quien-sien and Chiong A-cho exported tobacco to Hong Kong. And E. A. F. Ongcapin sent an interestingly mixed cargo to Hong Kong: sugar, tobacco, coconut oil, carabao hides, cabinet woods, and carabao horns.[69]

While these customs manifests indicate that Philippine Chinese were trading with Japan on their own account, they are inconclusive proof of their trading with other countries. Part of the cargoes to and from Hong Kong undoubtedly belonged to the China–Philippines trade, and we do not know the provenance or destination of the rest. But there is better evidence. In the 1880s the newspaper *La Oceanía Española* noted that although Chinese export operations were mostly in products like nests, sea cucumbers, and horns, the Chinese were more active in imports, particularly in cotton textiles, "English yarn for the textiles of the country," and rice.[70] It is possible that some of the "cotton textiles" came from China; but it is doubtful that any large quantity originated there. As for English yarn, Chinese trading in this product resulted from the needs of the Philippine textile industry, which met the competition of cheap English cloths by importing large quantities of English yarn to mix with its native fibers.[71] As previously noted, rice was a Philippine

68. PNA, Aduana, 24-9-1; 24-9-2.
69. PNA, Aduana, multas, 24-1-4; Aduana, 24-13-6; Aduana, 37-9-9.
70. *Los chinos en Filipinas*, p. 121.
71. Recur, pp. 105–07. This source gives a table of cotton yarn imports by weight for 1856 to 1871.

export to China from 1830 to 1870. Thereafter, as the Philippine population continued to increase and more and more land went into export crop production rather than into subsistence crops,[72] it became necessary for the Philippines to import not only rice, but wheat flour as well. The Philippine Chinese took the lead in the importation of these two products. Rice was brought in from Saigon, via Hong Kong.[73] Wheat flour, which also entered through Hong Kong, may have come from the United States or Japan; it did not come from China.

Available information does not enable us to estimate the share of the Philippine Chinese in trade with countries other than China. In 1897 it was estimated that Chinese paid one third of all import duties in the Philippines.[74] Victor Clark, writing in 1905, said that "over half the bulk of the goods passing through the Manila customs house is consigned to Chinese merchants, and of 489 importers in that city, 199 are Chinamen." [75] On the other hand, R. M. Ongcakwe, a Chinese exporter of sugar and importer of rice, said that in 1899 there were only 20 or 30 Chinese in the import business in Manila.[76] And Hsüeh

72. Legarda, "Foreign Trade," pp. 291–92.

73. Del Pan, Las Islas Filipinas, p. 229; Biography of Yang Chia-chung in Huang Hsiao-ts'ang, p. chia 196; Blumentritt, "Die Chinesen Manilas," p. 98. Hsüeh Fu-ch'eng, who did not give his sources, estimated that by the date of his writing (1890) Chinese rice imports into the Philippines ranged from 2,000,000 to 3,000,000 pesos in value per year. Ch'u-shih Ying-Fa-I-Pi ssu-kuo jih-chi (Diary of an Embassy to the Four Countries of England, France, Italy, and Belgium), Yung-an ch'üan-chi (21 ch., Shanghai, 1897), ch. 2, p. 22b. In 1879 rice imports were worth over 2,600,000 pesos, or about 15 per cent of Philippine imports; wheat flour imports amounted to over 400,000 pesos. Guía oficial para 1881, pp. 276–77. In 1883 wheat flour imports were worth over 650,000 pesos. Guía oficial para 1885, pp. 441–43. The United States consul in Manila reported that in 1889 over 2,400,000 pesos' worth of rice was imported from "China," 2,500,000 pesos' worth from "French possessions," and over 200,000 pesos' worth from "British possessions." From "China" 448,601 pesos' worth of wheat flour was imported. Alexander Webb, "Commerce of the Philippine Islands," Reports from the Consuls of the United States, 39 (May 1892), 155. Presumably this report and Hsüeh Fu-ch'eng's estimate were based on a common source.

74. Manuel Sastrón, Colonización de Filipinas. Immigración peninsular . . . (Manila, 1897), p. 109; Mencarini, p. 167.

75. Labor Conditions in the Philippines. U.S. Bureau of Labor Bulletins, 10 (1905), 834. It is not clear whether Chinese listed in various commercial and gazetteer-type publications as "principal Chinese merchants" are intended to be representative of Chinese importing–exporting firms or commission wholesalers. See, for example, Guía oficial de Filipinas (Manila, 1891), 3, 115, 140; Commercial Directory of Manila (Manila, 1901), p. 106; The Chronicle and Directory . . . (for years 1902–05) (Hong Kong, 1902–05).

76. Report of Philippine Commission, 2, 218–19. Ongcakwe's figure may refer to Chinese trading with China, of whom 23 were registered in 1886. Los chinos en Filipinas, pp. 103–04. On the other hand, Clark's high figure may include those whose names appeared but once on an invoice during the year, as well as those whose regular business was, or included, importing.

Fu-ch'eng wrote in 1890 that perhaps 20 to 30 per cent of all exporters of raw products in the Philippines were Chinese.[77] In the face of such incomplete and possibly contradictory information, we can only say that in trade with countries other than China the Chinese apparently had an important position in rice, wheat flour, and yarn importing, but we can make no estimate of their share of tobacco, abaca, and sugar exports.

The foreign trade of the Philippine Chinese had changed in another way by the 1890s. By 1891 (and possibly earlier than that) a Chinese-owned marine insurance firm in Hong Kong had established an agency in Manila.[78] By the turn of the century, some of the most important Chinese and mestizo import and commission agent firms in Manila were acting as agents of other Hong Kong insurance firms. E. F. Ong-capin, a large importer, was an agent for Man On Insurance Company, and Po On Marine Insurance and Godown Company. Limjap and Company, a commission house operated by the mestizo sons of Joaquín Barrera Limjap, besides being agent for Penang Khean Guan Insurance Company, Ltd., represented Po On and Chai On Marine Insurance Companies of Hong Kong. The shipping and commission agent firm of Viuda de Tan Auco was also an agent for the Po On firm. By 1902 five marine insurance firms owned by Hong Kong Chinese had registered agents in Manila, Iloilo, and Cebu.[79]

Thus it appears that the geographical expansion of the foreign trading interests of the Philippine Chinese was accompanied by the use of some Western-style institutions. Besides marine insurance agencies, Chinese-owned banks, for instance, were established by 1902.[80] Legarda has pointed out that the Western firms in Manila, starting out as commission agencies of companies in Europe and the United States, quickly began to assume other functions—as traders on their own account, investors in the products and industries of their host country, merchant bankers, and agents for marine insurance companies.[81] It would be of interest to know if Philippine Chinese firms which began as commission agencies also expanded their operations along these lines—perhaps in emulation of the foreign firms. We do know that such firms as Siy Cong Bieng and Company and the Yap Tico Company were shipowning

77. *Ch'u-shih Ying-Fa-I-Pi ssu-kuo jih-chi*, ch. 2, p. 22b.

78. Case of Uy Tiaoquieng, Manila, 1891, PNA, Defraudaciones de la contribución industrial, 5-12-13. The company was the On Tai Insurance Co. Ltd., for which Uy was agent.

79. *Commercial Directory of Manila*, pp. 121-26. The five companies are listed in *Census of 1903*, 4, 546.

80. *Census of 1903*, 4, 541.

81. "Foreign Trade," pp. 432-36.

trading firms with banking and insurance departments by 1920.[82] Francisco Yap Tico, by the early 1890s, had already established a combined commission agency and hemp and sugar exporting firm in Iloilo, which, by the turn of the century, had branches in Manila and Cebu.[83] It is not known whether he had developed his banking and insurance operations at that time, but it is possible that by the 1890s there were Chinese firms in the Philippines—Yap Tico's or others—which were beginning to become general merchandise and agency houses along the same lines as the Western firms.

To summarize, the Philippine Chinese continued to monopolize trade with China, but in trade with other countries they moved into the position of distributors and buyers for the Western import–export firms. For effective action in this role, credit systems and an economic organization characterized by the cabecilla–agent arrangement were developed. Late in the nineteenth century Chinese importers and exporters began to expand their trading to include countries other than China, so by the end of the century some Chinese firms appear to have been on the way to carrying out many of the functions typical of the Western firms.

The Chinese and Foreign Trade through Sulu

Besides the direct Philippines–China trade, the Chinese of Manila were interestingly involved in an entrepôt trade between Sulu and China. Although this trade was but a minor part of the total commerce of the Philippines and China, it is worthy of attention because of the way it was carried out and the way the Manila Chinese fitted into it.

The *tung-yang* junk route from Amoy traditionally included on its course Manila, the island of Panay, and Sulu. We have noted the encroachments of Western shipping on the China–Manila section of the tung-yang junk trade. By the 1840s a combination of Western and Chinese enterprise at Manila had also cut into the junk trade south of Manila—to Panay and Sulu—driving a wedge into the Amoy junk trade at Sulu by diverting part of it through Manila, as an entrepôt trade to China. (However, not all the goods brought back from Sulu were reexported to China. Some were consumed at Manila, some distributed to other parts of the Philippines.) [84]

82. Walter Robb, "The Chino in the Philippines," *Asia*, 21 (1921), 917, 962.

83. Ibid., p. 962; *Commercial Directory of Manila*, pp. xxxix, 106; *The Chronicle and Directory* . . . 1902, p. 691. A biography of Siy Cong Bieng appears in Huang Hsiao-ts'ang, p. chia 188. Advertisements for Siy Cong Bieng and Company appear in issues of the magazine *The Filipino People* for the year 1913. The firm is described as "Importers, Exporters, Consignees, Commission Agents, Owners of the steamers *Ban Yek* and *Tong Yek*."

84. Mallat, 2, 325; MacMicking, p. 244.

The organization of the Manila–Sulu trade was as follows: every year in March and April, certain Manila shipowners chartered small ships of 200 to 250 tons to Chinese for ventures to the trading mart at Sulu. A Chinese usually paid 600 to 700 pesos per month for use of a ship. Most of the cargo belonged to the shipowner. In addition, the shipowner loaned the Chinese 10,000 to 20,000 pesos, at interest rates of 20 to 30 per cent. If ship and cargo were lost, the Chinese owed nothing. If the venture proved successful, the shipowner received his profits and interest on the loan, and the Chinese made whatever he could over and above his expenses. Cargoes from Manila included an almost infinite variety of goods, mostly different kinds of textiles—from Europe, India, and China, as well as from native looms. Hardware, glassware, and iron were included. So was Patna opium, used at the court of the sultan of Sulu.[85] There were pottery and copper utensils from China, and Chinese nankeens were taken along because they were one form of currency at Sulu.[86]

On the way to Sulu the ships, which frequently numbered up to eight, stopped at Antique and Iloilo on Panay, where they completed their cargoes with rice, tobacco, coconut oil, and cheap sugar. At Sulu the height of the trading season was in June and July. Although some currency was available, most trade was on a barter basis. In exchange for their cargoes, the Chinese acquired swallows' nests, tortoise shells, sea cucumbers, sharks' fins, mother-of-pearl, wax, gold dust, and pearls. By September or October, the Chinese merchants were back at Manila, where the goods they brought were turned over to Chinese exporters for shipment to China.[87]

It is said that Chinese were financed for these yearly trips to the Sulu market because the difficult conditions of trading there required a patience and endurance no other trader wished to claim for himself.[88] However, it may be that roughly the same system of organizing and financing Chinese voyages was used for trading between Manila and the Bisayas—where markets were not so difficult—in the 1840s and 1850s.[89] Both the Sulu and the Bisayan trade appear to be instances of the same combination of Western capital and goods with Chinese enterprise.

85. Mallat, 2, 324. The American explorer, Charles Wilkes, noted the use of opium in the sultan's court in 1842. Wilkes, *Narrative of the United States Exploring Expedition During the Years 1838, 1839, 1840, 1841, 1842* (5 vols. Philadelphia, 1850), 5, 336–37.

86. Díaz Arenas, *Memoria*, p. 11; MacMicking, p. 241.

87. The Sulu-Manila trade is discussed by: Mallat, 2, 321–26; MacMicking, pp. 235–45; Lannoy, pp. 107–08; Díaz Arenas, *Memoria*, pp. 7–14.

88. Mallat, 2, 321–23; Lannoy, p. 108.

89. See above, pp. 53–55.

Not all of Sulu's foreign trade was channeled through Manila. There was also a vigorous foreign trade directly to Sulu and through Sulu to Mindanao and Palawan. Until 1876 Spain had been unable to exercise any kind of authority over the Sulu Archipelago. Even after that date, although a vague kind of Spanish suzerainty was acknowledged by the sultan of Sulu, and a Spanish military colony established at the town of Jolo, the archipelago continued to be largely independent of Spanish control.

In Chapter 1 it was mentioned that, between 1750 and 1850, Chinese took over the Moro sea-trade in the Sulu area while other Chinese penetrated Mindanao, buying up raw products for export to Sulu and China. After 1850 these conditions continued to exist, with some interesting developments.

The Moro sultan of Sulu maintained a residence at Jolo, on the north coast of the island of that name, and one at Maymbung, on the south coast. Both towns became emporia of foreign trade, their importing and exporting monopolized by certain Chinese merchants who were partners of the sultan. Whether or not the Spanish military governors at Jolo participated in this, their generosity in granting permits of residence in Mindanao to Chinese at Jolo—whatever their reasons may have been —was of assistance to Sulu's trade with Mindanao. Repeatedly during the 1880s, Spanish governors-general in Manila exhorted military governors in Jolo to observe the proper standards, granting such permits only to those Chinese who had already received general Philippine residence permits from the Manila authorities, and expelling from Mindanao those who had not. But these pleas were unavailing, and in 1891 the Manila government gave in to the point of granting residence permits to Chinese who could prove they had resided in Mindanao for at least two years. No new permits were to be granted for Mindanao.[90]

But the inflow of Chinese continued—secretly, through Borneo and Celebes, with the Chinese taking out of Mindanao an estimated 8,000,000 to 10,000,000 pesos in goods every year, without, as the Spanish bitterly noted, paying a centavo of head tax or *contribución industrial* to the Spanish coffers.[91]

The Spanish attempt to thwart Chinese penetration of Mindanao from outside the Philippines had political and cultural as well as fiscal motivations. In the last half of the nineteenth century the Spaniards

90. Joseph Montano, *Voyage aux Philippines et en Malaisie* (Paris, 1886), pp. 162–63; Comenge, pp. 42n–44n; *Chinos. Sus reglamentos . . .* , pp. 64–65, 70–71, 77; PNA, Gaceta de Manila, Sept. 29, 1888.

91. AMAE, China, 1889, Reclamación del gobierno chino, Ultramar to Estado, June 27, 1891.

were accelerating their campaigns against both the Moros and the other unconquered native peoples of Mindanao. They strongly suspected that the Chinese of Sulu were supplying munitions to their enemies, especially to the Moros. Joseph Montano, who visited Sulu in the 1880s, found possible evidence of this in the storehouses of Chinese merchants, where he encountered "a large stock of English powder and numerous cases of Enfield rifles, model 1857." [92] From a cultural point of view, the Spaniards feared that if the unconquered natives were exposed to Chinese merchants the success of Spain's mission in Mindanao would be jeopardized. It was bad enough that indios who had long been subdued, hispanized, and Catholicized were now being thrown into intimate relations with the Chinese. For those who were yet to be missionized, it could be worse. The frontier of Chinese penetration and contact with the natives, stabilized at the boundaries of the provinces of Tondo and Cavite from mid-eighteenth century to mid-nineteenth century, had now been pushed to the largely unconquered islands of Mindanao and Palawan, and the Spaniards were trying to stabilize it in these two areas. Thus, for cultural as well as political reasons, Spaniards believed that Chinese trade ought always to follow the Spanish flag, not oppose it.

Of the three most valuable products in Sulu's trade—mother-of-pearl, gutta percha, and almáciga—Mindanao furnished the latter two. The building of the transatlantic cable in the 1860s and 1870s created a large demand for gutta percha to be used as insulation. Singapore, the major market for this product, extended its influence eastward as the demand rose. Mindanao began exporting gutta percha by the 1880s, and for a time there was a boom in this product. The end of the boom was attributed to Chinese adulterations which made the Philippine product undesirable in the European market. Whether this was the real reason is not known. Nor can we determine how much gutta percha was shipped out of Mindanao to Singapore, because it was usually exported through Sulu (for which there are no trade statistics) to Sandakan or Labuan, from whence it entered Singapore as North Borneo gutta percha. [93]

Almáciga, used in copal varnish, was available in larger quantities on Palawan than on Mindanao. But at least some of the almáciga of Palawan went to Manila; all of Mindanao's went to Singapore, which

92. *China en Filipinas*, p. 160; *Los chinos en Filipinas*, p. 85; *La política de España en Filipinas* (Feb. 17, 1891), pp. 6-7; Montano, *Voyage*, p. 163; AMAE, 1897, Insurr. en Filipinas. Yncidente protección, Informe of Governor-general, 1891.

93. Penoyer L. Sherman, *The Gutta Percha and Rubber of the Philippine Islands*, Philippine Islands Bureau of Government Laboratories Publications, 7 (Manila, 1903), 7–8, 15–16; Sawyer, p. 142.

was the principal market for this product.[94] Singapore was also the source of Sulu's major import: cheap colored cottons made in Germany, which were distributed through Sulu to adjacent areas, including Mindanao.[95]

On Mindanao there were said to be about 1,000 Chinese residing. Some were around the Spanish military centers in Misamis and Cotabato. Others were in areas unconquered by the Spaniards. Either way, the Chinese seem to have preferred residing in coastal towns to traveling in the interior. They remained in their coastal stores, allowing the natives of the interior to bring raw products to them for sale or barter. Some of the jungle products exported by the Chinese of Mindanao were wax, tortoise shell, sea cucumber, and cinnamon, besides gutta percha and almáciga. The Moros also traded rice, maize, cacao, and coffee to the Chinese. In the 1880s it was estimated that some 1,000 Spanish tons of coffee were exported from Cotabato by the Chinese. And the natives of Misamis sold gold dust to the Chinese, who smuggled it out to Singapore at profits said to run at 40 to 50 per cent. The Mindanao Chinese also were involved in providing slaves for the Sulu market.[96]

We do not know the relationships between the Chinese of Sulu and those in Mindanao. But we do know that Sulu was the prime outlet for a number of important Mindanao (and some Palawan) goods, whose ultimate destination was Singapore. Singapore and Sulu were linked by fortnightly steamer service.[97] In a larger context, therefore, the Spanish–Moro struggle in Mindanao was part of a contest between Manila (assisted by Cebu and Iloilo) and Sulu to include Mindanao in their respective spheres of economic influence. The Chinese traders following the Spanish flag were not merely advancing their own economic frontier or that of their cabecilla, but were also extending the economic influence of Manila, Cebu, and Iloilo—expanding the area that looked to those port cities as markets and suppliers. The Chinese on the other side of the fence in Mindanao were, whatever the nature of their relations with Sulu Chinese, extending the area which looked to Sulu

94. Sawyer, pp. 142, 314, 345; *Guía oficial de Filipinas para 1885* (Manila, 1884), p. 808; Felipe Canga-Argüelles, "La isla de la Paragua," *Boletín de la Sociedad Geográfica de Madrid, 23* (1887), 236–37.

95. Montano, *Voyage*, pp. 162–63.

96. Felipe de la Corte y Ruano Calderón, "La isla de Mindanao y lo que contiene," *Boletín de la Sociedad Geográfica de Madrid, 22* (1887), 351–52; Sawyer, pp. 150, 332, 345, 373–74; Del Pan, *Las Islas Filipinas,* p. 297; Joseph Montano, "Excursión al interior y por el oriente de Mindanao," *Boletín de la Sociedad Geográfica de Madrid, 23* (1887), 41; AMAE, China, 1889, Reclamación del gobierno chino, Ultramar to Estado, June 27, 1891.

97. *Guía oficial . . . 1885*, p. 778; Montano, *Voyage*, p. 160.

for supplies and an outlet. And one may almost say that the line between Spanish and non-Spanish territory in Mindanao also marked the line between an area that felt a pull in the direction of Hong Kong and one that was oriented toward Singapore. Further research may very well demonstrate that in the late nineteenth century a southern limit of Hong Kong enterprise and an eastern limit of Singapore enterprise met in Mindanao.

4

Other Kinds of Economic Activity

Industries

SUGAR

In certain key industries, many of them involving export crops, the Chinese were notably active. Sometimes this was a matter of entering industries Chinese had never been in, sometimes a shifting of emphasis in the nature of Chinese activities.

Sugar is one of the oldest Philippine industries. It was established at some unknown, early date, possibly with Chinese participating from the beginning. We know that Chinese in the Philippines were dealing commercially in sugar as early as the 1720s,[1] and they may have been active in milling as well, since Philippine methods resembled those used in China—and may, in fact, have been learned from the Chinese.[2] However this may be, by the 1840s, if not earlier, the Chinese were active as both millers and refiners of sugar.[3]

At that time the most important sugar provinces were in Central Luzon: Pampanga, Pangasinan, Bataan, Bulacan, Batangas, and Laguna. Cebu, in the Bisayas, was also of some importance. The Chinese maintained in Manila and in each of these provinces *farderías*—literally, "packing plants"—which were actually refineries producing a crude, low-grade sugar. Each fardería sent its agents out to purchase raw sugar in loaf form. The loaves were encased in earthenware receptacles in the shape of inverted cones, called *pilones,* which allowed the molasses

---

1. PNA, Reales Órdenes, 37-1-3. Note a later mention in *Early American-Philippine Trade: The Journal of Nathaniel Bowditch in Manila, 1796,* ed. Thomas R. McHale and Mary C. McHale. Yale University Southeast Asia Studies Monograph Series, 2 (New Haven, 1962), 58.

2. An interesting description of Chinese methods in both milling and refining sugar is given in Li Ch'iao-p'ing, *The Chemical Arts of Old China* (Easton, Pa., 1948), pp. 154–58.

3. Zamora, 6, 101; Bowring, p. 250; Mallat, 2, 288; Buzeta, 1, 213–14.

to drain through the apex of the cone. Each pilón was about 18 inches in diameter at widest, 24 inches in height, and had a capacity of roughly 100 pounds of raw sugar. Once in the fardería the loaf was broken into three parts, the top part being the lightest in color, the middle part of medium darkness, and the part nearest the apex darkest because of its greater molasses content. All were bleached in the sun for a few days. Then the owner of the fardería would classify the sugar by its color, according to the Dutch scale, put it into small mat sacks, and sell it to a foreign merchant for export. This kind of "pilón sugar," when exported, ordinarily had to be sent first to a refinery in England or the United States. The advantage to exporting semi-refined sugar was that the lower grades in the Dutch scale—numbers 5 through 14, into which this kind of sugar fell—paid lower customs duties than sugar ready for immediate use. We do not know how much profit the Chinese made from this kind of "semi-refining" and packing operation, but the markup on one *pico* (about 140 pounds) of sugar thus processed was said to be around one peso. Besides sugar for export, the Chinese made a kind of semi-refined lump sugar for domestic use, which was called *caramelo.*[4]

Beginning in the 1860s the Philippine sugar industry underwent tremendous changes, characterized by new methods and a new regional emphasis. Foreign enterpreneurs provided loans and modern machinery, especially in the Iloilo–Negros region. Energetic Spaniards, Spanish mestizos, and particularly Chinese mestizos from Iloilo province established plantations in Negros. Hitherto sparsely populated, Negros now enjoyed a tremendous boom, economically and demographically. The sugar mills in this area were usually steam-powered rather than animal-driven. Bisayan sugar, although still crude, was granulated and of a higher grade than the "pilón sugar"; usually it was called "mat sugar," because of the kind of bags into which it was packed.[5] Centrifugal methods of refining may also have been used in some places, although the first centrifugal refinery is said to have been established in 1907.[6] In Central Luzon, too, steam mills began to replace the old vertical roller mills, especially in sugar mills owned by Spaniards.[7]

4. Petition of the "Alfareros de pilones de azúcar" of Tambobong, 1846, PNA, Bandos, 41-11-5; Díaz Arenas, *Memoria,* p. 49; *Los chinos en Filipinas,* pp. 117–19; MacMicking, pp. 281–83; C. W. Hines, *Sugar Industry of the Philippines.* Panama-Pacific International Exposition Pamphlets (Manila, 1915), pp. 2–10.

5. Jagor, pp. 304–06; Echaúz, pp. 12, 24–26, 35, 37; Sawyer, p. 303; *Census of 1903, 3,* 27–29; Hines, p. 10.

6. *Los chinos en Filipinas,* p. 118; Hines, p. 4.

7. Joaquin Rajal y Larré, "Memoria acerca de la provincia de Nueva Ecija en Filipinas," *Boletín de la Sociedad Geográfica de Madrid,* 27 (1889), 291, 293; Gregorio

These changes in sugar production, and the rise of sugar to the first or second spot among Philippine exports, were accompanied by the decline of the pilón method and the Chinese fardería. By 1915 almost all sugar exported was either of the "mat" variety or of the centrifugal type.[8]

Although the farderías declined, Chinese remained active in sugar brokerage, particularly in Batangas, where sugar crop loans at 15 to 25 per cent and subsequent foreclosure and acquisition of lands by Chinese brokers and moneylenders were not at all uncommon.[9]

ABACA

Abaca, as an important industry, dates from the 1820s when this product first entered the list of exports. It quickly found a dependable market in the United States, which remained the most important purchaser throughout the nineteenth century. From midcentury on, abaca and sugar alternated in first place among Philippine exports.[10]

The principal abaca areas were: the Bicol region of Southeastern Luzon, especially the provinces of Camarines Norte, Camarines Sur, Albay, and Sorsogon; and the Eastern Bisayas region, especially the islands of Leyte, Samar, and Cebu. The development of both the abaca and the sugar industries was stimulated by crop loans made by foreign firms. The opening of the ports of Legaspi, in Albay, and Tacloban, in Leyte, to world commerce in 1873 may have provided additional impetus.[11]

In the early years of its exploitation, abaca was produced by indio and mestizo growers and collected by Spanish or (Chinese) mestizo agents of foreign firms, or by provincial governors.[12] But after 1850 Chinese began to move into this industry both as buyers and as producers. Chinese buyers, unlike their competitors, did not ordinarily make advances on crops. Instead they established stores where they could barter rice and miscellaneous goods for abaca. In parts of the abaca

Flormata, *Memoria sobre la provincia de Pangasinan* (Manila, 1901), p. 20; Manuel Sastrón, *Filipinas. Pequeños estudios. Batangas y su provincia* (Malabong, 1895) (hereafter: Sastrón, *Batangas*), pp. 123–28.

8. *Los chinos en Filipinas*, p. 118; Hines, p. 13. *Farderías* were on their way out. But there were still plenty of them and they were sometimes lucrative. Joaquín Tan Angco, in 1883, had one in Malabong (Tambobong) which, by his estimate, netted him 3,000 pesos per year. PNA, Chinos, elecciones, 37-2-2.

9. Sastrón, *Batangas*, pp. 81–86; Lü Shih-p'eng, p. 340.

10. Legarda, "American Entrepreneurs," p. 153; *Census of 1903, 3*, 15.

11. José Montero y Vidal, *El Archipiélago Filipino y las Islas Marianas, Carolinas y Palaos* (Madrid, 1886), p. 234.

12. Jagor, p. 316; Sawyer, p. 285; *Los chinos en Filipinas*, pp. 114–15.

zone it was found that money was very scarce and rarely used, and small producers of abaca preferred business by barter. The Chinese also preferred it this way, offering better prices if paid in goods rather than cash.[13]

As producers of abaca the Chinese played a role rather unusual for them. It has been pointed out above that in general the Chinese eschewed agricultural endeavors. Abaca was something of an exception. In the most important abaca-producing regions some Chinese owned abaca lands, which they rented out to indio producers. Otherwise, it was the practice for a Chinese to lease small abaca "plantations" from their indio or mestizo owners. If the preliminary work of planting and cultivation had been done, the Chinese had only to lease the land for a short time, bring the crop to fruition, harvest it, have the abaca stripped, and send it off to "packing houses" (balers) in Manila for sale to exporters. But this practice, intended to produce a quick profit with a minimum of preliminary labor, could easily result in abuses, particularly the cutting and stripping of immature plants.[14] Outside the major abaca-producing areas, the Chinese are said to have owned abaca plantations in Iloilo and parts of Mindanao.[15] Their size is not known; but in the major abaca regions all holdings used for abaca productions were small.[16]

In the Bicol region and the Eastern Bisayas there was a wide range in the status and wealth of Chinese abaca buyers. Some were agents of a cabecilla in Manila; others were independent dealers. Some operated sari-sari stores having a total value of no more than 60 pesos;[17] others had bazares, luxury goods stores selling European furniture, fine plates, crystal, vases, European cottons, and Chinese silks, worth up to 4,000 pesos. Some of these bazar operators owned wagons and boats for taking their abaca to market.[18] It is of interest to observe that these

13. Petitions of Chinese industriales of Tacloban (1883) and various other Leyte towns (1887), PNA, Chinos, 22-22-12; Los chinos en Filipinas, p. 115.

14. Inventories of property: Tabaco, Guinobatan, Ligao, Polangui (Albay), and Bulusan (Sorsogon), PNA, Cabezas de barangay, chinos (1877), 49-1-10; Foreman, p. 330. "Packing houses" (Prensas para enfardar abacá) also baled tobacco. Chronicle and Directory . . . 1902, p. 679.

15. Testimony of Neil McLeod, Report of Philippine Commission, 2, 32.

16. M. M. Saleeby, Abacá (Manila Hemp) in the Philippines. Panama–Pacific International Exposition Pamphlets (Manila, 1915), p. 14.

17. Petition of Chinese of Naga, 1877, PNA, Cabezas de barangay, chinos, 49-1-10; Report of Intendencia subdelegado de hacienda, Leyte, 1877, in ibid.; Petition of Chinese of Jaro, Alangalang, San Miguel (Leyte), 1887, PNA, Chinos, 22-22-12.

18. Inventories: Yu Banco, Santiago Lim Saypo, Yu Punco, Emilio Asensi Yu Biaoco, Leon Tan Piengco, Bonifacio Co Cingco, PNA, Cabezas de barangay, chinos, 49-1-10.

bazares and their apparently affluent owners were found in rather obscure places like Carigara and Palo in Leyte, and Cagsaua in Albay.[19] One expects to find such luxury goods stores in Manila, or in only the largest provincial towns. The shop tax of 1852 established the luxury goods bazar as a category by itself—number one, paying the highest tax in the four-class shop tax scale. This classification was based upon the assumption that luxury goods bazares made their owners more money than any other kind of shop, which was probably true. Statistics of 1886 show that as of that date there were 53 Chinese owners of bazares in Albay, which amounted to over 30 per cent of the total number of Chinese bazar owners in the Philippines. Negros had 39, or over 20 per cent; the two together housed over 50 per cent of the Chinese bazar owners in the Philippines.[20] These figures are suggestive not only of the demand for luxury goods in the leading sugar province and the leading abaca province, but also of the supply of well-to-do Chinese merchants in these two regions.

TOBACCO

Tobacco was cultivated very early in the Philippines. But it first became of economic importance with the establishment of the government tobacco monopoly in 1780–82. This monopoly applied to the provinces of Northern Luzon, where the bulk of the tobacco was produced; the Bisayas, which also grew tobacco, were not included. Among the Northern Luzon tobacco-producing provinces were Ilocos Norte, Ilocos Sur, La Union, Pangasinan, Nueva Ecija, and the two tobacco monopoly provinces par excellence, Cagayan and Isabela. Under the monopoly there was almost no opportunity for private commercial or industrial enterprise. Government agents collected the tobacco from the growers and shipped it to Manila, where the government factory prepared it for export in leaf form or made it into cigars or cigarettes. The only place for private enterprise was in the transporting, which was done by contract, usually acquired by the mestizo and indio shipowners of Manila.[21]

For several years after its foundation, the tobacco monopoly was highly successful. But by the middle and latter part of the nineteenth century, for a variety of reasons, there came to be much agitation in

19. Note the lavish home and entertainment of the Chinese merchant "Narciso" in Cagsaua described by Montano (*Voyage*, pp. 92–95).

20. *Los chinos en Filipinas*, p. 101.

21. Buzeta, *1*, 251; MacMicking, p. 260.

favor of terminating the monopoly and opening the industry to free enterprise.[22] This was done in 1880.

Up to the 1870s, the Chinese had taken little interest in tobacco. Just before the government monopoly was abolished, however, Chinese storekeepers and moneylenders who had begun to settle in Cagayan found a situation suitable for their intervention. For a few years the government got behind in its payments to growers, and the hard-pressed cultivators (who, like the abaca-producers, were small holders) had to resort to the money-lender.[23] The loan contracts made, called *pactos de retroventa* (or *pactos de retro*), deserve some discussion here because of their prevalence in the Philippines—in tobacco-raising areas and elsewhere. The pacto de retro (contract of resale), founded in Spanish law, provided for the conveyance of the borrower's land to the lender, with an option to repurchase it for the sum of the loan. Until repurchase the debtor usually became the lessee or cash tenant of the lender. In the meantime, the lender often made further encumbrances upon the property, thus adding to the price of resale. Even if the borrower finally accumulated enough money to repurchase the land, he had to prove his right of option. This was sometimes difficult to do, since contracts were seldom made in the presence of a lawyer or notary, and were apt to be in improper form. The courts were full of cases involving the pleas of indios who had lost their lands in this manner. The pacto de retro was used by the mestizos of the Central Luzon rice-producing region in the late eighteenth century, and continued to be used by Chinese and mestizos in that area and in the tobacco region of Northern Luzon throughout the nineteenth century. Something like it continues to exist today in the *prenda,* or system of property-pawning.[24]

By use of the pacto de retro, Chinese moneylenders in Cagayan began to acquire lands from the indio cultivators. The Chinese did not work the lands themselves but rented them to the cultivators.[25] Chinese enterprise took a new course after the abolition of the government

22. Some reasons for its termination are given in H. O. Jacobson, *Tobacco in the Philippines.* Panama–Pacific Exposition Pamphlets (Manila, 1915), p. 2; Zaide, 2, 29–30. See also the discussion in Recur, pp. 49–65.

23. "The Chinese in the Philippines," p. 157; *China en Filipinas,* p. 103.

24. *Los chinos en Filipinas,* p. 27; "Contratos usurarios" in *Revista general de legislación y jurisprudencia,* 25 (Madrid, 1864), 174–77. The *Ordenanzas de buen gobierno* of 1768 warned against such contracts. See also the anti-usury law of 1848 in San Pedro, *1,* 144. Zúñiga noted the use of the *pacto de retro* by the mestizos of Central Luzon around 1800. Zúñiga, *1,* 364–65. On the mestizos' use of it during the nineteenth century, see Jagor, pp. 156, 302. On the *prenda* see Agaton P. Pal, "Barrio Institutions and Economic Change," *Philippine Sociological Review,* 7 (1959).

25. *Los chinos en Filipinas,* p. 27.

tobacco monopoly. Now Chinese began to pour into Cagayan and Isabela. In the wake of large Spanish-owned tobacco firms, like the Compañía General de Tabacos (Tabacalera), which bought up the best leaf, Chinese buyers began to move up the Cagayan Valley, purchasing cheaper grades and leftovers. Using Aparri at the mouth of the Cagayan River as their base, Chinese buyers made three-month trips up river toward Isabela.[26] Other Chinese established sari-sari stores in Cagayan Valley towns, selling groceries, palm wine, and textiles, and buying up tobacco at wholesale. So industrious were the Chinese that numerous stores were set up even in rather obscure places, such as the 18 sari-sari stores established by 1889 at Gamú, a town in Isabela.[27]

The success of Chinese buying and selling operations resulted from their willingness to barter goods from their stores for tobacco and from the cheapness of their operations. While other buyers stayed in Aparri, paying a packing and transportation fee to the indio cultivator for bringing the tobacco to them, the Chinese established their stores near the points of production. Small cultivators, eager for immediate cash or goods, could be induced to sell an unripe crop for one third what it would have brought if allowed to mature. And the Chinese buyers kept overhead down by transporting their purchases to Aparri themselves, instead of paying a fee. Once the tobacco reached Aparri, other Chinese sent it on to Manila by sea, to be kept in Chinese warehouses there for sale to cigar factories or exporters.[28]

Soon, Chinese in Manila were engaged in cigar and cigarette manufacturing, making cheap imitations of larger companies' brands. At one time there were as many as 200 Chinese cigar factories in Manila, some of them quite small, fly-by-night affairs. Manila's poorer people called their products "cigarros beri-beri," but smoked them anyway.[29]

After 1880, Philippine tobacco and cigars did not enjoy the status they seemed to deserve in world markets. This condition was blamed upon the Chinese, who, it was said, destroyed confidence in the Philippine product with their sales of unripe tobacco, and mixing of good with poor grades. But Del Pan, no friend of the Chinese, partly exon-

26. *China en Filipinas*, pp. 77, 79, 104; Lü Shih-p'eng, p. 399. In Ilocos Norte, as in the Cagayan Valley, the Chinese bought scrap tobacco while Tabacalera bought the good leaves. Camilo Millán, *Ilocos Norte. Descripción general de dicha provincia* (Manila, 1891), p. 150.

27. "Notario de Cagayan," PNA, Acuerdos de audiencia, 17-16-17. See also Letter of *superintendente subdelegado de hacienda,* Tuguegarao, 1886, PNA, Chinos, 22-22-12. By mid-1886 there were 36 Chinese shops in Tuguegarao, capital of Isabela, with an average value of 1,350 pesos each.

28. Jacobson, p. 8; *China en Filipinas,* pp. 77-79, 104; "The Chinese in the Philippines," p. 157; Sawyer, pp. 252-53; Lü Shih-p'eng, p. 399.

29. *Los chinos en Filipinas,* p. 120; Clark, p. 825.

erated them, pointing out that since the early 1860s there had been experimentation in crossing types of Philippine tobaccos which had not turned out well, and some poor quality Philippine tobacco had been sold in Europe even before the end of the monopoly.[30] Nevertheless, the Chinese must be accounted partly responsible. As in the case of abaca, fierce competition and the passion for quick and large profits caused some Chinese to produce poor quality goods that cost all Chinese goods the confidence of buyers.

INDIGO

This industry flourished in Central Luzon and the Ilocos region during the late eighteenth century and the first half of the nineteenth century. Its beginning apparently dates from some time in the eighteenth century when an Augustinian friar taught the technique of extraction to some Chinese mestizos of Tambobong (Malabong), who grew it first in Bataan. Later it spread to the areas mentioned above, becoming an export item in the trade with China. The practice was for mestizo buyers to make crop advances to indio growers, buy the crop, and send it to the Chinese of Manila. In Manila, the indigo was used by Chinese textile dyers or else put in earthenware jars and sent to China in a muddy or "liquid" form. During the nineteenth century other markets for indigo were developed, in Europe and the United States, which took the product in its "solid" form. To the end of the nineteenth century, exports to China continued to be in "liquid" form.[31]

During the most prosperous years of the industry, indigo production was centered in five provinces: Ilocos Sur, Pangasinan, Laguna, Pampanga, and Bulacan. Up to the 1840s the Chinese were content to buy at Manila from mestizo or indio wholesalers. But in the 1840s they began to function as buyers in Ilocos Sur, and by the 1880s indigo wholesaling was almost a Chinese monopoly.

Shortly after 1880, exports of indigo fell off, and the adulterations of the Chinese were blamed for the loss of foreign markets. It is true that the Chinese mixed good and inferior grades of indigo, as they did with tobacco. Undoubtedly this meant some loss of confidence in the Philippine product. But even opponents of the Chinese admitted that the issue was more complicated than that. Chinese adulterations may have caused indigo's decline in Ilocos Sur. But Laguna and Pangasinan, where some of the best indigo was produced, gave up because of inability to compete with Bengal and Java indigo. Finally, the develop-

30. *China en Filipinas*, p. 102; "The Chinese in the Philippines," p. 157; Del Pan, *Las Islas Filipinas*, p. 265.

31. Zúñiga, 1, 404–05, 493–94; MacMicking, p. 296; *Los chinos en Filipinas*, p. 115; *Census of 1903*, 3, 102.

ment of aniline dyes reduced the Philippine indigo industry to unimportance.[32]

RICE

Rice was always the staple food of the Philippines. Although it was grown everywhere, the real granary of the Islands was (and remains) Central Luzon. As provisioners of Manila and other Spanish settlements, the Chinese must have had a hand in rice wholesaling and retailing from the beginning of the Spanish period. A rice-dealers' gremio was among the Chinese occupational groups listed in the 1720s.[33] After 1755, when the Chinese retired from the provinces, the mestizos took over most of the coastwise trade between areas of rice surplus and deficiency. The mestizos of Tambobong (Malabong) and Pasig assumed a large share of the job of providing Manila with its rice. It was also in this period that the mestizos of Central Luzon were either acquiring rice lands through pactos de retro or leasing rice lands as inquilinos.[34]

When the Chinese moved back into the provinces after 1850 they again became coastwise shippers and wholesalers. The abaca regions of the Eastern Bisayas and Southeastern Luzon needed to import rice, particularly from Panay Island. Other regions of export crop concentration (like Cagayan and Isabela) also had rice shortages which had to be made up from other provinces.[35]

Besides the Chinese collectors who bought wholesale at the points of production, there were Chinese speculators who bought from producers or collectors, holding the rice in their warehouses while waiting the proper moment to put it on the Manila market. The retailing of rice was done in sari-sari stores or other small tiendas, both in Manila and in the provinces. In Manila there were also stores exclusively devoted to the sale of rice at retail. Some of these sold both hulled and unhulled rice, and violated the laws by selling in wholesale lots—over 1 *cavan* (about 2 1/3 bushels)—as well as at retail. Although the Chinese were quite important in the retailing of rice, they did not monopolize it during this period.[36]

32. *Los chinos en Filipinas*, pp. 27, 116; Jordana, p. 39; *Census of 1903, 3,* 98; Del Pan, *Las Islas Filipinas,* p. 223; Sawyer, p. 250. Indigo had been adulterated by indios, too, as early as the 1830s and 1840s. Díaz Arenas, *Memoria,* p. 50; MacMicking, p. 297.

33. PNA, Reales Órdenes, 37-1-3.

34. Zúñiga, *1,* 45–51, 206, 296, 334–35, 364–65; *2,* 57, 100.

35. Jagor, p. 152; Sawyer, p. 131; Bowring, p. 388.

36. Cases of Emeterio Lim Bunseng, Chua Puncho, Go Juyco, Go Yongco, 1894, PNA, Defraudaciones de la contribución industrial, 26-22-8; *Los chinos en Filipinas,* p. 114.

Almost no information is available on Chinese rice milling activities. That there were Chinese mills is indicated by the provision for them in category number four of the 1852 shop tax. A recent study of Chinese economic activities in the nineteenth-century Philippines mentions the existence of Chinese rice mills around Gapan, Nueva Ecija, but the author cites no sources.[37] It is known that there was at least one rice mill at Dagupan in Pangasinan by 1900, and Balayan, in Batangas, had 14 to 16 steam mills and many others of cruder variety by the 1890s.[38] But it is not clear whether these mills were Chinese-owned. In view of the fact that shortly before World War II it was estimated that the Chinese owned 75 per cent of all Philippine rice mills,[39] it would be highly desirable to be able to generalize about the extent of Chinese influence in this field as of the latter half of the nineteenth century. But the data at hand do not permit any conclusions.

Several references have been made to the change in status of the Philippines from a rice exporter to a rice importer by 1870. By the 1890s over 2,000,000 pesos worth of rice was being imported annually from "China," mostly by Philippine Chinese.[40] At the establishments of Chinese rice importers on Calle Anloague (present Juan Luna Street) in Manila, poor quality Saigon rice was skillfully mixed with good grades of native varieties and sold at low prices.[41] This trade reached its highest point—and the Philippine Chinese rice dealers their greatest success—during the Philippine Revolution of 1896–1902. During those years normal coastwise trade was interrupted, and a tremendous demand for rice developed in some areas. In this highly inflationary situation, Chinese importers "delivered the goods," picking up return cargoes of abaca, tobacco, and coconut products. It was said, probably with much exaggeration, that one trip would net 10,000 pesos profit.[42] Whatever the magnitude of profit, the Chinese probably emerged more solidly placed in the rice industry than before.

37. Lü Shih-p'eng, p. 399. The 1852 tax classifications are given in Los chinos en Filipinas, p. 101.

38. Flormata, p. 19; Sastrón, Batangas, pp. 123–28. LeRoy mentions the existence of rice mills owned by "foreigners," presumably meaning Westerners. James A. LeRoy, The Americans in the Philippines (2 vols. Boston, New York, 1914), I, 35.

39. Helmut G. Callis, "Capital Investment in Southeastern Asia and the Philippines," American Academy of Political and Social Sciences Annals, 226 (March 1943), 30.

40. Los chinos en Filipinas, p. 113; "The Chinese in the Philippines," p. 156; Blumentritt, "Die Chinesen Manilas," p. 98.

41. See note 73, Chap. 3.

42. Fukuda Shōzō, Kakyō keizai ron (On the Overseas Chinese Economy) (Tokyo, 1939), p. 368; Lü Shih-p'eng, p. 399.

MISCELLANEOUS INDUSTRIES

The activities of the Chinese in several minor industries, or industries in which Chinese influence was slight, may be sketched briefly. After the termination of the government's beverage monopoly in the 1860s, the distillation of rum and palm wine became an attractive occupation for the Chinese. Chinese distilleries—many of them quite small—were established in Iloilo, Cebu, Nueva Ecija, Pampanga, Bataan, Pangasinan, Batangas and Camarines Sur. In the Manila area there were at least ten moderately sizable Chinese distilleries by the 1870s. In general, the Chinese followed the same course in this industry that they did in tobacco: no effort was made to compete with large firms, like the Spanish-owned Ayala y Compañía. Instead, the Chinese contented themselves with manufacturing cheap rum and wine exclusively for the domestic market.[43]

In timber cutting and marketing the Chinese, encouraged by the favorable tax provisions of 1852, became prominent. The best stands of timber were on the eastern coast of Luzon in the provinces of Tayabas and Nueva Vizcaya. Cutting was done by contract, with indio, mestizo, and Chinese contractors in competition with one another. Mestizo and Chinese contractors used a piece-work system called *paqueao,* and they often made use of indio labor gangs rather than Chinese. No machinery was employed; cutting was by crosscut saw.[44]

In Manila there were by the 1890s at least nine fairly important lumber merchants, most of them located on Calle Lacoste. In order to increase their bargaining power with indio log contractors, and for the general purpose of mutual aid, the lumber dealers and box manufacturers organized the Ch'ung Ning She business association in 1888.

In other aspects of the lumber industry—cordwood and charcoal—there were many Chinese speculators, furnishing these commodities for sale to sari-sari and other small stores.[45] Immediately prior to World

43. *Guía oficial . . . 1891,* 3, 137, 141; *Guía oficial . . . 1885,* p. 799; Plauchut, p. 895; Sastrón, *Batangas,* pp. 113, 127; PNA, Chinos, elecciones, 37-2-2 (1877 and 1887); "Bataan," 1877, in PNA, Cabezas de barangay, chinos, 49-1-10; Case of Uy Oco, Nueva Ecija, 1876–78, PNA, Contribución industrial, 5-8-3; Sawyer, pp. 161, 242; Flormata, pp. 18–19; Sancianco, *El Progreso de Filipinas,* p. 94. In the contribución industrial "income tax" established in the 1880s, the small-sized Chinese distilleries were given a special rate of 100 pesos, as contrasted with rates of 360 pesos or 500 pesos paid by non-Chinese distilleries. Berriz, *Diccionario, 1,* 272–74.

44. Clark, p. 810; Sastrón, *Colonización,* pp. 100–01; Bernaldez Pizarro, p. 242.

45. *Guía oficial . . . 1891,* p. 126; Huang Hsiao-ts'ang, p. chia 72; Liu Chi Tien, *Hua-ch'iao,* p. 62; Case of Lim Simco (1891), PNA, Defraudaciones de la contribución industrial, 5-12-13; Cases of Go Juyco and Lao Joco (1894), PNA, Defraudación de la contribución industrial, 26-22-8.

War II it was estimated that the Chinese did 40 per cent of the timber cutting and milling in the Philippines.[46] Again, as in the case of rice, our information is so scanty it is impossible to tell what share they had in the late nineteenth century.

Sibucao, or sapanwood, was one of the oldest of Philippine exports. Produced by the provinces of Zambales, Pampanga, Pangasinan, La Union, and the island of Panay, sapanwood was an item of moderate importance in nineteenth-century Philippine exports to China and to Singapore. It is not known whether the Chinese cut the wood themselves. They did participate in its shipment to Manila, and the Manila Chinese monopolized its export to China.[47]

Of all the important export crops in the nineteenth century, coffee was the only one in which the Chinese had little or no influence. Although Mindanao coffee was purchased and exported by Chinese, this was but a small part of Philippine coffee exports. Cavite, Tayabas, and particularly Batangas were the real centers of the nineteenth-century Philippine coffee industry. Only in retailing did the Chinese handle coffee from these areas. There is no easy explanation for the absence of Chinese influence; but one reason was surely that the coffee industry centered on the Batangas towns of Lipa and Taal, both rich and inhabited by vigorous people who resisted Chinese intrusion. In fact, Taal was famous for never allowing the Chinese to settle there or take part in its business.[48]

In the discussion of Sulu's trade with Mindanao, mention was made of almáciga collection by the Chinese of Palawan. These Chinese also collected rattan and wax, with the aid of the Tagbanúa people, whom they kept in debt with advances on their collections. Sawyer, writing in the 1890s, was of the opinion that Tagbanúa social and economic life was being disrupted thereby, since the people had to neglect their crops and spend a great deal of time in the forests searching for jungle products to repay their Chinese creditors.[49] The Chinese were also active in the collection and shipment of products of internal trade and

46. Joseph Ralston Hayden, *The Philippines: A Study in National Development* (New York, 1950), p. 699.

47. Díaz Arenas, *Memoria*, p. 50; Sawyer, pp. 247, 249; Case of Santiago Galay Tan Chungco, Zambales, 1879, PNA, Defraudadores de la contribución industrial, 26-17-12; *Los chinos en Filipinas*, p. 121; *Commercial Directory of Manila*, p. 84; Bowring, p. 385; Del Pan, *Las Islas Filipinas*, p. 366; *Guía oficial . . . 1885*, p. 757; MacMicking, p. 307.

48. *Los chinos en Filipinas*, p. 119; Del Pan, *Las Islas Filipinas*, pp. 371–72; Sastrón, *Batangas*, p. 113; George H. Weightman, "The Philippine Chinese," p. 265. The reasons for Taal's and Lipa's resistance to the Chinese are unknown.

49. *Guía oficial . . . 1885*, p. 808; Sawyer, p. 314.

exclusively domestic use, like cacao, wax (for candles), fiber hats, mats, and bags, and coconut oil (used for illumination).[50]

Retail Trade

The position of the Chinese in Philippine retail trade has been most tenaciously maintained despite numerous attacks upon it. This aspect of Chinese activities, more than any other, has borne the brunt of anti-Chinese economic measures. It will be recalled that a major reason for the expulsion of 1755 was the desire of Spaniards, mestizos and indios to replace the Chinese in Manila's retail trade. In Part I it was pointed out that while the Spaniards were not very successful at this, the mestizos and indios did make progress during the century 1750–1850, so that by the latter date most of Manila's retailing was done by three groups: mestizos, Chinese, and indios, with the mestizos on the rise. Outside Manila, with the Chinese removed from most of the provinces, the indios and mestizos could enjoy a free hand in retail trade.

All this was changed between 1850 and 1898. By the latter year the Chinese had recovered their pre-1755 status of preeminence in Manila's retail trade, and occupied a very strong position in the retailing of almost every province. Those who suffered were the mestizo and indio retailers. Therefore, when anti-Chinese agitation began again in the 1880s, a major objective was to recapture a share of the retail trade for the mestizos and indios, in contrast to obtaining a foothold in retailing for Spaniards and mestizos as had been the case a century earlier. Furthermore, the spread of Chinese retailing activity to all parts of the Philippines meant that opposition to the Chinese retailer became, for the first time, an archipelago-wide issue.

Chinese retail establishments were, of course, of several kinds. In rural districts the characteristic type was the sari-sari store, which sold, at retail only, goods needed by the humble household. Its stock included a wide range of grocery items, and such other household staples as cordwood, coconut oil, soap, matches, maguey rope, candles, thread, needles, wrapping paper, buttons, cigars, tobacco, and betel nut.[51]

Although the Chinese store in a fixed location was in many regions a departure from the old system of periodic markets,[52] the Chinese did

50. *Los chinos en Filipinas*, pp. 27–28, 110; Sawyer, pp. 135, 314; Díaz Arenas, *Memoria*, p. 50; Lü Shih-p'eng, p. 400; *Guía oficial . . . 1885*, p. 801.

51. "Decreto de intendencia," Feb. 5, 1892, Berriz, *Anuario 1892*, p. 54; Case of Lao Joco, 1894, PNA, Defraudación de la contribución industrial, 26-22-8. Local detail is found in Lü Shih-p'eng, pp. 399–400; Bowring, pp. 345–46; PNA, Cabezas de barangay, chinos, 49-1-10; Rajal, pp. 295–97, 300, 310.

52. Nicholas Loney noted in 1857 the beginning of the permanent Chinese shop in Molo and predicted this kind of establishment would spread, although periodic

not ignore the old method. There is evidence of Chinese participation in periodic markets at towns where there was no Chinese store. In Pangasinan, for instance, Chinese merchants paid a special fee of 60 pesos for the right to trade in the periodic markets of that province.[53] Nor did the Chinese neglect itinerant peddling. In Luzon especially, Chinese ambulatory merchants competed successfully against indios and mestizos who had come to specialize in this activity. The indio and mestizo itinerant traders of Pampanga, Pangasinan, Tayabas, the towns of Taal in Batangas, and Tambobong (Malabong) near Manila, and the Bicol region, soon felt the pressure of Chinese competition, and many abandoned trading for agriculture.[54] Chinese ambulant merchants also visited periodic markets, although forbidden to do so by the licenses issued them.[55]

In urban areas, the ubiquitous sari-sari store catered to the poorer classes. In addition, there were several kinds of specialty stores: dry goods dealers, grocers, rice dealers, wood dealers, and so forth. But the principle of the "general store" persisted and was found at all levels. That is, besides the sari-sari store there were, on a somewhat higher level, "knickknack shops" (tiendas de chucherías) and "hardware stores" (tiendas de quincallería). These shops had in their stock, in addition to what normally would be considered hardware, such things as porcelains, toys, glasses, perfumes, mirrors, musical instruments, hats, clocks, writing paper, and paintings. Items of hardware were sold at both wholesale and retail; the non-hardware stock at retail only.[56]

The most expensive version of the "general store" was the bazar. The new export crop economy brought prosperity to many of those who participated in it, and the newly rich mestizos and indios developed a taste for luxury goods, mostly European imports.[57] The bazar, whether owned by Chinese or others, catered to this taste. The two largest Chinese-owned bazares in Manila were those of Chua Farruco, first located on Escolta and later at Number 6 Calle Nueva, and Mariano Velasco Chua Chengco, at Number 8 Calle Nueva. Their merchandise

markets would also continue. Bowring, pp. 400–03. On the location of some important markets see Miller, p. 417.

53. Bowring, p. 300; Ratzel, pp. 132–33. See also Lü Shih-p'eng, p. 399.

54. Los chinos en Filipinas, pp. 27–28, 64–65, 110; Testimony of Chas. I. Barnes, Report of Philippine Commission, 2, 187. Compare the discussion of itinerant traders in Miller, pp. 422–25.

55. "Ilocos Norte, 1891–2," PNA, Defraudadores de la contribución industrial, 26-17-12.

56. "Decreto de intendencia," Feb. 5, 1892, Berriz, Anuario 1892, p. 50; Carl C. Plehn, "Taxation in the Philippines," Political Science Quarterly, 16 (1901), 708. See also, Sancianco, pp. 91–92.

57. Legarda, "Foreign Trade," pp. 363–64; Benitez, pp. 243–44; Zaide, 2, 77–78.

included Viennese furniture, Parisian-made musical instruments, cooking stoves, cabinets, ornaments for carriages, dinnerware, lamps, galvanized iron for roofing, Chinese silks, European cottons and yarns of several grades and "an infinity of fancy goods from the best manufacturers of Europe." [58]

Most bazares and some hardware and sari-sari stores had large back rooms. These were supposedly for storage only, but were often used to display and sell articles sometimes more expensive and luxurious than those displayed in the outer room. Many dealers did not report their income from back-room sales, and in this way defrauded the tax collector. The Spanish officials, for their part, dealt harshly and perhaps indiscriminately with stores having back rooms, in a series of raids during the early 1890s. The Chinese complained that government regulations permitted the existence of back rooms if not used for sales, but that government officials were indiscriminately accusing everyone with a back room of illegal sales. Their protests were mostly unavailing.[59]

Many of the Manila retailers employed ambulant vendors, called *corredores,* who sold dry goods, hardware, and household needs from door to door. Often they went in pairs—one Chinese carrying the goods on a shoulder-pole, the other acting as salesman. It was said that all retailers who employed corredores decided among themselves each day's minimum prices, so as not to compete with one another.[60]

To summarize, Chinese retailers expanded their influence, both numerically, within Manila, and geographically, throughout the Philippines. Moreover, as demands for new imports developed, the Chinese entered new fields of retailing, beginning to handle European goods, notably textiles, hardware, and luxury items.

Artisans and Laborers

ARTISANS

From the earliest days of the Spanish colony in the Philippines, the Chinese had held a near monopoly on trades in Manila and in many

---

58. *Guía oficial . . . 1891,* p. 155; *Guía oficial . . . 1898,* advertisements.

59. *Los chinos en Filipinas,* p. 100, n. 3; Letter of gobernadorcillo de chinos to Central Revenue Administration, Sept. 12, 1891, PNA, Defraudaciones de la contribución industrial, 5-12-13. Several cases of this kind are found in this bundle and in 5-8-3 and 26-22-8.

60. Moya, p. 188; *Los chinos en Filipinas,* pp. 87, 104; Blumentritt, "Die Chinesen Manilas," p. 100; Sawyer, p. 186. Evocative descriptions of the Chinese door-to-door salesman and chocolate miller are given in T. H. Pardo de Tavera, "Los chinos (de mis recuerdos)," *Philippines Free Press* (July 8, 1916), pp. 28, 30.

other areas where Spaniards settled. Late in the eighteenth century indios and Chinese mestizos had begun to cut into the Chinese dominance in the Manila area.[61] But after 1850 the Chinese maintained or bettered their position in the trades where they were preeminent. The indios and mestizos made few gains; they either held on to what they had achieved, or slid back.

In Manila certain occupations which had been monopolized by Chinese since the sixteenth century continued to be. These were: dyers, barbers, sawyers, wax chandlers, bakers, confectioners, butchers, and tanners.[62] In a great many more occupations the Chinese were in the majority, but there were indio and mestizo competitors. These included: cooks, shoemakers, tailors, soap manufacturers, coachmen, smiths of all kinds, founders, masons, smelters, boilermakers, carpenters, cabinetmakers, and boat builders.[63] There were a few occupations in which the Chinese apparently had no interest. Indios and mestizos did Manila's fishing, river transporting, saddlemaking, engraving, and bookbinding.[64] On the other hand, there were two occupations which, because of their nature, were exclusively Chinese: herbalist and *pancitero*. Chinese drug practitioners, who numbered about ten in 1875, had a wide clientele including many well-to-do indios, mestizos, and Spaniards. Panciteros operated Chinese restaurants specializing in *pancit,* a noodle dish, probably of Chinese origin.[65]

Two new fields in which Chinese interest now began to be felt were drayage and furniture-making. Chinese had previously taken some in-

61. See Chap. 1, p. 28.

62. For sixteenth century occupations, see Salazar, "Chinese and Parián," BR, *7,* 227; Pedro Chirino, S.J., "Relation of the Filipinas Islands," 1604, BR, *12,* 192; Juan González de Mendoza, O.S.A., "History of the Great Kingdom of China," 1586, BR, *6,* 152; Purcell, *Chinese in Southeast Asia,* p. 590. For occupations in the 1720s, see PNA, Reales Órdenes, 37-1-3. The occupational gremios as of 1807 are listed in PNA, Bandos, 41-11-3, and the same for 1830 in PNA, Libro de capitación de chinos, 1830. Post-1850 references are: PNA, Defraudaciones de la contribución industrial, 5-12-13 (Letter of gobernadorcillo de chinos, Sept. 12, 1891); Blumentritt, "Die Chinesen Manilas," p. 98; Cavada, *1,* 52.

63. Clark, pp. 813, 815-18; Blumentritt, "Die Chinesen Manilas," p. 98; Foreman, p. 401; Buzeta, *2,* 245; *Los chinos en Filipinas,* pp. 32, 100-01, 122; Sawyer, p. 290; Moya, p. 185; Cavada, *1,* 52; Bowring, p. 183; González and Moreno, pp. 269-84.

64. Foreman, p. 401; Del Pan, *Las Islas Filipinas,* p. 358.

65. González and Moreno, pp. 269-84; *Los chinos en Filipinas,* p. 122; Blumentritt, "Die Chinesen Manilas," p. 99; Buzeta, *2,* 245; Mallat, *2,* 138. The reliance of many of Manila's Spanish and mestizo families upon the Chinese practitioner is a major theme of the novel *Sin título* by Francisco de Paula Entrala (Manila, 1881). In Manuel's wordlist of Hokkien Chinese contributions to Tagalog 20 per cent of the terms are names of foods or culinary terms; another 18 per cent are occupational terms—all of this significant lexical evidence of the nature of Chinese economic influence. *Chinese Elements in Tagalog,* pp. 109-12.

terest in drayage, since we find a wagonmasters' occupational gremio included in the tax classifications for the first decade of the nineteenth century. But their activities must have declined, since later occupational group lists do not include this classification.[66] However that may be, after 1850 the Chinese were increasingly active in drayage, especially the hauling of goods back and forth between ships and warehouses. By 1898 the Chinese were doing most of the hauling in the Manila area.[67]

The making of fine furniture had been developed as a local specialty by the indios of Paete in Laguna province. There were also a few furniture factories in Manila. After 1850 the Chinese began making furniture faster and cheaper than did indio craftsmen and, while the latter were able to continue in business, the Chinese took away their market except for the richer buyers.[68]

Furniture-making was not the only trade in which the Chinese matched speed and cheapness against the slower, more careful craftsmanship of the indio and mestizo. Crews of Chinese carpenters could put up a house faster than indios, but the indios stayed in business by doing more careful work. It was the same way with boilermakers. The Cavite Arsenal refused to hire either Chinese carpenters or boilermakers, on the grounds that indios, although slower, were more reliable.[69]

There is practically no information available on the Chinese as artisans outside of Manila. Victor Clark notes the Chinese dominance of woodworking trades in larger urban centers, but points out that such was not the case in less urbanized parts of the Philippines, since, in a predominantly rural or small town setting, most resident Chinese were merchants.[70] In lieu of any specific information on the subject there is a good rule of thumb to follow: It is likely that in any area of the Philippines the first Chinese penetration was made by merchants, probably of the sari-sari or chucherías type. Only later, as some urbanization developed, was there specialization in merchandising and the establishment of Chinese artisans.

Numerically speaking, the trades most often adopted by Philippine Chinese seem to have been cook, carpenter, and shoemaker. However,

66. PNA, Bandos, 41-11-3; Libro de capitación de chinos, 1830; Los chinos en Filipinas, pp. 42–43.

67. Plauchut, pp. 893–94; Los chinos en Filipinas, p. 122; "The Chinese in the Philippines," p. 154; Blumentritt, "Die Chinesen Manilas," p. 100.

68. Los chinos en Filipinas, pp. 110, 122; Clark, pp. 816–17; Sastrón, Colonización, p. 102.

69. Blumentritt, "Die Chinesen Manilas," p. 100; Los chinos en Filipinas, pp. 121–22.

70. Clark, pp. 813–14.

the 1903 census, which attempted to classify the Chinese by occupations, established general categories of "merchants," "salesman," and "laborers," which, if given finer definition, might well change the picture entirely.[71] Nevertheless, the Chinese were certainly prominent in the three trades listed above. Most of the cooks and shoemakers were Cantonese, and most Cantonese in the Philippines were either cooks or shoemakers.[72] A special form of encouragement was given Chinese shoemakers, perhaps unwittingly; Spanish tariff legislation protected domestically manufactured footwear, and since over 80 percent of the shoemakers in the Philippines were Chinese, passage of this law amounted to protection of a Chinese industry in the Philippines.[73]

LABORERS

Like artisans, Chinese laborers were found almost entirely in urban areas. Although some 11.6 per cent of all Chinese in the Philippines were classified as "laborers" by the 1903 census, most of them apparently were concentrated in just three places: Manila, Iloilo, and Cebu. One could therefore add a corollary to the rule of thumb just advanced: If merchants were the first Chinese to penetrate a given area, and artisans followed only with some urbanization, Chinese laborers were usually found only in urban areas where the volume of business—particularly exporting and importing—had reached a point requiring large amounts of factory, warehouse, and dock labor.

There had been Chinese laborers in the Philippines ever since the beginning of the Spanish period. But in the post-1850 period there were many more Chinese laborers than before, and they were put to a wider variety of uses. The situation was complicated by the growth of an urban proletariat in Manila during the nineteenth century, whose opportunities for employment were thwarted by the increased use of Chinese labor.[74]

The new export crop economy created a demand for cheap, efficient labor, especially on the part of the foreign firms in Manila, Cebu, and Iloilo, which used the Chinese as stevedores and warehouse laborers. In response to this demand, Chinese coolie-brokers in Manila began importing laborers from China. Some of these coolies may have been

71. Ibid., p. 736.

72. Blumentritt, "Die Chinesen Manilas," pp. 98–99; PNA, Padrones de chinos (Manila, 1894; Iloilo, 1894).

73. "In the same spirit the tailors are protected, i.e. allowed to overcharge the consumer to the extent of 40 to 50 per cent, the duty on imported clothes, which goes principally to the Chinese." Bowring, pp. 183, 296–97.

74. *Los chinos en Filipinas,* p. 122; Blumentritt, "Die Chinesen Manilas," pp. 98, 100.

signed to contracts with foreign companies. But the usual practice was for the coolie-broker to sell his "cargo" to Chinese cabecillas at perhaps 20 or 30 pesos per head. The individual laborer became a kind of indentured servant of the cabecilla until he had paid off this price. The cabecilla could use his laborers for whatever projects he might have, or hire them out in gangs to foreign companies for loading and unloading ships and working in warehouses. In the latter case the wages for all members of the gang were paid to him.[75]

From the foreign merchant's point of view, it was a convenience to use well-organized gangs and to pay only one person rather than each individual. When the United States took over the Philippines and the question of Chinese exclusion was debated, foreign businessmen in Manila who testified at hearings were almost unanimous in favoring inclusion of Chinese coolies, whatever other groups of Chinese might be excluded. Charles Ilderton Barnes, a partner in the merchant firm of Warner Barnes and Company, drily summed up:

> The man who wants Chinese coolies to assist him wants you to let the Chinese coolies in, Chinese carpenters and Chinese cooks, and Chinese servants . . . but I don't think they are favorable to other Chinese coming in whom they do not want. Everybody wants his own Chinaman.[76]

Foreign merchants were not the only users of Chinese labor gangs. The city of Manila increasingly employed them for public works instead of relying upon the obligatory corvée labor of 40 days per year owed by the indios.[77] Chinese owners of farderías needed 50 or 60 laborers per fardería. And balers of tobacco and abaca also made use of Chinese laborers. Finally, there were small groups of Chinese in Spanish-owned mining companies in Cebu, Ilocos, and Lepanto, where they worked without benefit of machinery.[78]

Coolie labor brokerage was a rich source of income to Chinese who participated in it. The wealthy Tan Quien-sien, whose career is outlined in Chapter 7, was among those known as a large supplier of coolie

75. Foreman, p. 119; Sawyer, p. 290; Testimonies of Edwin Warner, José Luis de Luzuriaga, A. R. M. Ongcakwe, Carlos Palanca [Tan Quien-sien], J. T. B. McCleod, William Daland, *Report of Philippine Commission, 2,* 17–19, 163–68, 218–19, 223–24, 309–10, 417; Moya, pp. 185, 189; Mencarini, p. 167.

76. Testimony of Barnes in *Report of Philippine Commission, 2,* 187–90. For other businessmen's opinions, see testimonies of Edwin Warner, Neil McLeod, and J. T. B. McCleod, in ibid., 2, 17–19, 32–36, 309–10.

77. *Los chinos en Filipinas,* p. 122.

78. Ibid., p. 118; Sawyer, p. 290; Testimony of Carlos Palanca [Tan Quien-sien], *Report of Philippine Commission, 2,* 223; Letter of *comandante* of Lepanto to Central Revenue Administration, 1877, PNA, Cabezas de barangay, chinos, 49-1-10.

labor.[79] Unfortunately no information is available on the profits derived from this business.

Monopoly Contractors

Among the innovations in Chinese occupations after 1850 none was more important than monopoly contracting. By the last half of the nineteenth century several imposts, both municipal and provincial, had been or were being established by the Spanish government. Among these were taxes on public markets, weights and measures, livestock slaughtering, cockpits, and a general impost on carriages, horses, and bridges.[80]

Prior to 1850 the Chinese were not allowed to bid on the monopoly contracts for collecting the taxes just mentioned. The only kind of contracts the Chinese held were for collecting Chinese taxes or for supplying meat to Manila.[81] When, in 1857, regulations were altered to allow the participation of foreigners in monopoly contract bidding, the Chinese quickly took advantage of the new opportunity. By the 1880s the Chinese were said to control 80 per cent of municipal tax contracts, and "not a few" provincial contracts.[82] The source of this claim, an anti-Chinese diatribe, may have exaggerated Chinese influence, but the data at hand are insufficient to allow us to confirm or deny this estimate. Whatever the percentage may have been, it is clear that Chinese interest in these contracts was considerable.[83]

Cockpits, established as a government monopoly in 1861, were a favorite interest of Chinese and mestizo contractors. Some of the richest, most prominent Chinese held cockpit contracts. In the late 1890s, Tan Quien-sien reportedly paid 68,000 pesos per year for the license for "the great cockpit of Manila and one other."[84] And in Cebu, two of

79. Testimony of O. F. Williams (U.S. Consul at Manila), *Report of Philippine Commission*, 2, 252.

80. *Los chinos en Filipinas*, p. 123; Sastrón, *Batangas*, p. 262; Rajal, pp. 323, 348. There was even a tax on Chinese theatrical presentations in Manila, from which the government derived a very small amount of revenue. Montero, *Historia*, 3, 453.

81. See contract of Juan Ong-Ganco, Oct. 1821, and contracts of Bartolomé Pitco, Sebastián de Niqua, and others, 1764–66, in PNA, "Legajo 15."

82. Montero, *Historia*, 3, 254, n. 2; *Los chinos en Filipinas*, pp. 20–21.

83. See PNA, Arbitrios: Pampanga, 28-10-4; Arbitrios: Cebú, 28-4-6; Rajal, p. 323. In 1881, of seven municipal contracts in Manila, the Chinese held five, the other two belonging to the prominent Chinese mestizo, Ildefonso Tambunting. *Guía oficial para 1881*, pp. 48–49.

84. Henry Norman, *The Peoples and Politics of the Far East* (London, 1900), p. 178. In this year, besides Tan Quien-sien, there were five other "farmers" in Manila. Ibid. The cockpit monopoly produced an annual revenue of 100,000–200,000 pesos. Plehn, *Pol. Sci. Q.*, 17 (1902), p. 145.

the wealthiest Chinese, Domingo Burgos Dy-Yangco and Ramón Lao Yuco, were also cockpit contractors in the 1890s.[85]

Much more lucrative were the opium monopoly contracts. Unlike the other monopolies, which involved merely applying a tax to some existing usage, the establishment of an opium monopoly required legalizing a practice hitherto frowned upon. The use of opium in the Philippines had been a problem since at least the second decade of the nineteenth century. The earliest available legislation on the matter is a proclamation of 1814 prohibiting the growth, importation, or use of the drug. Despite this interdict, the Philippine Chinese—at least those of Manila —were able to circumvent legislation by periodically renting parts of houses belonging to influential Spaniards who could be counted on to keep their activities secret, or to protect them if they were discovered.

By the 1820s and 1830s the Spanish government was beginning to reconsider its opium policies. In nearby China a market for opium had been developed, and it was argued by some that the Philippines, much closer to China than was India, could grow and sell opium to the Chinese market cheaper than British India was doing. In an effort to encourage such a development, a Royal Order of 1828 permitted opium culture in the Philippines on a strictly controlled basis, with the prohibition on domestic use to remain in force.[86]

Paralleling these policy developments was a general debate over the potentialities of opium as a source of government revenue. During the year 1843 a special commission investigated the pros and cons of allowing the Philippine Chinese to use opium under the control of a government monopoly. The commission reported favorably on the proposal and in December 1843 the opium monopoly was established on a limited basis. Six years later another commission reviewed the problem, coming to the same decision. In the course of the commission investigations a number of arguments, mostly of an economic and moral nature, were heard. Among others, the commission of 1849 solicited the advice of the ubiquitous China expert, Sinibaldo de Mas, who responded to the effect that from personal experimentation he had found opium no more debilitating than tobacco. More to the point, from personal obser-

85. PNA, Arbitrios, Cebu, 28-4-6. For further information on these two men, see PNA, Padron de chinos, Cebu, 1894.

86. The order of 1814 (December 1) is quoted in Comenge, p. 155 n. On the illegal use of opium by the Chinese prior to 1843, see Buzeta, 2, 246. The text of the 1828 royal order is found in Comenge, p. 164 n. The same text, and a summary of a related memorial by Bernaldez Pizarro, are available in "Estudios en el Archivo General de Indias de Sevilla," *Anales de la Real Academia de Farmacía, 19* (1953), 167–68.

vation he had learned that Chinese who used opium could work just as hard as those who did not.[87] Fortified by such arguments, and with the ever-present revenue question in their minds, the commissions decided in favor of the monopoly, giving the following reasons: (1) there was no conclusive evidence that opium caused physical damage; (2) the prohibition was impossible to enforce against the Chinese; (3) Spain's trade treaty negotiations with China were being jeopardized by such harsh treatment of Chinese subjects in the Philippines; (4) the monopoly was needed for revenue purposes.[88]

At first the scope of the monopoly was restricted to the Manila area, part of the Alcaicería de San Fernando being set aside as a government opium den. But in 1850 the holder of the monopoly, a prominent Spanish businessman, petitioned that contracts be let for nearby provinces as well, and it was after this date that the monopoly expanded to include the entire archipelago.[89]

In its final form the opium monopoly worked as follows: in each province where there were sufficient Chinese to make it worthwhile (non-Chinese were strictly forbidden the use of opium), monopoly rights were leased to a contractor on a three-year basis. He was to import opium,[90] store it in a specially-designated customs warehouse until ready for use, establish and supply as many government-licensed opium dens as the number of customers seemed to warrant, and prepare and sell opium to consumers. He might subcontract his monopoly as he wished, and was further empowered to select as many deputies as he needed to search out contraband. Furthermore, he had access to whatever law enforcement institutions were necessary to maintain his monopoly.[91]

Contracts were awarded to the highest bidders. For each triennium the government established a minimum bid figure, usually the amount of the previous triennial contract. Under this system the government, theoretically, could not lose, since bids—and hence revenue—would be higher with each letting. Indeed, they were higher; but when no profits were to be made, bidders simply boycotted the auction and the govern-

---

87. Comenge, pp. 152–60; Mas, *La Chine*, 2, 377.

88. Comenge, pp. 161–62.

89. Ibid., p. 157; PNA, Reales Órdenes, caja 108, núm. 12 and núm. 36.

90. Despite the royal order of 1828 permitting opium culture in the Philippines, little was grown, probably due to annoying regulations and the fact that the soil of the Manila area, to which the permission was limited, was unsuitable for this culture. MacMicking, pp. 301–03.

91. For contract terms, see Bando, Dec. 13, 1843, PNA, Acuerdos de audiencia, 52-24-8, and PNA, Rentas de anfión, 15-10-9.

ment was forced to lower the minimum bid figure, 5 per cent at a time, until it reached a more attractive level.[92]

Like other contractors, opium monopolists were taxed by the government at a rate of .5 per cent of the contract figure. Since by the 1880s the Spanish were attempting to establish a general 5 per cent income tax on most non-agricultural occupations, Carl Plehn, in an analysis of Philippine taxation, has reasoned that this tax applied to the profits from monopoly contracts as well. Hence, a tax of .5 per cent would suggest a profit of at least 10 per cent.[93] If we provisionally adopt this analysis we may obtain a very crude idea of the kind of profits possible from the opium contracts. Thus, the Cagayan contract for 1892–95, which amounted to 81,200 pesos, may have netted its owner in excess of 8,000 pesos over the three-year period. Likewise, the Manila contract for 1890–93, at 532,127 pesos, may have produced a three-year profit of over 53,000 pesos. Some of the other provinces having large contracts in the 1890s were: Leyte (about 64,000 pesos), Pampanga (over 62,000 pesos), Camarines (North and South) (over 52,000 pesos), and Samar (over 46,000 pesos). Although we have no figures for Iloilo, the fact that, by the 1890s, 100 opium dens were established there as against Cagayan's 40, suggests that the Iloilo contract was one of the largest.[94]

Though the possibilities for profit seem to have been considerable, the overhead on these contracts must also have been sizable. Opium had to be imported from British India, either via Hong Kong (for the northern part of the Philippines) or through Zamboanga or Jolo (for the southern Philippines). This operation alone could be expensive. Besides the shipping cost and the standard tariff on imported drugs, a contractor had to pay a special opium fee at the rate of 40 pesos per chest. Moreover, in 1890 a 50 per cent surcharge was added, which made the entire contract more expensive.[95]

92. PNA, Rentas de anfión, 6-2-9, 5-8-7, 37-2-10, 25-16-18; Ramo de anfión, 5-20-12.

93. Plehn, 16 (1901), 706; Real Órden, March 5, 1890, Berriz, *Anuario 1890*, p. 246.

94. PNA, Rentas de anfión, 15-10-9, 6-2-9, 5-8-7; Anfión, 42-5-7.

95. Real Órden, Sept. 18, 1847, Berriz, *Anuario 1888, 1*, 70; Letter of the opium contractor for Batangas to the Central Revenue Administration, 1890, PNA, Ramo de anfión, 5-20-12; Letter of opium contractor for Balabac to Central Revenue Administration, 1891, Rentas de anfión, 25-16-18; Letter of Camarines contractor, Sept. 1898, Rentas de anfión, 5-8-7. The ultimate source of Philippine-consumed opium is referred to in an article in the Spanish newspaper *La política de España en Filipinas*, June 7, 1891, p. 122. In 1873 some 17,163 kg. of opium, valued at 205,950 pesos, were imported from British India. González and Moreno, pp. 204–05. On opium costs, see also Plauchut, p. 886 and Cavada, 2, 375.

It was said that only rich Chinese held opium contracts. It is true that some of Manila's richest Chinese were opium monopolists, adding opium contracting to their several other business interests.[96] But in the 1890s, Chinese who were of the lowly sixth classification in the tax scale were among the bidders for opium contracts, even for some of the larger provinces.[97] In view of the sums involved, including an obligatory cash deposit of 5 to 10 per cent of the bid, one suspects that these sixth-class bidders were either borrowers from, or "front men" for, wealthier Chinese. Auctions for an opium contract were held simultaneously in Manila and in the capital of the province concerned. This arrangement tended to put the provincial Chinese, often less wealthy, in competition with the Manila Chinese. Speaking generally, it appears that the Manila Chinese were quite successful in obtaining the more valuable provincial contracts.

One of the most attractive contracts was that of Cagayan–Isabela (the two provinces being combined for this purpose), which is also of some interest because the ascent in its value illustrates the sharp increase in Chinese immigration in these two provinces. In 1869, the Cagayan–Isabela contract was leased for a three-year figure of 15,150 pesos. During succeeding triennia it rose gradually to 19,525 pesos in 1878. It jumped to 24,570 pesos in 1881, leveled off at 26,500 pesos in 1884, and then doubled with an 1887 figure of 58,610 pesos. While some of this increase may have been a reflection of other factors, such as increased operating costs and avid competitive bidding, a large share of it must be attributed to the considerable influx of Chinese into this area after the termination of the tobacco monopoly in 1880. In 1890 the figure for this contract again leveled off, at 58,869 pesos. But a question of disputed inheritance in 1892, and the hot competitive bidding that followed, drove the contract figure up to 81,200 pesos.[98]

The victor in the 1892 Cagayan–Isabela bidding was Federico Gamir Co Sequieng, a Manila Chinese merchant and cigar manufacturer with widespread opium interests. Unlike some Chinese contractors who

96. On the various interests of Joaquín Tan Angco, see PNA, Chinos, elecciones, 37-2-2, and Rentas de anfión, 6-2-9. The same kind of information about Joaquín Martínez Sy Tiongtay is found in Chinos, elecciones, 37-2-2; Rentas de anfión, 15-10-9; Case of Uy Tiaoquieng, 1891, Defraudaciones de la contribución industrial, 5-12-13; and Berriz, *Diccionario, 4,* 352–56. For the activities of Tan Quien-sien, see biographical sketch below in Chap. 7.

97. Cagayan–Isabela contract, 1890, PNA, Rentas de anfión, 15-10-9; Burias contract, 1891, Rentas de anfión, 6-2-9; Davao contract, 1894; Mindoro, 1897, Rentas de anfión, 5-8-7. Batangas contract, 1890, Ramo de anfión, 5-20-12; Leyte contract, 1897, Rentas de anfión, 25-16-18.

98. PNA, Rentas de anfión, 15-10-9.

preferred to bid on only the larger contracts, Co Sequieng built up a kind of territorial bloc of adjacent provinces in which he held opium contracts. At one time (1893) he held contracts for nine provinces, giving him a monopoly of opium distribution over much of Northern Luzon. However, most of these were small-scale contracts. The Cagayan–Isabela contract, the only large one he held, was acquired only over the opposition of the powerful Tan Quien-sien, who supplied a 15,000 peso loan in support of Co Sequieng's rival claimant.[99]

The opium monopoly was not an exclusively Chinese concern. Non-Chinese persons participated in various ways. Some of them held contracts, others were agents, partners, or bondsmen of Chinese contractors. The Manila contract, the most lucrative of all, was sometimes held by Spanish businessmen. In the early 1890s the Manila contractor was a prominent Spanish businessman, apparently the son of the 1850 contractor who had urged geographical expansion of the contracts. The 1890 Manila contractor was associated with a Spanish merchant and cigar-manufacturing firm which acted as Manila agent for opium contractors in Cavite and Bulacan.[100] The Cagayan–Isabela contract of 1892 was acquired by Co Sequieng with the aid of a non-Chinese agent and a non-Chinese bondsman. And a mixed partnership—Mariano Fernando Yu Chingco, Joaquín Tan Angco, and a Spaniard, Eulogio Mendoza—in 1890 held contracts for the provinces of Leyte, Samar, and Cavite.[101] Despite this participation by non-Chinese persons at the contracting level, the operators of dens and most of the various agents and subcontractors were and had to be, by the nature of things, Chinese.

Dens were established at a ratio of perhaps 20 to 30 Chinese per den. From the very beginning of the opium monopoly there was a status problem. Wealthy Chinese were reluctant to patronize dens used by the poor, and asked that they be allowed to establish "private" dens in their homes or places of business. Some Spanish officials made an alternative proposal that more luxuriously furnished dens be provided for those with status. Except in the case of Manila, which authorized "private" dens, no formal action was ever taken but local adjustments were made almost immediately, usually in the form of allowing those with standing in the community to use opium at home, provided they bought it

99. Ibid.; also, Ramo de anfión, 5-20-12, and Rentas de anfión, 37-2-10. For further information on Co Sequieng, see Chinos, elecciones, 37-2-2.

100. PNA, Rentas de anfión, 6-2-9, 5-8-7. The head of the cigar firm referred to was said to have some business connections with the two most prominent Chinese in Manila, Tan Quien-sien, and Chua Chengco. See also *Chronicle and Directory* . . . *1902*, p. 666.

101. PNA, Rentas de anfión, 15-10-9, 6-2-9. The contractor for Cavite in 1892 and 1896, and for Bataan in 1894 was a Spaniard. Rentas de anfión, 6-2-9, 5-8-7.

from the monopolist. A Spanish inspector of evident sincerity, who investigated Iloilo's government opium dens in 1896, found that, despite laws requiring that all dens be public (that is, open to all Chinese), 56 of the 100 licensed dens in Iloilo province were private. His horrified report to the central tax collecting administration in Manila was answered by a matter-of-fact statement that these adjustments had been common for several years in many parts of the Philippines, and were, in fact, the only way the monopoly could produce any revenue.[102]

The Philippine Revolution, beginning in 1896, caused serious damage to the opium business, as it did to many other businesses. In some provinces where revolutionary activities were strongest—in particular, Cavite—there was no security for Chinese property, and so many Chinese fled to Manila that the provincial contractor was forced into default for lack of customers for his opium. Elsewhere, it was a case of difficulty in moving the opium. Transportation was particularly a problem once Admiral Dewey blockaded Manila Bay, making it impossible to import more opium or to move what was already in Manila to other regions by sea. The result was that from 1896 to the end of Spanish rule in 1898 contracts went begging for bidders, or were taken on a month-to-month basis only.[103]

The Size and Independence of the Chinese Economy

It is clear that in the years between 1850 and 1898 the Chinese share in the Philippine economy increased markedly. The Chinese did not merely win back the position they had held before 1750; they exceeded any of their previous successes. The expansion of Chinese interests was both quantitative and geographical. Quantitatively, it involved increased Chinese influence in certain occupations and initial Chinese efforts in others. Geographically, the expansion of Chinese enterprise resulted in establishing for the first time something like a "Chinese economy" that covered the entire archipelago.

There is no way to measure the size of this Chinese economy or, to put it another way, the size of the Chinese share in the Philippine economy. As pointed out above, data are insufficient to allow quantification of Chinese activities in certain specific occupations. The same, un-

102. PNA, Reales Órdenes, caja 108, núm. 12, 36. Jagor, who visited the Philippines about 1860, found that besides the 478 government licensed dens that had been established, hundreds of persons were allowed to use opium at home. Jagor, p. 318, n. 244. Iloilo *visita*, 1896, PNA, Rentas de anfión, 6-2-9.

103. Cavite, 1896, PNA, Rentas de anfión, 6-2-9; Leyte, 1898, Camarines, 1898, Cavite, 1897, Bulacan, 1897, Batangas, 1897, Rentas de anfión, 5-8-7; and Rentas de anfión, 37-2-10 and 25-16-18, passim.

fortunately, holds true for the Philippine economy as a whole. The *Census of 1903*, which is the best source of statistical information, classifies by occupation only within color groups. That is, there is no general table of occupations which shows what percentages of each occupation are respectively "yellow," "white," "brown," or "mixed."

Nor is there any way to determine the size of the Chinese investment in the Philippines. Even partial estimates are impossible. On property ownership, for instance, the *Census of 1903* indicates size of private holdings by provinces only, not by "color," let alone nationality. The only other important statistical publication of this kind, Cavada's *Historia*, which presents the results of an inquiry of 1870, is uninformative on this point. Nor can we obtain estimates of even rural and urban landownership from the random references we have. Such references indicate the amounts of taxation derived from rural and urban real estate, but do not offer a nationality or color breakdown. The nearest indication is a reference in Cavada which indicates that in 1870 the Chinese, who constituted about .5 per cent of the Philippine population, owned about .5 per cent of all urban, income-producing houses in the archipelago.[104] This is, of course, of little use, since it concerns only houses, and does not indicate the values of the properties.

Another possibility would be to attempt to determine the net income of the Chinese, comparing it with that of other groups. Cavada provides figures on total net profits of *industriales*—that is, essentially, self-employed persons other than farmers, teachers, and lawyers. The net profits for 133,384 industriales in the Philippines in 1870 amounted to 32,508,511 pesos. Of this figure, 1,491,448 pesos, or about 4½ per cent, went to 3,200 Chinese industriales. Some 1,229,426 pesos, or slightly less than 4 per cent, went to 2,640 mestizos, including both Chinese mestizos and Spanish mestizos. Over 90 per cent of the 32,-508,511 pesos went to indio industriales. In per capita terms, the highest profits went to North Europeans and North Americans, the next highest to Spaniards. After this came mestizos and Chinese, at a rate of about 460 pesos each. Indio industriales had the lowest per capita profit figure.[105]

This information is unsatisfactory for at least two reasons. First, it considers only 133,384 self-employed persons, less than 3 per cent of the total population of the Philippines. Persons receiving wages and salaries are not included. Second, although the occupations included under the heading of industrial would encompass nearly all those en-

104. Cavada, 2, 395.
105. Ibid., 2, 412.

gaged in by Chinese, one cannot be very optimistic that the total figure for Chinese industriales bears any relationship to the total net profits of self-employed Chinese. Given the diffusion of responsibility and concealment of ownership characteristic of the cabecilla–agent system, this figure must be regarded with some skepticism. The fact that over 90 per cent of these profits seem to have gone to indios, and only 4 per cent to Chinese may be partially accounted for by the role of the indios as artisans and handicraftsmen outside the large urban areas. This explanation would account for the low per capita profits of the indio industriales. But the large share credited to indio industriales may be derived in part from dummy ownerships or Chinese businesses registered in the names of india wives. It would be helpful to have some other figures to check against. But here again the *Census of 1903* disappoints us: there are no statistics on income by "color" or nationality.

One rather far-fetched way to get at the size of Chinese profits would be to make use of the tax figures individually entered in the Chinese censuses of the 1890s. Since a 5 per cent income tax was standard, one could assume that a Chinese who paid 25 pesos' income tax had a net income of 500 pesos. But this tax was levied not on the basis of individually submitted returns, but on standard categories based on an estimated range of profit to be expected from certain kinds of occupations. Therefore, even if we could be certain of the completeness and accuracy of these censuses, to add an entire column of tax figures in a census and multiply the sum by twenty would result in an estimate so obviously inaccurate as to make unjustified the tremendous labor involved.

If we cannot measure the extent of Chinese economic influence, we can at least discuss how it came about and a few of its broader characteristics. To summarize what has been said previously, the Chinese were able to expand their economic influence because of three factors: liberalized Spanish policies, new opportunities offered by the new export crop economy, and Chinese business methods. Of the three, the last was perhaps the most decisive. Liberalized Spanish policies offered new opportunities to other groups as well as to the Chinese. The termination of the provincial governors' right to trade in 1844, for instance, opened up opportunities to anyone able to seize them. So did the development of an export crop economy. That it was the Chinese who were able to profit as they did was due particularly to Chinese business methods and financial backing. Especially striking is the contrast between the mestizos and the Chinese in wholesaling imports and collecting export crops. The mestizo practice of haphazard, speculative buying of export items, and leisurely disposition of imports by offering them in one periodic market after another, could not compete effectively with what came to be the characteristic unit of Chinese rural enterprise, the sari-sari or chucherías store. It was not that Chinese operations were so much less speculative than those of the mestizos; it was rather that the Chinese were more systematic in buying and in distributing.

Mention of the financial backing of Chinese enterprises during this period raises the question of the independence of what I have called the "Chinese economy." According to Uchida Naosaku's classification, the years under discussion here ought to correspond to a period of "compradore capital." What Uchida seems to mean by this expression is that although there was an "overseas Chinese economy" in each of the countries in Southeast Asia before the late nineteenth century, this Chinese economy, while maintaining a kind of independent continuity, subordinated itself to Western capital, Western forms of business organization, and, in particular, oriented itself toward the goal of most Western enterprises: the production of goods for markets in the West, and the distribution of Western imports in the Southeast Asian country in question. Not until the world depression in the early 1930s did overseas Chinese enterprise seriously begin to free itself from dependence upon world markets, and to gear itself to domestic consumer markets in the host countries.[106]

All this may be true enough, and more or less applicable to the Philippine Chinese during the period in question. But it does not directly answer the question of financial dependence. We have observed that advances from Western merchants or through the Banco Español–Filipino were major sources for financing Chinese commercial activities. We have also noted that the Western merchants attempted to put sales of imports to Chinese distributors on a strictly cash basis, beginning in the 1880s. Were the Chinese, particularly under the pressure of tighter credit, capable of forming their own commercial and industrial capital?

There is little doubt that capital was there, although not always readily available. By the 1880s and 1890s some of Manila's Chinese were believed to be worth as much as 60,000 to 80,000 pesos.[107] At least ten Manila Chinese were taxed on the basis of incomes in excess of 20,000 pesos for the year 1894.[108] Tax-farming contracts and coolie

    106. Uchida, *Overseas Chinese,* pp. 48–52. Uchida's argument is stated with particular reference to the replacement of Chinese enterprise by Western enterprise in mining and plantations, and is probably more applicable to the situation in Malaya than anywhere else.

    107. PNA, Chinos, elecciones, 37-2-2.

    108. PNA, Padrones de chinos, Manila, 1894.

labor brokerage had made some Chinese wealthier than had ever been possible before.[109] But how much of this capital was available for industrial or commercial purposes?

We have one tantalizingly brief reference to the existence of a Chinese bank in the Philippines by the mid-1880s.[110] Otherwise, the first such bank we are certain existed dates from 1902. Whatever the banking situation in the 1880s and 1890s, it is clear that personal loans of considerable size were made by Chinese businessmen. However, most of those we know about seem to have been for use in opium contracting. It is not clear whether Manila's wealthy Chinese regularly provided the same services as the Western merchants and the Banco Español–Filipino. It is, therefore, impossible to determine to what degree the Chinese economy was financially independent of outside sources of capital by the late nineteenth century.[111]

The Philippine Revolution, which lasted from 1896 to 1902, had a serious effect on the Chinese economy. Although many Chinese rice importers reaped rich profits, the lawlessness and unsettled conditions in several provinces caused severe property losses to a great number of Chinese. Not only did many Chinese retire from the provinces to the relative safety of Manila, but others fled the Philippines for China.[112] It is impossible to know how many business failures there were. But it is likely that the Philippine Revolution caused a breakdown of many of the economic networks built up by the Philippine Chinese, systems which had to be rebuilt after order was restored.

Even before the Philippine Revolution, the Chinese community in the Philippines had entered a new period of social and political insecurity, a consequence of cultural, social, and political questions implied in the economic changes just discussed. It is to these questions that we must now turn.

---

109. Comenge, p. 237.

110. "Today they count with the aid of a bank of their own, which advances funds on conditions no more onerous, although in a different form, than those of other known banks." *Los chinos en Filipinas,* p. 88.

111. On loans for opium contracting, see PNA, Rentas de anfión, 15-10-9. Tan Quien-sien, besides making loans to opium contractors, financed without interest the initial sugar operations of Miguel Malvar, an indio planter who became a hero of the Philippine Revolution. E. Arsenio Manuel, *Dictionary of Philippine Biography, I* (Quezon City, 1955), p. 269. For a discussion of a somewhat similar problem in Indonesia, see Williams, "Chinese Entrepreneurs," pp. 34–60; cf. also, G. W. Skinner, *Chinese Society in Thailand: An Analytical History* (Ithaca, 1957), pp. 99–109.

112. Liu Chi Tien, *Hua-ch'iao,* pp. 62, 64; Sastrón, *Colonización,* pp. 108–09. Damage to Chinese property in Cebu City amounted to 1,725,000 pesos. The Cebu Parián was also badly damaged. Foreman, p. 551.

PART THREE

Social Contraction

5

The Cultural and Social Context

Background

Before describing the position of the Chinese in Philippine society it is necessary to say something in broad terms about Philippine society as a whole and about the changes it was undergoing during the late nineteenth century. We will be dealing here with the social consequences of broad economic and cultural changes that were going on in the Philippines throughout the nineteenth century. Although these changes were multifaceted, we cannot discuss each facet here. We can only mention briefly those that seem to bear directly upon the social position of the mestizos and the Chinese.[1]

During the first two centuries of Spanish rule in the Philippines, before the development of crops for export and the rise of urban centers, indigenous political, social, and cultural institutions, once modified by the Spanish conquest, remained largely stable and unchanging. Below the small Spanish sector of Philippine society, composed of Spaniards and Spanish mestizos, who together formed the ruling class, the non-Spanish sector was uncomplicated in appearance. Its membership was mostly indio and among the indios there was a basic two-class division of notables and commoners. The Spanish government chose to rule indirectly through indio chieftains, or *caciques,* who were confirmed in their political power, becoming agents of Spanish authority. As gobernadorcillo, an indio chieftain had limited administrative and judicial authority over the indios of a town and its surrounding villages; as *cabeza de barangay,* a lesser cacique administered the tax and service

1. For discussion of cultural influences not dealt with here see especially Kano Tadao, *Tōnan Ajiya minzokugaku senshigaku kenkyū* (2 vols. Tokyo, 1946–52), passim.

obligations of a social unit of about 100 persons, which might be co-extensive with a village. The political power of the cacique was based not only upon his usefulness to Spain. Relative to the indios he governed, his power was based upon hereditary eminence of his family, the size of his supporting kinship group, or the number of unfree dependents he could command for agricultural labor.[2] Culturally, caciques and commoners shared in one or another local version of a hispanized Philippine culture, a blend of Spanish and indio elements, the most important feature of which was folk Catholicism.[3]

In the late eighteenth century complicating changes began to occur. There were attempts to develop crops for export, projects that finally began to bear fruit after 1820. Liberalized economic legislation opened up the Philippines to the currents of world trade, and with that, to a broader world of ideas and cultural influences as well. Furthermore, with the defection of most of the American part of the Spanish Empire and Spain's subsequent concentration of interest upon the Philippines, closer ties were developed between the metropolitan power and its colony. The interchange of persons between the Philippines and Spain was much more frequent than before. The level of hispanization rose appreciably—so much so that one can speak of a qualitative change in the nature of the hispanization of the Philippines in the nineteenth century.

The economic and cultural changes of this period had social implications. In the Philippines, the new opportunities for wealth brought by the export crop economy were shared with the indigenous population to a greater extent than in other European colonies of Southeast Asia. The crops for export were less likely to be produced on European-owned plantations than on relatively small holdings owned or leased by mestizos or indios. The result was the enrichment with a new form of wealth of certain mestizo and indio families. The acquisition of wealth made possible cultural opportunities hitherto undreamed of—the attainment of a more sophisticated grasp of Spanish culture. Once that was achieved, the lucky ones in turn promoted a still higher level of Spanish cultural life in the Philippines.

Those who possessed this new form of wealth—ownership or control of export-crop producing lands, and cash acquired from the sale of such crops—now began to make their influence felt socially and politically. Increasingly, land ownership and the possession of money became

2. Phelan, *Hispanization of the Philippines,* pp. 19–22; Robert B. Fox, "The Study of Filipino Society and its Significance to Programs of Economic and Social Development," *Philippine Sociological Review,* 7 (1959), 3–4.

3. Phelan, pp. 72–84.

the standards of wealth, rather than wealth measured by the number of unfree dependents one possessed. Status by landed wealth and the evidence of a relatively sophisticated adoption of Spanish culture replaced status by traditional marks. Finally, those who possessed these attributes formed a complicating "third class"[4] in the non-Spanish sector of Philippine society—neither hereditary notables nor hereditary commoners. Politically, they challenged those who held power hereditarily, and ultimately the entire Spanish-imposed political system with its limitations on native political authority. Let us examine these developments in detail.

In the late eighteenth century and throughout the nineteenth century, as Manila developed into an important urban center and as a modest amount of urbanization occurred in Cebu, Iloilo, and several other places,[5] new cultural phenomena began to appear. Of immediate importance to us was the development of a more sophisticated version of Spanish culture in the Philippines. This urban form of hispanization I will call filipinized Hispanic culture, to distinguish it from the less polished hispanized Philippine culture of folk Catholicism. Manila was the fount of this filipinized Hispanic culture. To the extent that the newly-rich mestizos and indios of the provinces either traveled to and from Manila themselves or sent their sons to Manila for an education, they could acquire a taste of this culture.[6] And it was the acquisition of this urban form of Spanish culture, together with the possession of wealth, that overcame barriers and opened doors to the rich. It was not that cultural standards were "lowered" to make room for those with money. It was rather that those with money could and did help create and share in a more sophisticated version of Spanish culture than any hitherto available in the Philippines.

The particular role of Manila in the social and cultural changes of the nineteenth century deserves brief discussion here. The essence of nineteenth-century cultural developments in the Philippines was a widening of horizons. Nowhere was this as true as at Manila, which acted as the focal point of culture change during this period. The

4. Manuel Azcárraga y Palmero, *La reforma del municipio indígena en Filipinas* (Madrid, 1871), pp. 17–19, 27, 50, 75–76.

5. Jimeno Agius, *Población y comercio,* p. 58; Montero, *Archipiélago filipino,* p. 322. As early as the 1820s there were thirteen places besides Manila that could be considered "urban." Bernaldez Pizarro, "Reforms Needed in Filipinas," p. 199. Bernaldez Pizarro's standard for "urban" is apparently a population in excess of 10,000. The same figure has been suggested as a general standard in Jack P. Gibbs and Kingsley Davis, "The International Study of Urbanization," *American Sociological Review,* 23 (1958), 504–14.

6. Benitez, *History of the Philippines,* pp. 243–44.

Philippines' tie to and dependence upon Mexico was broken, to be replaced by direct contact with Spain. The opening of the Suez Canal and the establishment of regular steamship service between Europe and Manila made for an increase in the flow of both persons and ideas. More and more Spaniards came to the Philippines, many of them settling in Manila. Several were bureaucrats, there being a tremendous turnover in administrative personnel during the nineteenth century.[7] Many other Spaniards were businessmen or professionals.

But Spaniards were not the only professionals in Manila. As the urbanization of Manila proceeded, and as more and more mestizos and indios entered law, medicine, and pharmacy, a small but highly important professional group, whose membership transcended ethnic lines, developed in Manila. For such people, an identity of professional interest and attitude was more important than differences in cultural practices. Another important leavening influence was provided by young mestizo and indio intellectuals returning from study in Spain. The new export crop economy had provided those families who benefited from it with the kind of wealth that enabled them to send their sons to Europe, particularly to Spain, for their higher education. The students traveling back and forth between Manila and Spain, and between Manila and their home provinces, transmitted ideas from Spain, through Manila, to the local regions.[8]

The urbanization of Manila and the development of more cosmopolitan tastes and a more sophisticated brand of Spanish cultural influence found expression in a variety of ways. For one thing, there was a gradual, but impressive—for a colonial Asian country—development of newspapers and periodicals in Manila after 1850. At first these were ephemeral in duration and quite limited in reader interest. But by the 1880s and 1890s, particularly under the stimulus of rising political dissidence, Philippine journalism developed along political lines. Although always subject to censorship, and reflecting the points of view of their predominantly Spanish publishers and staff members, Manila's periodicals nevertheless captured the flavor of the Colonial Spanish, or filipinized Hispanic culture that had developed.[9] Besides periodicals,

7. Corpuz, *Bureaucracy in the Philippines*, pp. 131–32. From a level of about 4,000 in 1810, the Spanish population of the Philippines reached heights of 13,500 in 1870 and 34,000 by 1898. BR, 52, 115–116 n.

8. Del Pan, *Las Islas Filipinas*, p. 347. The families of those studying in Europe were carefully watched by the Spanish government, which feared subversive political ideas would be spread through them. T. H. Pardo de Tavera, "History," *Census of 1903*, 1, 380.

9. Zaide, *Philippine Political and Cultural History*, 2, 98. MacMicking, writing in the middle of the nineteenth century, said: "A misconception appears as to the state of society in Manila, people at a distance for the most part labouring under the

there was some development of other forms of literature, particularly poetry and the novel in Spanish. Outstanding in this field were the social novels of Rizal, which reflect several different levels and kinds of hispanization, both urban and rural.[10]

Several theaters were maintained, presenting dramas and comedies in Spanish and in Tagalog. The Tagalog plays were an interesting blend of Spanish and native elements rendered in Tagalog dialogue by actors frequently dressed in Western style.[11]

Western style dress became characteristic of men of the upper class in Manila during the last decades of the nineteenth century. In household effects, as in dress, the increase in Western influence was noticeable. Those who had become wealthy from the sale of export crops indulged themselves in a taste for European luxury goods, particularly items of furniture, as well as European carriages in which to parade about.[12]

In sum, the final decades of the nineteenth century and the first twenty years of the following century witnessed a flowering of Spanish culture in the Philippines—a kind of cultural justification of 300 years of Spanish rule at the same time that demands to end that rule were being made. Spanish cultural influence was thus at its strongest at the time Spanish political influence was becoming the weakest it had been. The Philippine Revolution against Spain was a political, not a cultural revolt.

This rather paradoxical development contrasts sharply with the relationship between nationalism and culture in many other parts of Asia. Elsewhere in Asia, the combination of Western political pressure and cultural influence eventually produced new, culturally marginal elites, who sought to harmonize in a national framework the intellectually

---

erroneous impression that it remains stationary, and is today as much behind the rest of the world as it was 30 years ago; and that it can support no newspaper or other publication." MacMicking, *Recollections*, p. 202. A discussion of individual periodicals and nineteenth-century journalism in general is found in W. E. Retana, "El periodismo filipino," in *Aparato bibliográfico, 3,* 1493–1800. See also Jesús Z. Valenzuela, *A History of Journalism in the Philippine Islands* (Manila, 1933), Chaps. 4 and 5.

10. José Rizal, *Noli me tangere,* tr. as *The Social Cancer* by Charles Derbyshire (2d ed. Manila, 1912), and *El filibusterismo,* tr. as *The Reign of Greed* by Derbyshire (2d ed. Manila, 1912).

11. See W. E. Retana, *Noticias histórico-bibliográficas de el teatro en Filipinas, desde sus orígenes hasta 1898* (Madrid, 1909), and the anti-Tagalog but useful Vicente Barrantes, *El teatro tagalo* (Madrid, 1890). See also illustrations and biographical sketches in Arsenio Manuel's *Dictionary of Philippine Biography.* On progress in the arts generally, see Benitez, pp. 263–66; Zaide, 2, 99–102; Legarda, "Foreign Trade," pp. 365–66.

12. Benitez, pp. 243–44; Legarda, "Foreign Trade," p. 363.

attractive institutions of the West and a refurbished version of their own, emotionally valued indigenous tradition. In the early stages of Filipino nationalism there was little cultural ambiguity. The indigenous tradition had not been highly formalized at the time of the Spanish conquest, and there was no priestly caste to act as guardian of the tradition. Although Spanish political rule was indirect, through local magnates, Spanish cultural influence was direct and available to all from the beginning. Moreover, the local magnates who might have acted as leaders of an indigenous cultural revival became tied politically and culturally to the Spaniards. Finally, the weakness of Spain in the late nineteenth century made it evident that the remains of the indigenous tradition were not in imminent danger of being obliterated by organized Spanish efforts.

Thus, in the Philippines, nationalism did not involve fear that Western cultural and political pressure was about to destroy the indigenous tradition. When Rizal exalted the vigor of pre-Spanish Philippine civilization he did so purely as a device to promote Filipino morale and self-esteem. What he really prized was not Bathala, a pre-Spanish Philippine deity, but God, the divinity of Spanish Catholicism. Catholicism, not pre-Spanish beliefs, was the socially unifying element in Filipino nationalism. The nationalist leaders were urbanized mestizos and indios whose condition and opportunities were derived from the export crop economy, and whose orientation was toward some form of Spanish culture.

But Spanish cultural influence could provide only some of the ingredients of Filipino nationalism. As a national model for the Filipinos, Spain had certain deficiencies. Unsure of herself as a modern nation, torn between the old Spain and the new, she could offer little that was politically attractive to the Filipinos. Spanish liberalism did contribute masonic anticlericalism to Filipino nationalism. But other ideas, such as racial equality and the rights of the individual, were borrowed from the larger corpus of Western European liberalism.

That such ideas were available in the nineteenth-century Philippines is indicative of the fact that cultural influences other than the specifically Spanish were felt. Broader influences came from two sources: returning mestizo and indio students who had studied and traveled in other parts of Europe than Spain, and the North European and North American merchants residing at Manila. Implied in these influences was something broader than an urban colonial version of Spanish culture, a step beyond filipinized hispanism to a cosmopolitan Western cultural outlook. Those who developed such an outlook could not have been more than a small percentage of Manila's population. They formed a small but important cosmopolitan group—the so-called *ilustrado* ("enlightened") class—which transcended ethnic lines.[13]

Much of the nationalist leadership came from this cosmopolitan group, some of whose members remained in Europe and propagandized from there.[14] The nationalism they promoted involved an attempt to reconcile a reformed Spanish Catholicism—anticlerical, but still Catholic—with Western European liberal ideas derived from outside the Spanish context. Thus, from an intellectual point of view, the Filipino nationalism of this period was a matter of transferring the Spanish anticlerical battle to Philippine soil and attempting to harmonize a variety of European ideas. There was no real question of trying to integrate European ideas with native traditions. The symbols of nationalism, and sometimes the language, might be native, but the content —the vocabulary—was European.

To return to the filipinized Hispanic culture of Manila, a comparison of it with cultural developments in Netherlands India may be instructive. Wertheim has described the development of an "Indies Dutch" urban culture in nineteenth-century Netherlands India. This was a kind of hybrid style of life, or as he puts it, "mestizo culture," which was neither Dutch nor Indonesian, but a kind of Dutch life adapted to the local environment. Although the Dutch set the standards, this hybrid urban culture was shared by all groups. Yet it did not break down intergroup barriers. As Wertheim put it:

> Though Indo-Europeans, Indonesian Chinese and modern urban Indonesians were all of them equally imbued with the mestizo culture, they saw themselves as bearers *par excellence* of European, Chinese, and Indonesian cultural values. Paradoxically, however, the dwindling cultural differences tended to widen again, insofar as the various groups were also the supporters of divergent ideologies.[15]

The key to understanding the Philippine case is, again, the matter of religion. The absence of significant religious distinctions among the various Philippine ethnic groups, with the exception of the Chinese, made it possible for the process of sharing in the Philippine version

13. Legarda, "Foreign Trade," pp. 367–68, 447.

14. As one writer put it, boys who completed their higher education in Manila could be counted loyal, but those who completed it in Europe became *filibusteros* (agitators). Comenge, *Cuestiones filipinas*, p. 213.

15. W. F. Wertheim, *Indonesian Society in Transition. A Study of Social Change* (The Hague, Bandung, 1956), Chap. 7, esp. pp. 170–73, 182, 284–85.

of an urban "mestizo culture" to lead to a blurring of ethnic distinctions, and, probably, an increase in inter-ethnic social relationships—including relationships involving the Spanish sector of society.

But it ought to be noted that neither the urban filipinized Hispanic culture nor the transcendence of ethnic identification which it facilitated was shared by all classes—that is, all economic strata in Manila society. Wertheim apparently believes all economic classes shared in the urban "mestizo culture" of Netherlands India, but one cannot accept this for the Philippines. It is necessary only to observe the vigor of folk Catholicism in mid-twentieth-century Manila to realize the persistence of folkways in this urban environment.

Therefore, it should be emphasized that in Manila only the upper economic classes really participated in this new culture. And outside Manila (and a few other urban centers), in the rural areas, only the rich mestizos and indios were deeply affected by this cultural change. The overwhelming mass of the rural population was affected marginally, if at all. It is probable, although not verifiable, that these new cultural influences, as well as the new economic development, resulted in a larger gulf between the elite and the lower classes—especially in rural areas—than had hitherto existed.[16]

The Disappearance of the Mestizo Community

Throughout the nineteenth century, the most dynamic element in Philippine society was the Chinese mestizo. During the last half of the nineteenth century there were probably between 150,000 and 300,000 Chinese mestizos in the Philippines, in a mean Philippine population of about 5,500,000. In other words, the mestizos formed, as before, about 6 per cent of the total population.[17] In a half dozen provinces mestizos made up one third or more of the population, and in another half dozen they accounted for 5 per cent to 16 per cent of the local population. Elsewhere, their numbers were insignificant.[18]

With the large influx of Chinese immigrants after 1850 the mestizos began to modify their patterns of occupational specialization. Com-

16. Legarda, "American Entrepreneurs," p. 152.
17. Ferdinand Blumentritt, "Die Mestizen der Philippinen-Inseln," *Revue coloniale internationale*, I (1885), 253, 257; Foreman, *Philippine Islands*, p. 410; Francisco Ahuja, *Reseña acerca del estado social y económico de las colonias de España en Asia* (3 vols. Madrid, 1874–75), 3, 20–21; González and Moreno, *Manual del viajero*, pp. 51, 93; Lannoy, *Iles Philippines*, p. 113; Mas, "Internal Political Condition," p. 39. The figure of 5,500,000 is a rough equivalent of the 1877 census figure of 5,567,685. Jimeno Agius, p. 10.
18. Díaz Arenas, *Memorias históricas*, cuad. 17: "reseña de provincias."

petition from the Chinese drove many mestizos—especially those in Central Luzon—out of wholesale and retail commerce and into land-holding and the production of export crops. The same was true in the Iloilo area.[19] Mestizo occupational specialties thus became somewhat less like those of the Chinese and more similar to those of the indios.

In the pre-1850 period mestizo–indio group relations had been marked by rivalries, mostly over questions of local power and prestige. Wherever mestizo gremios existed they competed for these prizes with the *gremios de naturales* (indio gremios).

But by the late nineteenth century, all gremios–indio and mestizo alike—were becoming political anachronisms, both in the provinces and in Manila. In the provinces the judicial powers of the heads of the gremios, the gobernadorcillos, were being taken away by municipal judges, and their fiscal powers were transferred to a new Directorate of Local Administration. Stripped of the limited local power they had enjoyed, the gremios and their leading officers, the gobernador-cillos, now lost some of their reasons for existence. Local power increasingly fell into the hands of those with wealth. The Spanish government sought to attract the latter into service as gobernadorcillos and cabezas de barangay by changing these from hereditary offices into positions whose occupants were selected on the basis of wealth and real local power. But the members of the "third class" often refused to serve. The offices had no power or prestige. Indeed, the very title of gobernadorcillo—"petty governor"—reeked with a condescension that was intolerable to those whose cultural, social, and political pretensions were greater than any that had previously existed among the indigenes. Now that the gremios had lost their political significance and the ablest people in many towns declined to serve as officers there was very little reason to maintain them.[20]

In Manila, expansion and urbanization had brought the former sub-urban towns across the river from the walled city into the corporate limits of the expanded metropolis. While the old walled city, Intra-

19. *Los chinos en Filipinas*, pp. 27–28, 64–65. However, it is evident that some mestizos remained in commerce in Central Luzon, as, for instance, those of Dagupan and Calasiao in Pangasinan, who were still the preeminent traders of their region in 1901. Flormata, *Memoria sobre . . . Pangasinan*, p. 20. On the situation in the Bisayas, see Benitez, pp. 238–39; Echaúz, *Apuntes de la isla de Negros*, p. 24; and especially Jagor, *Travels*, pp. 303–05.

20. Azcárraga, *Reforma*, pp. 17–19, 36, 48–52, 76; J. P. Sanger, "The Judiciary," *Census of 1903*, 1, 402; Del Pan, *Las Islas Filipinas*, pp. 419–20; Legarda, "Foreign Trade," pp. 367–68. In 1786 the office of cabeza de barangay was made elective rather than hereditary. Phelan, pp. 122–23. This change presumably was related to the appearance of new standards of eminence.

muros, remained the religious and administrative center of Manila, the commercial and industrial centers lay across the river, in Binondo, Santa Cruz, Quiapo, and Tondo. The inclusion of these towns, once part of the separate province of Tondo, as part of the city meant the application of municipal government to them, thus replacing the old self-governing gremios.

But several of the gremios lingered on, both in the provinces and in Manila. As late as 1894 there were mestizo gremios in Binondo, Santa Cruz, Tambobong (Malabong), Tondo, Navotas, Pasig, Pagsanjan, Lingayen, Vigan and Cebu.[21] Paradoxically, the mestizo gremios were most persistent in Manila and in Central Luzon, where the cultural patterns of upper-class mestizos and indios were becoming so nearly uniform as to make the mestizo gremios seem as culturally anachronistic as they were politically obsolete. The primary reason for maintaining the mestizo gremios (and the indio gremios that also persisted in these places) was, I believe, that these bodies, particularly the ones in Binondo, had become social prestige groups whose members did not wish to dissolve them. In other words, although in other places the members of the "third class" refused to join the gremios and were uninterested in keeping them alive because membership reflected neither power nor prestige, in the places named above membership in either the mestizo or indio gremio was believed to be a mark of wealth and "Spanish-ness."

The mestizos of Manila and Central Luzon had taken the lead in creating the filipinized Hispanic culture in which upper-class mestizos and indios of those regions now joined. From at least the middle decades of the nineteenth century the mestizos had set the pace for the indios in customs and in style of living. The mestizos' wealth and the way they spent it made them the arbiters of fashion for Manila and Central Luzon. Although they built up their savings, sometimes into real fortunes, the Chinese mestizos were fond of gambling and ostentation, especially in dress. Besides entertaining guests with sumptuous banquets, mestizo families often expended great sums of money on feast days. This kind of behavior became a model for well-to-do indios.[22]

It is not surprising that the Chinese mestizos should have become envied models. In the localities where they were numerous they were among the wealthiest people and, what is perhaps more important, they

21. Del Pan, *Las Islas Filipinas,* p. 356; *Guía oficial de las Islas Filipinas para 1894* (Manila, 1894), p. 736.

22. Del Pan, *Las Islas Filipinas,* pp. 399–400; Mallat, *Les Philippines,* 2, 134–35; Buzeta, *Diccionario de las Islas Filipinas,* 2, 244; Comenge, pp. 214–15; Ratzel, *Die chinesische auswanderung,* p. 135.

were believed to be, as a class, wealthier than the indios. Hence, in some places in Central Luzon, everyone in the region claimed to be mestizo, even though this meant paying double tax. The best illustration of this kind of mestizo-craze attitude may be found in the character of Capitán Tiago in Rizal's novels. Capitán Tiago is an excellent example of an indio of means who wished to be regarded as a Chinese mestizo and was able to purchase for himself a place in the wealthy and famous Gremio de Mestizos de Binondo.[23]

The goals of socially mobile members of the non-Western sector of Philippine society were wealth and a Spanish cultural veneer. To be considered a mestizo, then, especially a member of a mestizo gremio, was to be considered wealthy and highly hispanized. In other words, although by the late nineteenth century upper-class mestizos and indios were equally imbued with the filipinized Hispanic culture they had created, there remained some additional prestige attached to being considered a mestizo, prestige that might be more important to a non-mestizo like Capitán Tiago than to most mestizos. Thus, the mestizo gremios continued to exist in some places. And indio gremios, whose members were unable to achieve recognition as mestizos, continued to exist in the same places as devices through which their members might claim that *they*—not the mestizo gremio—represented the ultimate in hispanism in the Philippines.

The most prestigeful of the mestizo gremios was the one in Binondo. It must be stressed that it was not the proximity of this gremio to the Chinese that caused it to resist being dissolved. Rather it was its location in Manila, which was not only the focal point of Chinese culture in the Philippines but also the center of Spanish culture. The proximity of the large Chinese community was likely to cause the lower-class mestizos of Binondo to be "more Chinese" than those anywhere else. But the upper-class mestizos were likely to be "more Spanish" than any other mestizos. It was the latter consideration that caused them to seek to maintain their gremio organization, and it was the upper-class mestizos who kept the gremios alive as social prestige groups instead of the sociopolitical bodies they had been.

Ever since the middle of the eighteenth century a contest for

23. Rizal, *Noli me tangere*, Chap. 6; James A. LeRoy, *Philippine Life in Town and Country* (New York and London, 1905), pp. 186–95. But the indio attitude toward the mestizo was not one of unmixed admiration. Many indios resented what they considered the harsh treatment given them by mestizo landlords and money-lenders. Jagor, p. 33; Mas, "Internal Political Condition," p. 64; Plauchut, "L'archipel des Philippines," *Revue des deux mondes*, 20 (1877), 904; Montero, *Archipiélago Filipino*, p. 151.

hegemony in Binondo had been waged between the mestizos and the indios. The mestizos claimed for themselves a preferential position in all public ceremonies in Binondo, basing their assertions on the claim that they were the heirs of the Chinese founders of the settlement. The practical advantages of preference were two: first, although each gremio had jurisdictional authority over matters limited to its own members, the question of who should be competent in questions affecting the general welfare or interest hinged upon which group was officially recognized as having precedence. Second, acknowledgment of precedence conferred prestige in a situation of petty rivalries.[24]

From the 1740s to the 1880s the question of precedence in Binondo was repeatedly raised, involving much paper work and litigation. Each time the question was settled in favor of the mestizos. But the competition persisted and by the 1880s, when the gremios had been stripped of their political significance, there was still a contest although the issue now was only social prestige.

In 1887, on the occasion of the celebration of Binondo's religious festival of La Naval, the matter came up again. The mestizos had long been the major source of financial support for this festival and had enjoyed a preferred status in its ceremonies. On this occasion the liberal Governor-general Terrero, whether out of idealism or capriciousness, reversed the usual order, giving precedence to the Gremio de Naturales. The mestizos and Catholic Chinese then withdrew from the festival. Their action—including, of course, the withdrawal of financial contributions—forced the cancellation of all but the final day of the scheduled eight-day celebration. When the parish priest attempted to oppose the governor-general's order he was removed from his position. Chinese and mestizo shops were shuttered and barred in protest and the social tension that developed in Binondo lasted for several days. Even when La Naval arrived the following year and the Colonial Office made the conservatives happy by restoring the traditional practice, the issue was not completely resolved. Agitation continued on both sides.[25]

Was there any significance to this incident? Concurrently, governor-general and clergy were at odds over a number of issues, and a group of mestizos and indios of Manila was daringly presenting a petition urging that the Spanish regular clergy be withdrawn from the Island.[26]

24. PNA, Gremios, 16-5-5.
25. Ibid.; El filibusterismo (Derbyshire tr.), pp. 151–53; Comenge, p. 223.
26. PNA, Gremios, 16-5-5; Archivo de PP Dominicos (Manila), T. 665 (Libro de memorias), pp. 105–108v; Gregorio Zaide, The Philippine Revolution (Manila, 1954), p. 29. See also LeRoy, Americans in the Philippines, I, 73–74 n.

Radical sentiment was mounting. Whether the La Naval question, seemingly a minor struggle for social prestige, was indeed related to these larger problems of anticlericalism and civil–ecclesiastical power rivalry is not clear. Conservative Spaniards thought it was. They considered Terrero's reversal of the order of precedence a dangerous change in the status quo at a time when preservation of the status quo, not encouragement of change, was needed.[27]

Both the Gremio de Mestizos and the Gremio de Naturales, in justification of their claims, styled themselves true "sons of Spain," eternally loyal to the mother country.[28] It is often asserted that the Gremio de Mestizos de Binondo was, formally at least, loyal to Spain and proud of its record of having always been on the Spanish side whenever revolts occurred.[29] Nevertheless, the restoration of the mestizos to the position of precedence was probably not an expression of Spain's dependence upon mestizo support, but rather an adherence to the conservative position that maintenance of the status quo, rather than flexible adaptation to change, was the policy needed to meet the rising political dissidence.

But if members of some of the mestizo gremios, especially the Binondo one, attempted to retain a vestige of their separate status for prestige reasons, they and other upper-class mestizos were in most social situations prepared to mingle with the upper-class indios on an equal basis. Azcárraga, writing about 1870, said that there was no reason to preserve gremio, tax, and other distinctions "between people born in the same towns, who have the same customs and speak a common language." [30] Del Pan, writing a few years later, argued that the gremios ought to be abolished because the distinctions they made were now artificial ones. They were anachronisms in an age when a man's status was judged by his ability rather than by ethnic considerations.[31]

It was this growing cultural uniformity, and the social communication that it facilitated that troubled conservative Spaniards, especially after 1850. Closer social relationships could lead to closer political relationships. From 1850 onward, therefore, one begins to find the "divide and rule" theme in Spanish writings about the mestizos and indios. Ironically for the Spaniards, their policy of recognizing cultural

27. Ibid.; Comenge, pp. 222–23.

28. Gremio de mestizos to gov.-gen., March 21, 1884; Gremio de naturales to gov.-gen., Nov. 19, 1888, PNA, Gremios, 16-5-5.

29. Comenge, pp. 216, 224; Gremio de mestizos to gov.-gen., March 21, 1884, PNA, Gremios, 16-5-5.

30. Azcárraga, *Reforma*, p. 91.

31. Del Pan, *Las Islas Filipinas*, pp. 347–56.

differences but seeking to bridge them with a program of hispanization had worked so well it now posed a threat to their rule. The members of the "third class" were culturally homogeneous. And the more hispanized and wealthy they became the more dissatisfied they were with their limited political opportunities. As Pardo de Tavera put it:

> Bigan, Taal, Balayan, Batangas, Albay, Nueva Caceres, Cebu, Molo, Jaro, Iloilo, began to be covered with solidly constructed buildings; their wealthy citizens would come to Manila, make purchases, become acquainted with the great merchants, who entertained them as customers whose trade they needed; they visited the Governor-general, who would receive them according to the position that their money gave them; they came to know the justices of the Supreme Court, the provincials of the religious orders . . . and, on returning to their pueblo, they took in their hearts and minds the germ of what was subsequently called subversive ideas and later still "filibusterismo". . . . Already the "brutes loaded with gold" dared to discuss with their curate, complain against the alcalde, defend their homes against the misconduct of the lieutenant or sergeant of the police force. . . . Their money permitted them to effectively defend questions involving money first, then, those of a moral character.[32]

The Spanish government was by no means unaware of these developments. To meet them it pursued a shifting policy: sometimes it made institutional and legal changes in recognition of cultural and social changes; other times (especially as revolutionary sentiment developed) it rigidly supported the status quo. One of the drastic changes made was a reorganization of the tax system. In the period after 1870 there was much discussion about abolishing the tribute or head tax paid by the indios and mestizos, replacing it with some kind of direct tax to be levied upon everyone. Finally, in the 1880s, the contribución industrial, a property and earnings tax levied on all self-employed persons, was established. With the establishment of this tax and the *cédula personal* (identification card) tax, the Spanish administration put an end to the tribute, long since an anachronism. The tribute dated from a time when it could be assumed that there was an absolute correlation between ethnic status and wealth. Now, as we have seen, there were rich indios and mestizos. And it was a source of annoyance to the revenue-minded Spaniards of that era that rich, urbanized indios were still paying a

32. Quoted in Benitez, p. 335.

mild tribute as their only tax, as if they had never left the villages.³³
The termination of the head tax was accompanied by the end of the
system of legal classification as mestizo and as indio. The Spanish
government thus recognized the merging of the mestizo and indio
social systems.

But more important than legal recognition was social usage. By 1900
the indigenous inhabitants of the Philippines, of whatever cultural background, called themselves and were called "Filipinos." By that time, too,
the unmodified term "mestizo" no longer referred to the Chinese mestizo, but had acquired the meaning it has today: Spanish mestizo or
Eurasian in general. James LeRoy, writing at the turn of the century,
observed that the Chinese mestizo did not insist on a separate distinction. Other mestizos did; but the Chinese mestizo was usually absorbed
into Filipino society within a generation.³⁴ LeRoy's observation is not
completely accurate, in that it disregards the Chinese mestizos who
"returned" to the Chinese community within a generation. But it is
correct as far as it goes. There was no longer a third ethnic status as an
alternative for Chinese mestizos. Their choice now was clearly defined
by themselves as "Filipino" or "Chinese."

But Spanish policy, characteristically made through a compromise
of the contradictory views of liberals and conservatives, contained both
the measures that abolished legal distinctions and the haphazardly
pursued policy of "divide and rule." Toward the Chinese mestizos the
liberal attitude was one of admiration and encouragement; the conservative, one of apprehension. Among all Spaniards a certain uneasi-
ness had developed as the mestizos began their rise to wealth and
prestige in the van of the "third class." If one surveys Spanish attitudes
toward the mestizo across the span of the entire Spanish period, an
interesting change appears. The first mestizos were hailed as being more

33. Del Pan, *Las Islas Filipinas,* pp. 345–58, 419–20; Sancianco, *El progreso de
filipinas,* pp. i., 104–18. See also Sancianco's summary of the work of the Junta de
Reformas Económicas of 1870 in ibid., pp. 11–15. Also Azcárraga, *Libertad,* Chap.
17, esp. pp. 228–40. For an opinion in opposition to universal direct taxation see
Ahuja, *3,* 11, 21–32. On the contribución industrial and cédulas personales see Berriz,
Diccionario, 1, 189–312; *12,* 206–45; Plehn, *16,* 691–92, 705–08; Berriz, *Anuario
1888, 1,* 502–04. There was also the *contribución urbana,* established 1878, a 5 per
cent impost on income derived from urban buildings, which was likewise applicable to
all groups. Berriz, *Anuario 1888, 1,* 502–04; LeRoy, *Americans in the Philippines, 1,*
55.

34. LeRoy, *Philippine Life,* p. 37. The use of the unmodified term "mestizo" to
mean "Chinese mestizo" is reflected in W. E. Retana, *Diccionario de filipinismos* (New
York and Paris, 1921), p. 127; Testimony of Benito Legarda, *Report of Philippine
Commission, 2,* 179; Gobernadorcillo de mestizos to gov.-gen., April 1841, PNA,
Gremios, 16-5-5.

intelligent and vigorous than the indios.[35] But by the 1740s, when mestizos were becoming numerous and prominent enough to have their own gremios, Padre Murillo Velarde complained that "now we have a querulous, discontented population of half-castes, who, sooner or later, will bring about a distracted state of society, and occupy the whole force of the government to stamp out the discord." [36] Still, in the 1790s, Spanish officials in Manila praised the mestizos for their energy, aid to the economy, devotion to Catholicism, and loyalty to Spain.[37]

In the first decade of the nineteenth century warnings were issued about the growing economic power of the mestizos. Zúñiga, noting the alienation of indio lands to mestizo moneylenders, protested: "If no remedy is found, within a short time the lords of the entire Archipelago will be the Chinese mestizos." [38] Ten years after Zúñiga, Tomás de Comyn observed:

> In the caste of the Chinese mestizos economy and cupidity go together with intelligence and energy to increase their funds, and, scattered through the principal towns of the islands, they are found in possession of the best lands and the most lucrative internal trading. There is excellent reason to predict that this industrious and knowledgeable people will be able, little by little, to draw to itself a mass of money of very great significance, although it is impossible to determine how much or to what destination it may ultimately go.[39]

Comments of the 1840s were in much the same vein.

> Almost all the retail commerce is in their hands and they may be counted the middle class of the Philippines.

> They are the proprietors, merchants and educated people of the country and will dominate public opinion.

> The Chinese mestizos will, within a century, have grown to at least one million by natural increase and immigration from China, and will possess the greater part of the wealth of the Islands.[40]

After the middle of the nineteenth century the mestizos could no

35. Francisco de Montilla, O.F.M., quoted in Gayo, "Ensayo histórico-bibliográfico" to *Doctrina Christiana,* pp. 72–73.

36. Quoted in Foreman, p. 214.

37. Report of audiencia, Jan. 25, 1797, San Pedro, *Legislación ultramarina,* 2, 523. Cf. Comenge, pp. 234–37.

38. Zúñiga, *Estadismo, 1,* 48–51.

39. Comyn, "Estado de las Islas Filipinas en 1810," p. 59.

40. Mas, "Internal Political Condition," pp. 64–65.

longer "be counted the middle class of the Philippines." The Chinese reassumed that position. But there was no letup in the engrossing of lands by mestizos. The new export crop economy, and an increase in population in the nineteenth century, raised the value of land and made landowning and export crop production an ever more attractive means of livelihood. Government legislation, easing the acquisition of good titles, encourage a trend toward land grabbing in the 1880s.[41] The mestizos were surely among the "grabbers." By the end of the Spanish period Retana (no doubt with some anti-mestizo exaggeration) was writing that the dire prophecies of Zúñiga's day had been realized: the mestizos had taken over half the lands of the country.[42]

Parenthetically, it may be noted that the acquisition of lands by the "third class" during the nineteenth century laid the foundation of what is sometimes popularly called the cacique class of Central Luzon in the twentieth century. It is sometimes assumed, especially in American writings about the mid-twentieth-century land problems of the Philippines, that the caciques of today are the descendants of the early indio chieftains.[43] I hope it is clear from the foregoing that such is not the case.

In the 1840s the Spaniards began to realize the political consequences of the rising "third class," especially its mestizo vanguard. The loss of

41. Del Pan, Las Islas Filipinas, pp. 338–39; Jagor, p. 305. There was also some Chinese interest in acquiring land, but mostly for speculative purposes. By 1870 foreigners (including Chinese) could own land and convey it to someone residing in the Philippines. But Chinese could not will or assign lands to persons in China. See Reglamento on sale of public lands, Jan. 19, 1883, in Comenge, p. 283.

42. "The future is theirs; even in politics." Notes to Zúñiga's Estadismo, 2, 526. Palgrave spoke of the Chinese mestizos as the "most bulky estate-owners." W. G. Palgrave, "The Far-Off Eden Isles"; Country Life in the Philippines Fifty Years Ago by a British Consul (Manila, 1929), p. 59. See also Testimony of Edwin Warner, Report of Philippine Commission, 2, 198–201.

43. For examples, see Alvin Scaff, The Philippine Answer to Communism (Stanford, 1955), pp. 86–87; Joseph E. Spencer, Land and People in the Philippines (Berkeley and Los Angeles, 1954), p. 125; and David R. Sturtevant, "Philippine Social Structure and Its Relation to Agrarian Unrest" (Ph.D. dissertation, Stanford, 1958), Chaps. 1, 2. A recent collaborative study of the Philippines dismisses the Chinese mestizo as of no importance after the first years of the Spanish period. Human Relations Area Files, Area Handbook on the Philippines, ed. Fred Eggan (4 vols. Chicago, 1956), 1, 440. By contrast, Filipino scholars now regard the social changes of the late Spanish period as a textbook commonplace. Zaide, 2, 77–78; Benitez, pp. 243–45; Corpuz, Bureaucracy in the Philippines, pp. 116–17; Legarda, "Foreign Trade," p. 363. Pardo de Tavera, perhaps the first Filipino scholar to comment on these social changes, put it as follows: "In the same manner as, by the arrival of the Spaniards, the old Filipino caciques were subjected to the Spanish officials, now the caciques, who dominated during the period of tutelary sequestration, found themselves immediately supplanted and converted into something lower than the new caciques of the economic order." Quoted in Benitez, p. 323.

Spain's American colonies and the extension to the Philippines of both
the politics of the Carlist Civil War and the political ideas current in
Europe awakened Spanish fears that the Philippines would go the way
of the American empire. Sinibaldo de Mas, in a secret report of 1842,
keynoted subsequent Spanish discussions of the mestizo. He offered two
alternative policies for Spain. If eventual independence of the Philippines from Spain were desired, then intermarriage and the enlargement
of the mestizo population ought to be encouraged by every means. This
was the course he preferred. But if Spain wished to retain the Philippines, then only a strict policy of divide and rule could be effective. In
particular, the indios and mestizos must be kept separated. Or, as he
put it, the brains and money of the mestizos must not be allowed to
become allied to the numerical strength of the indios. The separate
gremios should be maintained and their rivalries encouraged wherever
possible.[44]

Even before Mas's report a decree of the Philippine governor-general
ruled that in towns where there were two gremios (Binondo tacitly
excepted) the indio gremio should have precedence in affairs affecting
both.[45] The reasons for this ruling are not known. In any event, as
noted above, the gremios were on their way to extinction by the 1870s
and 1880s. Spanish conservatives seem to have made no formal effort to
retain them, but as political dissidence developed after 1870 the Spaniards were haunted by the fear of an indio revolution led by mestizos.
By the 1890s, when the Revolution did break out, the practice of
blaming everything—including the Revolution—on the mestizos, was
prevalent and was adopted even by some of the foreign merchants
residing at Manila. The mestizos were regarded as troublemakers, or, as
one person put it, "the worst class we have." [46] One author wrote during the Revolution that, unlike the indios and Spanish mestizos who are
loyal to Spain, the Chinese mestizos are insincere and seditious, evidence
of their Chinese heritage. They have joined themselves "ardently" to

44. Mas, "Internal Political Condition," pp. 31, 44–49, 61–65, 86–87. See also
Buzeta, 1, 214, who may have taken his comments from Mas's book.

45. Superior Decreto, Nov. 27, 1840, cited in PNA, Gremios, 16-5-5. There was
also an abortive attempt to force mestizos who lived in masonry houses to pay
double the ordinary mestizo tribute. Circulars of General Administration of Tributes,
Sept. 20, 1851, and Dec. 9, 1851, San Pedro, 8, 408, 410–11. The Spanish administration also attempted to institute classification of mestizos by physical appearance
rather than by status of paternal ancestor. Circular of Gen. Adm. of Tributes, Jan.
12, 1852, ibid., pp. 411–12.

46. Testimonies of Edwin Warner, R. W. Brown, Wm. Daland, Chas. Ilderton
Barnes, H. D. C. Jones, A. Kuensle, in *Report of Philippine Commission*, 2, 17–19,
167, 187–90, 198–201, 204–06, 216, 229; Comenge, pp. 213–14; *La política de
España en Filipinas* (June 23, 1891), p. 117 and (Sept. 13, 1892), p. 241; González
Serrano, *España en Filipinas* (Madrid, 1896), pp. 18–19.

the insurrection, "with their influence, their persons, and their funds." [47] Another Spaniard wrote: "The mestizo race is the major enemy of Spain, as contrasted with the indios, who are most loyal and grateful to the mother country." [48]

Unquestionably, many mestizos participated prominently in the Revolution in several ways—but not necessarily as mestizos. Many were partisans of the movement that favored reform over revolution. Still other mestizos were imprisoned by the Spaniards on suspicion of revolutionary complicity and released only after paying large ransoms. Their imprisonment was primarily a means of extortion.[49]

But the idea of mestizo "blame" (or credit) for the Revolution, or for all dissident activities, is unacceptable. Like many statements made by Spanish conservatives in the waning decades of the nineteenth century, it originates in a scornful reaction to the pretensions of Filipino nationalism. The practice was to label the indio a brute incapable of anything but animal's work; the mestizo a seditious outsider who filled him with subversive ideas.

Despite what Spanish conservatives might say, Sancianco, a Spanish-trained Chinese mestizo lawyer, pointed out that in the 1870s revolts against Spanish authority had been participated in by both mestizos and indios, and that it was futile for Spain to try to emphasize differences when those differences were being blurred in common action.[50]

Thus, in political action, as in cultural values and social relations, the mestizos and indios merged. The rich among them, who had kept alive the gremios as community organizations and as focal points of cultural distinction, now preserved the gremios only as prestige bodies for the wealthy and heavily hispanized few. The metamorphosis of the gremios from community institutions to small prestige organizations left the mestizo community without community institutions to keep it alive. By the end of the Spanish period it had disappeared, its members merging with the indios into a new Filipino society, or "returning" to the Chinese community. It is time we consider how the Chinese fitted into this changing milieu.

47. Eduardo Navarro Ordóñez, O.S.A., *Filipinas, estudios de algunos asuntos de actualidad* . . . . (Madrid, 1897), pp. 105–06.

48. Montero, *Archipiélago filipino*, p. 151.

49. LeRoy, *Americans in the Philippines, 1,* 279. See biographies of Telesforo Chuidian, Mariano Limjap, Roman Ongpin, and Francisco Osorio in Manuel, *Dictionary,* pp. 131–33, 248–50, 295–97. See also Foreman, p. 523; Liu Chi Tien, *Fei-lü-p'in hua-ch'iao shih hua,* pp. 43–45; T. H. Pardo de Tavera, *Biblioteca filipina* (Washington, 1903), p. 129; Sawyer, *Inhabitants of the Philippines,* p. 81; and biographical sketch of Luis R. Yangco in Samuel W. Stagg, *Teodoro Yangco: Leading Filipino Philanthropist and Grand Old Man of Commerce* (Manila, 1934), p. 28.

50. Sancianco, pp. 104–18, 223–37; Pardo de Tavera, "History," pp. 378, 380; Montero, *Historia, 3,* 595 n.; Valenzuela, pp. 43–44, 90–92.

6

The Position of the Chinese

During the 84 years from the 1766 expulsion to 1850 a condition of stability characterized the relations of the Chinese with other individuals and groups in Philippine society. For one thing, there was geographic stability: the Chinese were concentrated in the general region of Manila. There was also numerical stability, at a low level of about 5,000 resident Chinese. Undoubtedly, there was a considerable turnover in the persons that made up the Chinese community, but the level of population was kept constant at about 5,000. From an economic point of view, 5,000 Chinese was a sufficient number to carry out the functions that were considered customarily or necessarily "Chinese." There appears to have been little attempt on the part of the Chinese to extend their economic interests into new fields. And with but 5,000 Chinese in a total Philippine population of over 3,000,000, there was no cause for concern about the possibility of unemployment resulting from Chinese competition.

In the social realm, too, the position of the Chinese had been stabilized. Although geographically and occupationally limited, within those limitations the Chinese enjoyed somewhat more freedom of movement and confidence of personal safety than hitherto. The low level of Chinese population and increased size of Spanish military forces lulled Spanish fears of a Chinese insurrection. Accordingly, the Chinese had less reason to be apprehensive about a possible "preventive" massacre. The Chinese were no longer a source of intergroup violence.[1]

---

1. Díaz Arenas, *Memorias históricas,* cuad. 5: "población"; *Los chinos en Filipinas,* p. 95; Purcell, *Chinese in Southeast Asia,* p. 580. There was one exception to the condition of tranquility. In 1820, as a result of a cholera epidemic in Manila, there were riots and a number of foreigners, including some Chinese, were killed. But this was not the same thing as a large massacre of Chinese only. See "Events in Filipinas,

In sum, the Spaniards had finally realized their official objective of the seventeenth century: the reduction of the Chinese population to only those "necessary" to maintain essential economic services. And Philippine society had finally reached a kind of modus vivendi with its Chinese minority segment.

In the post-1850 period the freedom of immigration, geographical mobility, and economic opportunity suddenly available to the Chinese posed a threat to this condition of stability. The Chinese population expanded from about 6,000 in 1847 (in a total population of about 3,500,000) to perhaps 90,000 by the 1880s (in a total population of nearly 6,000,000).[2] As geographic barriers were lowered, the Chinese advanced into every province of the Islands, even into some areas where Chinese had never been before. Their expansion was occupational as well as geographic. Chinese began to enter trades and businesses that previously had not been considered "Chinese."

More important than demographic and economic expansion as such was the fact that this expansion occurred in a situation quite different from that of the Chinese expansion of the seventeenth and eighteenth centuries. Changed conditions—economic, social, cultural, and political —insured that when the reaction to Chinese expansion came, as it did come, in the form of a revival of old antagonisms against a minority group, the old antagonisms would be expressed within a new context and in a new way.

The revival of anti-Chinese sentiment meant that although economic opportunity and geographic mobility were now available to the Chinese on a greater scale than ever before, social and cultural resistance to them became greater than it had been for a century. For the mestizos and indios, economic achievement combined with cultural achievement to break down ethnic barriers. For the Chinese, economic achievement was accompanied by a social and cultural reaction to them that reinforced ethnic barriers. The Chinese response was to inaugurate a policy of organization and sinification of their community. Economic and cultural change in the Philippines, therefore, did not mean for the Chinese the disappearance of their community, as it did for the mestizos. Instead, the changes served to promote an awareness of solidarity; the Chinese became for the first time an organized community.

The reasons for the revival of anti-Chinese sentiment were basically of two types: cultural and economic. Putting it rather crudely, one may

---

1801–1840," BR, 51, 39–45. See also Pardo de Tavera's interpretation of these riots as a cacique reaction to new influences. Benitez, pp. 233–34.

2. See Chap. 2, p. 61.

say that because the Spanish despised the Chinese, who were rarely
if ever convertible into good Spanish Catholics, the more hispanized
the indios and mestizos became the more anti-Chinese they became. In
reaction to the anti-Chinese campaign that began in the 1880s, many
Philippine Chinese sent their children to China for their education,
and the Chinese community developed closer relations with China. The
more "Chinese" it became, culturally, the more likely it was to challenge
Spanish claims of cultural superiority with like claims of its own.

The cultural reaction to the Chinese was, in all probability, strongest
at the highest levels of Filipino society, where were found the most
heavily hispanized persons. For some of them the large influx of
Chinese meant economic competition. But cultural considerations were
probably as important as economic ones in their anti-Chinese outlook.
It is significant that a recent social distance study in Manila suggests that
anti-Chinese feeling among the white-collar classes appears to be closely
correlated with the level of westernization—not with the existence of
any economic competition. The higher the level of western cultural
influence, the stronger the anti-Chinese sentiment.[3]

In the nineteenth century the most westernized indigenes were likely
to be Filipino nationalists. The cultural outlook they espoused was
identified with Filipino nationalism. And Filipino nationalism was
directed both against the Spanish administration and the Chinese.
There are some indications that the Spanish sought to divert it from
themselves by directing it entirely against the Chinese.[4] Whatever the
case, Filipino nationalism was a source of pressure upon the Chinese
community.

Besides the cultural reaction, there were socioeconomic reasons for
the revival of anti-Chinese sentiment in the late nineteenth century.
The large volume of immigration after 1850 increased the Chinese
population at a rate faster than the natural increase of Philippine society
as a whole.[5] Of more importance, the increased number of Chinese and

3. Weightman, "The Philippine Chinese," pp. 257, 259.
4. See p. 152.
5. If the official figures of 1847 and 1903 are used for the Chinese (5,736 and
41,035, respectively), and the official figures of 1845 and 1903 for the Philippines
as a whole (3,488,258 and 7,635,426, respectively), the Chinese population grew 615
per cent, while the Philippine population as a whole increased by 119 per cent. The
figures used here for the Chinese do not fully reflect the growth during the Spanish
period because the 1903 census was taken after the decline in Chinese population
caused by the Philippine Revolution and the application of the Chinese Exclusion
Law by the American government. Moreover, the 1903 figure understates the size
of the ethnic Chinese population of that time because it includes only Chinese nationals. But even with these conservative figures, the comparison is impressive. Díaz

their geographical dispersion resulted in economic competition for other groups. To some extent, additional jobs created by the new export crop economy could take care of the increase in labor force. But the Chinese intrusion either drove out non-Chinese who had already been active in the export crop wholesaling business, or inhibited the attempts of those who had ambitions to enter that line. The same was true of occupations unrelated to the export crop business.

For mestizo merchants Chinese competition often forced a shift in activities. In Central Luzon the Chinese largely drove the mestizos out of retail trade, including the ambulatory peddling trade. The mestizos increasingly shifted their interests to agriculture.[6] In Manila, mestizo women who had sold native *sinamay* cloth on Calle Rosario were replaced by Chinese dealers selling imported textiles, and the mestizo shopowners of Santa Cruz were pushed aside by the Chinese. Some of these mestizos turned to speculation in government contracts. Others became skilled craftsmen.[7] At Tambobong (Malabong) to the immediate north of Manila, the mestizos appear to have maintained their control over a large share of the business of provisioning Manila.[8] But in the Bisayas the mestizos of Molo and Jaro cut back their trading interests in the face of more efficient Chinese competitors, and concentrated on their cloth weaving industry and the development of sugar production on adjacent Negros.[9] The fate of the mestizos of Cebu, after their abortive effort to stop Chinese penetration into interisland trade, is unclear. Jagor reported that in the 1860s most of the land on the island of Cebu belonged to these mestizos, but whether this condition was related to Chinese commercial competition is not known. In any event, there was still a small gremio de mestizos in Cebu as late as the 1870s, but there is no information available about its activities.[10]

Arenas, *Memorias históricas,* cuad. 5: "población"; Benitez, p. 242; *Census of 1903,* 2, 14.

6. See note 18, Chap. 5, for references. Del Pan, editor of the collection *Los chinos en Filipinas,* said that the decline of mestizo gremios in parts of Central Luzon was due to Chinese commercial competition. *Los chinos en Filipinas,* p. 18.

7. Ibid., pp. 18, 64; Del Pan, *Las Islas Filipinas,* pp. 69, 358. See also *La política de España en Filipinas* (March 3, 1891), pp. 19–20.

8. Del Pan, *Las Islas Filipinas,* pp. 357, 362.

9. See note 18, Chap. 5, and Jagor, p. 347. Note also Nicholas Loney's comments of 1859 on changing trade patterns, in Bowring, *Visit to the Philippine Islands,* pp. 406–11.

10. In Cebu it was not merely Chinese competition that damaged the mestizo wholesale trading operations. By Jagor's time foreign merchants were buying export produce directly from the producers, thus cutting out the high brokerage fee of the mestizos. Jagor, pp. 302–05. Chinese competition is supposed to have caused the decline of the mestizo gremio at Cebu City. *Los chinos en Filipinas,* p. 18. But one still

To the indios the intrusion of the Chinese certainly brought economic dislocations. But our information is far too sketchy to permit generalizations about such matters as the impact of the Chinese store upon the native periodic market. We do know that Chinese competition in ambulant trading in Central Luzon adversely affected the indios of Tayabas and those of the town of Taal.[11] We also know something about the effect of the Chinese upon Manila's indio population. The urbanization of Manila had produced a class of wage workers, who were now thrown into competition with Chinese coolies as labor for docks, warehouses, and public works. The government's use of Chinese labor gangs instead of indio labor for public works projects was a source of some hardship to the latter group. One anti-Chinese essay goes so far as to suggest that the decline in Manila's indio and mestizo population between 1855 and 1876, while that of other parts of the Philippines was increasing, could be traced to the inability of the indios and mestizos to find work in the city because of Chinese competition. According to this argument, economic misery was forcing indios either to leave the city or to avoid marrying and establishing families.[12] This is probably an exaggeration; but the competition of Chinese coolie labor must have had an important effect upon the indio labor force of Manila.

A third group affected by the Chinese intrusion was Spanish businessmen. Increasing immigration brought more Spaniards who wished to make their fortunes in commerce, either in Manila or in the provinces. At either location, the Chinese retailer stood in their way.

If cultural reaction was a reason for anti-Chinese sentiment among upper-class mestizos and indios, economic competition was more likely to be the reason for mestizos and indios of the lower classes. The combination of cultural and economic factors led to a revival of anti-Chinese sentiment and pressure on the Chinese—as a community—in the form of an anti-Chinese movement during the 1880s and 1890s. What were the objectives of the movement? The initiative is said to have come from Spanish businessmen in Manila. But in 1886 a petition urging the establishment of more restrictions on the Chinese was signed

---

hears of it in the 1870s. Spain, Instituto Geográfico, Catastral y de Estadística, *Censo de la población de España, segun el empadronamiento hecho en 31 de diciembre de 1877* (2 vols. Madrid, 1883–84), *1, 720*. And in the 1903 census there is still a separate entry for the *barrio* of the Parián, where the mestizos lived. *Census of 1903, 2, 156.* Cf. Foreman, p. 503.

11. *Los chinos en Filipinas,* pp. 27, 64.

12. Ibid., pp. 31, 67–68; Jagor, p. 317.

by 5,000 persons said to represent several segments of Manila society.[13] The stated motive was "to modify those excessive liberties through which evil conditions, generally among the middle and lower classes of the country, are visibly being established." [14] The two major demands of the petitioners were that the Chinese be forbidden to hold monopoly contracts for tax collection, and that the administration cease using Chinese labor gangs on public works projects.[15]

It is clear that these were not the only complaints against the Chinese. The books and numerous newspaper articles that discussed this issue during the 1880s and early 1890s made references to "unfair" business competition by the Chinese, tax frauds allegedly committed by the Chinese, inadequate tax rates applied to the Chinese, and the danger to the economy caused by Chinese speculations in currency, which were blamed for the monetary crises of 1856–61 and 1876.[16] Speaking generally, it appears that the four areas of most concern were Chinese competition in retail trade, coolie labor, monopoly contracting, and artisanry.

An examination of the timing of the anti-Chinese movement may help uncover some reasons for its development. In the 1880s the United States and Australia had virtually closed their doors to Chinese coolie immigration. There was some fear in Manila that the "yellow peril," turned away from other doors, would now visit the Philippines.[17] But aside from this broad, "international" reason, there were important domestic reasons. By the 1880s opponents of the Chinese could cite as evidence of danger the fact that thirty years' unrestricted Chinese immigration already had resulted in a Chinese hegemony in many aspects of the economy. Moreover, the development of coolie broker immigration in the 1870s and the consequent acceleration in Chinese immigration provoked fears of an irresistible yellow tide.

Three other events of the 1880s and early 1890s deserve attention. In 1879 a cholera epidemic struck Manila, taking a heavy toll of lives. A similar occurrence in 1820 had ended in the massacre of some foreigners, including Chinese. On the occasion of the 1879 epidemic the Chinese were accused of being agents of infection, because they traveled

13. *Los chinos en Filipinas*, p. 125.

14. "The Chinese in the Philippines," in *Report of the Philippine Commission, 1*, 153.

15. *Los chinos en Filipinas*, pp. 127–28.

16. Ibid., pp. 31, 37, 40, 44, 86–88, 100, 113–22; *China en Filipinas*, pp. 15–16, 19, 30, 49; "The Chinese in the Philippines," p. 156; Comenge, pp. 176–77, 179, 383.

17. *Los chinos en Filipinas*, p. 130. See also CSMJPKJC, p. 40a.

about from one part of the city to another.[18] It may have been this association of the cholera epidemic and the Chinese that caused Manila citizens to put pressure on the home government in Spain to impose rules of hygiene on the Chinese and to subject Chinese apothecaries to the same health requirements as other druggists.[19]

Of more importance as a background feature was the economic depression that hit the Philippines during the early 1880s. The reasons for this depression are not entirely clear, but a drop in the world market price of sugar was one of the conditions.[20] The combination of this depression and the economic and social dislocations in the Manila area caused by urbanization and the development of the export crop economy might have been partly responsible for generating feelings of discontent, which newspapers and publicists could turn in the direction of the Chinese.

Finally, there was the rising spirit of rebellion developing from the 1870s onward. It is possible that the anti-Chinese movement was partly a Spanish attempt to divert this political unrest into anti-Chinese channels, and at the same time make of the Chinese a scapegoat for the unhappy economic conditions. Manila's Spanish-language newspapers, in which the attacks on the Chinese were concentrated, were regulated and censored by the government. It can be said, therefore, that at the least the government was not opposed to the anti-Chinese movement.

It was the Spanish newspapers that kept the anti-Chinese campaign alive. In their columns, and in books,[21] one can find anti-Chinese opinions written by Spaniards of widely varying political viewpoints and occupational specialties—including a forestry specialist, a navy medical officer, and a writer of children's textbooks. The newspapers offered no editorial policies as such. *El Comercio* supported the Chinese, but

18. "Fei-lü-p'in hua-ch'iao shih-lüeh," p. 8.

19. *Los chinos en Filipinas*, p. 130; Bando, May 18, 1886, Berriz, *Diccionario, 14,* 278–80; Superior Decreto, April 28, 1888, Berriz, *Anuario 1888, 2,* 4. See also *La política de España en Filipinas* (Aug. 18, 1891), pp. 157–58.

20. Legarda, "American Entrepreneurs," in *Explorations in Entrepreneurial History,* 9 (1957), 156. Jordana (*La política de España en Filipinas,* July 12, 1891, pp. 133–34) blamed the Chinese for the depression. And Foreman (p. 120) indicates that the anti-Chinese campaign was a byproduct of the depression.

21. The books were: Jordana's *La inmigración china en Filipinas* (1888); *La inmigración china y japonesa en Filipinas. Documentos* (Madrid, 1892); and Comenge's *Cuestiones filipinas. 1ª. parte. Los chinos* (1894). Articles in the newspaper *La oceanía española,* edited by Del Pan, were collected and published as *Los chinos en Filipinas* (1886). Articles in the newspaper *El diario de Manila* were published as *China en Filipinas* (1889). See also the conservative Spanish newspaper *La política de España en Filipinas* (Madrid), issues of 1891 and 1892.

no one can tell why. All the other Manila papers attacked them, but in most cases their motives seem no more profound than support of a popular viewpoint and the sale of more newspapers.[22]

Yet two of the authors may be singled out because their views seem to be based upon broad principles. Rafael Comenge, writing in 1894, defends the conservative position. He finds that the Chinese invasion makes it impossible for Spanish businessmen to compete in provincial retail trade. The Philippines is surrendered to the Chinese and their mestizos (note the attempt to separate the mestizo from the indio and associate him with the Chinese), when it should be a field for Spanish enterprise. Moreover, the indio is not protected from the Chinese. Sheltered in an uncommercial Eden, the indio is unprepared; he has not learned the business skills needed to compete with Chinese merchants. It is therefore essential to return to the wise, protective paternalism of the seventeenth century.[23] Comenge, in short, is an echo of Bernaldez Pizarro, fifty years earlier.

At the other end of the Spanish political spectrum, in a moderate liberal position, stands J. F. Del Pan, who was responsible for most of the articles published in the collection Los chinos en Filipinas (1886). Del Pan argues that Chinese immigration should be regulated because the Chinese have inhibited the growth in the Philippines of that true middle class so essential to the strength of any country. It is not that the indio is so weak that he should not be exposed to the Chinese. It is rather that he is now so strong and has shown so much adaptability to commerce and trades that he needs protection for further growth.[24]

In brief, then, it appears that groups representing several shades of political opinion, for a variety of reasons, supported the movement to reduce Chinese immigration and to apply stricter regulations to those Chinese who remained. (Few people favored a complete expulsion of the Chinese).[25] The anti-Chinese writings in the newspapers and books of the period may have been partly responsible for the wave of vandalism that struck Chinese properties at this time.[26] In any event, the publication of Comenge's book in 1894 marked the end of the anti-Chinese agitation. After that date, the larger problems of reform and revolution claimed the attention of Manila's intelligentsia.

22. Los chinos en Filipinas, pp. 82–83; Retana, Aparato bibliográfico, 2, 1049; 3, 1558, 1569–70.

23. Comenge, pp. 176–78, 244, 402–05, 408–09; cf. articles in La política de España en Filipinas (Jan. 20, 1891), p. 4; (Sept. 1, 1891), pp. 176–77.

24. Los chinos en Filipinas, pp. 13–14, 64.

25. La política de España en Filipinas (Jan. 19, 1892), pp. 16–17.

26. SCJC, ch. 2, pp. 19a, 36a–36b.

In the anti-Chinese campaign of the 1880s and early 1890s there was never any question of massacre or revolt. The stable relationship established between the Chinese and the larger society prior to 1850 was beginning to break down. But there was no return to the extreme practices of the pre-1766 period. The methods of those who opposed the Chinese included the old technique of appealing to the home government for legislation, and the new technique of appealing to public opinion. The Chinese, for their part, reacted to this attack with combined domestic and international action. That they were able to take such action was partially due to certain developments within their community. Specifically, the Chinese were beginning to think of themselves as a community, and as a national minority, as indeed the Spaniards had begun to classify them.

Up to the nineteenth century the Spanish concept of empire included the idea that the conquered or pacified peoples became vassals of the Spanish king. In the nineteenth century, as Spain became a constitutional monarchy and began in some respects to resemble a modern nation, this bit of medievalism was replaced by the concept of "subjects of Spain." [27] In the process of defining those who were subjects of Spain one had to define those who were not. The Philippine Chinese thus became an international political problem as well as a domestic cultural problem.

Since traditional Spanish colonial policy, prior to 1800, made no provision for the presence of foreigners in any Spanish colony, the question of national status had been unimportant. The presence of the Chinese in the Philippines in the seventeenth century did not evoke legal arguments as to their status; it required instead a special section in the great Spanish compilation of legislation, the *Recopilación de Leyes de Indias,* a section not on foreigners in general, but specifically on the Philippine Chinese, with the title "De los sangleyes." It was not that the Spaniards were unaware that the Philippine Chinese might be considered subjects of the Chinese emperor. But the matter was of insufficient practical importance to require definition and distinctions along the lines of political status. The Philippine Chinese were, essentially, a cultural minority, not a national one.

But in the nineteenth century the changes in Spanish thinking just described and the opening up of China to formal diplomatic relations with the Western world, tended to pose the problem of the Philippine Chinese in political as well as in cultural terms. It may have been for these reasons that in the nineteenth century the old term *sangley* was much less used in official Spanish documents, and was increasingly re-

27. The expression "national races" was also used. *Los chinos en Filipinas,* p. 34.

placed by the word *chino*. Sangley stood for a cultural stereotype carrying pejorative overtones. Often it was followed, almost automatically, by the word *infiel*, "infidel." Thus *sangleyes infieles* became an invidious expression of the same style as the American "damnyankee." Chino, as an expression closer to cultural neutrality, may have been officially used as a kind of token concession of Chinese status as a national as well as a cultural minority. One should not make too much of this point. Whatever the official designation, in popular practice the Chinese continued to be called sangley, or, more commonly, one of the Philippine dialect-derived names, the Tagalog being *insik*.

Spain's attempt to obtain a trade treaty with China was undoubtedly a factor in the increasing tendency to treat the Chinese as a national as well as a cultural minority. From the 1840s on, discussions of policy toward the Philippine Chinese were made by the Spanish administration within the context of Spain's relations with China, and China's possible reaction to the treatment of the Chinese emperor's subjects.[28]

The official Spanish definition of the Chinese problem in national rather than in cultural terms inevitably raised the question of citizenship and naturalization. Ever since the late eighteenth century the basic status classifications of the Philippine Chinese had been "transient" (*invernado*) and "resident" (*radicado*). But these were administrative terms with cultural overtones. A "resident" Chinese was expected to be more reliable than a "transient" Chinese. He was also expected to pay higher taxes. But there was no question of his having any rights." [29]

Then, in the 1840s, the question of citizenship was raised. The previous classifications of "transient" and "resident" were retained. But it now became possible for a Chinese to go a step further and to become a Spanish subject. It is not entirely clear why this was allowed. It may have been a Spanish attempt to bind prominent Chinese to the regime by granting them whatever rights were inherent in the status of a Spanish subject. Since baptism had failed to insure loyalty, perhaps this method might succeed. The same analysis might apply to the granting of Spanish medals and honors to Chinese, a practice begun in the late nineteenth century.[30] But these are only assumptions about Spanish motives.

The probable motives of the Chinese are clearer. Without a consulate,

28. See Chap. 2, p. 49.
29. "Instrucción de 6 de abril 1783," Berriz, *Anuario 1888, 2,* 851 ff.; Superior Decreto, Jan. 24, 1804, Aug. 31, 1839, Dec. 20, 1849, Oct. 28, 1852, in San Pedro, 2, 467-76, 479-84, 486-90.
30. Órden de la Regencia, April 14, 1841, Berriz, *Anuario 1888, 1,* 604. The awards and titles given were the Medalla del Mérito Civil and the title of Caballero del Real Órden Americana de Isabela la Católica. See Comenge, p. 118 n.; Real Órden, April 5, 1884, PNA, caja 151, núm. 437.

or any other effective means of redress, citizenship was a straw to be grasped at in the hope it would provide the needed protection of one's property. Some of the richest Chinese took this step.[31] But the security of one's property may not have been the only reason for becoming a citizen. By a decree of 1892 it was ruled that henceforth Chinese who wished to marry indias or mestizas had first to accept baptism and then acquire citizenship.[32] Baptism alone was no longer sufficient. However, it is not known whether this provision was ever put into effect. Speaking generally, it appears that very few Chinese availed themselves of the opportunity to become Spanish subjects. The preconditions of citizenship included, besides residence in the Philippines (with good conduct) for a number of years, letters of reference from a half dozen officials. Baptism was another prerequisite.[33] There must have been also some kind of fee. The important thing to note here is the necessity of baptism, which added a cultural qualification to a supposedly political distinction.

The official tendency to consider the Chinese a partly national rather than a strictly cultural problem did not result entirely from Spanish rethinking or trade treaty negotiations with China. The admittance of other foreigners into the Philippines was also a factor. So long as the Chinese were the only foreigners, they could be covered by the special legislation entitled "De los sangleyes." But after 1800, and especially after 1850, as more and more Europeans and North Americans came to be admitted, the general problem of defining the status of non-Spanish subjects became pressing.

A note of ambiguity about the Chinese now appeared. If the Chinese were to be classed with other foreigners they would then be exempted from the various taxes they had been paying and the government would be out a valued bit of revenue. On the other hand, when it was in the interests of state policy to allow foreigners greater privileges in order to aid in developing the Islands, the Chinese could advantageously be included.[34] The result of this kind of thinking was an ambiguity in

31. Among them were Antonio Tong, a prominent exporter of the mid-nineteenth century, Joaquín Martínez Sy Tiongtay, Emilio Asensi Yu Biaoco, and Antonio Osorio Tan Quinco. See PNA, Reales Órdenes, caja 101, núm. 44; caja 147, núm. 174; caja 158, núm. 19; caja 160, núm. 101; caja 164, núm. 63, 192, and 199; caja 165, núm. 150; caja 166, núm. 187; caja 167, núm. 2. Tan Quinco was reputedly the wealthiest man in Cavite. His mestizo son, Francisco Osorio, was a martyr of the Philippine Revolution. See Manuel, *Dictionary*, pp. 296–97.

32. Comenge, p. 197; PNA, Reales Órdenes, caja 164, núm. 192.

33. Comenge, p. 228; PNA, Reales Órdenes, caja 101, núm. 44.

34. An unsigned article in the Spanish periodical *La política de España en Filipinas*, July 12, 1891, p. 141, says that the government in Spain explained its classification of Chinese with other foreigners as a matter of "high policy." Whether this may have referred to Spain's relations with China or with some third country is not known

the status of the Chinese before the Spanish administration, depending on the interests of the administration. When foreigners were given the right to own movable property, and later to own and entail real estate, the Chinese were included as foreigners. Likewise, when foreigners were to be subject to the *matrícula de comercio* and to Spanish commercial courts,[35] the Chinese were included as foreigners. But when it was a matter of taxation, the Chinese were considered to be, as before, no more than a cultural minority group. That the Spaniards were aware of the possible outcome of such a policy is suggested by the comments of one Spanish observer in the 1870s:

> The day that the Chinese government sends to Manila its own representatives to put into execution its treaties with the Government of Spain, in such a situation the status of the Chinese will come to be equal to that of other foreigners and the tribute that the Chinese pays now will be transformed into another impost on commerce, industry, etc., etc.[36]

But if the Chinese did not receive treatment equal to that of other foreigners, did they receive treatment equal to natives? It is clear that they did not receive the same treatment, but was this treatment really inequitable? In terms of geographic mobility it was. Although a Chinese could change his place of residence as easily as a mestizo or indio could, he was not as free to make temporary visits or to make trips back and forth between areas where he had business interests. Almost to the end of the Spanish period, the restrictions on Chinese movement remained in force. It was not that movement was prohibited, but rather that to do so required frequent petitions for licenses or extensions of licenses to the government in Manila, including fees on each occasion. These inconveniences could be gotten around with the connivance of local officials. But this, too, required money.[37] So, although the Chinese were no longer segregated, they were still hampered in their movements.

But in the nineteenth century the major area of distinction between

---

See also the revealing discussion in Órden del Gobierno Supremo, March 11, 1875, Berriz, *Diccionario, 12,* 26–27.

35. See Chap. 2, pp. 55, 59.

36. Ahuja, *3,* 20 (n. 5). Cf. Recur, *Filipinas,* p. 30, and Miguel Blanco Herrero, *Política de España en Ultramar* (2d. ed. Madrid, 1890), pp. 433–44.

37. "Circular del Gobierno Superior," 1867, Berriz, *Diccionario, 8,* 22–23; Superior Decreto, Sept. 28, 1888, ibid., *1,* 776–77; Comenge, p. 385; Superior Decreto, Sept. 26, 1888, *Chinos. Sus reglamentos* . . . , pp. 73–75. In the 1880s a license to go to the provinces cost a Chinese about 12 pesos. Non-Chinese foreigners received these licenses for a very nominal sum. AMAE, 1897. Insurrección en Filipinas. Yncidente protección. Commissioners to Terrero, Oct. 16, 1886; China, 1889. Reclamación del gobierno chino, Chang Yin-huan to Estado, Aug. 15, 1889.

the Chinese and other groups was taxation. In Part I it was pointed out that Spanish taxation policy in the seventeenth century was based on the philosophy of taxing heaviest those groups best able to pay (Spaniards and Spanish mestizos excepted). In accordance with this idea, the indios were taxed 14 reales (less than 2 pesos), the Chinese mestizos 24 reales (3 pesos), and the Chinese 81 reales (over 10 pesos).

The tax scale of the indios and mestizos remained about the same up to the middle of the nineteenth century, but that of the Chinese was undergoing some changes. From 1790 to 1828 it stood at a reduced figure of 54 reales (less than 7 pesos).[38] Then in 1828 the Chinese community was divided into classifications according to occupation, and the tradition of a uniform levy gave way to the principle of taxation according to categories of estimated income. The four classes established under this new "industrial" tax paid as follows: 120 pesos, 48 pesos, 24 pesos, and 12 pesos. Besides this occupational or "industrial" tax, the preexisting head tax and "community chest" tax were retained. So the totals, instead of ranging from 120 pesos to 12 pesos, according to class, were closer to a range of 127 pesos to 19 pesos.

In 1852 the Chinese were placed under a new version of the 1828 tax, a shop license tax called *patente industrial*. As in the 1828 tax, there was a graduated scale based upon estimated income, in this case depending upon the kind of shop. Again there were four classes. But these similarities were accompanied by significant changes. In the 1828 scheme the fourth class was established for employees of the first three classes, but the 1852 tax made all four classes apply to shopowners; employees were exempt from this tax. Another difference was that the first-class rate was less and the second- and third-class rates more than in 1828. The rates were: 100 pesos, 60 pesos, 30 pesos, and 12 pesos. The head tax and "community chest" taxes brought the highest total for a shopowner to about 107 pesos, and the lowest to about 19 pesos. But it must be noted that for a Chinese who was not self-employed (and only one in ten Chinese *was* self-employed),[39] the tax totaled less than 7 pesos.[40]

38. Made up of a head tax of 6 pesos (48 reales) and a "community chest" tax of 6 reales.

39. The evidence for this assertion is as follows: in 1870 only 3,220 *industriales* were counted in a total Chinese population of close to 30,000. Cavada, *Historia*, 2, 412. The 1885 *padron industrial* showed 6,512 industriales in an official count of 63,968 Chinese. *Guía oficial de Filipinas . . . 1885*, pp. 411–13. The padron industrial for the following year showed 6,679 industriales in a total official count of 66,934 (figures challenged by Del Pan and others). *Los chinos en Filipinas*, pp. 101–02. A 10 per cent sampling of the Manila Chinese census for 1894 revealed about 6 per cent industriales. Twenty per cent sampling of the censuses of Cebu,

Fifteen years later a new tax was added. The Chinese had always been exempt from the *polo*, or corvée service, to which the indios and mestizos were subject. During the nineteenth century there had been a growing tendency to commute this obligation with a cash payment called the *falla*. In 1867 the Chinese were made liable for polo service, which they could commute with the 3 peso falla. Thus, the rates now ranged from about 110 pesos to about 22 pesos for shopowners, and down to about 10 pesos for employees.[41] Taxation of the Chinese remained more or less on this basis from 1867 to about 1880.

Meanwhile, the indio tribute had been raised from 10 reales to 12 reales. With the addition of the miscellaneous fees and the 3 peso falla (if commutation of labor service were chosen), an indio was responsible for a total of 5 pesos. The mestizo tribute had been raised from 20 reales to 24 reales (3 pesos). Addition of miscellaneous fees and the falla brought mestizo taxes to 6½ pesos.[42]

It is clear that the ratios of Chinese taxes to indio taxes and mestizo taxes increased tremendously after 1828. Originally, the ratios had been approximately 5 to 1 and 10 to 3, respectively. Between 1790 and 1828 they were about 7 to 2 and 7 to 3. But after 1828 Chinese were taxed

---

Iloilo, and Cagayan for the same year or the adjacent year of 1893 found, respectively, 8 per cent, 12 per cent and 13 per cent industriales. PNA, Padrones de chinos, 1893, 1894. There were 2,589 industriales in 1867, in a Chinese population estimated by Jagor at 18,000. This would suggest that at that time perhaps 15 per cent of the Chinese were industriales. Scherzer, *Fachmännische berichte*, p. 164. In 1889, 2,956 industriales were listed in the Manila *matrícula de comercio*, a number approximately 10 per cent of the total Manila Chinese population. Circular of the Central Revenue Administration, Sept. 12, 1889, Berriz, *Anuario 1889*, p. 349. Spanish tax officials in 1889 estimated that 12–13 per cent of the Chinese were "dedicated to different industries." Real Órden, May 16, 1889, Berriz, *Annuario 1889*, p. 332. See also Sancianco's division of Chinese taxpayers (c.1880) into those who paid high rates (10 per cent) and those who paid low rates (90 per cent). Sancianco, p. 124; cf. ibid., p. 94. The figure of 10 per cent may underestimate the percentage of industriales. As pointed out in Chap. 3, cabecilla–agent relationships tended to conceal actual ownership. Nevertheless, it is clear that the majority of Chinese were not self-employed. The one radically high estimate of the proportion of industriales is that of Lannoy, who says that in the 1830s they made up almost 40 per cent of the Chinese population. Lannoy, p. 110. The development of the export crop economy and coolie immigration after midcentury may be responsible for the difference between Lannoy's figure and those of later years.

40. The head tax remained at 6 pesos, but the "community chest" tax was reduced from 6 reales to 2 reales. Plehn, *16* (1901), 704.

41. Montero, *Historia, 3*, 496; "Decreto de superintendencia," June 19, 1867, and Real Órden, Oct. 28, 1886, in Berriz, *Anuario 1888, 2*, 836 and 841; Sancianco, p. 8. See also Real Decreto, July 12, 1883 and "Decreto de la dirección general de administración civil," Dec. 2, 1885 in Berriz, *Diccionario, 11*, 218 and 257.

42. Circular of General Administration of Tributes, Sept. 20, 1851, San Pedro, *8, 408*; BR, *52*, p. 58, note 18.

according to occupation and estimated income while the indios and mestizos continued to pay a uniform tax at nearly the same low rate. Thus, by the 1870s the ratio between the highest rate paid by a Chinese shopowner and the rate paid by an indio was about 21 to 1; and between the same high rate and that of a mestizo, roughly 16 to 1. Even the lowest rate paid by a self-employed Chinese stood in a ratio of 4 to 1 with that of the indios and 3 to 1 with that of the mestizos. But, on the other hand, a Chinese who was not self-employed paid at a rate much closer to those of the indios and mestizos, the ratios being roughly 7 to 5 and 7 to 6½.

It was mentioned above (p. 140) that during the 1870s the Spanish administration was moving toward the establishment of direct taxation applying to all groups. The contribución industrial, promulgated in 1878 and gradually applied over the next decade, was just such a tax. It was created by extending the patente industrial of the Chinese to all social groups, adding more expensive categories and a near infinity of subclassifications. The contribución industrial was an income tax on most self-employed or high-salaried persons, with a tax scale ranging from 8 pesos to 600 pesos. As part of the transition to universally applied taxation according to income, the hoary tribute and miscellaneous taxes paid by the indios and mestizos were at last abolished in 1884. The system of polo service—and hence the falla—now underwent a period of confusing experimentation which need not concern us.

Because the contribución industrial was applied to all social groups— the Chinese included—on the same basis, we may disregard it in our further calculations of tax ratios between groups. The key tax for comparative purposes is the cédula personal, promulgated in 1884 and intended to provide revenue to replace that lost when the indio–mestizo tribute was terminated. Unlike the contribución industrial, which included the Chinese, the cédula personal tax was supposed to be applicable to all groups *except* the Chinese. The Chinese were to continue to pay their 6 peso head tax until a new cédula system could be designed especially for them. But instead the cédula personal system was partly applied to the Chinese community. Chinese paying taxes of 100 pesos or over were subjected to the cédula personal tax at the same rates paid by non-Chinese. In compensation, they were exempted from the 6 peso Chinese head tax.[43]

The cédula personal was an identification card, the possession of which was obligatory to all persons other than the Chinese (with the

43. "Reglamento de cédulas personales," July 15, 1884, Berriz, *Diccionario, 12,* 207 and 219; Superior Decreto, June 27, 1888, Berriz, *Anuario 1888, 1, 156.*

exceptions just mentioned). This card was both an identification document and a tax receipt and had to be shown on certain occasions, which were carefully defined. There were originally ten classes of cédula personal, but by the end of the Spanish period six new classes had been added. The class of cédula that one purchased depended upon the amount of direct taxes he paid, and hence, ultimately, on his estimated income. When there were only ten classes, the first-class cédula, appropriate to those with the highest estimated income, cost 25 pesos. The lowest cédula for which a price was charged (ninth class) cost 1½ pesos. Those who paid direct taxes of 400 pesos or more (or had incomes assumed to be at least 8,000 pesos) were obliged to acquire first-class cédulas. Second-class cédulas were appropriate to those with tax payments of 300 to 400 pesos. Third class applied to taxpayers of 200 to 300 pesos; fourth class to those of 100 to 200 pesos; fifth class to those of 50 to 100 pesos; sixth class to those of 12 to 50 pesos; seventh class to those of 8 to 12 pesos; eighth class to wives of seventh-class cédula holders; and ninth class to those paying taxes less than 8 pesos. Classes ten through sixteen were special categories, some of them without reference to income.

In its final form the cédula personal tax had a scale of rates as follows: first class, 37½ pesos; second class, 30 pesos; third class, 22½ pesos; fourth class, 12 pesos; fifth class, 7½ pesos; sixth class, 5¼ pesos; seventh class, 3½ pesos; eighth class, 3 pesos; ninth class, 2¼ pesos.[44] Bearing this in mind, let us consider the changes in the Chinese taxation scheme.

Although the contribución industrial was promulgated in 1878, it was applied very gradually to the Chinese, reaching full effect only in 1887. Since the contribución industrial was really a revised form of the Chinese patente industrial (or shop tax), it simply replaced the older tax. The main difference effected was at the highest tax levels. Instead of a top classification of 100 pesos' tax, as had been the case on the old patente industrial scale, there were now levels going up to 600 pesos. The "community chest" tax was finally abolished, but the Chinese continued to be subject to both the 6 peso head tax and the 3 peso falla. However, it was ruled that Chinese who paid a contribución industrial tax of 200 pesos or more were exempt from the head tax.[45] As pointed out above, the Chinese were not supposed to be subject to the cédula personal tax; but Chinese who paid taxes of 100 pesos or more were temporarily obliged to pay the rates appropriate to their tax contribu-

44. Plehn, 16 (1901), 690–92.
45. Real Decreto, June 14, 1878, Berriz, *Anuario 1888, 1,* 503.

tion. Thus, if we disregard the contribución industrial, since it was applied equally to all groups, the basic Chinese taxes during the 1880s amounted to 9 pesos (6 pesos for head tax and 3 pesos for the falla). And in addition, those who paid taxes of 100 pesos or more were subject to the cédula personal tax at the standard rates of 8 pesos to 25 pesos, but exempt from the head tax. Their highest tax total would be 28 pesos (with the addition of the falla).

Thus, during the middle and late 1880s, the highest range of Chinese taxation (28 pesos) was slightly higher than the highest range in basic taxes for other groups (25 pesos for a first-class cédula personal in the 1880s). But the basic rate for those not subject to the cédulas personales —9 pesos—was considerably larger than the minimum of other groups (1½ pesos for a ninth-class cédula personal).

As noted above, the retention of the 6 peso head tax in the tax structure for the Chinese during the 1880s was a temporary measure until a system of cédulas analogous to the cédulas personales could be devised for the Chinese. The Weyler–Becerra Reglamento, promulgated in 1889 and effectuated the following year, completed the changes in the Chinese tax system. By this law, the 6 peso head tax was abolished, to be replaced by a system of *cédulas de capitación,* or "head tax payment certificates." Nine classifications were established. The first included those Chinese paying total taxes of 400 pesos or more. The second was for taxpayers of 300 to 400 pesos; the third, 200 to 300 pesos; the fourth, 100 to 200 pesos; the fifth, 50 to 100 pesos. The sixth class included all other adult males not included in the first five classes; or, in effect, the first five classes were the self-employed shopowners and professionals, and the sixth was composed mostly of their employees. The seventh class was for women, the eighth for children under 14 and adults physically unable to work, and the ninth was for Chinese community officers and their wives. The tax scale was as follows: first class, 30 pesos; second class, 25 pesos; third class, 20 pesos; fourth class, 15 pesos; fifth class, 10 pesos; sixth class, 6 pesos; seventh class, 3 pesos; eighth and ninth classes, free. But because of surcharges, these base rates were expanded to become in reality the following scale: 48.90 pesos; 40.75 pesos; 32.60 pesos; 24.45 pesos; 16.30 pesos; 9.78 pesos; 4.89 pesos.[46]

Since the first five classifications on this scale were made on exactly the same principles as those of the cédulas personales, a comparison of the two systems ought to provide an answer to whether or not the Chinese were unfairly taxed in relation to other groups. It is apparent that with the addition of the surcharges to the Chinese tax, a Chinese of a

46. *Chinos. Sus reglamentos,* p. 18; Plehn, 16 (1901), 700.

certain income had to pay a somewhat higher cédula tax than anyone else having the same income. Specifically, in the 1890s, a Chinese whose income fell into the brackets prescribed for classes one through five would have to pay, on the average, 1⅔ pesos' cédula tax for every 1 peso paid by any non-Chinese in the same income bracket.

This lengthy discussion of the taxation problem has been presented here because claims of excessive and inequitable taxation were among the most important complaints of the Philippine Chinese. There is really no way to determine whether the taxes applied to the Chinese were excessive—in terms of Chinese profits, governmental needs,[47] or any abstract standards of fairness. But it is possible to comment on the equity of Chinese taxes in comparison with those of other groups.

Spaniards and mestizos often argued that, relative to other groups, the Chinese were not being taxed sufficiently, that the patente industrial, which had been established in 1852 to offset the business advantages of the Chinese, had failed to equalize the conditions of competition because it was too low and did not really reflect the wide ratio of Chinese incomes to those of other groups.[48] It may have been in response to arguments like this that the government established the Chinese cédulas de capitación at higher rates than the cédulas personales, on the ground that true equity required recognition of Chinese business superiority. We may get a better idea of Spanish thinking and policy, however, by surveying trends in Chinese taxation over the entire span of the nineteenth century.

When one does this, he is struck by three important features. The first is the growing disparity within the Chinese community between the taxes paid by the self-employed—particularly those with large incomes—and those paid by employees. Between 1828 and 1852, self-employed persons paid up to 127 pesos, while employees paid 19 pesos. From 1852 to 1880, the self-employed paid up to 109 pesos, while employees paid 9 pesos. The application of the contribución industrial to the Chinese in the 1880s meant that a self-employed Chinese might be liable for taxes ranging from 69 pesos to 600 pesos, while a Chinese employee was still paying only 9 pesos. Finally, with the addition of the cédula de capitación in the 1890s, a first-class taxpayer might be liable

47. In the mid-1870s expenses of the Spanish administration were ten times what they had been thirty or forty years before. Ahuja, 2, 25.

48. Sancianco, p. 121. The author of an unsigned article in *La política de España en Filipinas,* July 12, 1891, p. 141, complained that the Chinese should pay double the rates of income tax paid by other foreigners since other foreigners brought wealth into the Philippines and the Chinese brought nothing. See also ibid., Jan. 20, 1891, p. 2; Jan. 19, 1892, pp. 16–17. As early as 1859 complaints like this were heard. "Report of Governor Norzagaray," *Report of Philippine Commission, 1,* 152.

for almost 650 pesos, while an employee who purchased a sixth-class cédula was paying only about 8 pesos.

A second feature of the tax scheme was the consistently low rate for the employees. In the seventeenth and early eighteenth centuries employees (like all Chinese) paid 8 pesos. From 1790 to 1828, the rate was about 7 pesos. After a leap to 19 pesos in 1828–52, the employee rate returned to 9 pesos in the latter year and remained at about that level. Meanwhile, of course, the rates for self-employed Chinese continued to go up.

Thus it is clear that while taxes for all levels of the Chinese community were always higher than corresponding levels outside the community, the rate for the employees, who made up 90 per cent of the Chinese population,[49] was not excessive in terms of what Chinese had always paid in the Philippines. The real squeeze was at the top—on the 10 per cent of the Chinese community that was self-employed. It may well be that claims of excessive and inequitable taxation represented essentially the interests of this 10 per cent.

A third feature of importance was the circumstance that while the disparity between the rates paid by self-employed and employee within the Chinese community increased, the disparity between taxes paid by the Chinese and by other groups first widened, then narrowed. The application of the contribución industrial to all groups in the 1880s made tax rates more uniform and came closer than ever before to realizing the Spanish theory of taxation according to ability to pay. Not only did this narrow the rate gap between the Chinese and native groups, but it meant that foreigners other than the Chinese, hitherto tax-exempt, now paid at rates almost as high as the Chinese. Thus, there was nearly equitable taxation, whether the Chinese were compared with native elements or with other foreigners.

The Chinese should have been relieved at this development. Yet it is precisely in the 1880s, when taxation was approaching uniformity— when the difference between Chinese taxes and those of other groups was a matter of 3 or 4 pesos—that Chinese complaints of "excess" and "inequity" were loudest. Apparently, the fact of near uniformity was outweighed by the increase in rates for the upper class of the Chinese community. In other words, the real complaint seems to have been not inequitable taxation, but excessive taxation at the top. It is also worth noting that the contribución industrial applied a heavy tax to "middlemen," hitherto exempted by the "shop tax." [50]

49. See note 39.
50. See Chap. 3, p. 73.

The foregoing discussion has been concerned with legally established taxation. There is also the matter of extralegal taxation, the extent of which cannot, of course, be determined. Manila rumor had it that many governors-general were bribed by the Chinese upon beginning their terms of office. Weyler is supposed to have been furnished with household services, provisions, and gifts, and paid 80,000 pesos to withhold enforcement of certain laws harmful to the interests of the Chinese community. The practice of using the enforcement of certain laws as an instrument of extortion was apparently quite common. For instance, the government in Spain decreed in 1828–30 that the Chinese should be organized into barangayes, like the indios, to make tax collection and surveillance somewhat easier. Since the well-to-do Chinese were reluctant to act as cabezas de barangay, this law became a dead letter. But it was periodically revived as a means of extortion, notably in 1861 and 1877. Likewise, the bookkeeping law promulgated in the mid-1860s, intended to satisfy complaints of Chinese tax frauds, was used as an instrument of extortion. It called for the Chinese to keep a set of business records in Spanish as well as their ordinary set in Chinese. Like the barangay law, this one was bought off by the Chinese.[51]

It was in extortion like this, rather than the higher rates of legal taxation, that the inequitable taxation of which the Chinese complained really could be found. There were good reasons for the relationship of extortion and bribery existing between the Spanish officials and the Chinese. Spanish officials were poorly paid. Few of them had a transcendent interest in the welfare of the Philippines. They were in the Islands to make enough to retire in comfort to Spain. Under these circumstances it is not surprising that they should find it difficult to resist temptations to impose upon members of an almost defenseless minority group.

For their part, the Chinese reacted like members of such a minority in a situation where there were no guarantees, no right to negotiate freely or to obtain redress. The cultural baggage they brought with them to the Philippines was also important in conditioning their relationships with Spanish officials. It is often said that premodern China had a government of men and not of laws. Certainly the merchant in China did not depend upon the law to protect his property; he depended upon the kindness of the official. The good will of the official could be purchased with gifts and services, and the official could become a kind of protector

---

51. Real Cédula, July 26, 1863, Berriz, *Anuario 1888, 1,* 608; *Los chinos en Filipinas,* pp. 42–43, 92–93, 127; Sawyer, pp. 20, 291; Jagor, p. 348. See also PNA, Cabezas de barangay, chinos, 49-1-10.

or sponsor of the merchant's enterprises. If the official did not become a regular patron or "partner" of the merchant, the latter could expect at least periodic extortions, or demands for protection money. The official, in turn, was apt to consider the "squeezing" of merchants as part of his official prerogative. This pattern of merchant–official relationships and conduct was so thoroughly ingrained and generally accepted that even a Chinese emigrant from a farm family, without any commercial experience, would be aware of it and accept it as the natural mode of behavior.

Such was the case with the Philippine Chinese. It is true that during the 1880s and 1890s they increasingly defended their interests against government officials in the Spanish courts, hiring Spanish lawyers to assist them. Sometimes they won out over the government.[52] But there was still a strong, typically Chinese feeling among them that it was the men, and not the laws, that counted. Chinese community leaders in 1886 admitted as much when they said that whether or not a Chinese consulate was needed in the Philippines depended upon who was the governor. If the Philippine governor were a good man there was no need of a consulate.[53]

No doubt these Chinese attitudes, together with the attitudes of the Spanish officials and the minority status of the Chinese, combined to encourage extortion and bribery. In the nineteenth century extortion and bribery were certainly not new features of the relationship between the Chinese and the Spanish officials.[54] But given the dynamic nature of the Philippine economy during this period and the much greater possibilities for profit than had hitherto existed, both briber and bribed were playing for higher stakes than ever before. More important, the indios and mestizos who would one day rule the Islands were absorbing a lesson in official–minority group relationships.

While the government wrestled with the Chinese as a prospective issue in international politics, the popular attitude was one of unconcern about the political status of the Chinese. Indeed, it is of particular interest to note that after the establishment of American rule in the Islands in 1898 the term sangley disappears from usage to be replaced by a kind of semantic descendant or successor, "alien." "Alien," as

---

52. Corpuz, Chap. 3, and pp. 59, 105; PNA, Defraudadores de la contribución industrial, 26-17-2; Defraudaciones de la contribución industrial, 5-12-13; Contribución industrial, 5-8-3; Defraudación de la contribución industrial, 26-22-8.

53. SCJC, ch. 4, p. 21b.

54. It was said that in the seventeenth and eighteenth centuries it became the custom for Chinese to supply gratis all the household needs of officials in Manila. Los chinos en Filipinas, p. 17.

popularly used in the Philippines, does not mean any foreigner, nor even any Chinese who is not a citizen. It is a pejorative term referring to anyone who is culturally Chinese, Philippine citizen or not.[55] The definition is distinctly cultural, and not political.

For their part, the Chinese reacted to anti-Chinese pressure upon them as a group by withdrawing into communalism, stressing their "Chinese-ness," and, once China showed an interest in them, becoming what the Spanish government believed them to be, a national minority group.

55. This specialized definition of "alien" occasionally trips up those who rely on oral estimates of the number of "aliens" in order to estimate the number of Chinese nationals in the Philippines.

7

The Nature of the Chinese Community

During the last half of the nineteenth century the Chinese population responded to pressure upon it by developing a sense of community, by contracting socially into communalism. Institutions were developed to organize the Chinese as a community to deal with problems presented by the pressures from outside. By the end of the Spanish period a school had been established in order to prevent the assimilation of mestizo offspring into Filipino society. Even before that time, male descendants, usually mestizos, were claimed for the Chinese community by being sent to China for their education when their parents could afford to do so. Closer cultural relations were established with China, and political relations were inaugurated by the Philippine Chinese community leaders. Finally, there was a development of what might be called national consciousness (it is doubtful that it could be called nationalism) among the overseas Chinese in the Philippines.

Before beginning to discuss the Chinese community, some kind of caveat seems to be in order. What follows draws heavily upon Spanish government documents and the writings of Spanish and other observers. It is therefore essentially a view of the community from the outside. Even where publications of the Chinese community provide information about its institutions, the information is likely to be of a formal rather than a functional nature. The inner workings of the community cannot, therefore, be analyzed with any depth at all. We can only make inferences here and there.

Even the available documentation has certain internal inadequacies. This is particularly true of the census material for the 1890s in the Philippine National Archives. In accordance with the provisions of the Weyler–Becerra Reglamento of 1889, censuses of the Chinese (*padrones de chinos*), which had been made quinquennially, began to be made annually in 1890. Data included were name, sex, age, marital status, religion, place of residence, place of origin in China, occupation, and tax status. However, in making use of this material one finds many limitations. Due to the disorganized condition of the archives it was impossible to find a complete census for any single year, and for some provinces adjacent years' censuses had to be substituted. At least one volume of the Manila census is missing. Even where all volumes are present, some categories of information are not filled in or are entered in vague terms, there being little attempt to standardize usages. In addition, a number of Chinese undoubtedly escaped the census-taker (who was also the tax collector). Thus, the censuses of the 1890s available in the archives represent perhaps two thirds to three fourths of the total Chinese population.

Although these limitations rule out demographic analysis of the Chinese community, it nevertheless seems desirable to make use of these data for whatever general, qualified, "impressionistic" information they can give us about the Chinese community. On this basis, some sampling was done from four areas believed to be of key importance: Manila, Iloilo, Cebu, and Cagayan. Manila was selected because it was the largest center of Chinese settlement, somewhat over half of the Philippine Chinese being resident there. It also provided the largest urban concentration of Chinese. Iloilo and Cebu were chosen as areas where emphasis on sugar and abaca as export crops brought large increases in the Chinese population and, in the twentieth century, large urban concentrations of Chinese. Cagayan was included both as representative of a tobacco area and because it was and remained somewhat less urbanized than the other three areas. Of the Manila population, which probably totaled close to 50,000, only 22,110 names are accompanied by any substantial amount of data. From these 22,110, a 10 per cent sampling was made. For Iloilo province (Chinese population: 2,010), Cebu province (Chinese population: 1,447), and Cagayan province (Chinese population: 1,107), 20 per cent samplings were made. Except for Cagayan, where the 1893 padrón had to be substituted, the 1894 census was used. With this methodological description as background, let us proceed to investigate some of the features of the community.

Types of Immigration

The size of the Chinese community has been referred to on several occasions above. In the mid-1840s it stood at 5,736, representing no more than .14 per cent of the total Philippine population. In the 1903 census it appears as 41,035, in a Philippine population of 7,635,426 —in other words, slightly over 1 per cent of the total.[1] But between these two dates the Philippine Chinese population had reached a high point in the 1880s and 1890s. Some anti-Chinese writings give estimates as high as 120,000. Others settle for 90,000 to 100,000, or about a third more than official calculations showed.[2] An estimate of 90,000 to 120,000 would define the Chinese community as composing about 2 per cent of the total Philippine population.

The tremendous growth in the size of the community after 1850 was brought about by increased immigration, which, speaking generally, assumed two forms: coolie-broker and kinship-based; the relative amounts of each are not known. Coolie broker immigration developed after 1870 in response to the demands of foreign business houses in the Philippines. It was facilitated by the establishment of regular steamship service on a triangular route involving Amoy, Hong Kong, and Manila. Most of the coolie traffic was handled by the steamers of three Hong Kong firms: Butterfield and Swire's China Navigation Company, Jardine–Matheson's Indo-China Steam Navigation Company, and Russell and Company's China–Manila Steamship Company, which operated regular fortnightly service.[3] Besides these Hong Kong companies there were a few Philippine Spaniards, mestizos, and Chinese who occasionally sent individual steamers to the China coast. And after 1891 the Japanese N.Y.K. line entered the competition. The trip from either Hong Kong or Amoy could be made in less than three days and steerage rates were low. In the 1890s the cost of immigration for one person—including passage, food, and taxes—was said to amount to 50 pesos.[4]

The actual work of bringing over coolies was done by coolie-conductors, called by the Spaniards cabecillas. In this case, the ubiquitous term

1. See note 5, Chap. 6.

2. Los chinos en Filipinas, p. 95; China en Filipinas, pp. 12, 123, 127, 173; Felipe Canga-Argüelles, "La emigración española á Filipinas," Boletín de la Sociedad Geográfica de Madrid, 27 (1889), 205; Pablo Feced, Filipinas: esbozos y pinceladas por "Quioquiap" (Manila, 1888), p. 80.

3. Testimony of J. T. B. McCleod, Report of Philippine Commission, 2, 296–99; Chronicle and Directory . . . 1891, pp. 438–41; PNA, Entradas y salidas de chinos, July 14, 1895–Dec. 31, 1896; Comenge, p. 25.

4. González and Moreno, pp. 139–40, 474, and advertisements in back of volume; Real Órden, Oct. 30, 1889, Berriz, Anuario 1889, pp. 349–50; Chronicle and Directory . . . 1873, p. 404; Guía oficial de Filipinas, 1885, p. 855; PNA, Entradas y salidas de chinos, 1895–96; PNA, Cónsules, 34-5-8; China en Filipinas, p. 30; Chronicle and Directory . . . 1891, pp. 170, 190, 407, 443; Testimony of Carlos Palanca [Tan Quien-sien], Report of Philippine Commission, 2, 221; Chuang, in Hsia-men ta-hsüeh hsüeh-pao, 1 (1958), 105.

cabecilla can be taken as an equivalent of *k'e-t'ou,* or coolie-boss.[5] Once in Manila, the coolie was usually turned over to another "boss," also called cabecilla (*towkay,* roughly), whose activities were discussed in Chapter 3. This cabecilla was responsible for housing and feeding the coolie. Housing often took the form of a room which the cabecilla used by day for commercial purposes and by night as a dormitory for 40 or 50 coolies. During the 1880s, when the Spanish administration was particularly concerned about the hygienic aspects of the Chinese community, legislation attempting to curtail this practice was promulgated, the government even going as far as to specify how many meters' sleeping space should be allotted to each coolie.[6]

Newly-arrived coolies who had not yet been assigned to a cabecilla usually were housed in the office building of the gobernadorcillo de chinos, a building known as the Tribunal de Sangleyes. In the pre-1850 period, newly-arrived or transient Chinese were obliged to lodge in the Alcaicería de San Fernando, paying a rental fee which went into the city's coffers. There they could be watched over by a Spanish official, the Warden of the Alcaicería. But from 1843 on they had the option of staying in the Alcaicería or anywhere else in the Manila area. The decay and disuse of the Alcaicería resulted in the practice of new arrivals moving immediately into the Chinese community. Instead of being separated and watched by a Spanish official, they either went immediately to a cabecilla or lived in the Tribunal de Sangleyes under the care of a Chinese official, the gobernadorcillo.[7]

Coolie immigrants might first work as part of labor gangs, or perhaps as corredores (house-to-house vendors). In the latter case, there was some hope of improving one's condition. A corredor working for a cabecilla could often save enough money over a few years' time to enable him to open a chucherías or textile shop of his own, often in partnership with another ex-corredor.[8] Or, a newcomer might be used by his cabecilla as a stock clerk, with an opportunity to move up within

5. Comenge, pp. 32, 35; Real Órden, Feb. 1, 1889 and Superior Decreto, July 19, 1889 in Berriz, *Anuario 1889,* pp. 331, 334; Superior Decreto, Aug. 30, 1889, *Anuario 1890,* p. 298.

6. Moya, "Las Islas Filipinas en 1882," *Rev. de España,* 93 (1883), 189–90; "Bando del corregimiento," May 18, 1886, Berriz, *Diccionario, 14,* 280; *China en Filipinas,* pp. 48–49; "The Chinese in the Philippines," pp. 158–59.

7. Superior Decreto, Jan. 24, 1804, and Dec. 13, 1843, in San Pedro 2, 469 and 477; Superior Decreto, Dec. 20, 1849, ibid., 2, 479; PNA, Tribunal de sangleyes, 48-8-18; Buzeta, *1,* 138; 2, 258–59; Montero, *Historia, 3,* 63.

8. Montano, *Voyage,* p. 91; Plauchut, in *Revue des deux mondes,* 21 (1877), 893–94.

the business and eventually, having learned what he needed to know, to go out on his own.[9]

Kinship immigration appears to have followed a general pattern. Once a Chinese had established a foothold in the Philippines and achieved a modest measure of success, he either sent for, or else returned to China and brought back, a teen-aged son or nephew. Eventually, other relatives, usually adolescents, came over in the same way, until a kind of fragmentary family—minus females, usually—existed in the Philippines. Younger members could be used as agents or operators of branch stores. Or they might be kept in the original family store and apprenticed as clerks—or, with sufficient educational background, used as bookkeepers.[10]

Mention of kinship-based immigration raises the question of the general role of kinship in the Philippine Chinese community. In the contemporary Chinese community kinship plays a role of overwhelming importance.[11] On the basis of presently available information we cannot be certain of its role in the nineteenth century, but it may well have been as important then as today. This possibility is suggested by the high degree of concentration in the places of origin of the immigrants. In the four Philippine provinces from which census samples were taken, over 80 per cent of the Chinese were from four counties (*hsien*) in southern Fukien province: Chin-chiang, T'ung-an, Nan-an, and Lung-ch'i.[12] The greatest number, slightly over 50 per cent according to the samples taken, came from (or claimed to come from) Chin-chiang (which includes the city of Ch'üan-chou), followed by T'ung-an, Lung-ch'i (including the city of Chang-chou), and Nan-an, in that order. From this general area, twelve surnames are numerically predominant: Tan, Uy, Sy, Lim, Chua, Ong, Dy, Go, Co, Yu, Yap, and Que, in that order.[13] In sampling from the census data of Manila, Cagayan, Iloilo, and Cebu, it was found that two thirds of the persons in the samples had these surnames. The surname Tan alone accounted

9. Blumentritt, "Die Chinesen Manilas," *Globus*, 62 (1890), 98.

10. Amyot, "The Chinese of Manila," pp. 56, 57, 64. See also biographical sketches in Huang Hsiao-ts'ang, pp. chia 155, 158, 177, 187, 194, 196–97, 199; ibid., p. *chia tseng* 1.

11. Amyot, passim.

12. PNA, Padrones de chinos, Manila, Cebú, Iloilo (1894), Cagayan (1893). Smaller numbers of immigrants came from An-ch'i *hsien*, Hui-an *hsien*, Hai-ch'eng *hsien*, Hsing-hua *fu*, Amoy *t'ing*, and Feng-t'ing *ssu*. In more recent times Chin-chiang has continued to contribute 50 per cent of the immigrants. T'ung-an migrants have declined in number in the Philippines. Chuang, p. 97; Amyot, p. 32.

13. In the 1950s the surnames Tan, Lim, Chua, Dy, and Ong were the most important ones. Weightman, pp. 314–15.

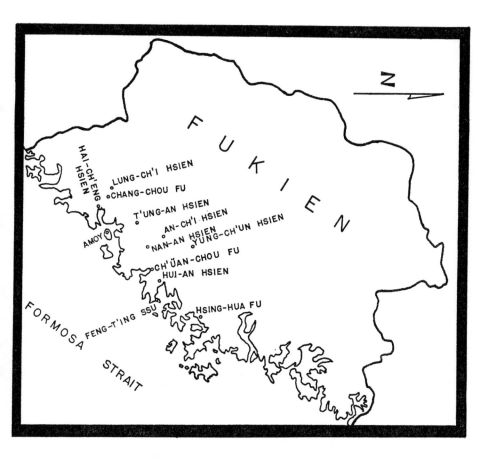

FUKIEN PROVINCE, CHINA

for over 10 per cent of the names. In the case of seven surnames—Tan, Sy, Chua, Ong, Dy, Co, and Go—over half the persons in the samples were from Chin-chiang.[14] If we assume that persons of the same surname from the same county were related, or would claim to be, and if the samples taken are at all meaningful, it appears that kinship must have been important. However, it may be remarked in passing that common surname associations, like those now existing among the Philippine Chinese, were apparently not formed until after 1898.[15]

In the Chinese community the sex ratio remained quite unbalanced during the nineteenth century. In 1870 official records showed 193 women in a Chinese population of about 23,000, a ratio of eight females per 1,000 males. Sixteen years later, official statistics registered 194 women (191 of them in Manila) in a Chinese population officially set at (in round numbers) 66,000. Thus, the ratio became 3 females per 1,000 males for the Philippines as a whole, and for Manila, where the Chinese population was close to 50,000, 4 females per 1,000 males. Another sixteen years passed, and the 1903 census found 517 China-born women in the Philippines, the total population of Chinese nationals being recorded as 41,035;[16] the ratio was now 13 females per 1,000 males. It appears, therefore, that although some increase in female population occurred between 1886 and 1903 the sex ratio remained quite unbalanced.

The Spaniards in the 1840s discussed the possibility of encouraging agricultural colonization by Chinese families, but little came of it.[17] It is doubtful that normal family patterns were at all common in the Philippine Chinese community. Most of the Chinese women in Manila were said to be prostitutes or concubines.[18] In 1870 approximately 40 per cent of the female Chinese population of the Philippines was under the age of 14, while only 5 per cent of the male population was in that category. This difference is suggestive of the importation of *mui-tsai*

14. PNA, Padrones de chinos, Manila, Cebú, Iloilo (1894), Cagayan (1893).

15. During the late Spanish period there were some regional and dialect group associations. But with the exception of the Cantonese *hui-kuan*, they existed in name only. Th same-surname associations were formed after them. *Fei-lü-p'in shang-hui wu-shih chou-nien k'an*, p. chia 2; Amyot, pp. 103–04.

16. Cavada, 2, 404; *Los chinos en Filipinas, pp.* 96, 104; *Census of 1903, 1,* 14. However, Tan Quien-sien testified in 1899 that in a Manila Chinese population of between 22,000 and 23,000 (his figures) there were about 2,000 women. *Report of Philippine Commission, 2,* 220. This would indicate a ratio of 100 females per 1,000 males. It is important to note that the 1903 figure includes Chinese nationals only.

17. Real Órden, Jan. 28, 1844; PNA, Reales Órdenes, caja 100, núm. 75.

18. "The Chinese in the Philippines, p. 153, Cf. Testimony of Carlos Palanca [Tan Quien-sien], *Report of Philippine Commission, 2,* 220.

for use as servants or, eventually, concubines. In the 1890s most of the women were in the 20–40 age range.[19]

It may be recalled that in 1890 the age of legal majority for Chinese was set at 14. If we use this as a standard, from 1870 to the 1890s enough children were brought over before the age of 14, and there were enough births in the Philippines so that the percentage of minors (under 14) in the total Chinese population remained about the same in the early 1890s as it was in 1870: 6 per cent in 1870 and 5 per cent in the early 1890s. Most of the minors, like the majority of Chinese women, resided in Manila. But there were so few of either that one could hardly call even the Manila Chinese population "settled" as a Chinese population. By contrast, the Chinese mestizos in the Philippines had, by 1870, an almost 1:1 sex ratio, and over 35 per cent of their population were under the age of 14.[20]

Intramural Rivalries

Since our view of the Chinese community is from the outside we can say very little about its class structure. It is likely that the basic division was between employer and employee, whose relationship frequently included a bond created by financial indebtedness.[21] Within the "employer" class there was probably some subdivision. Importers, brokers, and bazar owners were likely to be regarded as above owners of tiendas de chucherías, tiendas de sari-sari, and artisans' shops.

For census and tax purposes the Chinese were classified by the Spanish administration into two rough categories: *industrial,* meaning any self-employed merchant or artisan; and *jornalero* (wage-laborer), or *dependiente* (employee). Cabecillas (towkays) were among the industriales; their *personeros* (agents), although they did not work on a daily-wage basis, were classified with journaleros or dependientes. Whatever the terms used, the Chinese community was organized largely along paternal–dependent lines. In the four provinces sampled, the employee proportion of the Chinese population ranged from 75 to 90 per cent.[22] As pointed out above, the Spanish tax system increasingly discriminated between employers and employees. But whether this re-

19. Cavada, 2, 405; Bowring, pp. 311–12; PNA, Padrones de chinos, Manila, Cebú, Iloilo, (1894), Cagayan (1893).

20. Cavada, 1, 373; 2, 341, 404–05; PNA, Padrones de chinos, Manila menores (1894).

21. AMAE, Filipinas 1890. Supuestos atropellos . . . . Estado informe [1891?]; Ultramar to Estado, June 25, 1896.

22. PNA, Padrones de chinos, Manila, Cebú, Iloilo (1894), Cagayan (1893).

flected an actual widening of the gap between the two classes, economically and socially, it is impossible to say. Assuming a considerable opportunity for upward social mobility within the Chnese community, it is doubtful that the economic barrier between the two classes, whatever its width, would be a cause of disharmony.

The methods of achieving upward social mobility are a subject on which we have little reliable information. There exist a number of biographical sketches of successful community leaders, past and present, but these writings are remarkably lacking in specific detail. Moreover they are written according to standardized formulas, embodying the traditional *hua-ch'iao* (overseas Chinese) virtues of hard work and frugal living. Therefore, the most we can do is discuss what seem to have been general conditions of success.

Almost everyone, upon coming to the Philippines for the first time, went to work for someone else until he could afford to go out on his own. Those who joined relatives who had already pioneered had the best chance for rapid advancement. They started immediately as apprentice clerks or operators of branch outlets of the family store, with the possibility of owning the business later on. The immigrant brought over by a coolie broker, having no relatives to get him started, might have to work for some time as a warehouse or public works laborer in order to repay the cabecilla for advances on his passage money and the entry tax.[23] Only then did he have an opportunity to move into a job from which he could rise. He went into business for himself when he had saved enough to do so or could get someone to finance him.

For either kind of immigrant, the big break in his fortunes came when he acquired a wealthy patron, whether inside or outside the Chinese community. From then on it was a matter of expanding one's personal connections. How one attracted the attention of a patron or made personal connections, particularly with persons outside the Chinese community, is a subject that needs further research. But it is clear enough that although hard work and frugality were important conditions of upward social mobility, they were not enough, of themselves, to insure it. Personal connections were equally important.[24] One kind of personal relationship, baptismal *padrinazgo,* will be discussed below.

23. AMAE, Filipinas, sobre consulados chinos, 1887. Informe, Intendencia de Hacienda, 1881. The entry tax in the early 1890s was raised from 2 pesos to 20 pesos. AMAE, 1897. Insurrección en Filipinas. Yncidente protección. Estado informe, Jan. 2, 1896.
24. See biographical sketches in Huang Hsiao-ts'ang, pp. chia, 188, 197; biographies of Lucio Uy and Yap Anton in "Fei-lü-p'in hua-ch'iao shih-lüeh," pp. 30, 43; biographical sketch of Tan Quien-sien given below in Chap. 7; and Chuang, p. 114.

If a fairly high degree of upward social mobility reduced class antagonisms to a minimum, a more likely source of friction would be competition between dialect groups. But the homogeneity of the Philippine Chinese population made that kind of conflict improbable. The major division was between the Hokkiens of the four counties of southern Fukien and the Cantonese. But the latter formed such a small percentage of the entire community that it is doubtful there were real clashes between the two dialect groups. In the mid-nineteenth century the Cantonese population was composed of 500-odd *macanistas*. By the end of the century that number had increased to perhaps 3,000, including now Chinese from areas near Canton and Hong Kong, as well as Macao. The increasing commercial ties between Manila and Hong Kong were presumably of some importance as a reason for the numerical growth of Cantonese. Even so, at the end of the century the Cantonese were probably no more than 5 per cent of the total Chinese population.[25] They were numerous in only two places: Manila, where they formed almost 10 per cent of the Chinese population, and Iloilo, where they amounted to 8 per cent. In the city of Manila they tended to cluster together in several spots: in the old walled city (Intramuros), around Plaza Santa Cruz, and in various places in Binondo.[26]

Cantonese continued to specialize in the occupations of cook and shoemaker. But this is not to say that there were no wealthy Cantonese. On the contrary, the number of high taxpayers among Cantonese in Manila corresponded to their proportion of the population.[27] The Cantonese were aggressive, and there may have been occasional Hokkien-Cantonese skirmishes. But it is doubtful that there was anything like the dialect group competition for opium contracts and other prizes that occurred in Thailand.[28] In general, the two groups simply had little to do with each other. The Cantonese regarded the Hokkiens as crafty and untrustworthy; Hokkiens considered Cantonese to be "frivolous and unstable." [29] Although the two secret societies mentioned in Part I continued to exist throughout the nineteenth century,

25. Testimony of Carlos Palanca [Tan Quien-sien], *Report of Philippine Commission*, 2, 222.

26. PNA, Padrones de chinos, Manila, Cebú, Iloilo (1894), Cagayan (1893). In Binondo the Cantonese settled on the following streets: Escolta, Rosario, Nueva, David, Elcano, Jaboneros, Asuncion, Barcelona, San Jacinto, San Fernando, Santo Cristo, Lavezares.

27. PNA, Padrones de chinos, Manila (1894).

28. Letter of Fernando Sainz, O.P., parish priest of Binondo, Sept. 6, 1889, in Archivo de PP. Domínicos (Manila), T. 93, pp. 3v–4r; Moya, 93 (1883), 185; Skinner, *Chinese Society in Thailand*, pp. 140–43.

29. Amyot, p. 71; Weightman, p. 331.

it does not appear that they were representative of dialect group divisions as such.

There were, of course, political and personal rivalries within the Chinese community, some of which were partly brought into the open during disputed elections. In 1883 the reelection of Antonio Elizaga Yap Caong as gobernadorcillo de chinos was contested by a group of self-styled "principal citizens," who charged him and the alternate candidate, Marcelino Croquel Tan Pueco, with misappropriating 500,000 pesos' worth of relief funds contributed by the community during the 1879 cholera epidemic.[30]

A more serious battle occurred over the elections of 1892–93. A certain Pio de la Guardia Sy Pioco (alias Pio Barreto), who owned a sawyer's shop in Manila and was said to be worth about 20,000 pesos, was elected gobernadorcillo in 1892. Scarcely had he taken office, when he was suspended under charges of fraud. Manuel Pérez Tan Yaoco, the *teniente primero* (First Lieutenant), was appointed temporary gobernadorcillo. As the case against Sy Pioco dragged on, supporters of Tan Yaoco urged the government to permit a special election. They claimed that Sy Pioco was unworthy to hold office and should never have been elected in the first place. They pointed out his use of an alias, his previous involvement in a bribery charge, and his alleged campaign promises to "cover up" for those electors who did not pay the falla. They also complained that in his brief term of office the operating costs of the Chinese community hospital in Manila had been raised some 400 pesos per month, thus reducing the emergency cash reserve, while providing no better services than before. (Sy Pioco had answered criticisms with the claim that costs went up because more people were using the hospital.)

Sy Pioco's supporters replied that it was common knowledge in Manila that this incident was being used by a powerful person in the Chinese community who wished to consolidate his power by the election of his candidate, Tan Yaoco, as gobernadorcillo. They argued that since Tan Yaoco, as acting gobernadorcillo, already had full power to do whatever was necessary in the office, there was no need to have an election and allow the ambitious one to increase his power.

The Spanish administration hesitated. The civil governor of Manila pointed out that a power struggle among cabecillas had long been developing in Manila's Chinese community, and that to allow elections now might result in violence. Nevertheless, the government allowed an interim election in 1893, which was won by Tan Yaoco. The fol-

30. "Manila, 1883," PNA, Chinos, elecciones, 37-2-2.

lowing year, after Sy Pioco had been convicted of the charge against him and had exhausted all his appeals, another election was held, and once again Tan Yaoco was chosen gobernadorcillo, a position he resigned shortly thereafter.[31]

The Growth of Community Institutions

While these power struggles of a primarily personal nature were going on, there were institutional indications that the Manila Chinese community was beginning to mature and to assume the leadership of the Philippine Chinese community as a whole. In the pre-1850 period the main institutions of internal control in the Manila community appear to have been the two secret societies. After 1850 there was a growth of openly established, community-wide organizations. The Philippine Chinese of today attribute this to the relaxation of Spanish laws which had forbidden any organizations that might compete with the state.[32] This is probably true. But it is also possible to argue that the development of community-wide organizations is a reflection of an increased community awareness.

Of course, some of the organizations founded in this period were not as broadly inclusive. The establishment of commercial associations in the textile and lumber businesses has been mentioned in Part II. Among the other organizations established in Manila during this period was the Kwangtung Hui Kuan, founded shortly after 1850 in Santa Cruz by the growing Cantonese group. What little we know of its functions indicates that its major task was to take care of new arrivals by providing temporary housing and advances of money. It thus assumed for the Cantonese the function of lodging newcomers ordinarily carried out by the Tribunal de Sangleyes. Besides charitable aid, it probably exercised some authority in arbitrating disputes between Cantonese. To maintain its funds, the Hui Kuan regularly took a share of the wages or profits of Manila's Cantonese. A Kwangtung Hui Kuan was established in Iloilo about 1870.[33]

An organization of more importance because of its community-wide nature was the Gremio de Chinos. The term gremio, like cabecilla, was so widely used by the Spanish administration with reference to

31. Sources for this dispute are: "Manila 1893," "Manila, 1894," "Pio Barreto," in PNA, Chinos, elecciones, 37-2-2.
32. Liu Chi Tien, Hua-ch'iao, p. 62.
33. Letter of Fernando Sainz, O.P., Archivo de PP. Domínicos, T. 93, pp. 3r–4r; Liu Chi Tien, Hua-ch'iao, p. 62; "Fei-lü-p'in hua-ch'iao shih-lüeh," pp. 12, 91; Huang Hsiao-ts'ang, p. chia 152.

Chinese institutions that some confusion is almost inevitable. It will be recalled that since at least the early eighteenth century there were occupational gremios, headed by cabezas or cabecillas. There was also the Gremio de Chinos de Binondo, founded in the 1680s as a kind of combined municipal corporation and religious sodality. The Gremio de Chinos referred to here is separate from both of these.

The term Gremio de Chinos first appears about the year 1800 as the Spanish designation for a kind of vaguely defined, supramunicipal corporate organization of the Chinese in the Manila area.[34] With the destruction of the old Parián in 1790 and the dispersal of its former residents into Binondo and Santa Cruz, the center of the Chinese community—and hence, the location of the Gremio's formal apparatus—shifted to Binondo. This shift seems to have caused some popular confusion between the Gremio de Chinos and the old Gremio de Chinos de Binondo. The latter continued to exist. But as the municipal government of the city of Manila was extended to include Binondo, the Gremio de Chinos de Binondo lost its administrative character. It remained a kind of status group for Catholic Chinese with primarily ceremonial functions, involving particularly the Feast of La Naval.

The Gremio de Chinos also underwent some changes. Prior to 1850 the gobernadorcillo (capitán) de chinos, who acted as formal head of the Gremio, was chosen by a board of electors composed of ex-gobernadorcillos and *cabecillas de oficios,* or heads of the various occupational gremios, present and past. But in 1857 a group of Chinese petitioned the government that this method of choice did not really represent those with wealth and prestige in the community. The government responded by altering election regulations, substituting for the cabecillas de oficios payers of first- and second-class rates in the patente industrial. Ex-gobernadorcillos continued to be part of the electorate. But when there were none available, those who paid the first-class patente industrial tax would be substituted.[35]

Whether this petition and the government's action reflected any changes in wealth distribution or social organization within the community cannot be determined. As pointed out in Chapter 1, we do not know whether the occupational gremios had anything other than formal validity. It is probable that the 1857 petition represented primarily the reaction of those hit hardest by the new 1852 patente industrial tax.

34. Superior Decreto, Jan. 24, 1804, San Pedro, 2, 469.

35. *Guía de forasteros . . . 1847,* pp. 44–45; Superior Decreto, July 8, 1857 and July 15, 1857, Berriz, *Diccionario, 5,* 413; PNA, Chinos, elecciones, 37-2-2; Superior Decreto, May 14, 1861, Berriz, *Anuario 1888, 1,* 770.

Lith. par Bayot.   Imp. Lemercier à Paris

MÉTIS DE LA HAUTE CLASSE
en promenade.

Wealthy mestizos (probably Chinese mestizos) in mid-nineteenth-century dress. From Jean Mallat de Bassilan, *Les Philippines* (Paris, 1846).

METIS CHINOIS OU SANGLEY.

Chinese mestizos in mid-nineteenth-century dress. From Jean Mallat de Bassilan, *Les Philippines* (Paris, 1846).

MÉTIS ESPAGNOLS
en costume de promenade

Spanish mestizos in mid-nineteenth-century dress. From Jean Mallat de Bassilan, *Les Philippines* (Paris, 1846).

Lith par Bayot   Imp. Lemercier à Paris.

INDIENS TAGALES

pilant du riz.

Indios of the Tagalog region in mid-nineteenth-century dress. From Jean Mallat de Bassilan, *Les Philippines* (Paris, 1846).

Lith. par Bayot.   Imp. Lemercier a Paris

INDIENS PAMPANGOS

Indios of Pampanga province in mid-nineteenth-century dress. From Jean Mallat de Bassilan, *Les Philippines* (Paris, 1846).

The Chinese transportable kitchen. From J. A. Karuth, *Album der Philipinischen Inseln* (MS, Manila, 1858). (Original in the Ayala y Compañía Library, Manila. Photograph by courtesy of Don Fernando Zóbel de Ayala.)

A Chinese serving an open-air meal to some indios. From J. A. Karuth, *Album der Philipinischen Inseln* (MS, Manila, 1858). (Original in the Ayala y Compañía Library, Manila. Photograph by courtesy of Don Fernando Zóbel de Ayala.)

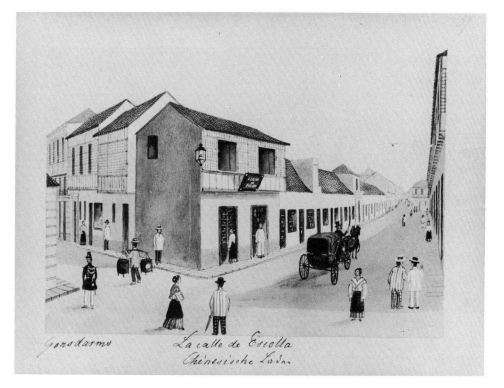

Escolta Street, Manila, about 1850. A street of Chinese shops. From J. A. Karuth, *Album der Philipinischen Inseln* (MS, Manila, 1858). (Original in the Ayala y Compañía Library. Photograph by courtesy of Don Fernando Zóbel de Ayala.)

門衙的造建所丹必甲人華爲僑華拉里岷代時牙班西

The Tribunal de Sangleyes, office of the Gobernadorcillo, Manila. From *Fei-lü-p'in Min-li-la Chung-hua Shang-hui san-shih chou-nien chi-nien k'an,* ed. Huang Hsiao-ts'ang (Manila, 1936).

Binondo Church, Manila. From *Fei-lü-p'in Min-li-la Chung-hua Shang-hui san-shih chou-nien chi-nien k'an,* ed. Huang Hsiao-ts'ang (Manila, 1936).

Forced to pay this tax, they sought some compensation in the form of possession of electoral rights.

The election law of 1861, with slight modifications, remained in force until 1887.[36] It provided for biennial elections of a gobernadorcillo, teniente primero (first lieutenant), *interventor* (comptroller), and *alguacil mayor* (chief constable). The elections were held as follows. On the appointed day, all ex-gobernadorcillos, industrial taxpayers of the first and second classes, and manufacturers of cigarettes and alcohol gathered in the Tribunal de Sangleyes in Binondo, under the supervision of the civil governor of Manila. Then, in a fashion similar to that used by the indios and mestizos in electing their officials, lots were drawn and an electorate of twelve chosen, the current gobernadorcillo being added to this as a thirteenth. Voting was by secret ballot, on which the electors were to write for each office the names of three favored candidates. For each office but gobernadorcillo, the person with the largest number of votes was considered automatically appointed. But for gobernadorcillo the practice followed that of the indios and mestizos. The person who received the largest vote and the runner-up were listed as first and second choices, and the incumbent gobernadorcillo as third choice. The list was then presented to the civil governor for his final choice.

Before choosing, he obtained from the parish priest and the Guardia Civil whatever information was available about the morality and wealth of the candidates. Chinese officials were supposed to be Catholics, but this regulation was not always observed. Financial considerations were at least as important as religion. Since the gobernadorcillo was ultimately responsible for the payment of Chinese taxes, it was important that he be wealthy. Also, since he must spend much of his time in his official capacity, he had to be sufficiently prosperous to be able to neglect his own businesses.

Although the civil governor could pass over the first and second choices and retain the incumbent if the new nominees appeared undesirable, in practice the first choice of the community was almost always approved. And although the government had a hand in the naming of the Chinese officials this was the extent of its intervention. There is no evidence that the government ever audited Chinese community records or otherwise intervened in the Gremio's activities once the election had been made.

The imposition of the contribución industrial, with its new system of tax categories, required some revision in the election laws. In 1887

36. PNA, Chinos, elecciones, 37-2-2.

it was ruled that the electorate was to include those Chinese who paid taxes according to the first five categories—from 400 pesos down to 60 pesos—besides the ex-gobernadorcillos and cigarette and alcohol manufacturers. The electorate that assembled for the 1887 election numbered 446,[37] in a Manila Chinese population of well over 40,000, an eloquent commentary on the oligarchic nature of Chinese community rule. The electorate was a small cabecilla elite; but it was probably as representative as the electorate had ever been.

During the 1880s there was criticism in Manila of the power of the Gremios de Chinos and the gobernadorcillo. It may be remembered that during the eighteenth century and the early nineteenth century the gobernadorcillo had been eclipsed by the cabecilla principal, the former office becoming honorary, while the cabecilla principal exercised the real power. But with the disappearance of the office of cabecilla principal in the 1830s the office of gobernadorcillo enjoyed a kind of renascence of power as well as prestige. By the 1880s it was a much-sought position, not only because of the financial perquisites attached to it, but because of the real power it embodied.[38] Critics of the Chinese argued that both the Gremio and the gobernadorcillo had too much power and were insufficiently subjected to state control and intervention. It was pointed out that the Gremio de Chinos, a "state within a state," had no basis in legislation; it had simply grown. So had the power of the gobernadorcillo. Indio and mestizo gobernadorcillos were in control of no more than a few thousand persons each. But the gobernadorcillo de chinos had under him tens of thousands in Manila, not to mention the tens of thousands in the provinces who were indirectly within his power.[39]

In response to these criticisms, the Spanish government in 1887 instituted a system of Chinese tenientes (lieutenants), who were to be appointed by the government, not elected by the Chinese community. There were twelve tenientes (popularly called by the Chinese "village elders": she-li lao-yeh) for the Manila area, and a teniente was to be appointed for each region in the archipelago where Chinese were numerous. They were to be responsible for keeping order among the Chinese assigned to them, collecting taxes, and keeping a record of all arrivals and departures in their jurisdictions. Of most importance, they were to

37. Ibid.; PNA, Gobernadorcillos, 49-13-7.
38. Superior Decreto, Dec. 20, 1849, San Pedro, 2, 479–84; Clark, *Labor Conditions*, p. 728; *Fei-lü-p'in shang-hui wu-shih chou-nien k'an*, p. chia 2.
39. *Los chinos en Filipinas*, pp. 20, 128; Feced, p. 79; *Gaceta de Manila* (Jan. 10, 1887); Letter of Fernando Sainz, O.P., Archivo de PP. Domínicos, T. 93, p. 6r.

be directly responsible not to the gobernadorcillo de chinos, but to the Spanish administration.[40]

This was obviously an attempt to cut into the power of the gobernadorcillo and at the same time reduce the Chinese community to fragments, each under a teniente responsible to the Spanish administration. It was not the first time such a program had been tried. As early as 1828 the government had attempted to organize the Chinese into barangayes like the indios and mestizos. Each barangay was to contain 50 to 100 Chinese, and to be under the charge of a cabeza de barangay, who would collect taxes, maintain order, and exercise surveillance over all movements of persons. He was to be responsible to the Spanish authorities, a procedure that would have had the same effect as that intended by the teniente system. But the Chinese who were to be appointed cabezas de barangay persistently refused to cooperate.[41]

The teniente program was more successful, at least formally. Tenientes were established. But as a practical measure, some degree of administrative subordination to the gobernadorcillo de chinos and the Gremio was necessary.[42] Over a long period of time, other conditions being constant, the institution of tenientes might have caused an erosion of the power of gobernadorcillo and Gremio. But in 1887 the end of Spanish rule in the Philippines was only a decade away.

Outside Manila, the Chinese of two provinces had enjoyed the privilege of electing their officials since at least the 1860s. By a decree of the Spanish administration in 1863 it was established that the Chinese of Cavite had the right to elect, on a biennial basis, a *teniente mayor* and four *alguaciles*. The electorate was composed of the twelve richest Chinese in the province plus the incumbent teniente mayor.

In Pampanga province, the three dictricts of San Fernando, Angeles, and Guagua likewise had electoral rights, each electing every two years a teniente mayor and two alguaciles. The elections were held in Bacolor, the capital of the province. As in Manila, twelve electors were chosen by lot, the thirteenth being the incumbent teniente mayor. The electorate included a mixture of high rate taxpayers and, after 1877, when the barangay system was applied to the Pampanga Chinese, cabezas de barangay.

The Chinese of Iloilo province obtained the right to elect a teniente mayor and five alguaciles in 1878. Thus, by the 1880s there were an

---

40. *Gaceta de Manila* (Jan. 10, 1887).

41. Real Órden, April 6, 1828, Berriz, *Anuario 1888*, 1, 780; *Los chinos en Filipinas*, pp. 42–43, 92–93.

42. For examples of gobernadorcillo–teniente relations, see PNA documents on "defraudación de la contribución industrial."

elected gobernadorcillo (with subordinate officials) in Manila and elected tenientes mayores in three other provinces.[43] But these offices, and for that matter, the Gremio de Chinos itself, were as much institutions for handling the dealings of the Chinese with the Spanish government as they were institutions for the benefit of the community. The gobernadorcillo and tenientes mayores presented petitions or executed the government's decrees. The alguaciles enforced the collection of taxes and the arrest of persons wanted by the Spanish government. But it is true that these officials were responsible for the settlement of matters internal to the community as well. Their functions thus involved both external relations and internal control.

Some institutions were of a purely internal nature. The most important of these was the Shan-chü Kung-so, a benevolent association founded in Manila in 1870 and known today as the Chinese Community. If the Gremio de Chinos became the major institution for handling community relations with other groups and the government, the Kung-so became the principal formal instrument for handling internal affairs. Its exact relationship to the Gremio de Chinos is uncertain. The contemporary Chinese community regards the two as one and the same. From documents now in the possession of the Kung-so[44] it is clear that the Kung-so was founded in 1870. But since it is evident from the Spanish documents that the Gremio antedates it, they cannot be the same. It is probable that the Gremio established the Kung-so as an organization for handling matters of internal concern to the community; or that the Kung-so was independently founded and the Gremio worked with it. That there must have been cooperation between the two is evident; the gobernadorcillo (capitán) was head of both.

There is a strong possibility that something similar to what happened in Semarang, Indonesia, occurred here. In nineteenth-century Semarang the Kong-koan, or Council of Chinese Officers, was responsible for establishing the Tjie Lam Tjay, which became an organization for supervising religious affairs, burying the destitute, and handling charitable matters of the community, while the Kong-koan remained the institution for handling community dealings with the government and with other groups.[45]

43. PNA, Chinos, elecciones, 37-2-2.

44. Liu Chi Tien, *Chung-Fei kuan-hsi shih* (A History of Sino-Philippine Relations) (Taipei, 1964), p. 559. On the history of the Shan-chü Kung-so see *Fei-lü-p'in Hua-ch'iao Shan-chü Kung-so ch'uang-pan Chung-hua Ch'ung-jen Tsung-I-yüan hsin yüan-yü lo-chien chi-nien k'an* (Chinese General Hospital. 65th Anniversary and Inauguration of the Newly Completed Buildings. Souvenir Program) (Manila, 1956), pp. 49 ff,, and "Fei-lü-p'in hua-ch'iao shih-lüeh," p. 7.

45. Donald E. Willmott, *The Chinese of Semarang* (Ithaca, 1960), p. 135.

In the Philippines the Shan-chü Kung-so, by the 1880s, administered the Manila Chinese cemetery and hospital, and, by 1899, the Anglo-Chinese School. The early history of the Chinese cemetery in Manila is obscure. As early as 1840 Mallat noted the existence of a Chinese cemetery at the La Loma site where it is located today. But its establishment apparently was more a case of necessity imposed by exclusion from Catholic cemeteries than an evidence of community concern. Just when the cemetery became a community project is not known. In the mid-1850s the gobernadorcillo and principales of the community petitioned the Spanish government for permission to improve the road leading to the cemetery. Although the community offered to finance the project, the government rejected the request because it involved the transfer of some land, which the Spanish were unwilling to allow.[46]

Community tradition has it that the cemetery really got its start when a certain Lim, campaigning for election as gobernadorcillo, promised to buy land for the cemetery if elected.[47] Once elected, he made good his promise, and he and his successors assumed jurisdiction over the land he had bought. The cemetery expanded in 1878 when Gobernadorcillo Mariano Fernando Yu Chingco bought a tract adjacent to the previous cemetery from the Provincial of the Dominican Order. The cost was 14,000 pesos, and another 33,980 pesos was spent erecting at the cemetery the Chong Hock Tong, a temple for commemorative purposes. Both cemetery and temple were now administered by the Kung-so. By 1880, then, the Chinese of Manila had a community cemetery, the major function of which was to bury the poor—those whose funds did not allow sending their bodies back to China.[48]

Another community resource was the Chinese hospital, the Ch'ung-jen I-yüan. The Chinese community dates this hospital only from 1891. But Spanish documents indicate that during the cholera epidemic of 1879 Antonio Yap Caong, who was then gobernadorcillo, collected 500,000 pesos and quickly set up a Chinese hospital in the La Loma region near the cemetery. This hospital was necessary both because of the number of casualties and because the Spanish government was attempting to keep the Chinese segregated from the Spanish population,

46. Mallat, 1, 174; Díaz Arenas, *Memorias históricas,* cuad. 10: "edificios públicos"; PNA, Tondo, 9-14-4.

47. Huang Hsiao-ts'ang, p. chia 122. This Lim is identified as a certain Lim Ong, who appears to have been a kind of early "culture hero" among the Philippine Chinese. See Lo, "China as a Seapower," p. 430.

48. Huang Hsiao-ts'ang, pp. chia 122–24; "Fei-lü-p'in hua-ch'iao shih-lüeh," pp. 7–8; biography of Mariano Fernando Yu Chingco in Huang Hsiao-ts'ang, p. chia 182. By the 1890s there were Chinese cemeteries in some other places; for instance, at Batangas, in the province of the same name. Sastrón, *Batangas,* p. 77.

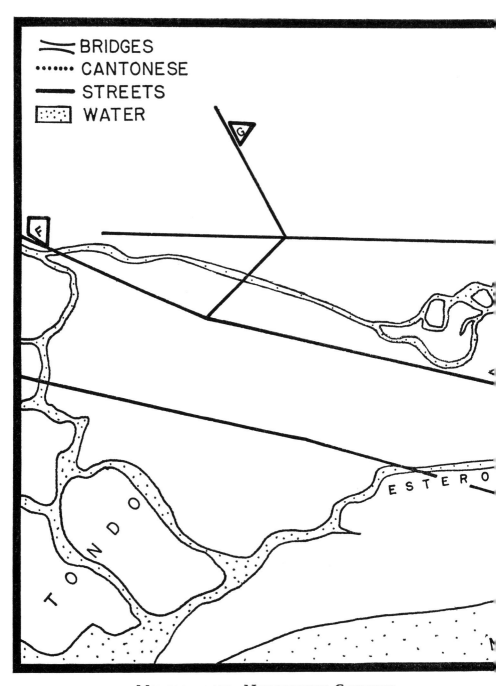

Manila in the Nineteenth Century

STREETS		LANDMARKS
1 Barcelona	12 Anloague	A Tribunal de Sang-
2 Madrid	13 Rosario	leyes
3 Asuncion	14 Nueva	B Puente de España
4 Elcano	15 San Vicente	C Plaza Santa Cruz
5 Santo Cristo	16 Dasmarinas	D Binondo Church

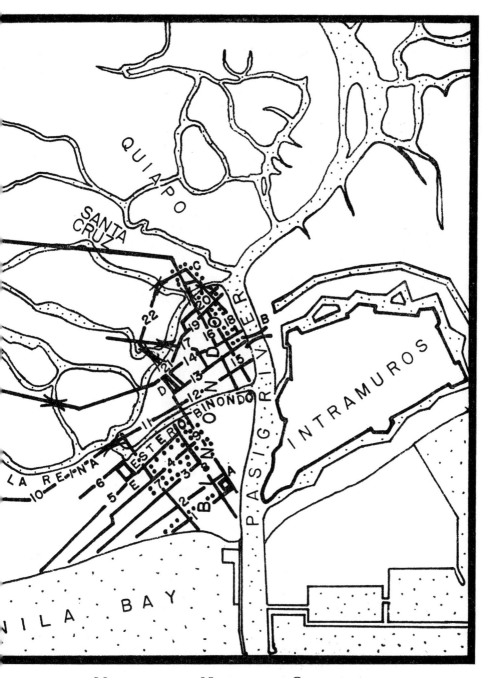

Manila in the Nineteenth Century

STREETS		LANDMARKS
6 Tabora	17 Norzagaray	E Divisoria Market
7 Lavezares	18 Escolta	F Chinese Cemetery
8 Jaboneros	19 San Jacinto	G Ch'ung-Jen Hospi-
9 San Fernando	20 David	tal
10 Lemery	21 Carballo	
11 Jolo	22 Lacoste	

and had closed the Hospital of San Juan de Dios to the Chinese, although normally they were admitted. Even had there been no epidemic there would have been a need for such a hospital. Besides being expensive, the treatment given at the Hospital of San Juan de Dios used Western medical methods, which were repugnant to many Chinese. There was need for a hospital that practiced Chinese medicine and offered charitable services to the poor. The Ch'ung-jen Hospital received an important boost in 1891, when Tan Quien-sien collected 30,000 pesos in the community and erected a hospital building at the La Loma site, south of the cemetery. Continuing support was provided at first by a tax on newly arriving Chinese immigrants; later, by monthly taxes on Chinese shops and a tax on Chinese returning to China. Either way, the administration fell to the Kung-so.[49]

Some mention should also be made of the Anglo-Chinese School (Chung-Hsi Hsüeh-hsiao), although it was established after 1898. During the last years of the nineteenth century, some of the wealthier Chinese sent their sons to China for higher education—some to receive traditional Confucian training, others to schools in Fukien that combined Western and Chinese learning.[50] There were no Chinese schools in the Philippines. But in 1899 the first Chinese consul-general, Ch'en Kang, son of Tan Quien-sien, who was using the old Tribunal de Sangleyes as his consulate, obtained the backing of some merchants and established a school in the consulate which subsequently became the Chung-Hsi Hsüeh-hsiao. At first, English language was the only Western subject offered.[51] In fact, the original intent of Ch'en Kang, himself a Confucian scholar of *chin-shih* rank, seems to have been to provide a combination of Confucian learning and practical commercial instruction aimed particularly at Chinese mestizos, who formed the majority of the first classes.[52]

Buddhist institutions also experienced some development during the last half of the nineteenth century. In 1881 the Fu Ch'üan temple was established in Zamboanga and eight years later two other temples opened in Manila.[53]

49. "Fei-lü-p'in hua-ch'iao shih-lüeh," p. 8; Huang Hsiao-ts'ang, p. chia 124; *Ch'ung-jen Tsung-I-yüan chi-nien k'an,* pp. 72, 111; PNA, Chinos, elecciones, 37-2-2.

50. *Los chinos en Filipinas,* p. 90; Huang Hsiao-ts'ang, pp. chia 163–64, 181.

51. IMH-AS, *ch'ing* 366, *fa* 161, Hsiao-lü-sung she-li ling-shih, Petition from Ch'en Kang, April 18, 1899, and same, July 30, 1899.

52. Biography of Ch'en Kang (Ch'en Tzu-yen) in *Nan-yang nien-chien* (Southeast Asia Yearbook) (Singapore, 1951), p. *kuei* 251; *Hsiao-lü-sung Hua-ch'iao Chung-Hsi Hsüeh-hsiao wu-shih chou-nien chi-nien k'an* ("Golden Jubilee. Anglo Chinese School, 1899–1949") (Manila, 1949), pp. 103, 287.

53. "Fei-lü-p'in hua-ch'iao shih-lüeh," p. 70; *China en Filipinas,* p. 135.

Newspapers, too, began to be published in Manila, although the first of them were short-lived. In 1888 a certain Yang Wei-hung, who was a kind of public relations man for Tan Quien-sien, founded a newspaper called the *Min Pu Hua Pao,* or simply the *Hua Pao.* Less than two years later (1890) he ceased publishing it under this name and put out a somewhat revised version called the *Min Pao,* which in turn collapsed after a short time due to financial difficulties. Two other newspapers that followed these first attempts, the *I Yu Hsin Pao* and the *Min I Pao,* founded in 1899 to promote the ideas of K'ang Yu-wei and Liang Ch'i-ch'ao, were also quite short-lived. This is not surprising, because the rate of literacy was not high in the Chinese community. It was said that most of the merchants could not write letters to relatives at home without the aid of their bookkeepers. The subject matter of these early newspapers appears to have been 50 per cent local and 50 per cent about events in China.[54]

Cultural Policies and Attitudes in Transition

The development of community institutions is indicative of the increasing tendency of the Chinese to think in communal terms and to orient themselves toward China. Simultaneously, the Spanish administration thought of them increasingly as an unassimilable minority, and, in fact, gave up most of its previous efforts to assimilate them.

Conversion to Catholicism had always been a major feature of Spain's program for assimilating the Chinese. In the Manila area a number of special institutions had been created for this purpose. Besides the mission settlements of Chinese in Binondo and Santa Cruz, a church had been erected for the non-Catholic Chinese in the Parián, and was serviced by the Dominicans. There was also the Dominican-operated Hospital of San Gabriel, located in Binondo, which cared for the medical needs of the Chinese, whether Catholics or not. It was said that over the years of its existence this hospital's treatment of Chinese patients resulted in 30,000 conversions to Catholicism. The San Gabriel Hospital was supported by the Chinese themselves, out of their "community chest" fund. But at the time of the general expulsion of Chinese in 1766 the hospital was closed and although for several years thereafter the Dominicans continued to treat the Chinese in private homes, supported by the "community chest" funds, the hospital was never re-

54. Biography of "Yang Hui-chi," Huang Hsiao-ts'ang, p. chia 191; Liu Chi Tien, *Hua-ch'iao,* p. 56; *Fei-lü-p'in yü hua-ch'iao shih-chi ta-kuan* ("Philippine Chinese Chronicle"), ed. Ch'en Hsiao-yü (2 vols. Manila, 1948), 2, *she* 3, 5; *Hua-ch'iao shih lun-chi* (Collected Essays on the History of the Overseas Chinese), ed. Kao Hsin (Taipei, 1963), pp. 109–11.

established. By the late nineteenth century Spanish agencies were providing no medical services specifically for the Chinese.[55]

When the Parián was destroyed in the early 1790s, the Parián Church was demolished with it and the parish removed to San Gabriel Church, near the old hospital in Binondo. But in 1843 it was ordered that the special Chinese parish be abolished, and the parish priest of Binondo (a Dominican) now assumed responsibility for all residents of Binondo, the Chinese included.[56]

We have already noted that when the Parián was destroyed its former residents were dispersed in Binondo and Santa Cruz, breaking down the isolation from non-Catholics that these two mission settlements were supposed to maintain. Binondo and Santa Cruz thus became cosmopolitan parishes. Moreover, in Binondo the Gremio de Chinos de Binondo, the religious–political organization founded by the Binondo Chinese Catholics in the seventeenth century, was now eclipsed in practical importance by the rising new Gremio de Chinos, the sociopolitical body that represented all the Chinese of the Manila area, Catholic and non-Catholic.

There is something ironic in the decline of the early Gremio de Chinos de Binondo and the rise of the new Gremio de Chinos, located in Binondo. The organization the Spaniards had hoped would provide loyal Catholic subjects declined, to be replaced by an organization that made demands for a Chinese consulate. Binondo, developed as a Chinese mission colony, became instead the center of what the Spaniards regarded as an unassimilable national minority.

We have noted that in the wake of the Chinese uprising of 1762 in which so many Catholics were involved the Spaniards lost confidence in the nominal acceptance of Catholicism by the Chinese as a basis for insuring Chinese loyalty. Not only were the special privileges given to Catholics revoked, but when immigration was allowed again classification was not by religion but by "transient" and "resident." During the nineteenth century, as economic considerations began to outweigh all others, the religion of the Chinese simply became unimportant and irrelevant. When the Spanish administration lowered the bars to Chinese settlement in the provinces it did so without qualifications as to religion. An 1839 decree on the subject of agricultural colonization did not insist that Chinese colonists be Catholics, but did lay upon hacen-

55. Juan Ferrando, O.P. and Joaquín Fonseca, O.P., *Historia de los PP. Domínicos en las Islas Filipinas.* . . . (6 vols. Madrid, 1870–72), 6, 152, 153 n., 154–58; Buzeta, 2, 259; Díaz Arenas, *Memorias históricas,* cuad. 10: "edificios públicos"; José T. Revilla, "Historical Notes on the Binondo Chinese Church," in *Program of the Solemn Festivities in Honor of Our Lady of the Most Holy Rosary.* . . . (Manila, 1958).
56. Ibid.

deros who used Chinese labor the obligation of seeing that those who were Catholics attended Mass and that those who were not received instruction and baptism.[57] But the agricultural legislation of 1850 and after says nothing about obligations of this kind. The old idea of grants of land to Catholic Chinese simply disappeared. Land grants were generally not available to Chinese at all, although the Chinese were not forbidden to acquire land. Freedom of residence was given to all Chinese, Catholic or not. And taxation was based upon income, not religious status. The practical rewards or benefits of formal acceptance of Catholicism were no longer available as such.

Finally, the practice of hair-cutting, once obligatory for all Chinese upon baptism, passed out of use. Dating from the 1580s, this custom had provoked some resistance, especially after the Manchu conquerors of China made possession of the queue mandatory for all Chinese. Cutting off the queues, it had been argued, prevented Catholic Chinese from returning to China where they might be useful in spreading the Faith. The argument in favor of the practice held that Catholic Chinese in the Philippines should be recognizable as such on sight, by the combination of Western-style haircuts and Chinese dress. Strict regulations were issued prohibiting Catholic Chinese from dressing like the indios and mestizos, and as late as 1804 one finds decrees that denounce the Catholic Chinese practice of disappearing into Philippine society by changing to native Philippine dress.[58] But in the late nineteenth century there were no decrees of this kind. Nor were there admonitions to Catholics to cut off the queue. Catholics, like non-Catholics, now dressed as Chinese in every way, or as indios or mestizos if they so wished. The matter had become unimportant.

From the Chinese point of view, too, Catholicism lost some of its importance. There was less reason than before to affiliate with it. Some of the practical advantages, such as reduced taxes, land grants, and freedom of residence, were no longer conferred on the basis of religious affiliation.

One of the most important motives for requesting baptism had always been the acquisition of a baptismal sponsor, who could be counted upon as a creditor, bondsman, and protector. This consideration continued to carry weight during the nineteenth century. Prominent Spaniards often acted as sponsors or godparents (*padrinos*), frequently giving their names to the Chinese. The Chinese usually retained their own names as well, as, for example, Mariano Velasco Chua Chengco. But when the Chinese part of the name was dropped, confusion of

---

57. Superior Decreto, Aug. 31, 1839, San Pedro, 2, 475.
58. Superior Decreto, Jan. 24, 1804, San Pedro, 2, 470.

Chinese and Spaniard often resulted so that it was then necessary to speak of "El Chino Mariano Velasco."

Godparentage (padrinazgo) of this kind was apparently a profitable arrangement for the godparent, who acquired a protégé who might have moneymaking talents. From the Chinese side, there was, besides the aforementioned advantages, the fact that this kind of patron–protégé relationship fitted well into Chinese cultural patterns. A Spanish writer of the 1880s denounced "these incomprehensible padrinazgos." [59] There was nothing incomprehensible about them; they fitted the interests and viewpoints of both sides.

But there is no reason to subscribe to the view of that time that "all the wealthiest Chinese are Christians." [60] It is clear from the census records of the 1890s that this was far from being the case. A survey of the three highest classifications of taxpayers shows that in Manila only 25 per cent of those in the highest income tax classes were Catholics, in Iloilo and Cagayan, 60 per cent, and in Cebu, 50 per cent.[61]

Clearly, it was possible to be highly successful, particularly in Manila, without becoming a Catholic. From a business point of view, there was probably less advantage to becoming a Catholic than there had been before. A Spanish padrino was helpful. But as a source of credit the Spaniard was now of less importance than the foreign merchant, who was ordinarily not a Catholic. Moreover, the power of some Chinese cabecillas was now sufficient to provide needed protection for those they might select as protégés.[62]

In yet another way, the importance of Catholicism was lessened. The presence of non-Spanish, non-Catholic foreigners in the Philippines and news about foreigners in China resulted in a growing awareness by the Philippine Chinese that Spain lagged behind other nations, both militarily and technologically. If one seriously wished to adopt a Western religion, as a source of power, the religion of the Spaniard was hardly the one, especially since the Spanish lack of strength might soon lose Spain the Philippines to some other master.[63]

But although the Spanish showed declining interest in converting the

59. *China en Filipinas*, p. 159. See also Comenge, p. 38.

60. "The Chinese in the Philippines," p. 155.

61. PNA, Padrones de chinos, Manila, Iloilo, Cebú (1894), Cagayan (1893).

62. Apropos the subject of cabecilla protection, an interesting phenomenon of the late nineteenth century was the appearance of several Chinese who assumed the uncommon Spanish surname of Palanca. It is almost certain that this was done in emula-tion of Tan Quien-sien (Carlos Palanca). It may have been mere copying, or a choice for luck. But it is not impossible that Tan Quien-sien and other Catholic Chinese acted as padrinos for newer arrivals, just as Spaniards had done for them.

63. See Felipe Canga-Argüelles, "Inmigración española al sur de Filipinas," *Boletín de la Sociedad Geográfica de Madrid*, 24 (1888), 205.

Chinese and the Chinese were less interested in Catholicism, the impact of Spanish Philippine Catholicism on the religious behavior of the Philippine Chinese—both Catholics and non-Catholics—was continuous throughout this period.

Over the years a marked syncretism in religious ceremonies and everyday religious behavior had developed among the Philippine Chinese. The Catholic Chinese of the Gremio de Chinos de Binondo celebrated the Feast of Our Lady of the Rosary (La Naval) with a procession through Binondo, their principalia leading the way, carrying tapers in the proper style for such a religious procession, but with the accompaniment of Chinese musicians and fireworks. Both Catholics and non-Catholics among the Chinese observed the Feast of St. Nicholas. The usual explanation of this is that it dates from the time when a certain Chinese, about to be attacked by a crocodile, called upon St. Nicholas for help. The crocodile was turned into stone and the Chinese was saved. Thereafter, the Chinese community venerated St. Nicholas as a special protector. For his festive day the Chinese of Manila, at great expense, built river barges in the shape of pagodas. On the saint's day the barges were towed up the Pasig River to a point near his shrine. Once the shrine had been visited, the barges were illuminated for the return down the river at night. Meanwhile, the Chinese community celebrated with feasting, visiting, and frequently with the presentation of performances in the Chinese theaters.

Among the cults brought over from China, the most popular were those of T'u-ti kung and Kuan Ti, regarded as gods of prosperity, Kuan Yin, and Ma-tsu. Here, too, there was syncretism. Kuan Ti was identified with "Santiago" and regarded as a protector of the Chinese. Kuan Yin and Ma-tsu, feminine deities, were frequently associated with the Virgin, in one or another of her manifestations. A very popular cult was that identifying the Virgin of Antipolo, Nuestra Señora de Buen Viaje y de la Paz, a protector of travelers to whom many miracles have been attributed, with Ma-tsu, the patroness and protector of those who go to sea, venerated by the people of southeastern China.[64]

One exclusively Chinese deity was Pun Tao Kong, a kind of culture hero who was venerated by the Teochiu and Hakka Chinese of Thailand, although with a completely different explanation of his significance than that given in the Philippines. In the Philippines Pun Tao Kong was and is believed to have been a crew member on one of the voyages of Cheng Ho to Southeast Asia. He went ashore at Jolo, where he met with mis-

---

64. Comenge, p. 332; Buzeta, 2, 244–46; Mallat, 2, 140; "The Chinese in the Philippines," pp. 155–56; PNA, Gremios, 16-5-5; Weightman, pp. 368–70; Amyot, pp. 97–98. On the Chinese theater in the Philippines see Barrantes, pp. 43, 44 n.

fortune, died, and was buried. His grave has become a kind of place of miracles. It is not known when the veneration of Pun Tao Kong began in the Philippines. The tradition has it that two Chinese merchants built a commemorative shrine for him about 1790. It is also said that Pun Tao Kong was the founder of the Chinese community of Jolo and subsequently its protector; that when Spanish naval forces shelled the town of Jolo in 1872 the preservation of the Chinese quarter was due to Pun Tao Kong's protection. Another possible reason why the quarter was spared was that some Chinese merchants were provisioning Spanish forces in their campaigns against the Moros that year.[65]

Another publicly manifested Chinese practice was the celebration of the "white-cock oath," which was given legal status by the Spanish government. This practice, which seems to be related to secret society ritual and is probably Popular Taoist in origin, was institutionalized by the Spanish administration as the only legal way for a non-Catholic Chinese to put himself under oath before testimony. A white cock was killed before the Chinese, who was then made to swear that the blood of the cock symbolized the shedding of the blood of his kinsmen if he should fail to tell the truth.[66]

The Growing Power of Gobernadorcillo and Gremio

Although several aspects of Spain's original plans to control Chinese immigration had fallen into disuse, the Spanish government retained a lively interest in the administration and particularly the taxation of the Chinese. Taxation was always the strong point of the government in its relations with the Chinese. But in administrative powers the government's control declined as the power of the gobernadorcillo and the Gremio de Chinos increased.

In the last few decades prior to 1850 there had been no institution strong enough to act effectively as spokesman for the Chinese community in its relations with the government or with other groups. The Gremio de Chinos was headed by a council composed of heads of occupational gremios and a virtually powerless gobernadorcillo. The electors of the 1830s and 1840s had difficulty finding anyone who would consent to hold office,[67] but shortly thereafter both gobernadorcillo and Gremio began to increase their power.

65. Huang Hsiao-ts'ang, pp. chia 200–01; Montero, *Historia*, 3, 606, 616 n.; Comenge, p. 118 n.; Weightman, pp. 369–70; Liu Chi Tien, *Fei-lü-p'in*, pp. 10–12. On Pun Tao Kong in Thailand see Skinner, *Chinese Society in Thailand*, pp. 138–39.
66. Buzeta, *1*, 110; Feced, p. 79.
67. MacMicking, pp. 40–41. "Ill health" was the most common excuse for "inability" to serve. PNA, Chinos, elecciones, 37-2-2 (elections of 1842, 1844, 1847, 1848).

We have already noted the transference to the gobernadorcillo of duties and responsibilities formerly incumbent upon the Warden of the Alcaicería de San Fernando. Besides supervising the housing of new-comers and transients, the Warden of the Alcaicería had the task of boarding arriving vessels with a treasury official, verifying the number of immigrants and the payment of their taxes, and collecting a fee for his services. With the end of the Alcaicería, these duties and fees were transferred from a Spanish to a Chinese official, the gobernadorcillo, with the Tribunal de Sangleyes taking the place of the Alcaicería as a place of residence.[68]

The Tribunal was also, as its name implies, a court of justice. The gobernadorcillo had always had jurisdiction in small claims cases where only Chinese were involved. Besides, like indio and mestizo gobernadorcillos, he had the responsibility of inaugurating fact-finding proceedings in criminal cases involving his community. He continued to discharge these responsibilities, with the advice and assistance of a council of eight principales chosen from among the wealthy and prominent members of the community. At some time during the 1870s and 1880s the gobernadorcillo also acquired from the government recognition of his right to take some part in all cases involving Chinese. In practice this meant that Chinese prisoners would be turned over to the gobernadorcillo first before being put on trial.[69]

Publications of the Manila Chinese community in recent years have claimed that the gobernadorcillos during the Spanish period were autocrats who held the power of life and death. But it appears that the council of principales assisted the gobernadorcillo in his judicial decisions.[70] And while there might not have been a formalized means of appealing his decisions, the fact that he was elected to office meant that he was probably limited to some extent by the opinions of the electorate.

Tax collection again became a function of the office of gobernadorcillo. During the eighteenth century and the first years of the nineteenth century, the cabecilla principal had assumed this responsibility, and for a time thereafter collection had been done by contractors. But from the

68. PNA, Tribunal de sangleyes, 48-8-18; Superior Decreto, Aug. 31, 1839, and Superior Decreto, Dec. 20, 1849, San Pedro, 2, 476, 479–84; Huang Hsiao-ts'ang, p. chia 3; Comenge, pp. 30–33.

69. Gobernadorcillo to gov.-gen., Sept. 1, 1881, and Jan. 31, 1882, PNA, Chinos, 37-12-6; Case of Lorenzo Tieng Chingco, Jan. 1885, PNA, Deportados, 5-5-16; Buzeta, 1, 106–07; Cheng Kuan-ying, Ch'en Ch'ien-shan [Tan Quien-sien] (Taipei, 1954), p. 12. This last book is a slightly expanded version of the author's "Ch'en Ch'ien-shan" in Hua-ch'iao ming-jen ch'uan (Biographies of Famous Overseas Chinese), ed. Chu Hsiu-hsia (Taipei, 1955), pp. 68–73.

70. Fei-lü-p'in shang-hui wu-shih chou-nien k'an, p. chia 2; Huang Hsiao-ts'ang, p. chia 3. See also PNA references in note 69.

1830s on the obligation fell upon the gobernadorcillo. It was more than an obligation; the perquisites attached to tax collecting were one of the most attractive features of the office of gobernadorcillo de chinos. After 1877, the barangay system, which had been bought off by the Manila Chinese, was imposed upon the Chinese in several other parts of the Islands. Through the Chinese cabezas de barangay in these areas the taxes were channeled to the gobernadorcillo in Manila and from him to the government.[71]

Tax collection was not the only connection between the gobernadorcillo and the Chinese in the provinces. Instances of property damage, anti-Chinese demonstrations, or maltreatment by officials were protested at the local level by local Chinese officials; but they were also reported to the gobernadorcillo in Manila.[72] Besides his other functions the gobernadorcillo controlled the Kung-so, assuming charge of the benevolent activities of the Manila community as well as whatever other matters concerned the Kung-so.

As the gobernadorcillo's powers and duties increased, so did those of the Gremio de Chinos. The change in the nature of the electorate, from occupational heads to highest taxpayers, may have had some bearing on the Gremio's increase in power but we cannot be certain. The Gremio had no specifically designated powers. The gobernadorcillo and his subordinates, the tenientes and alguaciles, had certain specified powers based upon law and custom, but the position of the Gremio de Chinos was anomalous. Normally, a gremio of its kind was a chartered municipal corporation. But the Gremio de Chinos was supramunicipal, and had simply grown into being as a kind of convenience, without any charter or formalized legal status. The government considered the gobernadorcillo its agent and the spokesman of the Chinese community. But in the 1880s the Gremio principales sought recognition of the Gremio (which included the gobernadorcillo) as the sole spokesman of the interests of the Chinese community.

The occasion of the Gremio's action was a petition regarding the handling of Chinese tax debtors. The large influx of coolie immigration in the late 1870s left a legacy of unemployed or marginally employed Chinese unable to pay their taxes. The government had tried various methods of dealing with debtors, principally by putting them

71. PNA, Cabezas de barangay, chinos, 49-1-10; Chinos, elecciones, 37-2-2; Superior Decreto, Jan. 8, 1887, Gaceta de Manila (Jan. 10, 1887).

72. PNA, Reales Órdenes, caja 160, núm. 156; AMAE, Filipinas, 1890. Supuestos atropellos. Chinese chargé to Estado, Dec. 23, 1890; China, 1889. Reclamación del gobierno chino. Estado to Ultramar, Oct. 17, 1889, and Ultramar to Estado, June 27, 1891.

to work on public projects in the Manila area or by sending them to the Marianas Islands as agricultural laborers. But neither method worked well. Wages were so low that the Chinese laborer could not earn enough to pay off his tax debt (and the fine that was added to it) except over a long period of time. Besides, there were not enough public works projects to take care of all the debtors, who were left languishing in the city jail at the expense of the government.

The Gremio stepped in with a petition in 1881, asking that penalties be waived and the Gremio allowed to pay all outstanding tax debts up to the end of the year. After that time, tax debtors, instead of being put to work, should be turned over to the Gremio for thirty days. If at the end of that period no way could be found to pay the money owed, the debtors should be deported to China at the Gremio's expense. The Gremio was also prepared to assume responsibility for surveillance of Chinese taxation, to see to it that there were no debtors. In this context, the Gremio now requested that its *junta de principales* be made the sole agent of the Spanish government in dealing with the Chinese community.[73]

This request, if granted, would have extended the fairly wide powers given the gobernadorcillo to the junta de principales (which included the gobernadorcillo), thus legalizing the Gremio on the same status as the gobernadorcillo. Instead of working through a single agent, the government would have to deal with a council. Moreover it would have recognized the Gremio's authority over all the Chinese in the Philippines, not just those in Manila—a recognition even the gobernadorcillo had not been given.

In reply to the petition the government acknowledged that current methods of dealing with debtors were harsh and apt to cause bitter feelings, particularly at a time when China was entering the family of nations and establishing consulates abroad. Under these circumstances, the Gremio was to be permitted temporarily to take care of tax debtors as requested. But its petition for recognition of its general authority over all Chinese was denied, and the power of the gobernadorcillo alone, under existing laws, was reaffirmed.[74]

Again in 1886 the Gremio offered to continue paying tax debts and financing the deportation of the insolvent. But again the government's acceptance was on a temporary basis only. And the Weyler–Becerra

73. Gobernadorcillo and principales to gov.-gen., Aug. 3, 1881, and Sept. 1, 1881; Opinions of Civil Governor and Treasury Intendency, 1881–82, all in PNA, Chinos, 37-12-6.

74. Opinion of Treasury Intendency, 1882, in ibid.; Superior Decreto, Jan. 14, 1882, Berriz, *Diccionario*, 9, 147–49.

Reglamento, put into effect in 1890, provided for heavy surcharges on the cédulas de capitación which the Chinese had to purchase, part of which went to build a fund for deportation, thus circumventing the Gremio's attempt to obtain control over tax matters.[75] From the Gremio's point of view insolvent tax debtors were not the only persons who should be deported. Drunkards, vagrants, and other undesirables were recommended by the Gremio for deportation, beginning in 1885.[76]

Of more importance, it was the Gremio, together with the gobernadorcillo, that filed protests against the anti-Chinese acts of the 1880s and 1890s and petitioned the Spanish administration to allow a Chinese consulate to be established in the Philippines.[77]

It was through the efforts of the Gremio that Chinese industriales of the first four tax categories finally achieved the same freedom to travel that non-Chinese had. When the cédulas personales appeared in 1884, Chinese who paid taxes over 100 pesos were obliged to purchase them. In a test case, Paulino Uy Pangco, a prominent Manila Chinese, contended that since the cédulas personales were used by non-Chinese as passports to travel at will through the provinces, a Chinese who had to purchase a cédula ought to have the same right, instead of having to acquire a special (and temporary) Chinese passport. Uy Pangco's claims were denied but the Gremio de Chinos pursued the question and in 1891 the government reversed itself, ruling that the Chinese cédulas de capitación were valid passports for Chinese of the first four tax classes (100 pesos and up), who could now travel about in complete freedom. Although this ruling affected only the first four classes, it provided for some improvement in the condition of the Chinese.[78]

In the same vein, the Gremio petitioned that Chinese who were subject to purchase of the cédulas personales should be exempt from paying the 3 peso falla. Finally, in 1892, the home government in Spain ruled that the surcharges on the cédulas de capitación were so large that to add the falla was excessive and inequitable. Therefore, the first four tax classes were exempted from the falla and were reimbursed their falla payments of the past two years.[79]

75. Superior Decreto, July 21, 1886, Berriz, *Diccionario*, 9, 149–50; Superior Decreto, Feb. 1, 1889, and Aug. 16, 1889, Berriz, *Anuario 1889*, pp. 330–31, 345; *Chinos. Sus reglamentos*, pp. 18, 29.

76. PNA, Deportados, 5-5-16.

77. SCJC, ch. 4, p. 21b. Archivo de PP. Domínicos, T. 665 (Libro de memorias), p. 111r.

78. Superior Decreto, April 6, 1891, *Chinos. Sus reglamentos*, p 78; "Reglamento de cédulas personales," July 15, 1884, Berriz, *Diccionario*, 12, 207, 219; Superior Decreto, July 5, 1888, Berriz, *Anuario 1888*, 2, 717.

79. Real Órden, Jan. 12, 1892, Berriz, *Anuario 1892*, pp. 158–60.

The petitions of the Gremio just described involved matters of immediate concern either to groups in the community or to the community as a whole. The Gremio and the gobernadorcillo were also prepared in the 1890s to support the complaints of individuals. In 1891 a series of government inspections of Manila's Chinese shops took place, covering particularly the stalls in the Divisoria Market that were rented by Chinese. Tax fraud charges were rampant. But the gobernadorcillo and Gremio supported the appeals through the Spanish courts, hiring Spanish lawyers to represent the Chinese merchants.[80]

Some of the appeals were successful; others were not. Whatever the outcome, it is of some importance to note that the gobernadorcillo and Gremio supported cases having only an indirect bearing upon the welfare of the community as a whole. It was nothing new for a gobernadorcillo to protest legislation or action he considered inimical to the interests of the community. But the support of individual claimants—as a consulate would do—does seem to have been without precedent when it occurred in the 1890s.

Tan Quien-sien and Hou A-p'ao: The Types of Leadership

The activities of the Gremio and gobernadorcillo probably softened the impact of Spanish legislation upon the Chinese community. Whatever success was achieved in this, as well as in the attempt to awaken China's interest in the plight of the Philippine Chinese, must be credited in part to the leadership of the Manila Chinese community. We have only fragmentary information about most of the leaders of the Manila community, but we do know more than a little about the man generally conceded to be the most powerful Chinese in the Philippines during this period.

In the annals of hua-ch'iao hagiography, few names are as luminous as that of Tan Quien-sien. Born of a poor family in T'ung-an hsien in 1844, he migrated to the Philippines about 1856. A kinsman started him in the textile business, and through hard work and good personal connections he prospered. When he became a Catholic his baptismal sponsor was Colonel Carlos Palanca y Gutierrez, who achieved fame as a leader of the Spanish forces in the Franco–Spanish intervention of 1858–62 in Cochin China. Tan Quien-sien assumed the name of his padrino, becoming Carlos Palanca Tan Quien-sien. Since he was usually

---

80. PNA, Defraudaciones de la contribución industrial, 5-12-13. For another instance of Gremio support of individual claims see AMAE, 1897. Insurrección. en Filipinas. Yncidente protección. Corregimiento de Manila to Gobierno Civil, Dec. 9, 1886.

spoken of by his more familiar Chinese name, Chuey-liong, the most common form of his name was Don Carlos Palanca Tan Chuey-liong, or Tan Chueco, as an abbreviation.

By the 1870s he was already a powerful man in the community. From 1875–77 he was gobernadorcillo, and again later he held this office. He also served as temporary or interim gobernadorcillo in 1885 and 1889. When not in office he moved behind the scenes powerfully, tending to dominate the community whoever might be in office.

His business interests expanded to include, among others, general importing, sugar exporting, coolie brokerage, monopoly tax contracting, and rice importing. There were few businesses in which he did not have some interest—through investments, if not actual participation. When American troops came to the Philippines in 1898, he billeted them in his godowns while he furnished coolies to build barracks. No one knew what he was worth financially but in 1894 he was taxed on the basis of an estimated year's income of 20,000 pesos.

Besides his terms as gobernadorcillo, he was active in community affairs in a variety of ways. He was one of the organizers of the Shan-chü Kung-so in 1870. When the Chong Hock Tong temple was erected in the cemetery, he was a member of the administrative board. He collected funds for the hospital and provided a new building in 1891. And he played a major role in the community's attempt to obtain a Chinese consulate during the 1880s and 1890s. Again, when the United States assumed control of the Philippines in 1898, it was Tan Quien-sien who urged the Ch'ing government to negotiate with the United States for a Chinese consulate in Manila. When that consulate was established in 1899, the Ch'ing government made his son the first consul, and rewarded Tan Quien-sien for his efforts by granting him the title of *Kuang-lu Ta-fu*.

Certain traditions have clustered about his name. It is said that he abolished vice in the Chinese community, that he put a stop to police extortions of the Chinese, obtained an abolition of the death penalty for crimes committed by Chinese, and, through his personal connections in high circles in Spain, kept Spanish legislation from being harder on the Chinese than it was. He was famous as an arbitrator of disputes and a philanthropist whose gifts were not limited to the Chinese community. His was the classic hua-ch'iao tale of "rags to riches"—followed by a life of community service and philanthropy.

When the Philippine Revolution broke out he did not commit himself to either side. When the Spanish government imprisoned a number of mestizos, charging them with conspiracy, Tan Quien-sien argued in behalf of some of them and helped secure their release. Otherwise his attitude toward Chinese mestizos was one of contempt, and he prevented the filipinization of his own son by sending him to school in China where he became a Confucian scholar. When the son was appointed consul there was an interim of a few months before he could get to Manila, during which time Tan Quien-sien served as acting Chinese consul.

He died in 1901, and some years later a statue of him was erected in the Chinese cemetery. There is no question that he is a kind of "culture hero" to the modern Chinese community.

The Spanish and Filipino reaction to Tan Quien-sien was mixed. For his services to the crown as gobernadorcillo the Spanish government bestowed upon him the Medal of Civil Merit and the Grand Cross of Isabel the Catholic. But the popular Spanish and Filipino reaction to him was that he was a master corrupter, one who was willing to go to any lengths to get what he wanted, and very ambitious to be Chinese consul. The character of Chinaman Quiroga in Rizal's El Filibusterismo is probably modeled upon him. Retana believed that the model for Chinaman Quiroga was Mariano Velasco Chua Chengco, but José Alejandrino, a friend of Rizal, later wrote that Carlos Palanca was the one. In view of the references to Chinaman Quiroga's desire to be consul, it appears that Alejandrino was right. Alejandrino also claimed that when Aguinaldo was setting up his revolutionary government, Carlos Palanca approached him about the possibility of an opium monopoly.[81] Whatever the pros and cons about this controversial character, it is evident that he was a powerful and usually effective force in the Chinese community during the late nineteenth century.

A leader of a different sort was Hou A-p'ao, known to the Filipinos he aided as José Ignacio Paua (or Pawa). The stories about him are so confusing it is difficult to sort out a credible series of facts. He was born near Amoy about 1856. Apparently he was active in secret society affairs in his youth and was regarded by some as a troublesome person who must be gotten rid of. Rather than resist his powerful opponents

81. "Fei-lü-p'in hua-ch'iao shih-lüeh," p. 5; Testimonies of Wm. Daland, Carlos Palanca [Tan Quien-sien], and O. F. Williams, Report of Philippine Commission, 2, 164, 219–25, 252; Feced, p. 79; Espasa-Calpe, ed., Enciclopedia universal ilustrada europeo-americana (72 vols. Barcelona, 1908?–30), 40, 89; Cheng, pp. 3–24; José Alejandrino, The Price of Freedom (Manila, 1949), pp. 227–28; Wen Hsiung-fei, Nan-yang hua-ch'iao t'ung-shih (General History of the Overseas Chinese in Southeast Asia) (3 vols. Shanghai, 1929), 3, 257–59; Huang Hsiao-ts'ang, pp. chia 179–81; PNA, Padrones de chinos, Manila (1894); Foreman, p. 127. The son was known in Manila as Ignacio Palanca Tan Chueco. AMAE, Filipinas. Sobre la creación de consulados chinos, 1887. Cólogan to Estado, July 28, 1898.

he took a ship to Manila, where he settled in Tondo and became a blacksmith. In the Philippines he maintained his secret society associations, and became a leader of the local branch of the Triad Society (*T'ien Ti Hui*).

When the Philippine Revolution broke out in 1896, the activities of the T'ien Ti Hui came into the open for the first time. Hou A-p'ao offered the services of himself and 3,000 supporters to General Emilio Aguinaldo, leader of the revolutionaries. It is not known whether Chinese troops were used during the Revolution. But Hou A-p'ao became a leader of Filipino troops, was promoted rapidly, and ultimately achieved the rank of general. He also set up a foundry in Cavite, where he melted down scrap metal in order to provide weapons for the revolutionaries.

When the Philippine Revolution was temporarily halted by the Peace of Biak-na-Bato in 1897, Hou A-p'ao retired with General Aguinaldo to Hong Kong. When the Revolution resumed, as a struggle against the new American forces in the Philippines, Hou A-p'ao returned to the Philippines, cut off his queue, and rejoined the Revolution. But his achievements during 1899 were more in the fiscal than the military realm. In Manila, in Bulacan, and especially in the Bicol region, he collected money for the Revolution—particularly from Chinese, but from non-Chinese as well. Presumably his secret society connections were of some assistance here. In any event, he collected 386,000 pesos in the Bicol region alone. But the Revolution was doomed to defeat, and Hou A-p'ao retired from action in 1900. He had married a Filipina of Albay province and he settled there, becoming active in local politics but otherwise living the life of a retired general until his death in 1922.[82]

Hou A-p'ao's commitment to the Philippine Revolution was unusual for a member of the Chinese community. As a general rule, the Chinese seem to have refrained from overt commitment to either side. Their method was simply to wait and be prepared to do business with whoever might be victorious.

With the decline of Spanish power it became evident that a transfer of sovereignty was inevitable. The future of the Chinese community, as a community, was unclear. So were the futures of Chinese individuals.

82. Liu Chi Tien, *Hua-ch'iao,* p. 57; Wen Hsiung-fei, *3,* 256; Edwin Wildman, *Aguinaldo, A Narrative of Filipino Ambitions* (Boston, 1901), pp. 105–06; Gregorio Zaide, "Chinese General in the Philippine Revolution," *Fookien Times Yearbook, 1955* (Manila, 1955), pp. 155–60; Juan F. Villasanta, "General Aguinaldo Recalls General Paua," ibid., *1956* (Manila, 1956), pp. 145, 152; *Fei-lü-p'in yü hua-ch'iao shih-chi ta-kuan, 2, she* 21. A picture of Hou A-p'ao in Western-style clothing is found in Sun Yat-sen's revolutionary journal *Min Pao,* No. 9 (December. 1, 1906) (Photolithographic ed. 4 vols. Peking, 1957).

Tan Quien-sien, the Gremio principales, and the Shan-chü Kung-so negotiated for a Chinese consulate. Most of the Chinese simply waited and suffered the damages of the anti-Chinese campaign of the 1880s and the recklessness of the revolutionaries. Hou A-p'ao sought an individual solution—a radical solution, consistent with his secret society background—by becoming not a Chinese leader but a Filipino leader.

The Problem of Community Consciousness

Reference has been made in the preceding pages to the development of community consciousness among the Philippine Chinese. Let us examine the problem again here.

One important factor was simply the homogeneity of the community. In this the Philippine Chinese were quite unlike most overseas Chinese communities, where dialect group feuds had to be overcome before some semblance of unity could be achieved. In the Philippines, on the contrary, the Cantonese were not significantly numerous. Intracommunity struggles were likely to be on a personal rivalry basis, rather than a dialect group basis.[83]

A second consideration was the fact that the decline of Spain's power in the Philippines left the Chinese on their own. Someone else would soon assume Spain's place, perhaps the anti-Chinese Filipino nationalists. The Chinese were not afraid that the community would be decimated by a massacre, but decimation could as easily be effected by expulsion and exclusion, and the economic position won since 1850 could be lost by a reversal of government policy. Moreover, at the leadership level in the Chinese community it must have been evident that anyone who based his future on the power of Spain might go down with a sinking ship. As Spain's power declined with no certainty about who would take Spain's place, the Chinese leaders were left with nothing to depend upon but their own resources. The charitable projects of the community, beginning with the founding of the Kung-so in 1870 and continuing through the establishment of the cemetery and the hospital, deserve mention here. The disappearance of the San Gabriel Hospital, the termination of the Spanish-instituted "community chests" in 1884, and, combined with these developments, the restrictions placed by the Spanish upon the use of institutions provided for the general public, put the Chinese on their own. But these services could have been carried out by individuals for their kinsmen, or cabecillas for their

83. "Pio Barreto," in PNA, Chinos, elecciones, 37-2-2; Opinion of Central Revenue Administration, Oct. 3, 1881, PNA, Chinos, 37-12-6.

dependientes. The Spanish government, in fact, did get some cabecillas to make good the tax debts of their dependientes.[84] The fact that such institutions were provided by the community, and were established primarily to aid the poorer members of it, is strong evidence of the community awareness of the Chinese leaders.

A third significant point is that closer relations with China underlined for the Philippine Chinese the fact of their own cultural distinctiveness. The tremendous number of new arrivals from China could not but change the character of the community. Moreover, travel to China and back became so easy that the population turnover was greater and closer ties could be maintained with the mainland.

Finally, and most important, the pressure of the anti-Chinese movement drove the Chinese together as a community. Considered a community by others, they so considered themselves. They organized as a community and, ultimately, acted to check assimilation and to reclaim mestizos for their community by founding the Anglo-Chinese School.[85]

What part was played by Filipino nationalism in the anti-Chinese pressure that drove the Chinese together? The Filipino nationalist movement was aimed at both the Spanish government and the Chinese. But the Chinese were a secondary target. The killing of Chinese and the destruction of Chinese properties during the Revolution were not simply by-products of conflict; but neither were they major objectives.

There is a contrast here with the first organized nationalist activities in Indonesia, which were explicitly aimed at the Chinese. In Indonesia, the Sarekat Islam movement included an Indonesian reaction to increasing Chinese commercial competition and rising nationalism among the Indies Chinese. But it had broader cultural and social motives, in opposition to Dutch policies. Filipino nationalism was not provoked by the Philippine Chinese. There were Filipino economic grievances against the Chinese; but Filipino nationalists, knowing the weakness of Spain, and aware that those grievances could be taken care of once they achieved the ruling position held by the Spaniards, largely ignored the Chinese and concentrated most of their attention on overthrowing Spanish power. Perhaps the key difference between Indonesian and Filipino nationalism at this early stage was the difference in relative strengths of the Netherlands and Spain. Sarekat Islam had to be aimed at the Chinese because in 1912 the Dutch were too strong to be attacked directly.

84. Circular of Central Revenue Administration, Sept. 12, 1889, Berriz, *Anuario 1889*, p. 346.

85. Compare the historical development of communalism in Malaya as analyzed in Maurice Freedman, "The Growth of a Plural Society in Malaya," *Pacific Affairs, 33* (1960), 158–68.

Filipino nationalism, almost entirely Western in content, with little ambiguity in its objectives, could direct itself almost exclusively at a weakened Spain.

Another consideration in the development of community awareness and community action among the Philippine Chinese was the position of the Chinese leadership. In the Netherlands Indies the Chinese nationalist movement could be led only by a new elite in Chinese society, one that was not tied to old practices. In the officer system established by the Dutch, Chinese officers were not elected by the community; they were appointed by, and served only at the pleasure of, the Dutch. Therefore, they tended to be dependents of the colonial government rather than representatives of the Chinese community. When the Chinese of Netherlands India began to embark upon a nationalist course the Chinese officers were not sufficiently independent to take the lead.[86]

In the Philippines there is a rather striking contrast. The Chinese community's appeal for a consulate is not to be construed as an expression of "nationalism." Although it was a radical departure from previous action, the move was not taken by new elements in community leadership or new organizations established for that purpose. The initiative came from the Gremio de Chinos and the Shan-chü Kung-so, both headed by wealthy men who might have been expected to be personally satisfied with the status quo, and from the gobernadorcillos, who were supposed to be dependents of the Spanish administration. But all these institutions were freer from colonial governmental control than was usually the case in other parts of colonial Asia. The Gremio and Kung-so had been organized on community initiative and were not limited by defined powers or dependence upon the government. And the gobernadorcillo, unlike the officers in the Netherlands Indies, was elected by his community and was almost never replaced by the government. He was, of course, somewhat more independent than he would ordinarily have been because of the declining power of Spain. In short, then, the comparatively large area of self-government achieved by the Philippine Chinese community and the weakness of the Spanish administration allowed greater flexibility and more independence to existing Chinese leadership.

This interpretation contradicts the statements of the contemporary Chinese community about its nineteenth-century antecedent. The view one finds in the contemporary community's publications is one in which, prior to 1906 when the Chinese Chamber of Commerce was founded, community organizations were rudimentary and ineffectual,

86. Williams, *Overseas Chinese Nationalism,* Chap. 4.

gobernadorcillos were almost always creatures of colonial rule or de-
spots in their own interest, and only the heroics of Tan Quien-sien
prevented the situation from being worse than it was.

One must beware of a Chamber of Commerce bias in these publications. The cemetery and hospital were not founded by Tan Quien-sien
alone, nor was he the only one to seek a consulate. It is likely that the
community institutions of the late nineteenth century were, in fact, a
necessary precondition to the establishment of a China-sponsored Chamber of Commerce. During the late nineteenth century there was, in
some overseas Chinese communities, a general trend toward supralocal
and suprakinship organizations—toward *hui-kuan* which were same-
province organizations, and toward kung-so or hui-kuan at the community-wide level.[87] When we know more about the conditions that
brought about their development we will be in a better position to
talk about the period prior to the establishment of China-sponsored
Chambers of Commerce.

When the Spanish administration first tried to apply a new income
tax to the Chinese in 1828, over 1,000 Chinese fled to the hills and
some 800 left for China.[88] A half century later, the application of new
taxes and the launching of an anti-Chinese campaign were met with
greater calmness by the Chinese. They responded with a tactic that was
old: petitions directed to local authority. They added a tactic that was
unprecedented: an appeal directed to China.

87. Uchida, *Overseas Chinese*, pp. 43–44. Cf. also Uchida's *Nihon kakyō shakai no
kenkyū* (Overseas Chinese Society in Japan) (Tokyo, 1949), pp. 347–58, 363.
88. Zamora, *Biblioteca de legislación ultramarina, 6, 104.*

PART FOUR

China: The Added Dimension

8

The Philippine Chinese Look to China

The Philippine Chinese appeal to China for consular protection in 1880 was the first known attempt by their community to establish a political relationship with China. Their action may be attributed both to their insecurity, in light of events in the Philippines, and to their awareness of the response that could be expected from China. The fact that such a request was made reflected changes in the Philippines, both inside and outside the Chinese community. That it was made with any hope of a favorable response from China was due to consciousness of China's changing attitude toward the overseas Chinese.

The request evidently was made by the Shan-chü Kung-so. In a Chinese document of 1888 it is suggested that the Chinese ambassadors in Spain maintain contact with the hui-kuan in the Philippines.[1] Since at least some of the Philippine Chinese who communicated with Chinese officials about a consulate were Hokkiens, this could not refer to the Kwangtung Hui-kuan. The Fukien Hui-kuan was not established until later.[2] It is therefore most likely, since the term "hui-kuan" was sometimes substituted for the term "kung-so,"[3] that the body referred to was the Shan-chü Kung-so.

The appeal complained of excessive and inequitable taxation, insecurity of property against theft or damage, and the extortionate practices of Spanish officials. The conditions under which this appeal was sounded were discussed in Chapter 6. Given the circumstances, it was logical enough that the wealthy and powerful leaders of the community

---

1. WCSL, ch. 75, p. 21.

2. "Fei-lü-p'in hua-ch'iao shih-lüeh," p. 3; Huang Hsiao-ts'ang, *Fei-lü-p'in Min-li-la Chung-hua Shang-hui k'an,* p. chia 5.

3. See H. B. Morse, *The Gilds of China* (2d ed. London, 1932), pp. 35 ff.

would take some action to ensure the community's future and their own. Practical need and personal ambition combined to urge this act.

It was evident that simple negotiation with local Spanish officials was insufficient to protect Chinese property. The Chinese leaders, strong enough within the Chinese community, were not sufficiently strong in their relations outside it. A Chinese consul, behaving as Western consuls did in China, might be strong enough.

Personal ambition was not absent. Tan Quien-sien, for one, coveted the position of consul-general of the Philippines. The fact that a Singapore Chinese had been named consul-general in that city was an encouraging sign.[4] And even if someone from China were appointed to the highest post, the consuls and vice-consuls would probably be local Chinese.[5]

This prospect would be appealing to a Philippine Chinese because it offered the realization of hitherto unattainable ambitions. If holding public office in China was a prized ambition that could not ordinarily be realized without a Confucian education, here was an opportunity to approximate the ideal by achieving a Chinese office without having to acquire the Confucian education and pass the examinations. The office of consul was a greater prize than that of gobernadorcillo. Although the latter office carried some powers the consul might not have, it was an office devised by the Spaniards and its incumbent had prestige only in relation to the Philippine Chinese community. A consul would hold a Chinese office, recognized in the Chinese bureaucratic system, and would be in a position of prestige vis-à-vis China as well as the Philippine Chinese.

But the decisive reason for the petition was simply an awareness that intervention by China was possible and that it produced good results. In 1880 the efficacy of China's intervention in overseas Chinese matters had but recently been demonstrated in an amelioration of coolie labor recruiting practices and an improvement in the condition of Chinese coolies in Cuba. The fact that the latter case involved Spain was a pointed lesson to the Philippine Chinese that Spain could be made to yield if China intervened. Therefore, the timing of the Philippine Chinese consulate request was dictated not merely by the promulgation of a new Spanish tax law (contribución industrial, 1878), and the de-

---

4. Liu Chi-hsüan and Shu Shih-cheng, *Chung-hua min-tsu to-chih Nan-yang shih* (History of the Colonization of Southeast Asia by the Chinese People) (Shanghai, 1934), pp. 253–54.

5. CWHKCC, ch. 15, p. 11b; Ch'en T'i-ch'iang, *Chung-kuo wai-chiao hsing-cheng* (The Administration of China's Foreign Relations) (Chungking, 1943), p. 163.

velopment of an anti-Chinese campaign in the Philippines, but also the recent evidence that China could successfully negotiate with Spain.[6]

China's aroused interest in the overseas Chinese dated only from the 1860s. The traditional Chinese view that overseas emigration was, at best, of no concern to Chinese officialdom had been evident in China's unwillingness to act in response to the loss of "unfilial" Chinese lives abroad.[7] Reference was made in Chapter 1 to the letter of a Fukien official in 1605 answering a Spanish letter which justified the 1603 massacre of Chinese in Manila. The Chinese official said that overseas Chinese, as deserters of the tombs of their ancestors, were unworthy of China's protection. A similar answer is attributed to a Chinese official in 1740, when the Dutch wrote from the Netherlands Indies to explain their massacre of Chinese during that year. This official is supposed to have expressed a lack of sympathy for those who would abandon their ancestors in quest of money.

Other traditional attitudes—that overseas migrants were likely to include political dissidents who were to be feared, and that it was better to attract foreign traders to China under the aegis of the Chinese tributary system than to let Chinese carry the trade abroad—found expression in an imperial edict of 1712, forbidding Chinese to trade and reside in Southeast Asia. Five years later another edict allowed those already abroad to come home without fear of punishment. But in 1729 still another edict announced that a date must be set after which those overseas would not be allowed to return.[8] Despite these edicts, and the harsh penalties registered in the Ch'ing dynasty law code, the *Ta-Ch'ing lü-li*,[9] little was done to prevent Chinese from going abroad. Since the laws were neither rescinded nor enforced they provided a fruitful source of extorted funds for local officials whenever a wealthy Chinese returned from abroad.

This condition began to change in the 1860s. The first indication was a clause in the Chinese peace treaty with Britain in 1860, which acknowledged the right of Chinese to go to British colonies, sail on British ships for that purpose, and make contracts with British subjects to that end. Eight years later, in the Burlingame Treaty with the United States, China acknowledged the general right of its citizens to leave the

6. WCSL, ch. 84, p. 1b.

7. H. F. MacNair, "Relations of China to Her Nationals Abroad," *Chinese Social and Political Science Review*, 7 (1923), 30.

8. Ta Chen, *Emigrant Communities in South China* (New York, 1940), pp. 49–51; Ta Chen, *Chinese Migrations*, U. S. Bureau of Labor Statistics Bulletin, 340 (Washington, 1923), pp. 16–17.

9. Quoted in H. F. MacNair, *The Chinese Abroad; Their Position and Protection* (Shanghai, 1924), pp. 1–2, and in Chen, *Emigrant Communities*, pp. 50–51.

country. Within ten years after that time the Chinese had begun to establish consulates abroad, one purpose of which was to protect the lives and property of overseas Chinese.[10]

In the case of the Philippines, the hitherto local interest of Fukien and Kwangtung became a national policy concern in the 1860s and after. In 1864 China signed a general treaty with Spain, one part of which referred specifically to the Philippine Chinese. The conclusion of this agreement climaxed long years of effort on the part of the Spanish. Ever since the 1820s Spanish commercial agents had been attempting to acquire from China treaties granting special trading advantages. After the Opium War Spain sought a treaty similar to those given the Great Powers. Sinibaldo de Mas was sent to Macao in the mid-1840s as a special envoy, but he was ignored by the Kwangtung–Kwangsi governor-general and soon withdrew. Thereafter, Spain maintained merchant-consuls in some Chinese treaty ports, officials who were not recognized by the Chinese as consuls. In 1858 the Spaniards tried again to negotiate, seeking to facilitate Chinese immigration to the Philippines as well as to improve trade conditions.[11] But it was not until 1864 that Mas could arrange a treaty, which was signed in Tientsin by Ch'ung Hou, Superintendent of Trade for the Northern Ports, and Hsüeh Huan, a member of the Tsungli Yamen (the Chinese "foreign office").[12]

Much of the content of this treaty was taken directly from treaties recently signed with other nations. It included a statement of the right of Chinese to migrate to Spanish territories and to sign contracts to do so. But there is in addition a striking passage of specific concern to the Philippine Chinese.

> Art. 47: Chinese merchant vessels, without limitation of number, shall be at liberty to trade with the Philippines, and shall be

10. MacNair, *Chinese Abroad*, p. 313; Chen, *Emigrant Communities*, pp. 52–53; Ch'en T'i-ch'iang, p. 195; Knight Biggerstaff, "The Establishment of Permanent Chinese Missions Abroad," *Chinese Social and Political Science Review*, 20 (1936), 17–19, 22, 24, 33; L. Tung, *China and Some Phases of International Law* (Shanghai, 1940), pp. 112–15, 142–43.

11. AMAE, Filipinas, 1890, Supuestos atropellos á súbditos chinos en Mindanao, Chinese Chargé to Estado, May 27, 1895; China, 1889. Reclamación del gobierno chino, Chang Yin-huan to Estado, Aug. 15, 1889.

12. PNA, Reales Órdenes, caja 97, núm. 2, 3, 100; caja 99, núm. 37; caja 100, núm. 126; caja 111, núm. 90; caja 118, num. 94; *Guía de forasteros en las Islas Filipinas para el año 1860* (Manila, 1860), p. 68; Bécker, *Historia relaciones exteriores de España*, 2, 668; Mas, *La Chine*, 2, 114–21 (cf. pp. 434–38); *Ch'ing-shih kao* (Draft History of the Ch'ing Period) (Peiping, 1928), *pang-chiao chih*, ch. 7, p. 8b.

treated as those of the most-favored nation. Should Spain hereafter concede any fresh advantages to the merchants of another nation, Chinese merchants shall enjoy them like the merchants of the most-favored nation.[13]

The wording of this treaty article is rather curious. While including all Chinese merchants as "most-favored," it appears to single out the merchant *vessels* for special encouragement—this, at a time when the junk trade had declined to a volume of two or three vessels per year. It is possible that the expression "Chinese merchant vessels" was intended to encourage either a revival of the junk trade or a development of trade in Chinese-owned Western-style vessels.[14]

Another interesting question is why the article was included at all. The documentation pertaining to the treaty negotiations is not informative on this point.[15] Presumably, the Chinese negotiators wanted such a clause and the Spanish negotiator did not. Although Spain wished to encourage Chinese trade and immigration to the Philippines, she had no desire to be restricted in her power to treat the Chinese there however she wished. The logical explanation for this treaty article is that China, knowing Spain's eagerness for the treaty and her weakness in comparison with the victorious powers of 1860, was prepared to grant a treaty on the same terms as those of 1860 but only with some concession in return.

Although this treaty was signed in 1864 and went into effect three years later upon ratification by both sides, it was some years before the Chinese made a move to implement Article 47. Meanwhile, the treatment of Chinese coolie laborers in Spanish Cuba had become an issue. Ch'en Lan-pin, who had been appointed the first Chinese ambassador to the United States, Spain, and Peru in 1875, and had earlier participated in a Chinese commission which examined conditions in Cuba, signed an immigration treaty with Spain in 1877. It provided for most-favored-nation treatment for Chinese subjects in Cuba, gave permission for the establishment of Chinese consulates in Cuba, and provided for the control of conditions of emigration from China and of labor on Cuban plantations. Nevertheless, it permitted the Spanish administra-

---

13. G. E. P. Hertslet, ed., *Treaties &c. between Great Britain and China; and between China and Foreign Powers. . . .* (2 vols. London, 1908), *I*, 512–22.

14. Writing in the mid-1880s, J. F. Del Pan, commenting on this part of the treaty, observed that no Chinese-owned ships had come to the Philippines for the past fifteen years. *Los chinos en Filipinas*, p. 126.

15. *Ch'ou-pan i-wu shih-mo* (The Management of Barbarian Affairs from Beginning to End) (Peiping, 1930), T'ung-chih period, ch. 28, pp. 31b–37b; AMAE, Negociaciones, siglo xix, núm. 208, leg. 74.

tion to restrict the areas of travel and residence of the Chinese in Cuba, and promised that any advantages China might grant to other parties in emigration agreements would be enjoyed by Spain as well.[16]

Almost all the provisions of this treaty applied specifically to Cuba, and did not include other Spanish territories. Although coolie labor was sent to the Philippines, the conditions of its impressment and transportation were apparently not bad enough to warrant attention. Chinese emigration to Cuba was primarily coolie labor to work on Cuban plantations. Since the nature of emigration to the Philippines was quite different, the 1877 treaty could not be applied. Further negotiation would be necessary.

The request for consulates, made by the Philippine Chinese in 1880, was forwarded to Li Hung-chang, Superintendent of Trade for the Northern Ports, who dominated the handling of China's foreign relations at that time. Li wrote to the Tsungli Yamen, China's foreign office, suggesting a preliminary investigation similar to that done in Cuba and, eventually, the establishment of consulates. The Tsungli Yamen referred the matter back to him and Li wrote to Ch'en Lan-pin, China's ambassador to Spain, Peru, and the United States, instructing him to secure Spanish approval of the proposed innovation. Ch'en approached the Spanish Foreign Office, but was told that the Foreign Office must first consult with the Spanish Colonial Office and the Philippine governor-general. There the matter rested until the end of Ch'en's tenure in office the following year.[17]

When Cheng Tsao-ju became ambassador in 1881 the negotiations were resumed, but with no more success than before. The Spanish Foreign Office pointed out that the 1864 treaty did not specifically provide for Chinese consulates in the Philippines. A new agreement would be necessary, but that would have to await news of the Philippine reaction to the proposal. While waiting, Cheng Tsao-ju sought specific evidence to support the claims of unfair treatment and excessive taxation made by the Philippine Chinese. To do so, he revived Li Hung-chang's idea of an investigating commission to collect the information and testimony needed. It could also be a means of gathering general information about the Philippines for use by the consuls appointed in the future. Finally, sending such a commission would demonstrate to Spain that China was serious about the protection of the Philippine Chinese and determined to follow through to the end on the consular negotiations.

16. W. F. Mayers, *Treaties between the Empire of China and Foreign Powers* (5th ed. Shanghai, 1906), pp. 204–08.

17. CSMJPKJC, p. 5a; LWCKCC, ser. 2, *p'eng-liao han-kao*, ch. 19, p. 21a; WCSL, ch. 84, p. 1b; AMAE, Filipinas. Sobre creación consulados chinos, Estado to Ultramar, Aug. 28, 1880.

Cheng Tsao-ju therefore wrote the Spanish Foreign Office expressing China's interest in making such an investigation. His letter was ignored. He also wrote to China with this suggestion, and the proposal was accepted by Li Hung-chang and the Yamen. But nothing was done to implement it pending arrival of news of the Philippine reaction.[18]

Months lengthened into years. Administrative bodies in the Philippines avoided responding to the question, despite periodic promptings from Spain. Finally, in the middle of 1885, five years after the original request, the Philippine authorities sent back a negative reply. On the basis of this reply Spain declined to consider the proposal.[19]

The time span between question and answer might not have been so long had the Chinese ambassadors been able to press unremittingly for a reply. But they were limited in the amount of time they could remain in Spain. As ambassador to three countries the Chinese minister had to choose a point of residence in one of the three, leaving the affairs of the other two in the hands of subordinates. Most of the time he remained in the United States and had to negotiate through the chargé d'affaires in Madrid. Furthermore, in Cheng Tsao-ju's case, a series of damage claims arising from anti-Chinese riots in the western United States kept him busy in Washington. Another possible deterrent to additional travel to Spain was the fact that 80,000 *taels* were drained from Cheng's embassy fund to be loaned to the China Merchants Steam Navigation Company, an enterprise supported by Li Hung-chang.[20]

The Sino-Spanish consulate negotiations entered a new phase with the appointment of Chang Yin-huan as China's ambassador in 1885. Chang, a native of eastern Kwangtung, had specialized in the study of foreign relations. Before leaving China on his mission he consulted first with Li Hung-chang and with the Spanish Minister in Peking, Leopoldo de Alba Salcedo. Then he stopped at Canton, where he discussed overseas Chinese affairs with the governor-general of Kwangtung–Kwangsi, Chang Chih-tung.[21]

While Chang Yin-huan was still at Canton in early 1886, four merchant leaders from the Chinese community in the Philippines, Yap

18. WCSL, ch. 84, pp. 1b–2b; CSMJPKJC, p. 7a; AMAE, 1897. Insurrección en Filipinas. Yncidente protección, Chinese chargé to Estado, June 11, 1883.

19. AMAE, Filipinas, Sobre creación consulados chinos, opinions of Philippine treasury, civil administration, cabinet, 1881, 1884, 1885; Ultramar to Estado, Sept. 15, 1885.

20. Arthur W. Hummel, ed., *Eminent Chinese of the Ch'ing Period (1644–1912)* (2 vols. Washington, 1943), 1, 61; CSMJPKJC, pp. 106a–106b. In 1890, 60,000 taels were loaned from this embassy fund to the China Merchants Company. Ibid. In 1886 the Haikwan, or Customs tael, was equal to approximately US $1.22 and Mex $1.45.

21. Hummel, 1, 61; CWHKCC, ch. 15, p. 10b.

Liong-quin, Tan Chuey-liong, Lim Cong-jap, and Co Chi-lui, arrived
in Hong Kong with a petition asking for a Chinese consulate in the
Philippines. Three of these four men cannot be identified with certainty.
"Yap Liong-quin" may have been Francisco Manzano Yap-Tico, one of
the most prominent persons of the time with the surname "Yap." A
more likely identification is with Antonio Yap Caong, who was
gobernadorcillo between 1883 and 1885. The fact that "Yap Liong-
quin" appears first in this listing would suggest that he headed the small
delegation. Also, it is known that Yap Caong applied for and was
granted a visa to make a trip to Hong Kong for health reasons.[22]

"Tan Chuey-liong" is, of course, Tan Quien-sien, the only one of
these four who can be definitely identified. "Lim Cong-jap" is more
than likely Joaquín Barrera Limjap, a prosperous sugar, tobacco, and
hemp merchant originally from Fukien, who founded a prominent mestizo family in Manila. "Co Chi-lui" may be Federico Co Sequieng, the
opium contractor, who was gobernadorcillo in 1888. Or it may be a
rich and prominent Manila merchant named Juan Lecaros Co-Lico.

The petition these four emissaries brought contained the signatures
of 290 persons who favored establishing a Chinese consulate in the
Philippines. Chang Yin-huan met the four merchants in Hong Kong
and discussed their petition with them and with the directors of the Tung
Wah Hospital and some of the merchants of Hong Kong.[23]

A word about the Tung Wah Hospital may not be out of place here.
Founded in Hong Kong in the early 1870s, by a combination of govern-
ment and private (Chinese) initiative, it began as a hospital offering
Chinese-style medical treatment. But its directors, wealthy and influential Chinese, quickly became a committee for presenting to the Hong
Kong government petitions relating to Chinese affairs. The directorate
went further. By the early 1880s it was corresponding directly with
Canton officials and with the Japanese government. It also acted as a
center for collecting famine relief funds for China from the overseas
Chinese. And there is some indication that the Tung Wah directorate
acted as a kind of information center and advisory board for Chinese
officials concerned with overseas Chinese affairs. Further research may
well demonstrate that Hong Kong was, as Chang Chih-tung indicated
it was, a listening post for overseas Chinese affairs, and that the Tung
Wah directors were the central clearinghouse for information.[24]

22. CWHKCC, ch. 15, p. 10b; PNA, Chinos, elecciones, 37-2-2.
23. CWHKCC, ch. 15, p. 10b.
24. G. B. Endacott, *A History of Hong Kong* (London, 1958), pp. 156–57,
245–46; R. C. Hurley, *Handbook to the British Crown Colony of Hongkong and
Dependencies* (Hong Kong, 1920), p. 105; C. A. Middleton Smith, *The British in*

This tendency of a benevolent foundation to assume political functions is characteristic of overseas Chinese benevolent organizations founded in the late nineteenth century. The Shan-chü Kung-so in the Philippines may be cited as one example. Others are the Chung Wah Kung Saw, founded in 1851 in San Francisco, and renamed in 1862 Chung Wah Wui Kwoon (Chinese Six Companies), the Chung-hua Hui-kuan in Yokohama, established in 1873, and the Chung-hua Hui-kuan of Kobe, organized in 1891. All assumed political functions and carried out many of the same duties later taken over by the Chinese Chambers of Commerce.[25] It is possible that all of them were, sooner or later, in touch with the Tung Wah directorate in Hong Kong.

The directors of the Tung Wah advised Chang Yin-huan that plans should be made for establishing consulates not only in the Philippines but in other places where there were Chinese. The expenses of such projects could be worked out after other plans had been completed.[26] There were already Chinese consulates in Japan, the United States, Hawaii, and, as a result of the 1877 emigration treaty with Spain, in Cuba. The only consulate in Southeast Asia was in Singapore, an office opened in 1877 and later given the title of consulate-general for Southeast Asia.[27]

Chang Yin-huan and Chang Chih-tung now memorialized jointly, suggesting that there be two consulates-general for Southeast Asia, the second one to be, presumably, in Manila. Although the consuls-general in these establishments were to report on the affairs of the overseas Chinese to the Chinese ambassadors in the appropriate European countries, they were also to be in touch with the Kwangtung–Kwangsi governor-general, who, since he was so much closer to them than the ambassadors in Europe, could advise them more quickly. Also, since most of the Chinese in Southeast Asia sooner or later came to Hong Kong, the Chinese governor-general at Canton was in a position to be in constant touch with overseas Chinese news throughout Southeast Asia. Besides these consulates-general, overseas Chinese could be appointed as consuls and vice-consuls in other parts of Southeast Asia. By choosing from among the rich local Chinese who would be willing to serve for the honor alone, a drain on China's treasury for official salaries could be avoided.

China and Far Eastern Trade (London, 1920), pp. 203–04; SCJC, ch. 2, p. 36b; ch. 4, pp. 19a–19b.

25. Uchida, Overseas Chinese, p. 44.
26. CWHKCC, ch. 15, pp. 10b–11a.
27. Ch'en T'i-ch'iang, pp. 148, 153, 161, 165; Liu and Shu, pp. 253–54.

Chang Yin-huan and Chang Chih-tung now revived the idea of an investigating commission as a prerequisite to establishing consulates. But their idea was that it should be commissioned by Chang Chih-tung rather than by authorities in Peking, and that the commissioners would not limit themselves to the Philippines but cover all of Southeast Asia and Australia as well. To head this commission, Chang Yin-huan and Chang Chih-tung chose Brigade-general Wang Yung-ho, a native of Lung-ch'i hsien in Fukien, who had resided abroad for a time. His assistant was to be the Expectant Prefect Yü Ch'iung, a man from Hsin-ning hsien in Kwangtung, who among other occupations had held the office of Chinese consul at Nagasaki. Accompanying them would be a small retinue of secretaries. The inspection trip was supposed to require some eight months' time, at an estimated expenditure of 1,380 taels per month. The money was to be drawn from that part of the Canton Maritime Customs receipts normally set aside for legation expenses.[28]

There was also the question of transportation. Chang Chih-tung favored sending the commissioners on a warship of the new Chinese Navy, to give an impression of negotiation from strength. He cited as precedent a previous Chinese naval exercise in Southeast Asia. But Chang Yin-huan cautioned against the idea on the grounds that it would unnecessarily arouse suspicions and resistance. More decisive opposition to the idea came from Li Hung-chang. Since Kwangtung had no ships of its own, Chang Chih-tung wired Li Hung-chang about the availability of a Navy ship and the advisability of using it. Li replied in the negative on both counts. Since Wang and Yü would not be empowered to negotiate for consulates, but merely to investigate conditions, he could see no advantage and some possible disadvantage to using a warship. In any case, no suitable ship was available. The ironclad despatch boats of the Pei-yang Squadron had all been sent to Vladivostok, and the Nan-yang Squadron's despatch boats were already committed to a naval exercise and patrol mission off the Korean coast. Therefore, the two commissioners would have to take a commercial vessel.[29]

The limitations of the commission's authority were also discussed at this time. Chang Chih-tung argued that, in the Philippines at least, the two commissioners should be empowered to negotiate with the Spanish governor-general for an improvement in the condition of the Philippine Chinese until Chang Yin-huan could arrange for a consulate. Chang Yin-huan and Li Hung-chang favored an investigation only. The commission's limitations seem never to have been defined, and it did present

28. CWHKCC, ch. 15, pp. 11b–13b.
29. WCSL, ch. 68, pp. 5a, 6a–7a.

petitions to local authorities in at least two of the areas it visited, the Philippines and Australia. The Dutch, however, were very strict about prohibiting anything beyond casual observation in their territories. In fact, Wang Yung-ho and Yü Ch'iung could not get visas to visit the Netherlands Indies until they entitled their inspection trip a "pleasure cruise." [30] While these discussions were going on, Chang Yin-huan had sailed to the United States to take up his duties. Once there, he resumed and maintained contact with both Chang Chih-tung and Li Hung-chang.

In August of 1886, just as Wang and Yü were about to depart on their "pleasure cruise," a new petition from the Philippines reached them. Signed by a certain Kuan Wen-tou and others, it complained of recent outbreaks of robbery and arson in Camarines and elsewhere. The damage to Chinese properties totaled 200,000 pesos. The merchants who sent this petition requested that commissioners be sent to arrange for consulates. They were prepared to pay the expenses of the commission and urged that the commissioners arrive on warships in order to give the most forceful impression possible.[31]

Regardless of these requests, Wang and Yü boarded a commercial vessel as planned and traveled with funds from the Maritime Customs. They left Canton late in August, going first to the Philippines. From there they traveled to Sulu, Singapore, Malacca, Penang, Rangoon, Deli (Sumatra), Batavia, Semarang, Surabaya, and to various places in Australia. In all, twenty cities were visited. The entire trip, which was expected to require eight months, took twelve. Even then, several places the commissioners had hoped to visit, such as Siam, Indo-China, and Borneo, had to be left out.[32]

In general, the Wang Yung-ho Commission was well received everywhere it went, both by the local Chinese and by colonial officials, the latter having sometimes received advance notice of its coming. In the Philippines, where it remained for well over a month, the Commission investigated differential rates in personal taxes and alleged instances of extortion, robbery, and property damage, with particular concentration on the recent claim of losses amounting to 200,000 pesos. The commissioners drew up a petition to the Spanish governor-general, requesting that he investigate and punish those responsible for damage and loss of Chinese property. They also sent a report to Chang Yin-huan, who forwarded it to the chargé d'affaires in Madrid. The Spanish Foreign Office replied that the governor-general would be ordered to

30. WCSL, ch. 68, pp. 6a–6b; SCJC, ch. 2, pp. 19a, 37a; Foreman, *The Philippine Islands*, p. 120 n.
31. WCSL, ch. 68, p. 6; SCJC, ch. 2, p. 19a.
32. WCSL, ch. 74, pp. 22a–23a; CWHKCC, ch. 23, pp. 15a–16a.

punish those responsible and to pay indemnities to the injured. But nothing further is heard of this matter and it is doubtful that anything was done. The commissioners had arrived during the height of the anti-Chinese campaign, just after citizens of Manila had sent to Spain a petition for more restrictions on the Chinese. Under these conditions, for the Colonial Office in Spain or the harassed Governor-general Terrero in Manila to act in behalf of the Chinese would have required going against a strong tide of public opinion.[33]

Just as the investigating commission was leaving on its tour, an imperial rescript ordered Chang Yin-huan to resume negotiations for a consulate. Although he directed the chargé in Madrid to initiate discussions, Chang did so reluctantly. He believed that Southeast Asian affairs should properly be included in an enlarged area of jurisdiction for the Kwangtung–Kwangsi governor-general. He would have preferred simply to let Chang Chih-tung nominate a Philippine consul-general and request a visa for him from the Spanish government. But since there was no provision for a provincial governor to negotiate directly with a foreign state these duties necessarily fell upon him, as China's ambassador to Spain. Chang Yin-huan also preferred having some evidence to take with him when he went to Spain. But the latest report from Wang and Yü indicated that the petition of Kuan Wen-tou was not necessarily reliable. With no further information coming from Chang Chih-tung, and upon the urging of Li Hung-chang that he ought to delay personal negotiation no longer, Chang Yin-huan finally went to Madrid in May 1887, some nine months after being directed to resume negotiations.[34]

Once again there were delays. A division in Spanish views now appeared. The Foreign Office clearly favored the consular project. Its analysis was that if consulates were not established China might take action in any of three ways. She could denounce the present treaty, in which case it might be difficult to negotiate another one as good. Alternatively, China might attempt to mobilize international pressure on Spain to permit the consulates, giving China the same rights other nations enjoyed in the Philippines. China had, in fact, followed this course in Cuba. Finally, given the imperial rivalries of the European Powers in the area around the Philippines and the way these Powers hungrily watched the decline of Spanish rule, China, if it took military

33. WCSL, ch. 74, pp. 23a, 25a; SCJC, ch. 2, pp. 23b, 36a; ch. 3, p. 65a; AMAE, 1897. Insurrección en Filipinas, Yncidente protección, Commissioners to Terrero, Oct. 16, 1886; Ultramar to Estado, Feb. 17, 1887; PNA, Reales Órdenes, caja 155, núm. 18.

34. WCSL, ch. 71, pp. 9a–9b; SCJC, ch. 2, pp. 76b–77a; ch. 3, pp. 64a, 65a, 86a; WCSL, ch. 84, p. 3a.

action in behalf of its nationals, could surely count on European allies. It was simply too dangerous to have a rebellious, dissatisfied national minority provoking incidents in the Philippines. A consulate-general should be established, the administration of Chinese affairs should be made completely consistent with treatment of other foreigners, and there should be continuous communication between Spanish-speaking Chinese consuls and Chinese-speaking Spanish officials. The dangerous isolation of the Chinese community could no longer be allowed to continue. The Foreign Office, therefore, communicated its support to the Chinese.[35]

The Philippine authorities saw the problem differently. They argued that consular protection was unnecessary because the Chinese had the same rights to own property and do business that a Spaniard or indio enjoyed. The same justice was available. Chinese who believed their gobernadorcillo was unjust could make use of Spanish courts. As to protection, the Spanish government made special efforts to protect the Chinese by allowing them to form their own gremio. No other foreign group could do so.

A second general argument was that the establishment of consulates would make it impossible to collect certain extra taxes from the Chinese. These were needed for revenue, to equalize competition, to keep the surplus earnings of the Chinese from being sent to China, and to exercise limited control over immigration. Given the anti-Chinese sentiment current in the Philippines, if the Philippine government were now to put Chinese taxes completely on the same basis as those of other foreigners it would be accused of favoring this unpopular minority group.

Thirdly, a consulate would usurp many of the functions of the gobernadorcillo and Gremio, and sound the death-knell for both. But the consulate could not do everything these institutions had been doing. It would be necessary for the Philippine government to establish an expensive administration like the Singapore Chinese Protectorate and to staff it with linguistically-trained Spaniards—this at a time when revenues from the Chinese to support such an administrative apparatus would be declining.

Finally, the establishment of a consulate would be an invitation to the Chinese to use gunboat diplomacy. The consul would make demands and China, perhaps aided by others, would support them with gunboats. Spain was weak and China's naval strength was growing. As one Spanish writer had put it, the China of the 1880s was not the weak China

35. AMAE, 1897, Insurrección en Filipinas, Yncidente protección, Estado to Ultramar, Oct. 17, 1887; Estado nota, 1890; Filipinas, 1890. Supuestos atropellos á súbditos chinos en Mindanao, Estado to Ultramar, Jan. 2, 1896.

of the 1840s, and the Chinese had "made a special point of having the first ship of their new ironclad squadron visit Manila before any other port." Perhaps the Philippine government could move in the direction of reforming the existing administration of Chinese affairs. But a consulate could not be tolerated.[36]

The Foreign Office and Colonial Office were now deadlocked over the question, the latter accepting the Philippine view. China sought to force an end to this stalemate by appointing Yü Ch'iung as consul and asking the Foreign Office for its agreement. But the Foreign Office was unwilling to go against the wishes of the Colonial Office.[37] The matter was therefore taken to the Spanish Council of Ministers, where it was decided in April 1889 to accept the idea in principle but to indicate the impracticality of implementation in the near future.[38]

When Chang Yin-huan heard of this he decided to try a different approach. Since the Wang Yung-ho Commission had not furnished him with all the statistics he needed, Chang had to use a combination of official Spanish tax figures and information culled from various places. But what he collected seemed to demonstrate that since 1867, the date of effect of the 1864 treaty, the Chinese in the Philippines had paid much higher taxes than other foreigners, despite the presence in the treaty of Article 47, which gave "most-favored" status to Chinese merchants in the Philippines. It seemed clear to Chang that the Chinese were receiving "least-favored" treatment. He therefore demanded an indemnity of almost 10,000,000 pesos, the difference, as he calculated it, between what the Chinese should have paid in taxes and what they had actually paid since 1867. This indemnity claim he now attempted to use as a countermeasure to the intransigence of the Colonial Office.[39]

Another new tactic was the use of international law. Since the Spaniards insisted that they were not obliged to allow a Chinese consulate because none was provided for in the 1864 treaty, Chang Yin-huan now sought advice from specialists in international law. On their advice he soft-pedaled his arguments based on Article 47, which, after

36. Same sources as in note 19, and AMAE, 1897, Insurrección en Filipinas, Yncidente protección, Cólogan to Estado, May 10, 1897; Recur, *Filipinas*, pp. 19–21, 30, 72. Cf. Jordana, *Inmigración China*, pp. 24, 46. A Chinese warship is known to have visited Manila in 1877. It may have been the vessel referred to here. *Guía oficial de Filipinas, 1879*, pp. 56–57.

37. AMAE, Filipinas, Sobre creación consulados chinos, Chinese chargé to Estado, June 3, 1887.

38. Ibid., Política, núm. 45.

39. SCJC, ch. 4, pp. 10b–11b, 12a–13b, 17b; WCSL, ch. 84, p. 3a; AMAE, China, 1889, Reclamación del gobierno chino, Chang Yin-huan to Estado, Aug. 15, 1889.

all, included only the category of Chinese merchants. Instead he argued that since Article 50 gave "most-favored" status to Spanish subjects in China, the principle of reciprocity obliged Spain to give the same rights to all Chinese in Spanish territories. Furthermore, he relied upon the customary right of ambassadors to name consuls in the territories of their ambassadorial competence, whether or not specifically provided for by treaty. But Chang Yin-huan was aware that arguments based upon international law were not likely to be of much effectiveness as long as Spain continued to resist.[40]

The Spanish queen-regent now issued a new regulation on consulates in Spanish colonies which, among other things, provided that hereafter the Colonial Office, not the Foreign Office, should have jurisdiction. Since Chang Yin-huan could negotiate only with the Foreign Office, and the support or opposition of the Foreign Office was now irrelevant, Chang soon returned to the United States.[41]

With Chang Yin-huan back in Washington, negotiations about the consulate lagged. But a minor matter affecting the Philippine Chinese now came briefly to the fore. During the 1880s there developed some opposition in the Philippines to the Chinese apothecaries practicing there. There was probably some relationship between this opposition and the existence of a cholera epidemic in 1879, but the complaints of their competitors—Spanish physicians and Spanish and German druggists—were a more immediate factor.

In June 1887 the Philippine governor-general issued a decree providing that Chinese apothecaries should henceforth be subject to all the health and sanitation laws observed by non-Chinese druggists. The Chinese chargé in Madrid protested on behalf of the Philippine Chinese, arguing that the nature of the Chinese pharmacopoeia made it impossible to follow the same regulations. The Spanish Colonial Office responded by exempting Philippine Chinese apothecaries from normal sanitation regulations, provided they could produce herbalists' licenses from medical halls in China, certified by Spanish consuls in China. Even with such licenses, they were to be allowed to sell only to Chinese persons. And the Colonial Office made it clear that tolerance of Chinese herbalists on this basis was temporary and could be terminated on six months' notice.

The Chinese chargé, who was in touch with Tan Quien-sien in Manila, conveyed the news of his negotiations and the outcome. He also collected certificate forms in Madrid and sent them through Chang

40. SCJC, ch. 4, pp. 27a–27b, 29a; WCSL, ch. 71, p. 10a.
41. WCSL, ch. 84, p. 3a; SCJC, ch. 4, pp. 33b–34b, 38a.

Yin-huan to the Kwangtung–Kwangsi governor-general, who then filled in the names of practitioners in the Philippines, had the certificates stamped by a British official in Hong Kong rather than a Spanish consul, and sent them to the Philippines. The Governor of Fukien also participated in similar fashion. These certificates apparently were accepted in the Philippines, although there were some instances of harassment of herbalists as late as 1890, as well as some discrimination in taxation. But in 1892, apparently under the pressure of Chinese diplomacy, the Spanish abolished the special tax classification for Chinese apothecaries, making their tax uniform with that paid by other druggists.[42]

But while Chinese diplomacy was winning minor victories for Chinese herbalists it was no more successful than before in the consulate matter. Now that Chang Yin-huan had left Spain, the Tsungli Yamen attempted to negotiate with Spanish ambassadors in China. But the latter were instructed by their Foreign Office to leave all negotiations to Madrid.[43] Meanwhile, on the chance that consulates could eventually be established in the Philippines, there was some discussion among Chinese officials about how they ought to be financed and what facilities ought to be provided for the overseas Chinese.

The delegation of four Chinese merchant leaders from the Philippines that had met Chang Yin-huan at Hong Kong in 1886 had proposed that the Philippine Chinese bear the expenses of consulates established in the Archipelago. The Philippine Chinese were prepared to guarantee expenses to the amount of 12,000 taels per year. Wang Yung-ho and Yü Ch'iung found similar attitudes in the other overseas Chinese communities they visited. Wang and Yü were concerned that China's prestige would suffer from the European colonial powers' knowledge that China's consulates had to be financed by locally supplied funds, but no one else seemed worried. The Tsungli Yamen, meanwhile, had delegated to Chang Chih-tung the responsibility for deciding how the Philippine consulates ought to be financed.

Chang Chih-tung suggested that the Singapore precedent should be followed. Legation funds should be used for the establishment of

42. Victor Balaguer, *En el Ministerio de Ultramar* (2 vols. Madrid, 1888), *1*, 456–57; Sawyer, *Inhabitants of the Philippines*, p. 290; Berriz, *Diccionario*, *1*, 11; *Anuario 1888, 2*, 4; *Anuario 1892*, p. 55; PNA, Reales Órdenes, caja 159, núm. 467, 318; SCJC, ch. 5, pp. 18b–19a, 38a–39a, 65b–66a; CSMJPKJC, p. 28b; *La política de España en Filipinas* (April 12, 1892), p. 99; AMAE, 1897, Insurrección en Filipinas, Yncidente protección, Yamen to Tsui Kuo-yin, June 19, 1890; China, 1889, Reclamación del gobierno chino, Ultramar to Estado, June 27, 1891.

43. WCSL, ch. 75, p. 21; AMAE, Filipinas, Sobre creación consulados chinos, Real Órden, Jan. 24, 1891, in Estado nota, Jan. 22, 1891.

the consulate-general and the first year's salaries and expenses. For consul-general, Chang nominated Wang Yung-ho, a Hokkien who would be more acceptable to the Philippine Chinese than Yü Ch'iung, who was a Cantonese. Once established, Wang could name wealthy Philippine Chinese to be consuls and vice-consuls in various parts of the Archipelago, serving without salaries. After the first year, a combination of local donations and consular fees would be sufficient to make further outlay from China's treasury unnecessary. As possible fees to be collected, Chang Chih-tung suggested taxes on persons arriving or leaving the Philippines, and taxes on coastwise shipping craft owned by Chinese.

The same general plan could be used for other parts of Southeast Asia. Once the Philippine experiment had proved itself, consulates-general could be established in every colonial capital of Southeast Asia, as Wang and Yü had recommended; and these consulates-general would then establish satellite consulates in their areas of jurisdiction. The finances would be handled in the same way. And since funds derived from fees would vary in amount from area to area and from year to year, surplus funds from consulates in one part of the area could be transferred to those in another where there was a deficit.[44]

The Tsungli Yamen had its doubts about this method of financing, as did Chang Yin-huan. The Yamen pointed out that although the Singapore consulate had been successfully financed for a time by local contributions, these had fallen off to a point where they failed to provide more than a small fraction of consular expenses. The same thing had happened in Cuba; initial enthusiasm had been followed by disinterest. The Yamen also feared that local financing provided too many opportunities for corruption. Consulate personnel would make demands of local Chinese under the guise of "consular expense"; the final result would be a waning of interest, and hence of contributions, on the part of the localities.[45]

The Tsungli Yamen's argument reflected its conservative, "go slow" view of this problem—it did not wish to alarm the European powers by taking precipitate action of any kind. Chang Chih-tung took an opposite stand. Not only did he favor establishing a Philippine consulate as soon as Spain would issue a visa, but he had plans for using Chinese warships in connection with consular protection. As early as October of 1885 Chang Chih-tung had memorialized that a fleet of five

44. SCJC, ch. 2, p. 37b; WCSL, ch. 74, pp. 23a, 25b–27a; WCSL, ch. 84, p. 3b; CWHKCC, ch. 15, pp. 11b–12a.

45. WCSL, ch. 75, pp. 20a–20b; WCSL, ch. 71, pp. 10a–10b.

or six warships should be built and maintained exclusively to come to the aid of the overseas Chinese—both those in Southeast Asia and those in Hawaii and the Western Hemisphere. Their function would be to make a show of strength whenever the commerce of the overseas Chinese in any particular area appeared to be threatened. The fleet could be held together or dispersed according to the needs of the moment. An Overseas Naval Superintendent (*Wai-yang hai-chün t'ung-ling-yüan*) could be put in general control of the fleet's operations, although in Southeast Asian matters the Kwangtung–Kwangsi governor-general (Chang Chih-tung himself) would have jurisdiction.

The funds for this project were to come from overseas Chinese contributions. If overseas merchants could afford to pay the heavy taxes foreign governments levied upon them, surely they could afford to pay for something of benefit to them. Besides, they could be rewarded for their contributions with grants or honors of some kind, such as broadening the quotas of scholars and degree-holders from their home areas, or sending them Imperial autograph tablets to hang in their hui-kuan or kung-so.[46]

When the consulate question began to be discussed, Chang Chih-tung proposed that part of the fees collected by consuls be set aside to provide a boat-building fund. Wang Yung-ho and Yü Ch'iung were instructed by him to sound out the communities they visited on this matter. And it was Chang Chih-tung who urged that Wang and Yü travel through Southeast Asia in a warship in order to give an impression of negotiation from strength.[47] Clearly he favored a strong policy, to uphold Chinese prestige. Gunboat diplomacy, a technique learned by China at such expense from the Europeans, should now, in his view, be applied to China's advantage. Chinese naval forces, which had made their last great show of strength in the fifteenth century, were now supposed to cruise Southeast Asian waters again. But while the fleets of Cheng Ho in the fifteenth century sought to encourage Southeast Asian traders to come to China under the aegis of the tributary system, Chang Chih-tung's nineteenth-century squadron would seek to encourage Chinese to go and trade in Southeast Asia— with the knowledge that they had the support of Chinese forces.

Chang Chih-tung probably had some interest in overseas Chinese commerce for its own sake, but he was also interested for broader reasons. Of foremost importance were the remittances of the overseas Chinese to their relatives in China. Chang Chih-tung estimated that

46. SCJC, ch. 5, p. 84a; CWHKCC, ch. 13, pp. 12a–13b.
47. CWHKCC, ch. 15, p. 11b; WCSL, ch. 74, p. 22b; WCSL, ch. 68, p. 6a.

these amounted to $20,000,000 annually. They were of incalculable benefit to Kwangtung and Fukien, where rapidly increasing populations caused severe economic strains. Emigration acted as a mitigating factor; so did the remittances of the emigrants. But if emigrants could find no security of livelihood abroad they would return to compound the population problem of the coastal provinces. Besides remittances, overseas Chinese contributions were of proven importance for famine relief and the development of China's defenses. Finally, the overseas Chinese were a valuable source of information about their countries of residence. To the extent that China showed an interest in them, they would keep the lines of communication open.[48]

Chang Chih-tung's interests in the overseas Chinese were, thus, primarily economic in nature. The sending of gunboats to protect their commerce might uphold China's prestige, but it was also a means to a more tangible end—the nurturing of overseas Chinese commerce, source of remittances to relatives and contributions to public projects in China.

But were Chang's interests entirely economic? Among his proposals was one suggesting that where consulates were established, part of the consular fees and contributions collected should be set aside to provide for the establishment and maintenance of Confucian academies (*shu-yüan*), which would teach overseas Chinese youth the traditional social virtues of *li, cheng,* and *i.* Chang was prepared to take the lead in this by purchasing sets of the Classics for use in the shu-yüan to be established in the Philippines.[49]

But was this apparent cultural interest genuine? On the contrary, the idea of establishing shu yüan appears to be another means to the same economic end. In fact, it offers an interesting parallel to Chang Chih-tung's famous *t'i-yung* analysis, in which the application of Western techniques became the means of saving Chinese culture. Chang's idea that Chinese in China should add Western techniques to their basically Confucian foundation was paralleled by his belief that Chinese overseas, in the midst of Western or Westernized cultures, needed a dose of Confucian culture. But in neither case was the cultural addition intended merely to bring about a kind of optimum balance. Both ideas had the same ultimate objective: the preservation of traditional China as Chang knew it. In China, one added the new in order to protect

48. CWHKCC, ch. 15, pp. 8a–9a, 10a; CWHKCC, ch. 13, p. 13b; WCSL, ch. 74, p. 25a.

49. WCSL, ch. 74, p. 26b. Chang Chih-tung hoped local contributions would be sufficient to establish hospitals and provide funds to employ lawyers to defend Chinese interests. CWHKCC, ch. 15, p. 11b.

the old. Overseas, one saved the old in China by infusing the old into the new, which then would support the old. It is doubtful that Chang's purpose was either to create really Confucian societies abroad or to prepare overseas Chinese for careers as intellectuals and bureaucrats in the mainland civil service. Rather, it was to encourage them to invest in the support and maintenance of a Confucian China.

The use of Confucianism together with consulates is an interesting blend of old and new. Chang Chih-tung's project—never realized— was not the only such instance. Since there was no other ideology available in the late nineteenth century to those who wished closer ties between China and the overseas Chinese, Confucianism, a non-nationalistic ideology, had to be used for what were essentially national purposes. In this function it appears, for instance, in the first nationalist association founded in the Netherlands Indies.[50]

When Chang Yin-huan left office in 1889 negotiations with Spain over a Chinese consulate in the Philippines had reached a stalemate. Invocations of the 1864 treaty and arguments based on international law had met with delaying tactics by the Spanish Foreign Office and the outright opposition of the Colonial Office. Chang's continued claims for indemnities on the basis of the alleged inequitable taxation of the past several years were likewise unsuccessful. It was clear that, although Spain would be willing to reform current abuses in answer to specific complaints, there was little hope under existing conditions of either reparations for the past or a consulate to guard the future.[51]

Chang Yin-huan's successor, Tsui Kuo-yin, arrived in Spain in May 1890, intending to resume negotiations. But urgent matters in the United States required his return to Washington after less than one month's stay in Spain. Shortly thereafter, a Spanish Foreign Office spokesman announced that the Spanish opposition to a consulate had been made clear to China so there was no point in continuing negotiations.[52]

But from the Chinese point of view several specific problems needed discussion. There were complaints from Manila about the new system of cédulas de capitación; anti-Chinese incidents had continued to occur and were regularly reported to China; there were charges that the expulsion of Chinese who had secretly entered Mindanao was being carried out harshly, without giving the Chinese an opportunity to dispose of their assets; the Chinese druggists were harassed; and the law of 1889 making children of 14 responsible for a full tax burden

    50. Williams, *Overseas Chinese Nationalism*, pp. 54 ff.; cf. Willmott, *Chinese of Semarang*, p. 25.
    51. SCJC, ch. 8, p. 5a; WCSL, ch. 75, p. 29a.
    52. CSMJPKJC, pp. 36b, 41a; WCSL, ch. 84, p. 3b.

stimulated complaints that in practice even 12-year-olds were being regarded as fully responsible.[53]

As before, the efficient handling of such questions seemed to require a consulate. The problem was to force Spain to reopen the suspended negotiations. Tsui Kuo-yin now began to cast about for some new way to deal with Spain. One possibility involved the sale of Spanish lottery tickets in China. The Philippine Government Lottery, established in 1833, had expanded its sales of tickets to Shanghai by the early 1860s, and to Japan, Singapore, and British India by at least the 1880s. Wherever there were Spanish consular establishments in Asia, the consuls were directed to encourage the sale of the tickets, which were a source of revenue for the Spanish administration in the Philippines.

The lottery also provided a lucrative business for European and Chinese merchants in Manila, who shipped the tickets abroad. In fact, the Philippine government's treasury administration complained in 1881 that there was a scarcity of lottery tickets available to prospective purchasers in Manila because so many had been sent abroad. In the 1880s and 1890s three fourths of all Philippine lottery tickets were bought by Manila's European and Chinese merchants, bundled, and sent to China. The proceeds from their sales produced profits at a 10 per cent rate, which these merchants deposited in Hong Kong banks.

The tickets enjoyed a broad popularity among Chinese. In Amoy it was the practice for groups of 10, 20, or up to 50 Chinese to band together in order to buy a fraction of a Philippine lottery ticket. And in far-off Cuba, Chinese laborers, who had no other hope of getting back to China, bought Philippine lottery tickets. Those who were lucky paid passage for themselves and their friends or kinsmen.

In China the sale of the lottery tickets had expanded from Shanghai to the other treaty ports. By 1885 the Spanish were negotiating with the Ch'ing government for formal permission to sell tickets in the interior of the country. China's interest in this question was now aroused. Admiral Ting Ju-ch'ang, who headed a naval exercise cruise to Japan and the Philippines about 1889, was instructed to find out what he could about the sale of Philippine lottery tickets to Chinese. When he reported that three fourths of the Philippine government's lottery revenue came from ticket sales in China, Tsui Kuo-yin thought he had the new weapon he was looking for.[54]

53. AMAE, 1897, Insurrección en Filipinas, Yncidente protección, Issues pending, Sept. 14, 1890; China, 1889, Reclamación del gobierno chino, Reclamación por el impuesto, 1891; Ultramar to Estado, June 27, 1891; Chinese chargé to Estado, Jan. 28, 1890.

54. Berriz, *Anuario 1888*, 2, 407, 414, 417; WCSL, ch. 84, pp. 3b, 4b–5a; *La política de España en Filipinas* (Jan. 20, 1891), pp. 11–12; "Amoy," *Reports from*

In February of 1891 Tsui suggested a reorientation of China's policy with respect to the Philippine consulate. He noted that Chang Yin-huan had used indemnity claims as a countermeasure to Spanish intransigence. Tsui now suggested that China replace this countermeasure with a more effective one: prohibition of the sale of Philippine lottery tickets in China. If the lottery revenues were vital to Spain, and he believed them to be, this action should bring Spain to the point of at least reopening negotiations about a Philippine consulate for China.

But this measure was not intended solely for bargaining purposes. It had virtues of its own. In the 1860s the sales of Philippine lottery tickets at Shanghai had amounted to an estimated 480,000 taels (about 735,000 pesos). By 1891 total sales in China, by Tsui's reckoning, must have become three times that. Thus, over a thirty-year period, between 10,000,000 and 20,000,000 taels had been drained out of China to Spanish coffers. The result was the same as if Spain had extended its taxation to Chinese territory. And even if, as Spain claimed, excessive taxation of the Chinese in the Philippines was an internal matter with which China could not interfere, no less was the sale of Spanish lottery tickets in Chinese territory a domestic matter, which China could unilaterally terminate without Spanish interference. Such a termination, even if it did not cause Spain to reconsider the Philippine consulate question, would at least stop the drain of Chinese money to the Philippines.

But there remained the problem of how to protect the Philippine Chinese until a consulate could be established. Tsui Kuo-yin favored a modified form of Chang Chih-tung's gunboat idea. Instead of a special "overseas Chinese protection fleet," prepared to go wherever there was trouble, Tsui favored occasional cruises to the Philippines by existing naval units. In this way the Spaniards could be kept aware of China's strength and her constant interest in the Philippine Chinese. A consulate could be prohibited by the Spanish government, but (so Tsui believed) there was no easy way to prohibit naval visits. Chinese agents could accompany the fleets on these visits and gather information about the Philippine Chinese.

Tsui emphasized that these policies could be carried out only with the prior understanding and agreement of the other Western nations about what China intended to do. For instance, foreign cooperation in not selling Spanish lottery tickets in the foreign concessions would

the Consuls of the United States, 38 (1892), 155; SCJC, ch. 4, pp. 47b–48a. The fleet commanded by Ting Ju-ch'ang, which had been sent out under Chang Chih-tung's encouragement, later visited Singapore, Batavia, Siam, Penang, and Burma. E. H. Parker, John Chinaman and A Few Others (New York, London, 1902), p. 251.

be essential. But since both this and the naval cruises were policies directed exclusively at Spain, and were not matters of common concern to the Powers, insuring their cooperation ought not to be difficult.

Tsui's proposals, more specific than Chang Chih-tung's, were also more realistic. Chang Chih-tung advocated a show of force as a general policy with respect to the overseas Chinese. Tsui Kuo-yin realistically proposed that this kind of diplomacy be directed at only one country for a specific purpose. In detail, Tsui Kuo-yin described the weakness of Spain and the probable success of using gunboat diplomacy against her. It is evident that he believed he had found not only a tactic for a specific purpose, but a safe opportunity to reverse upon the West its own tactics. The West could now be shown how much China had learned, and a kind of minor revenge might be gained for her previous losses to the gunboat diplomacy of the Western Powers. Spain was Western enough to make it seem like revenge, but weak enough to make it possible.[55]

We do not know the outcome of Tsui Kuo-yin's plans. It is known that in the early 1890s the sale of Philippine lottery tickets was forbidden in parts of Fukien and Kwangtung. But the fact that the revenues from the lottery, after falling off during the 1880s (perhaps a reflection of Sino–Spanish tension), rose during the next decade, suggests either that there was no widespread prohibition in China or that it was ineffective. Even had this policy been put into effect, it is doubtful that it would have proved as severe a blow to the Spaniards as Tsui Kuo-yin thought. Even at the highest point in their revenue production (1897), the lottery tickets yielded only about 6 per cent of all Philippine revenue.[56]

The Philippine Chinese continued to send petitions of grievances to China. By 1894 and 1895 their complaints focused upon the sudden increase in the entry tax from 2 pesos to 20 pesos within 14 months' time. There were two levels of opposition: coolie brokers and cabecillas were upset because the increases pushed up their business costs; while the penniless masses of Chinese, whose complaints were now reaching Li Hung-chang through his trusted emissaries, claimed that they were encountering severe hardships because of the usurious interest rates charged by the cabecillas for the money lent to pay the entry fee.[57]

55. WCSL, ch. 84, pp. 3a–7b.
56. *La política de España en Filipinas* (May 10, 1892), pp. 123–24; Sawyer, p. 416; China, Inspectorate-general of Customs, Statistical Series, *Customs Decennial Reports, Amoy, 1892–1901* (Shanghai, 1906), p. 117; AMAE, Correspondencia embajadores y legaciones, China, 1886–95.
57. See documents in AMAE, Filipinas, 1890. Supuestos atropellos á súbditos chinos en Mindanao, especially Estado informe [1891–]; Ultramar to Estado, June 25,

Then in 1896 the consular question came once again to the fore, pushed there by the eruption of the Philippine Revolution. Anti-Chinese incidents accompanied the Revolution from its first day and the Spanish were unable to guarantee the protection of anyone's life or property. There was now an opportunity to reopen the consular question.

In October 1896 the Tsungli Yamen raised the question with the Spanish Minister in Peking, proposing either a new treaty or a renegotiation of the existing one. At this juncture a telegram arrived in China from Tan Quien-sien, asking consular and gunboat protection, to be furnished by a third country if China were unable to do so. The Manila Chinese were immediately concerned about the fate of some Chinese laborers working for the Spanish armies, whose services had been arranged for by the Gremio de Chinos in Manila. More broadly, indio hostility toward Chinese laborers working for the Spanish seemed to prefigure indio hostility toward all Chinese. There were stories that the revolutionaries intended to kill all Spaniards and all Chinese.

China now turned to Great Britain, requesting that British gunboats be sent to Manila harbor and that the British consul in Manila assume responsibility for protecting the Chinese. The Spanish, although apprehensive about the nature of British interest in the Philippines and where the involvement of Britain in this affair might lead, realized their own inability to protect the Chinese. Preferring the British to some less friendly power, they agreed in December 1896 to allow the British consul to assume temporary and unofficial advisory responsibilities over the protection of the Chinese.

But the agent of contact between the British consul and the Chinese community was not Tan Quien-sien, but another prominent Manila merchant, Yang Shu-te. The Ch'ing government realized that Tan Quien-sien's position was equivocal. He was partly dependent upon the Spanish for his position, and he had made a profitable business out of protecting the Chinese. Therefore, between December 1896 and July 1898 the practice was for Yang Shu-te to report Chinese complaints to the British consul, who negotiated with the Spanish or the revolutionaries for redress. Tan Quien-sien's attempts at intervention and claims to fees for services were rebuffed.[58]

The question of a Chinese consulate continued to be discussed. The Manila Chinese had ambivalent feelings about it. They recognized that

---

1896; Chinese chargé to Estado, May 27, 1895; and in China, 1893–94–95, Reclamación de legación china.

58. AMAE, 1897, Insurrección en Filipinas, Yncidente protección, passim.; IMH–AS, ch'ing 366, fa 161, Hsiao-lü-sung she-li ling-shih, Yamen to Liang-Kuang gov.-gen., Dec. 5, 1896; Communication from Cólogan, Dec. 7, 1896; Report of Yang Shu-te, with annexes, April 14, 1897.

only a consulate would be strong enough to protect them, and they were aware that the gobernadorcillos double-taxed them. But looking at the Singapore experience they could not but be apprehensive about the "squeeze" possibilities if a consulate were established. To avoid this problem, Sir Robert Hart, Inspector General of the Chinese Maritime Customs, had proposed that foreigners in the Customs Service be sent abroad as Chinese consuls. But this was a solution acceptable neither to China nor to Spain.[59]

Finally, in July of 1898, with only a shadow of her authority remaining in the Philippines, Spain conceded the establishment of a Chinese consulate on a temporary basis until the end of the disorders. Until the new consul arrived, Tan Quien-sien was to be acting consul. When the United States assumed control over the Philippines, the consulate was confirmed as a permanent one and the first consul arrived in January 1899.[60]

From the eighteen-year period of Sino–Spanish negotiations over the protection of the Philippine Chinese certain points of view on both sides stand out and are worthy of comment. Chang Chih-tung's interest in the Philippine Chinese and his views on the overseas Chinese generally have already been examined. Li Hung-chang was interested in a Philippine consulate because the China Merchants Steam Navigation Company, of which he was patron, had begun to carry cargoes from Manila to the China coast, and he hoped to expand the operation. He also viewed the overseas Chinese, in the Philippines and elsewhere, as useful because of their contributions to famine relief and coastal defense in China.[61]

Some years before this, in 1867, the Tsungli Yamen had suggested the possibility of making use in the Chinese bureaucracy of overseas Chinese who had a knowledge of foreign techniques.[62] But the interest of most officials in the overseas Chinese was economic in nature. The

59. AMAE, 1897, Insurrección en Filipinas, Yncidente protección, Interview with Li Hung-chang, in Spanish consul-gen., Shanghai, to Estado, April 11, 1896; Cólogan to Estado, Nov. 5, 1896; Spanish minister to Estado, Nov. 25, 1890; SCJC, ch. 4, p. 28b.

60. AMAE, Filipinas, Sobre creación consulados chinos, Estado to Wu T'ing-fang, July 20, 1898; PNA, Reales Órdenes, caja 167, núm. 359, 482; Liu Chi Tien, Hua-ch'iao, pp. 61–62; Testimony of Wm. Daland, Report of Philippine Commission, 2, 164.

61. SCJC, ch. 4, p. 13a; LWCKCC, ser. 2, p'eng-liao han-kao, ch. 31, pp. 30a–30b; AMAE, Filipinas, Sobre creación consulados chinos, Ultramar to gov.-gen., June 26, 1883; Biggerstaff, pp. 17, 22, 33; Tung, pp. 112, 114. A Philippine Chinese famine relief contribution of Mex $15,220 is recorded in the Singapore Chinese newspaper Lat Pao, June 20, 1893. I am indebted to Wen Chung-chi for this reference.

62. Immanuel C. Y. Hsu, China's Entrance into the Family of Nations; The Diplomatic Phase, 1858–1880 (Cambridge, 1960), pp. 161, 171–72.

importance of overseas Chinese contributions to famine relief and coastal defense, and their remittances to relatives were the principal arguments for protecting the overseas Chinese.[63] In a sense, one can see here a projection overseas of the traditional Chinese bureaucratic attitude toward the merchant, except of course, that the "squeeze" was for public welfare, not for private use. "Squeeze" or not, the relationship was primarily economic and eminently practical.

One looks in vain for any evidences of a philosophical Pan-Sinism in the writings of Chinese officials of this period. The overseas Chinese communities were considered worthy of protection not because they were little bits of China scattered about the globe, but because they were merchant communities whose earnings—and perhaps "know-how"—were suddenly of value to China's "self-strengthening" effort. There was, of course, very little about these communities that was culturally attractive to a Chinese official. They were colonial communities whose leading elements were merchants, not scholar–officials. Given the absence of nationalism and the presence of traditional Chinese social values, and granting the mercantile nature of overseas Chinese society at that time, it is not surprising that China's official interest took this form.

But national self-pride also was certainly involved, at least by the 1890s when almost every country of consequence, Japan included, had a consulate at Manila. Chinese prestige demanded the same for China.[64]

The economic motivation is clearly visible in Hsüeh Fu-ch'eng's observation that the total of remittances and contributions from Singapore since the consulate was established there amounted to twice the cost of maintaining that office.[65] Chang Yin-huan, too, captured the spirit if not the statistics when he lamented the wasting of overseas Chinese earnings on gambling and opium (he might have added taxes), while "only 10 in 100,000 make remittances."[66]

This argument has direct applicability to the Philippine Chinese. It was on the use of Philippine Chinese earnings that the Sino–Spanish argument centered. As early as 1844 one finds Spanish officials suggesting that Chinese immigrants should be brought to the Philippines

63. Chen, *Chinese Migrations,* p. 55; Ch'en T'i-ch'iang, pp. 195, 204–05, 215; Biggerstaff, pp. 17–24; SCJC, ch. 4, p. 47a.

64. AMAE, China, 1893–94–95, Reclamación de la legación china, Estado to Ultramar, May 30, 1893; Filipinas, Sobre creación consulados chinos, Ultramar, núm. 47, 1890.

65. AMAE, 1897, Insurrección en Filipinas, Yncidente protección, tr. from diary of Hsüeh Fu-ch'eng; Cólogan to Estado, Nov. 5, 1896. China, 1893–94–95. Reclamación de la legación china, Estado to Ultramar, May 30, 1893.

66. SCJC, ch. 4, p. 47b.

only in families, because only in this way would they be likely to spend their earnings in the Philippines rather than send them to China.[67] The opium monopoly, like the higher taxes levied upon the Chinese in the mid-nineteenth century, was both a valuable source of government revenue and a way to get the Chinese to leave some of their earnings in the Philippines. During the anti-Chinese campaign of the 1880s one of the strongest complaints against the Chinese was that they brought nothing to the Philippines and spent nothing while there; they only took money away. This argument is a familiar one; it echoes the Spanish complaints of the Manila Galleon days, when the Chinese were accused of draining away all the wealth of Manila.

During the 1880s and 1890s the leaders of the Manila Chinese community were almost constantly in contact with officials in China and the Chinese ambassadors to Spain. The Spaniards were not unaware of this development. They attempted, unsuccessfully, to keep the Manila Chinese from sending any telegrams without first notifying the Spanish authorities of their contents.[68] Despite this pressure, complaints on various subjects continued to be sent out by the Manila Chinese, particularly during 1889 when Tan Quien-sien was interim gobernadorcillo.[69] That both the provisions of the new Weyler–Becerra Reglamento and the decrees on Mindanao were modified and liberalized in the early 1890s must have been due to the combined efforts of the Gremio de Chinos, the Shan-chü Kung-so, and Chinese ambassadors to Spain. The Gremio's function was to make local protest; the Kung-so kept in touch with officials in China and Chinese ambassadors to Spain.

The softening of the impact of Spanish legislation and policies was a small gain. The consulate was achieved only as Spain gave up the Philippines. But the significance of this period was the establishment, even before the founding of a consulate in 1899, of a working political relationship between the Philippine Chinese (with the Manila community leading the way) and China. In addition, the publication of newspapers carrying reports about China and the founding of the Anglo–Chinese School, with its emphasis on Confucian learning, were harbingers of a closer cultural tie between the Philippine Chinese and China. The new school, by providing an emphasis on Confucianism and commercial studies, prepared its students for lives in which their economic function was commerce and their social status that of a cultural minority. By identifying their minority status with Confucian

67. Real Órden, Jan. 28, 1844, PNA, Reales Órdenes, caja 100, núm. 75.
68. CSMJPKJC, p. 28b.
69. PNA, Reales Órdenes, caja 158, núm. 388; caja 159, núm. 318; caja 160, núm. 156.

culture the backers of the school made a formal declaration of cultural affiliation with China.

Faced by an uncertain future, the Philippine Chinese drew closer together, becoming for the first time a unified community. They sought aid from China, in political form and in cultural form as well. Thus, when the United States set the final seal of rejection upon full participation of the Chinese in Philippine society by encouraging both Filipino nationalism and Chinese cultural exclusivism, the way had already been prepared for the Philippine Chinese to survive, not only as a community, but as a community whose cultural orientation was specifically Chinese.

9

The Philippine Chinese at the Turn of the Century

In 1850 the Chinese in the Philippines were a largely unorganized group of individuals living in the Manila area, possessing an important economic function in that region but in danger of losing it to the Chinese mestizos. They readily intermarried with the indios and their mestizo offspring were being assimilated into a developing Filipino society.

Fifty years later the Philippine Chinese were an organized community with members in every part of the Philippines. They had reclaimed from the mestizos the status of "middle class of the Philippines" and had gone on to acquire much greater and more diversified economic interests than ever before. Assimilation of the Chinese had not ceased, but the Chinese community now actively opposed it. Moreover, the Chinese community had established political relations with China, thus adding a new dimension to its status in the Philippines.

From the viewpoint of governmental authority in the Philippines, the "Chinese problem" before 1850 had been essentially a Manila problem. It had also been almost exclusively a problem for Spaniards. The anti-Chinese campaigns of the seventeenth and early eighteenth centuries were primarily Spanish campaigns against a Manila Chinese population that outnumbered the Spaniards (but not the indios). Expulsions were based on Spanish jealousies of Chinese competitors; massacres resulted from Spanish fear of the Chinese numerical majority. The indios were involved only to the extent of being Spanish-led troops and learning from the Spaniards certain cultural attitudes toward the Chinese. But from the standpoint of competition, the indios, save for those in the native weaving industry in certain places, were not really affected. The seventeenth-century Chinese did not usurp positions from an already existing urban work force; they created positions where none had existed.

In the middle and late eighteenth century, as a new native elite began to develop and as indios and mestizos began to compete with the Chinese, attempts to expel the Chinese from Manila's retail trade came to involve native as well as Spanish interests. But the problem was still limited to the Manila area. It was only after 1850—when the numerical weight of the Chinese, both in Manila and elsewhere, became greater than ever before, when Chinese scattered to all parts of the Islands, and when mestizos, and to a lesser extent indios, had achieved an important position in the country's economy—that opposition to the Chinese for the first time became archipelago-wide and involved all groups in Philippine society.

The changed social and economic environment, together with the beginnings of Filipino nationalism during this period, had broad implications for the future. The origins of the economic nationalist movement of the mid-twentieth-century Philippines, which is aimed particularly at the Chinese, may be traced to the period 1850–98. It is true enough that Filipino cultural attitudes toward the Chinese, which provide a psychological background for economic nationalism, originated in an earlier period. But the basic economic, social, and political conditions date from the late nineteenth century, when Chinese economic interests first became archipelago-wide, when Chinese competition for the first time seriously affected non-Spanish elements in Philippine society, when Filipino nationalism had its genesis, and when the Chinese community first began to attach itself to China. Given all these conditions, it was almost inevitable that Filipino nationalism would eventually express itself against the economic power of the Chinese, and that earlier attempts to expel the Chinese from retail trade for the benefit of Spaniards would be followed, in time, by a retail trade nationalization movement for the benefit of Filipinos.

One may well speculate about what would have happened had Spanish policy not reopened the gates to a new influx of Chinese immigrants. It has been pointed out already that in the 1840s many predicted that the mestizos would eventually hold a kind of economic hegemony in the Philippines. Had all relevant conditions remained constant—the size and geographic restriction of the Chinese community, especially—it is not unlikely that the mestizos would have increasingly taken over the economic position of the Chinese. The Chinese might have been gradually assimilated or, in the face of increasing mestizo competition, might have chosen to leave the Philippines because there were no longer substantial profits to be made. In this way, trade—retail and otherwise—and industry might have become "nationalized" by natural means, and there might not be a "Chinese problem" in the twentieth-century Philippines.

When we turn to the contemporary scene, we find that in the mid-twentieth century a sizable portion of the Filipino elite is made up of families founded by Chinese immigrants. The fact of their part-Chinese origin is now of little significance, politically or socially. It is impossible to determine what percentage of the Philippine population of today would be classified as Chinese mestizo according to the Spanish standards, let alone what percentage of the contemporary elite fits that category. But it is generally agreed that a large segment of the current Philippine leadership is Chinese mestizo in family background.

In their attainment of prominence in Philippine economic, social, and political life the mestizos partially realized the predictions made about them in the early and middle nineteenth century. That they did not fully live up to the economic predictions may be attributed to increased Chinese competition. Their success otherwise may be credited to their closer association with the indios and their identification of themselves as Filipino.

It is instructive to compare the history of the Chinese mestizos in the Philippines with that of the native-born children of Chinese in other parts of Southeast Asia for what we can learn about the general problem of the assimilation of overseas Chinese into local societies. A recent article by Skinner contrasts and seeks to account for the rapid assimilation of the descendants of Chinese in Thailand in pre-twentieth-century times and the prolonged delay in the assimilation of Chinese descendants in Java. With what we know about the Chinese mestizos in the Philippines we are now in a position to compare them to Chinese descendants in Thailand and Java.

In Thailand prior to the early twentieth century, Chinese were normally assimilated into Thai society by the third or fourth generation. They behaved completely as Thai and were readily accepted as such by the Thai. Upon reaching majority, descendants of Chinese had complete freedom to opt for membership in either Thai society or the local overseas Chinese society. Those who chose membership in Chinese society were regarded as Chinese; those who chose to be Thai were so regarded. Because there was no colonial ruler in Thailand there were no confusing cultural and legal problems. Unlike native cultures elsewhere in Southeast Asia, Thai culture had never lost prestige through the superimposition of a favored European culture by a colonial conqueror. Nor had the Thai incurred the liabilities in legal status often placed by a conqueror on a conquered people. There was no cultural or legal disadvantage attached to assimilation to the Thai. Given these conditions, Thai culture, which also contained certain elements familiar to the Chinese (notably Buddhism), was attractive to the Chinese. Finally, there were no special Sino–Thai organizations comparable to the mestizo gremios in the Philippines that might retard assimilation.

In Java the descendants of Chinese immigrants formed a special group known as *peranakan* Chinese, or simply "peranakans." For several generations they identified themselves as Chinese and remained apart from Indonesian society. Their cultural life was a creation of blended Chinese and Indonesian elements. They were, in other words, neither Indonesian nor completely Chinese. Although they were in many ways culturally Indonesian they resisted assimilation into Indonesian society for a number of reasons. Javanese culture, as the culture of a conquered people, lacked prestige and there were legal liabilities attached to identifying oneself as Javanese. Dutch culture, as that of the conqueror, was attractive but not really available. In the classic "plural society" of Java, ethnic lines and class lines were identical. The peranakan Chinese, classified always as Chinese, were the middle class of Java. Assimilation toward the Indonesians meant a move downward. Upward social mobility meant moving toward the Dutch. But there was no way for the peranakans to move. They could not change status. Even those who tried to move toward assimilation to Javanese society had difficulty being recognized as anything but Chinese. Caught between an attractive but inaccessible Dutch culture and a partly attainable but unattractive Javanese culture, the peranakan was fixed where he was. And the peranakan social system he developed served as an "assimilation trap"—a half-way house between "Chinese" and "Indonesian." [1]

The historical experience of the Chinese mestizos in the Philippines was somewhere between these two extremes, with segments of similarity to each combined with features that were uniquely its own. The mestizos, like the peranakans, formed a distinct group with a culture of its own, a mixture of Chinese and indigenous elements. Where there were enough mestizos to form gremios assimilation was retarded. Like the peranakans the mestizos had a recognized legal status, established by the colonial government.

1. G. William Skinner, "Change and Persistence in Chinese Culture Overseas: A Comparison of Thailand and Java," *Journal of the South Seas Society, 16* (1960), 87–96. See also Skinner's "Java's Chinese Minority: Continuity and Change," *Journal of Asian Studies, 20* (1961), esp. pp. 356–60, and his "Chinese of Java," pp. 2, 8. The expression "assimilation trap" is Skinner's.

Nevertheless, the mestizos were assimilated to indio society (or perhaps it is better to say to Filipino society) more rapidly than the peranakans were to Javanese society. Indeed, where mestizos were not numerous they may have been assimilated as rapidly as Chinese descendants were in Thailand. The most important reason for the pattern of mestizo assimilation in the Philippines was the nature of Spanish cultural influence and the native response to it. In Indonesia the Dutch, prior to 1900, sought to maintain indigenous society as it was, influenced as little as possible by Dutch culture. The Spanish, by contrast, sought to hispanize the Philippines. Thus, although indio culture lost prestige as the result of the conquest, the Chinese could still be assimilated to the indios because both of them were heading in the same direction—toward the acquisition of Spanish culture, which was equally available to both. The indios were almost all Catholics. The india mothers of mestizos were, therefore, almost inevitably Catholic and raised their children in that faith. Hence there was no religious barrier to continuous intermarriage of mestizos and indios. Moreover, the mestizo was regarded from the start as a special kind of Filipino, not a local Chinese. And he could rather easily switch legal status to that of indio.

Finally, Philippine society was not a classic plural society. Ethnic and class lines were not congruent. And, like Thai society, it was open and accepting toward those who regarded themselves as (in the Philippine case) Filipinos. Mestizos could adopt Spanish surnames and personal names and be accepted as Filipinos. Why not? Indios were doing it too in the nineteenth century. Or they could even retain Chinese surnames (which they combined with Spanish personal names) and be accepted as Filipinos, once they adopted Filipino dress and attitudes. Indeed, the very question of what was "Filipino" in dress and attitude was, to an important degree, decided by mestizos.

During the century 1750–1850 the assimilation patterns of the Chinese mestizos in most parts of the Philippines—places where there were no gremios—were much like those in Thailand. Where there were gremios a pattern like that in Java apparently existed, although it is doubtful that assimilation was ever retarded for as many generations as it was in Java. In the period after 1850 the pattern everywhere in the Philippines resembled that in Thailand, with the added factor that those mestizos who were not quickly assimilated into Filipino society were quickly reclaimed by the Chinese community.

The rise of the Chinese mestizo to social, economic, and political prominence is an important phenomenon in modern Philippine social

history. It is part of a process of social change that began in the middle
of the eighteenth century and was characterized by the rise of a new
elite whose leading element was mestizo. It is true that the policies of
the American regime in the Philippines after 1898 brought about some
important social changes—notably, the rise of an urban middle class.
But the origins of modern Philippine society must be found in the
social changes of the late eighteenth century and the nineteenth century.
The period 1850–98 saw the acceleration of those changes under the
influence of the new export crop economy, with all that it meant in
terms of new wealth, new material and intellectual demands, and open-
ness to foreign ideas as well as foreign trade.

In the social changes of the nineteenth century we may find some
aids to our understanding of the relations between the Chinese community and its host society in that period. Specifically, why did the
anti-Chinese agitation of the 1880s fail to result in anything like the
massacres and revolts that had characterized earlier periods? One explanation is, of course, the presence of larger military forces in the
Philippines in the nineteenth century than the Spaniards of the seventeenth century commanded. But one may also mention the social
changes of the nineteenth century, and hence the change in the nature
of anti-Chinese agitation. The massacres of the seventeenth century
were the action of a small group of outnumbered, frightened Spaniards
in a fortress city on the edge of Asia. The nineteenth-century agitation
took the form of a newspaper campaign in an urbanized environment,
where there were not only more than a few Spaniards but a great many
indios and mestizos whose interests were as much threatened as the
Spaniards' were. The Spaniards might fear a revolutionary movement
by the mestizos and indios. But on the subject of opposition to the
Chinese there was no doubt of mestizo–indio cooperation with Spain.
In the seventeenth century that cooperation was a matter of native
loyalty as subjects of Spain and acceptance of Spanish-taught cultural
biases against the Chinese. In the nineteenth century it was also a question of personal interest as economic competitors of the Chinese.

As for the Chinese, their revolts in the seventeenth century were
reactions to economic repression, or else desperate acts impelled by
expectation of massacre by the frightened Spaniards. In the nineteenth
century the very size of the opposition made it apparent that a fear-
driven massacre was out of the question. There was no cause for
desperation on the Chinese side. Economic repression in the nineteenth
century was more a threat than a reality. The liberal Spanish economic
policies of the post-1850 period had given new economic opportunity
to the Chinese. Now it was a matter of holding on to economic gains

rather than seeking to open closed doors. So long as there were less radical means of staving off the threat of policy changes, there was no need to resort to revolts.

But in addition to the seventeenth-century revolts there was the 1762 uprising, in which the Chinese rejected Spanish Catholicism and sought to make the English invaders, instead of the Spaniards, rulers of the Philippines. Superficially, there is some similarity between this situation and that existing during the last decades of the nineteenth century when Spain's hold on the Philippines was loosening. Why not a revolt in the hope that some other country might step in and take the place of the Spaniards? The obvious difference is that in 1762 the English were already invading the Philippines and appeared to be winning; it was a case of watching the tide of battle and picking a winner. In the 1880s and 1890s the battle had not begun and the most likely opponent of Spain was a revolutionary force of mestizos and indios, from which, if it were successful, the Chinese could expect no better treatment than they were receiving from the Spaniards. Thus, in all these ways, the social context of the renewed anti-Chinese agitation of the 1880s and 1890s was a determining factor for both the form taken by the agitation and the nature of Chinese response.

The other important factor was the international context. In the seventeenth and eighteenth centuries the Spanish could massacre Chinese in the Philippines with the knowledge that even though Fukien and Kwangtung officials might be concerned, there would be no large-scale retaliation from the Chinese government. But in the late nineteenth century the Spaniards were aware of China's new interest in the overseas Chinese, and Spanish consciousness of China's developing naval strength acted as a deterrent to reckless action.

From the Chinese side, the revolts of the seventeenth century were made in the knowledge that the only help the Philippine Chinese might get would come from Chinese adventurers. No aid was to be expected from China. One of the reasons for such revolts was precisely the impossibility of aid from China, which made drastic methods the only course of action. In the nineteenth-century context, revolts were unnecessary because China's aid was available.

Another determinant of Chinese action may well have been the changes in the Chinese community itself. In the seventeenth century uprisings were usually the work of restless, newly-arrived Chinese, while the propertied elements deplored such disturbances.[2] In the nineteenth century the community as a whole was wealthier than before

---

2. Schurz, *Manila Galleon*, pp. 82–83.

and there was in all probability a larger propertied class than ever. Furthermore, it is likely that such institutions as the cabecilla and the coolie broker made possible closer individual supervision and social control. The Chinese, in short, were better organized than they had been, and their leaders were probably better able to restrain reckless elements.

The ties formed between the Philippine Chinese and China during this period were tentative and not yet firm. Likewise, the internal organization of the Philippine Chinese community was incomplete. Nevertheless, the period 1850–98 may be regarded as not only a critical era in terms of the survival and future of the Philippine Chinese, but as a necessary period of preparation for both the closer bonds to China and the more sophisticated Chamber of Commerce community organization that were to follow.

From China's point of view, the relationship appears to have been primarily one of financial contributions from overseas in exchange for promises of honors and consular protection. But the new relationship also involved defining the position of the Philippine Chinese—like all overseas Chinese—in Chinese society. In 1894 an imperial decree abrogated the old prohibitions of trade and residence aboard, long since unenforced.[3] The Philippine Chinese were now legally free to return to China without being subjected to harassment by local officials. They now had the same rights and opportunities as any Chinese.

But although the economic and social betterment of the family's position in China was the ultimate objective of overseas labor, that ideal was attainable only by securing the economic and social position of the emigrant while he was abroad. The renewal of anti-Chinese sentiment in the Philippines threatened the economic and social status of the Chinese there. Thus, the Philippine Chinese had first to seek definition of their position in Chinese society in order to insure their position in the economy and society of the Philippines.

3. Chen, *Emigrant Communities*, p. 55.

Appendices

Appendix A: Glossary of Chinese Names and Terms

Amoy t'ing 廈門廳
An-ch'i hsien 安溪縣
bazar 百貨
bí-tiam kah-li-si 米店甲黎司
capitán 甲必丹
Chang Chih-tung 張之洞
Chang Ho Hui 長和會
Chang Yin-huan 張蔭桓
Ch'en Kang (Ch'en Tzu-yen) 陳綱 (陳紫衍)
Ch'en Lan-pin 陳蘭彬
Cheng Ch'eng-kung 鄭成功
Cheng Chih-lung 鄭芝龍
Cheng Ho 鄭和
Cheng Tsao-ju 鄭藻如
Chin-chiang hsien 晉江縣
chin-shih 進士
Chong Hock Tong 崇福堂
Chua 蔡
Mariano Velasco Chua Chengco 蔡德淺 (蔡永明)
Chung-Hsi Hsüeh-hsiao 中西學校
Chung-hua hui-kuan 中華會館
Chung Wah Kung Saw 中華公所
Chung Wah Wui Kwoon 中華會館
Ch'ung Hou 崇厚
Ch'ung-jen I-yüan 崇仁醫院
Ch'ung Ning She 崇寧社
Co 許
Co Chi-lui 許志螺
Dy 李

Feng-t'ing ssu 楓亭司

Fu Ch'üan ssu 福泉寺

Fu Lien I Pu Shang Hui 福聯益布商會

Go 吳

gîn tiam kah-li-si-iâ 銀店甲黎司耶

Hai-ch'eng hsien 海澄縣

Hou A-p'ao 侯阿保 (侯甫鮑，侯甫胞，侯寶華)

Hsing-hua fu 興化府

Hsüeh Fu-ch'eng 薛福成

Hsüeh Huan 薛煥

hua-ch'iao 華僑

Hui-an hsien 惠安縣

Hung Men 洪門

I Ho Chü Pu Shang Hui 義和局布商會

I Yu Hsin Pao 益友新報

k'e-t'ou 客頭

ko 哥

kongsi 公司

kuan 官

Kuan Fu Tzu Hui 關夫子會

Kuan Ti Yeh Hui 關帝爺會

Kuan Wen-tou 官文斗

Kuang-lu Ta-fu 光祿大夫

Kwangtung Hui Kuan 廣東會館

Lang Chün Hui 郎君會

Li Hung-chang 李鴻章

Lim 林

Lim Cong-jap 林光合

Lim Ong 林旺

Lung-ch'i 龍溪

Ma-tsu 媽祖

Man On 萬安

Min I Pao 岷益報

Min Pu Hua Pao 岷埠華報

mui-tsai 妹仔

Nan-an hsien 南安縣

On Tai 安泰
Ong 王
Po On 普安
Pun Tao Kong 本頭公
Que 郭
Shan-chü Kung-so 善舉公所
shang-lü 商旅
she-li lao-yeh 社里老爺
shu-yüan 書院
Benito Siy Congbieng 施光銘
Sy 施
Tan 陳
Carlos Palanca Tan Quien-sien 陳謙善
      (Tan Chuey-liong) 陳最良
Tan Samto 陳三多
Manuel Pérez Tan Yaoco 陳文耀
T'ien Ti Hui 天地會
Ting Ju-ch'ang 丁汝昌
towkay 頭客
Tsui Kuo-yin 崔國因
T'ung-an hsien 同安縣
Tung Wah Hospital 東華醫院
tung-yang chen-lu 東洋針路
T'u-ti-kung 土地公
Uy 黃
Lucio Herrera Uy Mayan 黃馬元
Wai-yang hai-chün T'ung-ling-yüan 外洋海軍統領員
Wang Yung-ho 王榮和
Yang Shu-te 楊樹得
Yang Wei-hung 楊維洪 (楊滙溪)
Yap 葉
Yap Liong-quin 葉龍欽
Yu 楊
Mariano Fernando Yu Chingco 楊尊親
Yü Ch'iung 余璚
Yung-ch'un hsien 永春縣

Appendix B: A Partial List of Gobernadorcillos de Chinos at Manila, 1875–1898

1875–77: Carlos Palanca Tan Quien-sien
1877–79: Mariano Fernando Yu Chingco
1879–81: Unknown
1881–83: Antonio Elizaga Yap Caong
1883–84: Antonio Elizaga Yap Caong
1885 (interim): Carlos Palanca Tan Quien-sien
1885–87: Mariano Ocampo Lao Pengco
1888 (interim): Angel Aldecoa Lim Ange
1888–89: Federico Gamir Co Sequieng
1889 (interim): Carlos Palanca Tan Quien-sien
1890–92: Mariano Ocampo Lao Pengco
1892–93: Pio de la Guardia Sy Pioco (Pio Barretto)
1893–94 (interim): Manuel Pérez Tan Yaoco
1894–96: Gavino Tan Tiongco (Tan Suyjiong)
1896–98: Juan Pina Tan Chuaco

Bibliography

1: Unpublished Material

The major source of unpublished material for this study was the Philippine National Archives in Manila, which contains a large collection of official documents from the period of Spanish rule in the Philippines (1565–1898) that had never before been systematically exploited for research purposes. During a one year stay I was able to photograph there enough material to fill 6,000 feet of microfilm, most of it about the Chinese in the Philippines, which has been deposited at the University of California, Berkeley.

A description of the contents and condition of the Archives is found in my article cited below. However, a word or two should be said about the large bodies of material in the collection that proved especially valuable for this study. One useful group of material was the royal orders and decrees emanating from Spain, together with related documentation. These were found in a series of 168 metal file boxes, called *cajas*, whose contents cover the years 1660 to 1897. The most useful for this study were those files covering the years 1750 to 1898—roughly cajas 25 to 168. There is a guide to this series of royal orders in the form of a chronological register, which lists without comment the title of each royal order. This register has been microfilmed and is available at the University of California.

The Archives contains almost 300 volumes of *padrones de chinos,* or census and tax registers of Chinese residents. Enumerations of the Chinese were made approximately once every five years until 1890, when they began to be made annually. Most of the volumes of padrones in the Archives are from the 1890s. Several of the volumes from 1890–1900 are now available on microfilm at the University of California. For further discussion of the padrones, see Part III above.

Most of the documents in the Philippine National Archives are kept in bundles according to rough subject classifications. Among these, the most useful were four bundles on the *contribución industrial* tax, identified as 26–17–12, 5–12–13, 5–8–3, and 26–22–8; six bundles on the opium monopoly (*anfión*, 5–10–9, 6–2–9, 5–8–7, 5–20–12, 37–2–10, 25–16–18); two bundles on elections within the Chinese community (Chinos, elecciones, 37–2–2 and Cabezas de barangay, chinos, 49–1–10); and a single bundle on mestizo, Chinese, and indio relations in Binondo (Gremios de naturales, mestizos, y chinos, 16–5–5).

A word is in order about the numerical system for identifying the bundles. The bundles in the Archives had no identifying numbers or letters according either to sequence or physical location. Therefore, the numbers used here represent an arbitrary device developed by me to aid in identifying individual bundles, and were based upon physical location. That is, the three numbers were to represent the case, shelf, and position on the shelf at which the given bundle might be found. Thus, the expression "16–5–5" located this bundle at space 5 on shelf 5 of case 16.

This system was worked out at the time the Archives were housed in the old Bilibid Prison. When the collection was transferred to new quarters at the University of the Philippines Library in 1953 no attempt was made to keep the bundles in the same case-order or shelf-order as at Bilibid. The identification system used here thus became valueless as a means of locating specific bundles. However, the contents of individual bundles were not dispersed but remained together. Also, the bundles that were microfilmed were marked with the numbers I had assigned them. So these bundles, when located, ought to be easily identifiable. It is for this reason that the assigned numbers have been retained here even though they are valueless as locating devices. They can at least indicate which materials go together in a given bundle.

II: Published Works in Western Languages

Ahuja, Francisco, *Reseña acerca del estado social y económico de las colonias de España en Asia*, 3 vols. Madrid, Imp. de J. Noguera, 1874–75.

Alejandrino, José, *The Price of Freedom*, Manila, M. Colcol and Co., 1949.

Amyot, Jacques, S.J., "The Chinese of Manila: A Study of Adaptation of Chinese Familism to the Philippine Environment," Ph.D. dissertation, Dept. of Anthropology, University of Chicago, mimeo., 1960.

Aube, Th., "Manille et les Philippines," *Revue des deux mondes*, 22 (1848), 329–55.

Ayerbe, Marqués de, "Sitio y conquista de Manila por los ingleses en 1762," *Tres hechos memorables de la marina española en el siglo xviii*, Madrid, Impreso por Fontanet, 1907.

Azcárraga y Palmero, Manuel, *La libertad de comercio en las Islas Filipinas*, Madrid, J. Noguera, 1872.

———, *La reforma del municipio indígena en Filipinas*, Madrid, J. Noguera, 1871.

Balaguer, Victor, *En el Ministerio de Ultramar,* 2 vols. Madrid, M. Tello, 1888.

Bécker, Jerónimo, *Historia de las relaciones exteriores de España durante el siglo xix,* 3 vols. Madrid, J. Ratés, 1924–26.

Benitez, Conrado, *History of the Philippines*, rev. ed. Boston and New York, Ginn and Company, 1954.

Berriz, Miguel Rodríguez, *Diccionario de la administración de Filipinas*, 15 vols. Manila, M. Perez, 1887–88.

———, *Diccionario de la administración de Filipinas. Anuario 1888,* 2 vols. Manila, M. Perez, hijo; *Anuario 1889, Anuario 1890, Anuario 1891, Anuario 1892*, Manila, M. Perez, hijo, 1889–93.

Biggerstaff, Knight, "The Establishment of Permanent Chinese Missions Abroad," *Chinese Social and Political Science Review,* 20 (1936), 1–41.

Blair, Emma H. and James A. Robertson, *The Philippine Islands, 1493–1898*, 55 vols. Cleveland, Arthur Clark Co., 1903–07.

Blanco Herrero, Miguel, *Política de España en ultramar*, 2d. ed. Madrid, Francisco G. Pérez, 1890.

Blumentritt, Ferdinand, *Die Chinesen auf den Philippinen*, Leitmeritz, 1878.

———, "Die Chinesen Manilas," *Globus*, 62 (1890), 97–100.

———, "Die mestizen der Philippinen-Inseln," *Revue coloniale internationale*, 1 (1885), 253–61.

Bowring, John, *A Visit to the Philippine Islands*, London, Smith, Elder and Co., 1859.

Buzeta, Manuel, O.S.A. and Felipe Bravo, O.S.A., *Diccionario geográfico, estadístico, histórico de las Islas Filipinas*, 2 vols. Manila, José C. de la Peña, 1850–51.

Catálogo de la exposición cartográfica y documental de Filipinas, Madrid, 1946.

Cavada y Méndez de Vigo, Agustín de la, *Historia geográfica, geológica y estadística de Filipinas*, 2 vols. Ramirez y Giraudier, 1876.

Census of the Philippine Islands Taken under the Direction of the Philippine Commission in the Year 1903, 4 vols. Washington, Government Printing Office, 1905.

Chang, Y. Z., "Sangley, the Merchant-Traveller," *Modern Language Notes*, 52 (1937), 189.

Chaunu, Pierre, *Les Philippines et le Pacifique des Iberiques (xvie, xviie, xviiie siècles)*, Paris, S.E.V.P.E.N., 1960.

Chen, Ta, *Chinese Migrations*, U.S. Bureau of Labor Statistics Bulletin, 340, Washington, Government Printing Office, 1923.

———, *Emigrant Communities in South China*, New York, Institute of Pacific Relations, 1940.

China, Inspectorate-general of Customs, Statistical Series, *Customs Decennial Reports, Amoy, 1892–1901*, Shanghai, Inspectorate-general of Customs, 1906.

China en Filipinas. Colección de artículos publicados en el Diario de Manila. . . . , Manila, Establecimiento tipográfico de Ramirez y Cª., 1889.

"The Chinese in the Philippines," *Report of the Philippine Commission to the President*, 1 (1900–01), 150–59.

Los chinos en Filipinas, ed. La Oceanía Española, Manila, Est. tip. "La Oceanía Española," 1886.

Chinos. Sus reglamentos y sus contribuciones, comp. El Faro Administrativo, Manila, Establecimiento tipo-litográfico de Ramirez y Cª., 1893.

The Chronicle and Directory for China, Japan, and the Philippines [title varies], Hong Kong, "Daily Press," 1873, 1891, 1902–05.

Clark, Victor, *Labor Conditions in the Philippines*, U.S. Bureau of Labor Bulletin, 10, Washington, Government Printing Office, 1905.

Comenge, Rafael, *Cuestiones filipinas. 1ª parte. Los chinos*, Manila, Chofré y Cª., 1894.

Commercial Directory of Manila, Manila, n.p., 1901.

Comyn, Tomás de, "Estado de las Islas Filipinas en 1810," in *Las Islas Filipinas. Progresos en 70 años*, ed. J. F. del Pan, Manila, Imprenta de "La Oceanía Española," 1878.

Concepción, Juan de la, R.A., *Historia general de Filipinas,* 14 vols. Manila, Impr. del Seminario Conciliar y Real de San Carlos, 1788–92.

"Contratos usurarios," *Revista general de legislación y jurisprudencia,* 25 (1864), 176.

Corpuz, O. D., *The Bureaucracy in the Philippines,* Quezon City, University of the Philippines Press, 1957.

Craig, Austin, *Rizal's Life and Minor Writings*, Manila, Philippine Education Co., 1927.

De la Costa, Horacio, S.J., *The Jesuits in the Philippines*, Cambridge, Harvard University Press, 1961.

Delgado, Juan, S.J., *Historia sacro-profana, política, y natural de las Islas del poniente llamadas Filipinas*, Manila, Imp. en el Eco de Filipinas de D. Juan Atayde, 1892.

Del Pan, José Felipe, *Las Islas Filipinas. Progresos en 70 años*, Manila, Imprenta de "La Oceanía Española," 1878.

Díaz Arenas, Rafael, *Memoria sobre el comercio y la navegación de las Islas Filipinas,* Cádiz, Impr. de Domingo Féros, 1838.

———, *Memorias históricas y estadísticas de Filipinas*, Manila, Imprenta del "Diario de Manila," 1850.

Echaúz, Robustiano, *Apuntes de la isla de Negros,* Manila, Chofré y Cª., 1894.

Endacott, G. B., *A History of Hong Kong*, London, Oxford University Press, 1958.

Fairbank, J. K., *Trade and Diplomacy on the China Coast,* 2 vols. Cambridge, Harvard University Press, 1953.

Feced, Pablo, *Filipinas: esbozos y pinceladas por "Quioquiap,"* Manila, Ramirez y Cª., 1888.

Fernández, Pablo, O.P., *Dominicos donde nace el sol*, Barcelona, Tall. Gráf. Yuste, 1958.

Ferrando, Juan, O.P. and Fonseca, Joaquín, O.P., *Historia de los PP. Dominicos en las Islas Filipinas . . .* , 6 vols. Madrid, Imp. y estereotip. de M. Rivadeneyra, 1870–72.

Flormata, Gregorio, *Memoria sobre la provincia de Pangasinan*, Manila, Impr. "La Democracia," 1901.

Foreman, John, *The Philippine Islands*, 2d. ed. New York, Charles Scribner's Sons, 1899.

Freedman, Maurice, "Chinese Kinship and Marriage in Early Singapore," *Journal of Southeast Asian History, 3* (Sept. 1962), 65–73.

———, "The Growth of a Plural Society in Malaya," *Pacific Affairs, 33* (1960), 158–68.

———, "Immigrants and Associations: Chinese in Nineteenth Century

Singapore," *Comparative Studies in Society and History, 3* (1960), 25–48.

García Ageo, Gabriel, "Memorandum on the Chinese in the Philippines," *Report of the Philippine Commission to the President, 2* (1900–01), 432–47.

Gayo, Jesús, O.P., "Ensayo histórico–bibliográfico," *Doctrina Christiana; Primer libro impreso en Filipinas,* Manila, University of Santo Tomas Press, 1951.

Gemelli Careri, Giovanni, *A Voyage to the Philippines,* Manila, Filipiniana Book Guild, 1963.

González Fernández, Ramón, and Moreno Jérez, Federico, *Manual del viajero en Filipinas,* Manila, Est. tip. de Santo Tomás, 1875.

González Serrano, Valentín, *España en Filipinas,* Madrid, R. Velasco, 1896.

Guía de forasteros en las Islas Filipinas para el año 1847, Manila, Colegio de Santo Tomás, 1847.

Guía de forasteros en las Islas Filipinas para el año 1860, Manila, Amigos del País, 1860.

Guía oficial de Filipinas . . . 1879, 1881, 1885, 1891, 1898, Manila, various publishers, 1879–98.

Hayden, Joseph Ralston, *The Philippines: A Study in National Development,* New York, Macmillan, 1950.

Hertslet, G. E. P., ed., *Treaties &c. Between Great Britain and China; and Between China and Foreign Powers* . . . , 2 vols. London, printed for H.M.S.O. by Harrison and Sons, 1908.

Hines, C. W., *Sugar Industry of the Philippines,* Panama–Pacific International Exposition Pamphlets, Manila, 1915.

Horsley, Margaret Wyant, "Sangley: The Formation of Anti-Chinese Feeling in the Philippines," Ph.D. dissertation, Columbia, 1950. Available from University Microfilms, Ann Arbor, Michigan.

Hsu, Immanuel C. Y., *China's Entrance into the Family of Nations: The Diplomatic Phase, 1858–1880,* Cambridge, Harvard University Press, 1960.

Human Relations Area Files, *Area Handbook on the Philippines,* ed. Fred Eggan, 4 vols. Chicago, University of Chicago Press for HRAF, 1956.

Hummel, Arthur W., ed., *Eminent Chinese of the Ch'ing Period (1644–1912),* 2 vols. Washington, Government Printing Office, 1943.

Jacobson, H. O., *Tobacco in the Philippines,* Panama–Pacific International Exposition Pamphlets, Manila, 1915.

Jagor, Feodor, *Travels in the Philippines,* London, Chapman and Hall, 1875.

Jensen, Khin Khin Myint, "The Chinese in the Philippines during the American Regime, 1898–1946," Ph.D. dissertation, University of Wisconsin, 1956. Available from University Microfilms, Ann Arbor, Michigan.

Jimeno Agius, José, *Población y comercio de las Islas Filipinas,* Madrid, Est. tip. de El Correo, 1884.

Jordana y Morera, Ramón, *La inmigración china en Filipinas,* Madrid, M. G. Hernández, 1888.

Lannoy, J., *Iles Philippines*, Bruxelles, Impr. de Delevingne et Callewaert, 1849.

La Perouse, Jean François de Galaup de, *A Voyage Around the World in the Years 1785, 1786, 1787, and 1788*, 3d. ed. 3 vols. London, printed for Lackington, Allen and Co., 1807.

Laufer, Berthold, "The Relations of the Chinese to the Philippine Islands," *Smithsonian Miscellaneous Collection*, 50 (1908), 248–81.

Legarda, Benito, Jr., "American Entrepreneurs in the 19th Century Philippines," *Explorations in Entrepreneurial History*, 9 (1957), 142–59.

———, "Foreign Trade, Economic Change, and Entrepreneurship in the Nineteenth Century Philippines," Ph.D. dissertation, Harvard, 1955.

LeRoy, James, *The Americans in the Philippines*, 2 vols. Boston, New York, Houghton Mifflin Co., 1914.

———, *Philippine Life in Town and Country*, New York and London, G. P. Putnam's Sons, 1905.

Lo, Jung-pang, "China as a Seapower, 1127–1368," Ph.D. dissertation, University of California (Berkeley), 1957.

MacMicking, Robert, *Recollections of Manilla and the Philippines During 1848, 1849, and 1850*, London, Richard Bentley, 1852.

MacNair, H. F., *The Chinese Abroad; Their Position and Protection*, Shanghai, Commercial Press, 1924.

———, "Relations of China to her Nationals Abroad," *Chinese Social and Political Science Review*, 7 (1923), 23–43.

Mallat de Bassilan, Jean, *Les Philippines; histoire, geographie, moeurs, agriculture, industrie et commerce des colonies espagnoles dans l'Oceanie*, 2 vols. Paris, A. Bertrand, 1846.

Manuel, E. Arsenio, *Dictionary of Philippine Biography*. Volume One, Quezon City, Filipiniana Publications, 1955.

Marcaida, Juan Bautista, *Empresas agrícolas, con chinos, en Filipinas*, Manila, n.p., 1850.

Mas, Sinibaldo de, *La Chine et les puissances Chretiennes*, 2 vols. Paris, L. Hachette, 1861.

———, *Informe sobre el estado de las Islas Filipinas en 1842*, 2 vols. Madrid, n.p., 1843.

———, "Internal Political Condition of the Philippines, 1842," BR, 52, 29–90.

Meilink–Roelofsz, M. A. P., *Asian Trade and European Influence in the Indonesian Archipelago between 1500 and about 1630*, 'S-Gravenhage, Martinus Nijhoff, 1962.

Mencarini, Juan, "The Philippine Chinese Labour Question," *Journal of the Royal Asiatic Society, North China Branch*, 33 (1899–1900), 157–84.

Miller, Hugo L., *Economic Conditions in the Philippines*, 2d. ed. Boston and New York, Ginn and Co., 1920.

Montano, Joseph, *Voyage aux Philippines et en Malaisie*, Paris, Hachette et cie., 1886.

Montero y Vidal, José, *El Archipiélago Filipino y las Islas Marianas, Carolinas, y Palaos,* Madrid, M. Tello, 1886.

———, *Historia general de Filipinas,* 3 vols. Madrid, M. Tello, 1887–95.

Morga, Antonio de, *Sucesos de las Islas Filipinas,* ed. W. E. Retana, Madrid, V. Suárez, 1910.

Moya y Jiménez, Francisco de, "Las Islas Filipinas en 1882," *Revista de España, 85–94,* 1882–83.

Navarro Ordóñez, Eduardo, O.S.A., *Filipinas, estudios de algunos asuntos de actualidad,* Madrid, Imp. de la Vda. de M. Minuesa de los Ríos, 1897.

Norman, Henry, *The Peoples and Politics of the Far East,* London, T. F. Unwin, 1900.

Palgrave, W. G., *"The Far-Off Eden Isles"; Country Life in the Philippines Fifty Years Ago By a British Consul,* Manila, National Book Co., 1929.

Pardo de Tavera, T. H., "Los chinos (de mis recuerdos)," *Philippines Free Press* (July 8, 1916), pp. 28, 30; (July 15, 1916), pp. 26, 28.

———, "History," *Census of 1903, 1,* 309–410.

———, *Una memoria de Anda y Salazar,* Manila, Imprenta "La Democracia," 1899.

Pastells, Pablo, S. J., "Historia general de Filipinas," in Pedro Torres Lanzas and Francisco Navas del Valle, ed., *Catálogo de los documentos relativos á las Islas Filipinas existentes en el Archivo de Indias de Sevilla.* 9 vols. (Barcelona, 1925–36), 1–9.

Phelan, John L., *The Hispanization of the Philippines,* Madison, University of Wisconsin Press, 1959.

Philippine Islands. Real Audiencia Chancillería, *Colección de autos acordados de la Real Audiencia Chancillería de Filipinas,* 5 vols. Manila, Ramirez y Giraudier, 1861–66.

Plauchut, Edmond, "L'Archipel des Philippines," *Revue des deux mondes, 20* (1877), 447–64, 896–913; *21* (1877), 885–923.

Plehn, Carl C., "Taxation in the Philippines," *Political Science Quarterly, 16* (1901), 680–711; *17* (1901), 125–48.

La política de España en Filipinas, 8 vols. Madrid, 1891–98.

Purcell, Victor, *The Chinese in Southeast Asia,* London and New York, Oxford University Press, 1951.

Rajal y Larré, Joaquín, "Memoria acerca de la provincia de Nueva Ecija en Filipinas," *Boletín de la Sociedad Geográfica de Madrid, 27* (1889), 290–359.

Ratzel, Friedrich, *Die Chinesische auswanderung,* Breslau, J. U. Kern, 1876.

Recopilación de leyes de los reynos de las Indias, 2d ed. 4 vols. Madrid, Antonio Balbas, 1756.

Recur, Carlos, *Filipinas: estudios administrativos y comerciales,* Madrid, Impr. de Ramón Moreno y Ricardo Rojas, 1879.

Relación verdadera del levantamiento que los Sangleyes o Chinos hizieron en las Filipinas, y de las vitorias que tuvo cõtra ellos . . . 1640 y 1641, Sevilla, I. Gomes, 1642.

Retana, W. E., *Aparato bibliográfico de la historia general de Filipinas,* 3 vols. Madrid, Imp. de la sucesora de M. Minuesa de los Ríos, 1906.

———, *Archivo del bibliófilo filipino,* 5 vols. Madrid, Imp. de la Vda. de M. Minuesa de los Ríos, 1895–1905.

———, *Diccionario de filipinismos,* New York, Paris, "Extrait de la Revue Hispanique," 1921.

———, "El periodismo filipino," *Aparato bibliográfico, 3,* 1493–1800.

Rizal, José, *El filibusterismo,* tr. Charles Derbyshire as *The Reign of Greed,* 2d. ed. Manila, Philippine Education Co., 1912.

———, *Noli me tangere,* tr. Charles Derbyshire as *The Social Cancer,* 2d. ed. Manila, Philippine Education Co., 1912.

Saleeby, Najeeb, *History of Sulu,* Manila, Bureau of Printing, 1908.

Sancianco y Goson, Gregorio, *El progreso de Filipinas. Estudios económicos, administrativos y políticos. Parte económico,* Madrid, Vda. de J. M. Pérez, 1881.

San Pedro, Joaquín Rodríguez, *Legislación ultramarina,* 16 vols. Madrid, Imp. de los señores Viotas, Cubas y Vicente, 1865–69.

Sastrón, Manuel, *Colonización de Filipinas. Inmigración peninsular . . . ,* Manila, 1897 [Malabong, Asilo de huérfanos, 1896].

———, *Filipinas; pequeños estudios; Batangas y su provincia . . .* Malabong, Asilo de huérfanos, 1895.

Sawyer, Frederic H., *The Inhabitants of the Philippines,* London, Sampson Low, Marston and Co., 1900.

Scherzer, Karl von, *Fachmännische berichte über die österreichisch-ungarische expedition nach Siam, China, und Japan (1868–1871),* Stuttgart, J. Maier, 1872.

Schurz, William Lytle, *The Manila Galleon,* New York, Dutton, 1939.

Sherman, Penoyer L., *The Gutta Percha and Rubber of the Philippine Islands,* Philippine Islands Bureau of Government Laboratories Publications, 7, Manila, Bureau of Public Printing, 1903.

Skinner, G. William, "Change and Persistence in Chinese Culture Overseas: A Comparison of Thailand and Java," *Journal of the South Seas Society, 16* (1960), 86–100.

———, "The Chinese of Java," *Colloquium on Overseas Chinese,* ed. Morton Fried (New York, Institute of Pacific Relations, 1958), 1–10.

———, *Chinese Society in Thailand: An Analytical History,* Ithaca, Cornell University Press, 1957.

———, "Java's Chinese Minority: Continuity and Change," *Journal of Asian Studies, 20* (1961), 353–62.

Stagg, Samuel W., *Teodoro Yangco: Leading Filipino Philanthropist and Grand Old Man of Commerce,* Manila, University of the Philippines Press, 1934.

Sturtevant, David R., "Philippine Social Structure and Its Relation to Agrarian Unrest," Ph.D. dissertation, Stanford, 1958.

Tung, Ling, *China and Some Phases of International Law,* Shanghai, 1940.

Uchida, Naosaku, *The Overseas Chinese. A Bibliographical Essay Based on the Resources of the Hoover Institution,* Hoover Institution Bibliographical Series, Stanford, Stanford University Press, 1959.

United States Library of Congress, *A List of Books (with References to Periodicals) on the Philippine Islands in the Library of Congress,* comp. A. P. C. Griffin, Washington, Government Printing Office, 1903.

United States Philippine Commission, 1899–1900, *Report of the Philippine Commission to the President,* 4 vols. Washington, Government Printing Office, 1900–01.

Valenzuela, Jesús Z., *A History of Journalism in the Philippine Islands,* Manila, The Author, 1933.

Van Leur, J. C., *Indonesian Trade and Society. Essays in Asian Social and Economic History,* The Hague and Bandung, W. van Hoeve, 1955.

Wang Gungwu, *A Short History of the Nanyang Chinese,* Singapore, Eastern Universities Press, 1959.

Webb, Alexander, "Commerce of the Philippine Islands," *Reports from the Consuls of the United States,* 39 (May 1892), 146–55.

Weightman, George H., "The Philippine Chinese: A Cultural History of a Marginal Trading Community," Ph.D. dissertation, Cornell, 1960. Available from University Microfilms, Ann Arbor, Michigan.

Welsh, Doris V., *A Catalogue of Printed Materials Relating to the Philippine Islands, 1519–1900 in the Newberry Library,* Chicago, Newberry Library, 1959.

Wertheim, W. F., *Indonesian Society in Transition. A Study of Social Change,* The Hague and Bandung, W. van Hoeve, 1956.

Wickberg, Edgar, "The Chinese Mestizo in Philippine History," *Journal of Southeast Asian History,* 5 (March 1964), 62–100.

——, "Early Chinese Economic Influence in the Philippines, 1850–1898," *Pacific Affairs,* 35 (1962), 275–85.

——, "Spanish Records in the Philippine National Archives," *Hispanic American Historical Review,* 35 (1955), 77–89.

Wilkes, Charles, *Narrative of the United States Exploring Expedition during the Years 1838, 1839, 1840, 1841, 1842,* 5 vols. Philadelphia, Lea and Blanchard, 1850.

Williams, Lea, *Overseas Chinese Nationalism; the Genesis of the Pan-Chinese Movement in Indonesia, 1900–1916,* Glencoe, Free Press, 1960.

Willmott, Donald Earl, *The Chinese of Semarang,* Ithaca, Cornell University Press, 1960.

Wu Ching-hong, "A Study of References to the Philippines in Chinese Sources from Earliest Times to the Ming Dynasty," *Philippine Social Sciences and Humanities Review,* 24 (1959), 1–181.

——, "Supplements to a Study of References to the Philippines in Chinese Sources from Earliest Times to the Ming Dynasty (?–1644)," *University of Manila Journal of East Asiatic Studies,* 7 (1958), 307–93.

Zaide, Gregorio, "Chinese General in the Philippine Revolution," *Fookien Times Yearbook* (Manila, 1955), 155–60.

————, *Philippine Political and Cultural History,* 2 vols. Manila, Philippine Education Co., 1949.

Zamora y Coronado, José María, *Biblioteca de la legislación ultramarina en forma alfabética,* 7 vols. Madrid, Alegría y Charlain, 1844–49.

Zúñiga, Joaquín Martínez de, O.S.A., *Estadismo de las Islas Filipinas,* ed. W. E. Retana, 2 vols. Madrid, Imp. de la Vda. de M. Minuesa de los Ríos, 1893.

III: Published Works in Chinese and Japanese

Quotation marks around the translated title of a Chinese work indicate that it is the English version given on the title page; it may or may not be a close translation. The author's English equivalents are given without quotation marks.

Chang Chih-tung　張之洞　　　　　, *Chang Wen-hsiang-kung ch'üan-chi* 張文襄公全集 (Collected Works of Chang Chih-tung), 229 chüan, Peiping, 1928.

Chang Yin-huan　張蔭桓　　　　, *San-chou jih-chi* 三洲日記 (A Diary of Three Continents), 8 chüan, Peking, 1896.

Ch'en Ching-ho　陳荊和　　　, "Fei-lü-p'in hua-ch'iao ta-shih chih," 菲律賓華僑大事誌 (A Chronicle of Important Events regarding the Overseas Chinese in the Philippines), *Ta-lu tsa-chih* 大陸雜誌 , 6 (1953), 137–54.

————, *Shih-liu shih-chi chih Fei-lü-p'in hua-ch'iao* 十六世紀之菲律賓華僑 (The Philippine Chinese in the Sixteenth Century), Hong Kong, 1963.

Ch'en T'i-ch'iang　陳體強　　　, *Chung-kuo wai-chiao hsing-cheng* 中國外交行政 (The Administration of China's Foreign Affairs), Chungking, 1943.

Cheng Kuan-ying　鄭冠英　　　　, *Ch'en Ch'ien-shan* 陳謙善 (Tan Quien-sien), Taipei, 1954.

Ch'ing-chi wai-chiao shih-liao 清季外交史料 (Historical Materials on Foreign Relations in the Late Ch'ing Period), 243 chüan, Peiping, 1932–35.

Chuang Wei-chi　莊為璣　　　　, "Fu-chien Chin-chiang chuan-ch'ü hua-ch'iao shih tiao-ch'a pao-kao 福建晉江專區華僑史調查報告 (Report of an Investigation into the History of the Overseas Chinese of Chin-chiang Special District, Fukien), *Hsia-men ta-hsüeh hsüeh-pao, she-hui k'o-hsüeh pan* 厦門大學學報, 社會科學版 , I (June 1958), 93–127.

Fei-lü-p'in Hua-ch'iao Shan-chü Kung-so ch'uang-pan Chung-hua Ch'ung-jen Tsung-I-yüan hsin yüan-yü lo-chien chi-nien k'an 菲律賓華僑善舉公所創辦中華崇仁醫院新院宇落建紀念刊 ("Chinese

General Hospital. 65th Anniversary and Inauguration of the Newly Completed Buildings. Souvenir Program"), Manila, 1956.

"Fei-lü-p'in hua-ch'iao shih-lüeh" 菲律賓華僑史畧 (A Short History of the Philippine Chinese), *Fei-lü-p'in hua-ch'iao shang-yeh ming-lü* 菲律賓華僑商業名錄 ("Philippine-Chinese Business Guide and Pictorial Directory"), Cebu, Manila, 1953.

Fei-lü-p'in Min-li-la Chung-hua Shang-hui san-shih chou-nien chi-nien k'an 菲律賓岷里拉中華商會三十週年紀念刊 (Thirtieth Anniversary Commemorative Publication, Manila Chinese Chamber of Commerce), ed. Huang Hsiao-ts'ang 黃曉滄 , Manila, 1936.

Fei-lü-p'in Min-li-la Chung-hua Shang-hui wu-shih chou-nien chi-nien k'an 菲律賓岷里拉中華商會五十週年紀念刊 ("Golden Book, 1955. A Fiftieth Anniversary Publication of the Philippine Chinese General Chamber of Commerce"), Manila, 1955.

Fei-lü-p'in yü hua-ch'iao shih-chi ta-kuan 菲律賓與華僑事蹟大觀 ("Philippine Chinese Chronicle"), ed. Ch'en Hsiao-yü 陳笑予 , 2 vols. Manila, 1948.

Hsiao-lü-sung Hua-ch'iao Chung-Hsi Hsüeh-hsiao wu-shih chou-nien chi-nien k'an 小呂宋華僑中西學校五十週年紀念刊 ("Anglo-Chinese School, 1899–1949. Golden Jubilee"), Manila, 1949.

Hsüeh Fu-ch'eng 薛福成 , *Ch'u-shih Ying-Fa-I-Pi ssu-kuo jih-chi* 出使英法義比四國日記 (Diary of an Embassy to the Four Countries of England, France, Italy, and Belgium), *Yung-an ch'üan-chi* 庸盦全集 (Collected Works of Hsüeh Fu-ch'eng), 21 chüan, Shanghai, 1897.

Li Hung-chang 李鴻章 , *Li Wen-cheng-kung ch'üan-chi* 李文忠公全集 (Collected Works of Li Hung-chang), 165 chüan, Nanking, 1908.

Liu Chi-hsüan 劉繼宣 and Shu Shih-cheng 束世澂 , *Chung-hua min-tsu to-chih Nan-yang shih* 中華民族拓殖南洋史 (A History of the Colonization of Southeast Asia by the Chinese People), Shanghai, 1934.

Liu Chi Tien 劉芝田 *Chung-Fei kuan-hsi shih* 中菲關係史 (A History of Sino–Philippine Relations), Taipei, 1964.

————, *Fei-lü-p'in hua-ch'iao shih-hua* 菲律賓華僑史話
(Historical Stories of the Chinese in the Philippines),
Taipei, 1958.

————, *Hua-ch'iao yü Fei-lü-p'in* 華僑與菲律賓
(The Overseas Chinese and the Philippines), Manila, 1955.

Liu-shih-wu nien lai Chung-kuo kuo-chi mao-i t'ung-chi
六十五年來中國國際貿易統計 ("Sta-
tistics of China's Foreign Trade During the Last Sixty-Five Years"), comp.
Yang Tuan-liu 楊端六 (C. Yang), Hou Hou-p'ei 侯厚培
(H. B. Hau), and others, National Research Institute of Social
Sciences, Academia Sinica, *Monographs, 4,* Peiping, 1931.

Lü Shih-p'eng 呂士朋 , "Hsi-ling shih-chi Fei-lü-p'in hua-ch'iao
chih shang-yeh huo-tung" 西領時期菲律賓華僑之商業活動
(Commercial Activities of the
Chinese in the Philippines during the Spanish Period), *Ta-lu tsa-chih*
大陸雜誌 , *13* (1956), 356–59, 396–400.

Tsui Kuo-yin 崔國因 , *Ch'u-shih Mei-Jih-P'i-kuo jih-chi* 出使
美日秘國日記 (Diary of an Embassy to
the United States, Spain, and Peru), *Hsiao-fang-hu-chai yü-ti ts'ung-ch'ao*
小方壺齋輿地叢鈔 , comp. Wang
Hsi-ch'i 王錫祺 , 64 chüan (1897), chih 帙 12.

Wen Hsiung-fei 溫雄飛 , *Nan-yang hua-ch'iao t'ung-shih*
南洋華僑通史 (General History of the Overseas
Chinese in Southeast Asia), 3 vols. Shanghai, 1929.

Wu Ching-hong 吳景宏 , "Chung-Fei kuan-hsi chih niao-k'an chi
ch'i shih-liao yen-chiu" 中菲關係之鳥瞰及其史料研究
(A Bird's-eye View of Sino–Philippine Rela-
tions and a Study of Their Historical Sources), *Ta-lu tsa-chih* 大陸
雜誌 , 8 (1954), 329–37.

————, "Hua-ch'iao tui-yü Fei-lü-p'in wen-hua ti kung-hsien" 華僑對
於菲律賓文化的貢獻
(Contributions of the Overseas Chinese to Philippine Culture), *Ta-lu tsa-
chih* 大陸雜誌 , 9 (1954), 350–53.

Yanai Kenji 箭內健次 , "Hi-tō shinajin no chihō hatten ni
tsuite" 比島支那人の地方發展について
(On the Geographical Dispersion of the Philippine Chinese), *Nampō Minzoku* 南方民族 , 7 (1942), 1–28.

————, "Ma-ni-ra no iwayuru 'Parian' ni tsuite" マニラの謂パリアンに
就いて (On the So-called 'Parian' of

Manila), Taihoku Teikoku Daigaku Bunsei Gakubu, *Shigakka kenkyū nempō* 台北帝國大學文政學部，史學科 研究年報 , 5 (1938), 189–346.

———, "Ma-ni-ra Tondo-ku no shinajin no hatten" マニラトンド 區の 支那人の發展 (The Growth of the Chinese in Tondo Ward of Manila), *Minami Ajiya Gakuhō* 南亞細亞 學報 , 2 (1943), 35–64.

Index

Italicized page numbers refer to maps.

Abaca (Manila hemp), 112; as export, 47, 56, 77, 83, 84, 103; Chinese trade in, 55, 87, 96–98; region, Chinese in, 62; crop, 96, Chinese growers of, 97

Ageo, Gabriel García, quoted, 50

Agius, Jimeno, cited, 54 n.

Agriculture, 6; efforts of Philippine government to attract Chinese to, 15, 18, 24, 49–50, 56, 174, 190–91; Chinese in, 24, 51, 55–58, 97, 122 n., 191, 197; development of export crops, 24, 29, 45–48, 67, 86, 107, Chinese in, 62 (see also Abaca; Indigo; Sugar; Tobacco), production, 121–22, 143; mestizos in, 56, 77, 107, 121–22, 135, 149; government attempt to establish large plantations, 56–58; capital for, 74 (see also Inquilinos; Moneylenders); indio traders in, 107

Aguinaldo, Gen. Emilio, 201, 202

Ahuja, Francisco, quoted, 157

Albay province, 140, 202; number of Chinese in, 62; abaca in, 96; bazares in, 98

Alcaicería de San Fernando, 28, 81, 84, 115; function and population, 23; Warden of, 38, 171, 195

Aldecoa y Compañía, 76

Alejandrino, José, cited, 201

Algeria, 46 n.

Alguaciles, 181, 183, 184, 196

Almáciga (mastic), 55, 91–92, 105

Amoy, 21, 22, 170, 172 n., 201, 229; immigrants from, 38; junk trade, 82, 83, 88; European shipping to, 84

An-ch'i hsien, China, 172 n.

Angeles, Pampanga, 183

Anglo-Chinese School (Chung-Hsi Hsüeh-hsiao), 188, 204, 235–36

Anglo-Chinese War, Second, 60

Antique, Panay, 89

Aparri, 100

Apothecaries, Chinese, 109, 152, 223–24, 228

Arévalo, Pariancillo at, 12

Artisans. See under Chinese; Indios; Mestizos

Asia: Philippine trade with, 46; nationalism and culture, 131–32; colonial, 205; Spanish consuls in, 229. See also Southeast Asia

Augustinians, 16, 101

Australia, 151, 218, 219

Ayala y Compañía, 104

Azcárraga y Palmero, Manuel, quoted, 139

Babuyanes Island, 57

Bacolor, Pampanga, 183

Balayan, Batangas, 103, 140

Banco Español–Filipino de Isabel II, 69–70, 122, 123

Banks, 69–70; Chinese, 87–88, 123

Barangayes, 183; Chinese, 196. See also Cabezas

Barnes, Charles Ilderton, quoted, 112

Bataan province: number of Chinese in (mid-1700s), 12; mestizo population, 25; Chinese in sugar industry, 94; indigo crop, 101; Chinese distilleries, 104

Batanes Island, Chinese colonists, 57

Batangas, Batangas, 140; Chinese cemetery, 185 n.

Batangas province: Chinese in, 76; Chinese in sugar industry, 94, 96; Chinese distilleries, 104; coffee, 105

Batavia, 219

Bazares, 97–98, 107–08, 175

Bengal, 101

Bernaldez Pizarro, Manuel, 46 n.; quoted, 51 n., 74 n.; views on Chinese, 153

Biak-na-Bato, Peace of (1897), 202

Bicol region, 107, 202; Chinese economy in, 62, 97–98; abaca in, 96

Bigan, 140. See also Vigan

Binan ("mestizo town"), 34